Chinese Art

CHINESE ART

JUDITH AND ARTHUR HART BURLING

BONANZA BOOKS · NEW YORK

PREFACE

THIS IS A BOOK about Chinese art and about the role that art has played in the history of China and the lives of its people. The material that it contains has been accumulated during a lifetime (actually two lifetimes) of study, and particularly in the twenty years which we spent in different parts of China in search of firsthand knowledge and confirmation of the data that we had acquired in the outside world.

We could never have obtained all the information of which this volume represents the essential elements without the generous hospitality and friendship of the many Chinese scholars, collectors, dealers, artists, writers, poets, and others who so unstintingly shared with us their time, their wisdom, their knowledge, and their experience.

At the time of Pearl Harbor, the well-known collector, Sir Percival David, who was passing through Shanghai, found himself trapped, as were we, in an enemy-occupied country. He told us he was particularly interested in Chinese painting, and we arranged for him to meet some of the Chinese authorities on that subject. We did not know what lay in store for us. We were cut off from all contact with our own countries and realized that any day we might be interned.

The Chinese, too, lived in a country occupied by an enemy, but that did not prevent us from meeting almost daily with such Chinese authorities on art as T. Y. Chang, Wu Hu-Fan, C. C. Wang, Long Chin San, and Ch'ien Tso-t'ieh, among others. For hours at a time theories of art were propounded, old paintings were scrutinized, tea was sipped, poems were quoted, and perhaps some special piece of porcelain or jade might be examined and discussed. We met in just the way that Chinese scholars have met, even in times of crisis, since the early periods of their history. After one of these gatherings Sir Percival David said: "I learn more about Chinese art in one afternoon here than in ten years of study in London."

Many of our Chinese friends are now shut off from contact with us, others are homeless refugees or are seeking to rebuild life in a strange land. To all of them—wherever they may now be—we offer this book as a small token of our gratitude and admiration of a great people and a great civilization.

We want to thank the collectors, and the directors and staffs of the many museums in the United States, Canada, and England, who have so generously given us photographs of their pieces to illustrate this book. Many of them have offered invaluable hints and suggestions; and, although space does not permit us to list them all, we should like to express our gratitude for special courtesies to the staff of the Metropolitan Museum of Art in New York, and especially to Alan Priest who read a section of the manuscript while it was in preparation; to Charles F. Kelley and Prudence Nelson of the Art Institute of Chicago; Laurence Sickman and Carol Tucker of the William Rockhill Nelson Gallery of Art in Kansas City; Dr. Kojiro Tomita of the Museum of Fine Arts, Boston; Dr. A. G. Wenley of the Freer Gallery of Art, Washington, D. C.; Dr. Hoopes of the City Art Museum of St. Louis; Wilbur D. Peat of the John Herron Art Institute, Indianapolis; Paul L. Grigaut and William A. Bostwick of the Detroit Institute of Arts; Russell A. Plimpton of the Minneapolis Institute of Arts; Robert P. Griffing, Jr., and Gustav Ecke of the Honolulu Academy of Arts; Gordon Bailey Washburn of the Carnegie Institute, Pittsburgh; Helen E. Fernald of the Royal Ontario Museum of Archaeology, Toronto; Jean Gordon Lee of the Philadelphia Museum of Art; Sir Leigh Ashton of the Victoria and Albert Museum; and Basil Gray of the British Museum, London.

We are grateful, too, to our editor, Bryan Holme, and to Lois Dwight Cole and other staff members of Studio–Crowell who have put so much understanding and effort into making this book what we all wanted it to be.

Because of the wide field we have tried to cover in this one volume, and in order to avoid confusion, we have referred to most of the Chinese painters only by their most commonly known name, omitting the various sobriquets and "secret" names which it was their custom to assume.

Chinese art is so universal and so timeless that, as will be seen by the bibliography, during these last decades it has been the subject of study by scholars of all nationalities. Yet there is no comprehensive book dealing with Chinese art written by a Chinese. They have never made any attempt to state their case, or to contradict the many misconceptions which have grown up around the subject in foreign lands. We hope that this volume will do for them what they have been too modest to do for themselves and show how the love of art and the appreciation of fine craftsmanship has permeated every phase of Chinese life.

If we have succeeded in conveying some sense of the true spirit and dignity of Chinese art we shall feel we have repaid a small part of the debt we owe to those who taught us about their art, and who, at the same time, gave us a new conception of the meaning of friendship.

CONTENTS

Introduction: THE ART OF CHINA   9

I: THE ART OF COLLECTING

I   *COLLECTING CHINESE ART*   14

II   *COPIES AND IMITATIONS IN CHINESE ART*   27

III   *DISTINGUISHING THE GENUINE FROM THE FALSE ARTICLE*   34

II: THE ARTS OF THE BRUSH

IV   *CALLIGRAPHY AND PAINTING*   40

III: THE ARTS OF THE POTTER

V   *POTTERY AND PORCELAIN*   127

IV: EARLY CHINESE CULTURE EXPRESSED IN BRONZE

VI   *BRONZES*   208

V: THE ARTS OF THE CARVER

VII   *SCULPTURE IN STONE AND WOOD*   230

VIII   *JADE*   251

IX   *THE CARVING OF IVORY*   272

VI: OTHER EXPRESSIONS OF THE CRAFTSMAN

X   *ARCHITECTURE*   277

XI   *FURNITURE*   289

XII   *LACQUER*   296

XIII *TEXTILES, EMBROIDERY, COSTUMES, AND CARPETS*   307

XIV   *ENAMEL, METALWORK, AND JEWELRY*   326

VII: MEANINGS IN CHINESE ART

XV   *SYMBOLISM AND SUBJECTS*   337

      APPENDIX
         Commonly Occurring Symbols   360
         Table of Dynasties, Periods, and Reigns   362
         Bibliography   364
      Subject Index   375
      List of Illustrations   383

Introduction

THE ART OF CHINA

FOR OVER four thousand years the art of China has served to interpret a civilization, and has satisfied the cravings of a whole people for beauty in their daily life, and in their religious and family ceremonies.

In many parts of the world it has been assumed that art was a luxury to which men would give no thought until all their material needs had been satisfied. It was believed that art represented something useless that had no special function except, perhaps, the desire of some individual to try to create beauty. Such an attitude was unknown in China. In that country art was one of the necessities of life. Beautifully designed objects were created for definite purposes —utilitarian, symbolic, or ritual—and they were a basic part of the scheme of existence.

This applies not only to the work of the artist but also to that of the artisan, for the Chinese craftsman brought a love of beauty to each object that he turned out. When he first had to design a bowl for cooking food, or drinking tea or wine, or a jar to hold oil or water, he considered the best way of utilizing the material in which he was working, and how it would best suit the purpose for which it was intended.

Art in China was not something apart, to be understood and enjoyed merely by the aesthete and the initiated. It was not confined to the paintings made by and for scholars; but the innate "sense of rightness" showed itself in the rice bowls and teapots and cooking utensils that were made by, and for, the humblest people. Such objects were just as right in design and decoration as were the elaborate and costly articles of jade and porcelain made for the use of the Imperial Court. Even with the simplest means they achieved fine results.

This "sense of rightness," this love of fine craftsmanship has been handed down from generation to generation. One afternoon in Peking we accompanied a tourist who had decided to have some changes made in a set of pewter vessels she had acquired. We went from one shop to another all along the streets of the metal workers. While most of the men were poor and would have welcomed the money, they all refused to do what she wanted because they felt that her designs were not suitable for the material. "Pu hao k'an" ("It would not look right") they all invariably said.

China has had the longest continuous art history of all civilizations, and her art has reflected all phases of her history, but it is only within the last half century that Chinese art has begun to be studied on any sizable scale by English and American scholars. It is probably because most people have been accustomed to considering that all great art originated in Greece and Italy that the vast range and scope of true Chinese art has so long been neglected. Its bronzes have never been surpassed; its noble sculptures, and its superb landscape paintings were made centuries before men of the Western world could forget their obsession with man and turn to the contemplation and study of nature.

So little has been known about Chinese civilization that there has been a tendency to doubt that their art is as old as they claimed. It is only in the light of excavations made within the last thirty or forty years that the Western world has begun to recognize that the Chinese had accurately recorded their own history, and that bronzes and pottery which would have been classified as about 200 B.C., less than twenty-five years ago, are now conceded to be more than a thousand years older.

It is because of a long-continued and developing tradition throughout the centuries that Chinese art has attained its perfection. André Gide, in his work *Thesée,* shows how a strong, able, and courageous individual is able to find his way out of the maze where he was imprisoned, but only because he had clung tightly to the thread which linked him with the past. In the same way, Chinese art has been deeply rooted and built up on firm foundations. There has never been any long and complete break in the continuity of their art and culture. There were no Dark Ages in Chinese as in European art. Different arts reached their highest development at different times, and all the arts experienced normal cycles of rise and decline, but there was no complete cessation.

There were many periods of political and social upheaval, but, for the most part, art continued on its way, serenely ignoring external events. Art was at its height in the Sung period (960-1279). At that time China was in a state of upheaval not unlike that of the present day, with the Tartars and Mongols sweeping down from the north, invading and then conquering the whole country. But there is no sign of any disturbance in the delicate exquisite paintings, or in the cool perfection of the porcelains of that dynasty.

The Chinese artists and craftsmen did not need to act as conscious historians. The things they created give us the best picture of what kind of people they were and how they lived. Those who have studied the true art of China will never again be able to use such terms as "quaint" or "exotic," "amusing" or "pretty" in describing it. They will have grasped the sweep and grandeur, as well as the austere simplicity and strength, of the best specimens of Chinese art.

It is essential to emphasize this simplicity and grandeur because, unfortunately, whenever we speak of Chinese art someone is sure to start talking about "curios." That word at once brings to mind porcelain mandarins with shaking heads, ingeniously carved ivory balls, heavy, dust-collecting, intricately worked teakwood tables, and all the other bric-a-brac that formerly cluttered up the homes of persons who had returned from China.

The traders who flocked to China in the last century were seldom connoisseurs of art, and the objects which they collected and brought home with them reflected their own taste, and that of the period in which they lived, rather than that of the Chinese. Seeking the grotesque and the curious they found it, but such things have no more connection with true Chinese art than ships inside bottles, or the Lord's Prayer written on the head of a pin, have with the fine art of the Western world.

The Chinese themselves have a vast literature about their art. We have seen many books dating as far back as the Sung dynasty (960-1279) which deal with antiques—ancient pottery, bronzes, pictures, and jades—for even at that time the Chinese were greatly concerned with studying their past. In the whole of that literature there is no reference whatever to any of the things that we in the West associate with "Chinese curios."

It is particularly regrettable that Chinese art should have long been judged by the poorest products of its craftsmen, often by objects which the Chinese made in a spirit of condescension to suit what they considered to be the taste of the Western barbarians, because true Chinese art has developed according to strict canons of good taste. The best Chinese artists and craftsmen have adhered to the principle that beauty is simplicity, and that every line or curve of an art object, or a picture, must be essential and not superfluous. To achieve "a sense of rightness" one must feel that nothing can be added and nothing can be taken away.

Nowhere has the value of the blank space, and the lack rather than the excess of ornament, been better understood. One of the greatest Chinese philosophers, Lao Tzŭ, the father of Taoism, expressed this idea 2500 years ago when he said: "Clay is moulded into a vessel; the utility of the vessel depends upon its hollow interior. Doors and windows are cut out in order to make a house; the utility of the house depends on the empty spaces."

At an exhibition of modern Chinese paintings in Shanghai we overheard a visitor tell the artist she would like to buy one of his pictures—a bird on a bare branch. She explained to him, however, that she considered the painting too empty and suggested that he add a few more branches and leaves.

"If I did that," the Chinese artist answered, "there would be no room for the bird to fly."

Another illustration of the difference between the true art of China and the amusing, and often charming, little objects that their craftsmen sometimes make was voiced by an American architect as he looked at a collection of Chinese art. He pointed to some small Sung vases, moulded in simple classic forms, and remarked that if any one of them were enlarged until it was as high as a tall building it would still be impressive and right because of the fine proportions and perfect balance. Only a piece of true art can stand this test.

While the obsession with "curios" still prevails among some sections of the general public, in the case of certain scholars the pendulum has swung too far in the other direction, and there is a tendency to shroud the whole subject of Chinese art in an atmosphere of obscure and forbidding profundity.

In China, art has never been divorced from the life of the people. It was utilitarian and functional tens of centuries before these words, and what they mean, had entered into the consciousness of the Western world. The ancient bronzes, for example, which are now considered priceless works of art were created, many nearly four thousand years ago, to meet the daily necessities of life—a butcher's chopping block, suits of armor and trappings for chariots and horses, libation cups, cooking utensils or incense burners. Everything down to the flower pots and vases created in the last century was conceived to fill some utilitarian, ceremonial, or decorative need.

The insistence that art is a part of life applies equally to the decoration. Pattern and ornament have a meaning and convey a message to the mind just as a poem does. During the latter part of the eighteenth century, and also during the nineteenth, there was a great demand in the West for overloaded and over-decorated objects. To satisfy this vulgar taste of the Victorians, certain Chinese craftsmen were instructed to add design after design to the same object, the final result being as ugly and meaningless to a cultured Chinese as a page with different poems printed one over the other would be to an American.

So much have the Chinese considered art a part of life that they have even carried the principle of the yang and the yin, one of the most important symbols in Chinese philosophy, into the objects that they created.

When we first went to China we often noticed differences in size and shape between the two parts of a pair of vases, tables, bowls or hangings. In Peking, an old Chinese connoisseur explained to us this apparent lack of symmetry. He walked over to a large pair of covered Ming jars and pointed out that one was taller and thinner, while the other one was shorter and squatter. The first, he said, represented the male (yang), and the other the female (yin) element. Those are the two components which comprise the two elements that are always essential for a perfect whole. They represent motion and repose, light and darkness, heat and cold. These two elements cover all phases of life, and each carries within itself the essence of the other. The yang and yin are forever opposed, and yet must eternally unite.

A question we have often been asked is why one should insist on a thing being old when the new may be just as good. The main charm in collecting antiques is that they give us "a physical presentment of a world which has disappeared," and the Chinese themselves have been the greatest collectors of antiques, each generation wishing to have examples of the art of its forefathers. This desire has, of course, led to the copying of antiques; such copies were not considered as forgeries, but simply as reproductions of beautiful objects of which the originals could not be obtained. From the earliest periods of Chinese history we read of the paintings, bronzes, jades, and potteries of earlier periods being imitated, even to the extent of copying the marks and seals.

In some cases copies are almost as fine as the originals, and well worth collecting. Copies which are old in themselves, and which are objects of art because they were made with great care and skill, cannot, however, be classed with imitations made within the last generation. Porcelain making, for instance, was formerly carried out under the personal supervision of high officials who knew that if they produced fine enough work to win the approval of the emperor they might expect great honors. Work done in large quantities, and purely for commercial gain, during the present century cannot compare with the earlier production, and hence cannot be considered "just as good."

Quite apart from the question of whether a modern copy can compare with the original, the true collector knows the thrill of holding in his hands a delicate piece of porcelain, or a fine antique painting, and realizing that this fragile object, fashioned by a man's hands, has withstood and defied centuries of violence and change.

Original antique Chinese pieces will, of course, continue to become more and more rare. With such fragile things as pottery, porcelain, and paintings, there has always been a great amount of breakage and damage in the natural course of time, as well as destruction caused by wars, revolutions, and other upheavals.

As early as the Ming dynasty (1368-1644), Kao Lien in his Tsun Shêng Pa Chien thus concluded his discussions of the Kuan and Ko wares of the Sung dynasty: "It is impossible to foretell to what point the loss of these ancient wares will continue. For that reason I never see a specimen but my heart dilates, and eye flashes, while my soul seems suddenly to gain wings, and I need no earthly food, reaching a state of exaltation such as one could scarcely expect a mere hobby to produce. My great grief is the thought that those who come after me will hear the names of these wares, but never see the wares that bore these names."

The answer to the fear of Kao Lien that specimens of the Kuan and Ko wares might one day no longer exist, and to the realization that much of irreplaceable beauty in all forms of Chinese art must eventually be lost to mankind, is contained in a passage from H. M. Tomlinson's book *Galleons Reach*. He attributes to a thoughtful Chinese gentleman living in Malaya an observation regarding a collection of old porcelain: "They may all go some day. . . . The world is rough and it is careless. But these things have been done, and so they cannot be lost. They have been added and they cannot be taken out of the sum."

Chapter I

COLLECTING CHINESE ART

THE EARLIER WRITERS of books on Chinese art could not foresee the ever widening horizons that have opened up in the course of the excavations on neolithic sites at Yang-Shao in Honan, and in many other parts of China, the Shang-Yin discoveries on the site of the old capital of Yin at Anyang, and the Chou finds at Loyang and other centers. These discoveries have not only opened up new fields of Chinese archaeology, but they have also confirmed the statements made by the Chinese that their art was far older than was believed in other countries.

Even now it is only the surface of this vast field for exploration that has been scratched, and our knowledge of Chinese art is still far from complete. According to the Taoist teachings anything which is static, and incapable of further growth, is already dead, and it is only where there can be growth and renewal that life exists. Chinese art, and the study and appreciation of Chinese art, is still very much alive.

The modern approach to the subject, which is almost entirely of an archaeological nature, has been extremely useful in extending the frontiers of knowledge but it has interested only a limited circle. It is still mainly due to the emergence of individual collectors with sufficient wealth, leisure, taste, and scholarship, that the general public has had the opportunity of seeing and admiring the true art of China.

Many of these collectors started without archaeological preparation, and frequently without great knowledge of either China or art, but they depended for the acquisition of their art objects upon that sixth sense with which some collectors are said to be endowed. The Chinese have a term for it, "K'ai mên chien shan," which means, "Open the door and you see the mountain."

One collector who undoubtedly possessed this sixth sense was George Eumorfopoulos, a businessman, who had been engaged in the import and export trade between the Orient and the West. He was able to appreciate specimens of Chinese art when they first appeared on the London market and when nobody but he realized their beauty or value. Without relying on mechanical devices, or seals, or marks, he made practically no mistakes in judgment.

The last time we saw him was shortly after the British Museum and the Victoria and Albert Museum had jointly acquired his collection. It was in the summer of 1938, and he had been away in the country, but he came back to London and opened his house in Chelsea so that we could see him and his Chinese treasures before we sailed for the United States.

The world-famous collector was waiting in the hall to greet us. He was a short man, with a small pointed white beard, eyes at once benign and penetrating, and the most charming old-world manner. Although seventy-five years old, he had not lost any of his unquenchable enthusiasm. One look around the drawing room and the adjoining rooms showed us that the house was fuller than ever of specimens of every type of Chinese art.

"We see that you only disposed of one collection in order to make room for another," we said.

"Oh, well, you know what it is to be a collector. It is something for which there is no cure."

We were in China when George Eumorfopoulos died in December 1939, and the Chinese deeply regretted his loss because they realized that through his unfailing instinct for collecting what was best and most representative in their art, he had definitely added to the sum of Western knowledge on that subject.

For instance, he was one of the first to appreciate and acquire specimens of Han and T'ang pottery tomb figures and animals when they first began to appear on the London market. These objects, scorned at first by most experts, have contributed enormously to our understanding of early Chinese civilization.

When one of the first pieces of Sung porcelain, a fine Chün yao type bulb bowl, was shipped to London nearly half a century ago, nobody had ever seen anything like it. A dealer showed it to Eumorfopoulos and said disparagingly: "I don't know what kind of thing this is. It says on the invoice that it is a Sung [pronouncing the word to rhyme with 'dung']." The collector said immediately that he liked it very much and bought it for a few pounds. His purchase was scoffed at by other collectors, but, a few years later, fine specimens of Sung Chün yao were among the most appreciated, and highly priced, of Chinese wares.

George Eumorfopoulos did not speak or read Chinese, and never visited that country until 1935, when he went as one of the London Selecting Committee to choose pieces for the great Exhibition of Chinese Art, which opened in Burlington House, London, that year, and which, for the first time, accorded Chinese art the dignity it merited. It was his instinctive understanding that put him far ahead of all other collectors, for, as the Chinese put it: "He may not have known Chinese, but he had a Chinese heart."

An earlier type of collector was George Salting, whose beautiful porcelains were practically all of the Ch'ing dynasty, mostly of the reigns of K'ang Hsi, Yung Chêng, and Ch'ien Lung (1662-1795). He was an eccentric figure whose fortune had been made in Australian wool. He lived in cheap, cramped quarters, grudging every penny spent on anything except the Chinese objects which seemed to represent for him all the beauty and warmth of life. The prices he paid for those porcelains were far higher than similar pieces would cost today, but, although it was as hard to get money from him for any other purpose as "to pluck a feather from a porcelain bird," when it came to his one passion he never balked at the cost.

One of the curators of the Victoria and Albert Museum told us that, as a young man, he had once sent a note to Salting and asked for permission to bring an American couple, who were very anxious to look at some of his newly acquired pieces. But, after the appointment was made, the woman was suddenly taken ill. The curator called, in person, to apologize to Mr. Salting and explain that the visitors would be unable to come. "That's a fine thing" the collector answered crossly. "And what about the cake? My housekeeper made me buy a cake at Fuller's this morning, and I paid two shillings for it. You will have to take it back to them yourself, explain the whole thing, and make them return my money."

Then there was the time when Salting went to fetch the Crown Prince of Sweden (another ardent collector of Chinese art), who happened to be in London, to a meeting of connoisseurs of Chinese art. Before leaving he made careful inquiries about buses. Someone remarked: "You are surely not thinking of taking the Crown Prince in a bus?"

"What else can I do?" came the reply. "If I call a cab I'm afraid he'll expect me to pay the fare."

Naturally to such a man museums which would look after and display the treasures that he loved so greatly, but for which he had no room in his small flat, were a godsend. From 1887 on he sent his pieces to the Victoria and Albert Museum, where they formed the bulk of their earliest collection of Chinese art.

The museum had cases made and provided the proper care. There the collector could go as often as he liked, open the cases, fondle his pieces, display them to friends and rivals, and yet not be forced to take a larger place, or be put to the expense of entertaining visitors. When he died, in 1910, he left his entire collection to the nation.

While there are still admirers of the later finely finished and beautifully decorated products of the Chinese porcelain kilns, such as those in the Salting Collection, many present-day connoisseurs prefer the earlier specimens of Chinese art. Not only the exquisite Ju, Kuan, and Ko wares of the Sung period (960-1279), and the magnificent bronzes of Shang and Chou (1766-221 B.C.*), but also neolithic types of pottery dating all the way back to 3000 B.C. and earlier.

Another well-known British collector of Chinese art is Sir Percival David. He and George Eumorfopoulos were devoted personal friends, but they had an entirely different approach when it came to acquiring pieces. "Eumo" selected his specimens by the method which the Chinese call "with heart and eye" and by the accumulated experience acquired in handling and studying art objects

* Traditional dates.

16

Pair of gallipots, Tz'ŭ Chou ware. Sung Dynasty. Samuel C. Davis Collection.

Blue and white vase with magnolia design, reign of K'ang Hsi (1662-1722). Salting Collection.

Peach-shaped cup, kuan yao, with warm gray glaze. Sung Dynasty. Eumorfopoulos Collection.

Bronze water buffalo. Last part of Middle Chou.
Alfred F. Pillsbury Collection.

Above: Tomb figurine of woman. T'ang Dynasty
or earlier. Eumorfopoulos Collection.

Right: Jadeite figure of Kwan Yin. 19th century.
Jacob Ruppert Collection.

Three-color vase, *famille jaune,* reign of K'ang Hsi (1662-1722). B. Altman Collection.

Peach bloom flower vase. Reign of K'ang Hsi (1662-1722). W. T. Walters Collection.

Chinese export porcelain plate from the dinner service of George Washington, decorated with Order of Cincinnati (1785).

White jade covered vase in form of large lotus
flower. 18th-19th century. T. B. Walker Collection.

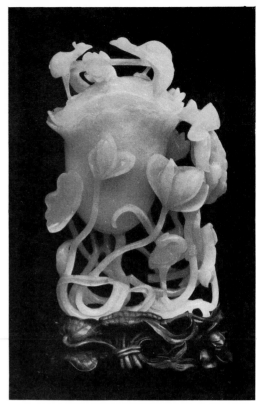

Blue and white conical Ming bowl with design
of Three Friends—pine, prunus, and bamboo.
Late 14th—early 15th century. Herbert C. Hoover
Collection.

for many years. But not for Sir Percival was the "heart and eye" method. He always wanted proof. He bought only pieces that bore marks and inscriptions. Many of the finest objects have none, but those he usually ignored. Everything had to be painstakingly identified and authenticated. The Chinese dealers and collectors all knew this characteristic and catered to it. They ransacked old Chinese books and libraries to find records that would bear testimony to the genuineness of a painting or a piece of porcelain.

Sir Percival told us the following story which shows that he knows how the Chinese feel about him, and does not resent it. One afternoon in Hong Kong he was asked to the home of a wealthy Chinese collector. After they had examined the pieces together exhaustively, and probably exhaustingly, for several hours, his Chinese host got up and said:

"Now I am going to show you my greatest treasure."

Sir Percival waited eagerly, wondering what he was going to see even more wonderful than the objects already displayed. Then the Chinese came back, followed by an amah carrying a small baby in her arms. "Look!" he exclaimed. "This is my very greatest treasure. My first son. A boy. Do you want to see his mark?"

The collection, which can be seen now at the Percival David Foundation of Chinese Art in London, is a wide and varied one, and every piece is perfect. It does not include many specimens of the very early periods of Chinese art because the collector never cared for things that had been buried in the earth.

In China the role of the art connoisseur and collector has been an important one. While many artists and craftsmen worked under Imperial patronage, there were others of more independent spirit who preferred to work for a patron who would allow them to express themselves in an individual manner, and to live far removed from the academic restrictions and intrigues of the Court.

The names of some of these art patrons became as famous as those of the artists, and the fact that a piece of jade or porcelain or a picture was once included in their collection gives it added prestige and value. When a painting was added to a collection, the owner affixed his seal to the work, and the seal of a well-known collector is often considered a proof of authenticity as well as of merit.

Such a collector was Hsiang Yüan-p'ien (1525-1590), a wealthy and important Ming expert, whose seal appears on one of the great landmarks of the art world—the fourth-century Ku K'ai-chih painting in the British Museum.

In China we ascertained that Hsiang Yüan-p'ien had been a pawnbroker in addition to being an artist, critic, collector, connoisseur, and one of the most celebrated writers on art of the sixteenth century. Chinese connoisseurs showed us that pieces with his seal were numbered in a manner still used by pawnbrokers, and pointed out that, as a pawnbroker, he often wrote on his pictures how much he had paid for them, something that no other collector ever did.

This fact does not detract from his reputation or standing. Many great European fortunes were originally derived from the same source, and many famous Western collections were started with art objects on which money had been loaned, the original owners having been unable to redeem their pledges. It does, however, explain the unevenness of Hsiang's collection.

Another important Chinese collector, chiefly of paintings and calligraphy, was An Ch'i (born 1683), the son of a Korean who worked in the family of a Manchu minister. He had such excellent judgment and taste that his seal on a painting stamps it as genuine.

Being public-spirited men, An Ch'i and his father undertook to rebuild the city wall of Tientsin with their own money. This civic enterprise took six years and cost so much more than had been anticipated that An Ch'i was forced to spend his entire fortune. He was finally obliged to sell his whole collection to meet the rising costs.

An Ch'i wrote several books on art, and in one of them he relates how, during the building of the wall, he had been unable to purchase certain pictures, and that these had later "haunted him in his dreams."

AMERICAN COLLECTORS

Dr. Hu Shih, the Chinese philosopher-statesman, who was formerly ambassador to the United States, maintains that one of the most important foundation stones of American friendship for China has been the forming of collections of Chinese art objects in this country by American museums, private collectors, and individual scholars. This observation reveals an important truth, for it is only as we learn more about this great art, with its recorded history of over four thousand years, that we can begin to understand the Chinese people. Of past history, of long dead emperors, of battles fought long ago, of social and political turmoil, little if any information remains to us. But what does remain are the vessels that the Chinese made for their daily needs and for use in religious and family ceremonies, as well as their paintings, sculptures, and other art objects. It is these things that give us a key to the life lived by the people of China from the most remote past to the present day.

In the early days of the American republic, George Washington had a complete dinner service of Chinese Export porcelain. "Blue and white" porcelains, as well as Export porcelains decorated in colored enamels in Canton (of the type mistakenly called Lowestoft), and other Chinese objects were brought back by New England sea captains and were to be seen in many American homes. There was, however, little general interest in Chinese art in the United States until the opening of the Centennial Exhibition in Philadephia in 1876. Since that time many magnificent collections have been formed by American admirers.

One of the first important American collectors of Oriental ceramics was William Thompson Walters, a merchant, railroad president, and art collector of Baltimore, Maryland, who died in 1894. He was particularly interested in Ch'ing monochrome porcelains, the jewel-like colors of which were so brilliant and satisfying that they needed no decoration. His collection, which can now be seen at the Walters Art Gallery in Baltimore, also includes specimens of Ming porcelains and some earlier pieces.

Toward the end of the nineteenth century, Benjamin Altman, who founded the department store in New York that bears his name, formed a large collection of Chinese porcelains. This included many specimens of large K'ang Hsi vases of the "famille verte" and "famille noire" type. He donated his entire collection to the Metropolitan Museum of Art in New York.

An outstanding American collector, who was among the first to recognize the beauty of early Chinese art, was Charles Lang Freer. He retired from business while still young, after having amassed a fortune by the sale of railroad cars. Through his close friendship with James Whistler, who had been so greatly influenced by Oriental painting, Freer became an ardent admirer of Chinese culture.

Charles Freer also enjoyed the friendship of Professor Ernest F. Fenollosa, whose knowledge of Chinese art was entirely derived from Japanese sources, because he had studied it in Japan. Professor Fenollosa tried to dissuade Freer from going to China, but Freer felt that it was essential to have lived in China in order to achieve some insight into Chinese standards of art and philosophy. Guided by his own judgment, Charles Freer traveled throughout China, purchasing the masterpieces of pottery, sculpture, bronze, and painting which formed the basis of the fine collection in the Freer Gallery of Washington, D. C.

Until about twenty years ago, most of the Chinese art collections in the United States were concentrated in the East—New York, Washington, Boston, Philadelphia, and Baltimore. Since then important collections have been formed and made available to the public in every part of the country—for instance in museums in Detroit, Chicago, Kansas City, Indianapolis, Minneapolis, Cleveland, Cincinnati, Toledo, St. Louis, Denver, Seattle, and at various centers in California. There are also splendid collections in Ontario, Canada, and in Honolulu.

In the city of Minneapolis alone there are such outstanding collections as that of Alfred F. Pillsbury, who specialized in archaic bronzes, and Thomas Barlow Walker, who assembled, among other things, a remarkable group of jades of all periods.

One of the most carefully selected and beautifully displayed collections of Chinese art is the one at the William Rockhill Nelson Art Gallery in Kansas City, which was opened as recently as 1933.

While there still remains a vast field for excavation, discovery, and interpretation, the Western world already understands more about the artistic creations of China than about any other phase of Chinese civilization, and this is largely due to the pioneer work of enthusiastic collectors.

With most collectors, the pleasure of finding and acquiring art objects and antique pieces comes first. Few of them start with much knowledge of Chinese history or art. The collector soon realizes, however, that the smallest object is characteristic of the nation which produced it, and he inevitably comes to understand more about the men who created the things he admires. A growing understanding of art, history, and archaeology is frequently the result, and not the cause, of the acquisition of a Chinese collection.

In order to admire a Chinese painting, a sculptured figure, or a piece of porcelain, it is no more essential to understand fully the Buddhist, Taoist, or Confucian philosophies than it would be to make a profound study of Western religions and philosophies before visiting a collection of American or European art.

Chinese art can be appreciated if it is judged by the same standards as all other art. Of course, the greater the knowledge, the deeper will be the understanding. Everything that an artist knows, is, and thinks goes into and influences his work, but it is not necessary for the spectator to follow him in all his experiences. The artist should always be able to communicate some understanding of his conclusions or feelings. One of the great achievements of the Chinese artist has been the fusion of the spiritual and material, so that his art can be enjoyed for its outward beauty alone should certain of the deeper symbolism elude the casual Western observer.

It is always the simple beauty, the universality, the timelessness of Chinese art which appeals irresistibly to people of so many nationalities and draws them on to become ardent students and collectors.

Although the men we have already mentioned have been wealthy and were able to purchase collections important enough to donate to museums, the acquiring of Chinese pieces has not been confined to the rich. One finds excellent individual specimens of Chinese art in modest homes in almost every part of the world—a family teapot, fruit bowl, lacquered chest or painted screen, a carved ivory figure or an enamel plate, for instance. Such is their universal appeal that their owners are often not particularly aware that they are Chinese, or even that they are old. They have become a part of the common heritage. Almost all the traditional flower patterns and motifs used in fabrics and wallpapers had their origin in China, and designs on most of the dishes and bowls and vases we use, even if not Chinese, are derived from Chinese designs. Yet all these things are now accepted without thought of their origin.

The decoration on a piece of Chinese art conveys a definite message to the Chinese mind, but it is possible for the Westerner to enjoy it without understanding that message. If you look at a porcelain bowl with a bamboo design, you can still admire it without knowing that the design is intended to affirm that the bamboo bends but never breaks, even in the strongest gale, just as the true gentleman will never break under the worst afflictions. A vase depicting little children at play delights you even if you do not know that it conveys the wish that the recipient will have many children and that they will all have successful careers. Even the shapes of various objects have meanings. A bride's lacquered powder box has a finely curved rim which expresses the wish that her happiness will continue without end just as the rim is rounded without any break. These decorations or shapes are beautiful, but the added knowledge of their meaning makes each work of art still more interesting.

When it comes to paintings it is equally easy to admire a picture without any special training—but your interest will be heightened if you realize that you, as well as the artist, are intended to be the little figure that is usually seen in a Chinese landscape, and that you should imagine yourself to be walking along the banks of the river, or climbing a mountain, and enjoying the scenery on the way. That is why the perspective is seldom static. Neither you, nor the artist, is standing in front of an easel; you, and he, are actually moving through the scene depicted. If you see a picture of birds on a branch you may find it charming, but you will be still more enchanted if you know that the bird on the branch is singing gaily because he knows that he has wings and can fly if the bough breaks.

None of this is peculiarly Chinese—it is universal. This universality and serenity, so well understood by the Chinese, has led to the increasing use of Chinese objects in interior decoration throughout the world. Once the unfortunate idea that Chinese art consisted of quaint and fantastic things was shown to be false, it was realized that well-chosen Chinese pieces could be used harmoniously in any tasteful setting.

The oldest things are particularly well adapted for the most modern rooms. Examples are the classic forms of Shang and Chou bronzes and early pottery, the strong functional forms of Han pottery, and the simple vigor of T'ang horses and figures. The simplicity and delicacy of form and color which characterize Sung porcelains and paintings render them equally suitable for modern or classical settings; and Ming art, with its opulent outlines and rich clear colors, forms a perfect complement to Baroque types of decoration. The charm and decorative quality of Ch'ing dynasty carved jades, ivories, porcelains, and pictures blend admirably with rococo and Chippendale rooms.

Andrea Palladio, the famous Italian architect who died in 1580, said his criteria of good design were "utility, timelessness and beauty." The same criteria might well be used in the selection of Chinese art objects.

As opposed to the decorator, the collector will not stop with the purchase of certain pieces to decorate a room. Or, one should say, the true collector *cannot* stop, because there is always the possibility of making a discovery. He starts with simple, inexpensive pieces, studies and compares them, and gradually exchanges good pieces for better ones as his knowledge increases. Although there are wealthy collectors who will buy an object only because it is the best of its kind, there are many student collectors with equal taste and discrimination and knowledge, but with limited means, who are just as happy to find carefully repaired specimens of rare old pieces which are as fine and have as much historical interest as do the more expensive perfect ones.

A friend of ours asked a Chinese expert in Peking how to distinguish between an original piece and a later copy. He replied: "Compare, compare, compare." Another old Chinese collector, when asked the same question said: "Yen ching yeh hsin," which means "With eye and heart."

When the eye and heart are sufficiently developed by the study and handling of many pieces, there is the deep rewarding satisfaction of finding that one not only has learned to distinguish between different periods of Chinese art, but has also learned much about another civilization.

Art is meant to lead men's thoughts away from what is mean and ordinary to an understanding of what is fine and beautiful in life and in nature. This is especially true of Chinese art which is the means by which the Chinese people have traditionally expressed their soul and aspirations. As one grows in understanding of Chinese art, one finds one has also acquired a key to the spiritual and intellectual nature of the Chinese people during the last forty centuries.

Specimen of the calligraphy of Mi Fei. (Palace Museum, Peking)

Chapter II

COPIES AND IMITATIONS
IN CHINESE ART

IN THE EIGHTH century B.C. there lived in the state of Ch'u a minor official named Ho. He was a man of the greatest integrity, who felt that if truth and honesty did not prevail the inevitable outcome would be the ruin of the state.

One day, when digging his garden, he found in the earth a piece of ancient sacrificial jade. At that time antiques were already highly valued, and Ho did not even consider keeping for himself an object that had once been used in Imperial rites, but went off at once to the Court to present his find to the Duke of Ch'u. The Duke handed the piece to his experts who examined it and pronounced it to be an imitation.

Ho indignantly protested this opinion, and offended the experts who retaliated by persuading the Duke that the man had deliberately tried to play a hoax upon his ruler. They worked up the Duke's feelings to such a pitch that Ho was condemned to lose his right foot as a punishment for deceiving the head of the state.

Ho, now a lame man, kept the piece of jade carefully wrapped in silk, and polished it frequently and carefully.

Some years later the Duke died. Ho knew that the jade was genuine, and he felt he could not live until both the jade and his own honor were cleared of the aspersion that had been cast upon them. Again he made his way to the Court and presented the piece of jade to the new Duke. Once more the experts insisted that it was a copy, and the enraged Duke ordered Ho to lose his other foot.

Now reduced to the status of a crippled beggar, Ho lived on because he felt certain that truth must prevail in the end.

Eventually the Dukedom passed into other hands. Fearful as he was of further punishment, Ho felt it was imperative for him to appear before the third Duke. The poor, emaciated, old man, propped up by his crutches, wept as he told his story. His grief, he explained, was not caused by his mutilations, but by the thought that a genuine jade, and a loyal man, had both been maligned.

The Duke ordered the piece of jade to be examined again, and this time the experts agreed that it was a genuine antique. The Duke was now anxious to heap honors upon Ho to compensate him for his sufferings, but the old man refused to accept anything. He said that his only purpose and desire in life had been that truth should prevail, and now he would return to his village and die in peace.

This is the classic story of how experts may disagree, and, to this day, when a difference of opinion arises among experts in China, someone may remark: "Remember the jade of Ho."

Almost as old as Chinese art itself is the custom of imitating the art works of earlier periods. This was not necessarily done with intent to deceive. Once a perfectly satisfactory form had been devised for a cooking utensil, an incense burner, a water container, or a rice bowl, it was easier for each generation of craftsmen to continue copying it than to endeavor to create something new. The Chinese did not seek novelty for its own sake, and were quite content to imitate forms and decorations which they found to their liking.

Quite early in Chinese history, however, there arose a desire to own "antiquities." Perhaps sooner, and more strongly, than did the people of any other race, the Chinese experienced a compelling urge to collect specimens of the art works of their ancestors. When these were not available, imitations were ordered, so that in Sung times we have records of copies being made of Shang and Chou bronzes and of early pottery. This tradition continued unbroken, and we find reproductions of Sung porcelains, paintings, and books being turned out in the Ming dynasty, and copies of Ming art objects being created in the Ch'ing dynasty.

Naturally when a dynasty or a reign ended everything did not immediately change. The same artists or craftsmen would continue working with the same materials, and in the same traditions, for many years. It was only by degrees that a new mode superseded an old established one, with the result that we frequently find typical Ming vases bearing K'ang Hsi marks, or pieces of porcelain that, by all critical standards, should have been made in the reign of K'ang Hsi, or Yung Chêng, but which bear the Ch'ien Lung seal. Such pieces cannot be called imitations.

In the earlier periods of Chinese art, even when paintings or other objects were deliberate copies bearing false date marks, they are still frequently beautiful in themselves, and well worth collecting, even though their value may be less than that of the original.

It was only within the last few decades, when a considerable demand arose abroad for Chinese pieces, that the manufacture of spurious Chinese "antiques" assumed the proportions of an important industry created for the purpose of deceiving purchasers. Fortunately the majority of Chinese dealers did not lend themselves to these attempts at deception, and many deplored them. We knew many dealers in Peking, Canton, Shanghai, and other places who were scrupulously honest in their dealings, and who cheerfully refunded money at any time if their clients were not wholly satisfied with their purchases.

There was one large store on Nanking Road in Shanghai where the Chinese proprietor carefully classified all his stock into four categories, and told intending purchasers to which one the piece in which they were interested belonged. He described them in the following manner:

1. "Genuine old piece"   Indicating period, etc.
2. "Old imitation"   The piece is old in itself, but is a copy of a still older one.
3. "Imitation old"   Recent copy of an old piece.
4. "New piece"

This man fixed his prices in accordance with these groupings and did not attempt to deceive even the most unwary tourist.

On the other hand some dealers had very little knowledge of their wares. They had never made a serious study of porcelain, or any other antiques, and were interested only in making a profit. These were the men who referred to all their wares as "very old" and knew nothing of periods. Both types of dealers are of course to be found in every country.

A Chinese philosopher of the Sung dynasty, Chu Hsi (1130-1200), wrote: "In every human mind there is the knowing faculty; and, in everything, there is its reason. The incompleteness of our knowledge is due to our insufficiency in investigating into the reason of things. The student must go to all things under Heaven, beginning with the known principles and seeking to reach the utmost. After sufficient labor has been devoted to it, the day will come when all things will suddenly become clear and intelligible." *

It is only by experience and the handling of many pieces that the novice becomes the expert—there is no substitute for the "compare, compare, compare" method of learning.

In many parts of China we saw numbers of Chinese craftsmen busily engaged in making copies of antiques. For instance, in Honan, there were factories that poured out streams of imitations of the Han and T'ang clay tomb figures and other objects found in the graves of that region. The same clay of which the originals were made is always at hand, as well as a constant supply of fine models, so that it takes considerable experience to detect the forgeries.

Stone heads of Buddha and Kwan Yin, which were represented as having been broken off sculptures in the old cave temples, were turned out by the hundred in Peking, because the right kind of stone could be procured there. Similarly, stone carvings of horses, chariots and riders modeled after those seen in the bas-reliefs in the Han tombs were sold as dating from the Han dynasty, although corresponding originals have not been found. This is an instance of creating a new "antique" to meet the artistic taste of the purchaser.

There would appear to be no limit to the ingenuity of the Chinese when it comes to imitating the more valuable specimens of works of art, as is illustrated by the following incident.

Sir Percival David's insistence on evidences of authenticity has caused many dealers to regard his catalogue as the Bible of their business. When we were in

* Translated by Dr. Hu Shih in *Religion and Philosophy in Chinese History.*

London in 1938, the late Mr. Brankston of the British Museum discussed with us an experience he had had when he went to China to visit the porcelain kilns at Ching-tê Chên. The director of one of the kilns had said to him: "I wish you would ask Sir Percival David next time he makes a catalogue to show pictures of both sides of each piece. How can we tell what the other side looks like?" Mr. Brankston regarded this as touching evidence of the man's scholarly interest in this particular ware—delicately painted Ch'ien Lung porcelain of the rare and costly Ku Yüeh-hsüan type.

Two years later we met Mr. Brankston again in Shanghai, and he reminded us of this conversation. "You remember my telling you about that chap in Ching-tê Chên who said he wished David had shown both sides of each piece in his catalogue? Well, now I know why. A collection of the most perfect copies of every piece of porcelain of the Ku Yüeh-hsüan type illustrated came on the market in Paris. Even experts might have had a hard time recognizing them as imitations had it not been for the fact that they were decorated on only one side, the other being left completely blank."

Fortunately, there is usually some slip which enables the careful observer to detect the forgery. It is quite rare for a "perfect crime" to be perpetrated, even in the realm of art forgeries.

At certain times there has been a special vogue for particular types of "antiques" and then elaborate plans have been made for the large scale production of such objects. One instance is the demand which arose in the United States for wooden statuary, and which kept a large number of wood-carvers in Peking busy turning out thousands of "Ming" statues and statuettes for several years before Pearl Harbor. They were referred to as "American dealers' cargo."

Many of them were made of old stolen telephone poles, but the more costly and elaborate ones were carved from old coffins or the roof beams of old temples, so that the wood was of the correct period and impregnated with the fumes of incense.

As far as color goes, even the original wooden statues would have been painted and repainted many times—often in gratitude by persons whose prayers in the temples had been answered—so that the freshness would give no conclusive indication of period. Also, as these statues were exposed to the elements, even in the course of only a few decades the paint would have worn off on the more exposed sections, and the copies took care to imitate this effect. Wood, however, is a sensitive material which lends itself less readily to fraud than does stone, and it is comparatively easy to detect imitations. Apart from the inferiority in the modeling of the hands and feet and hair, these new pieces feel harsh to the touch, and do not have the smoothness and softness of the genuine old piece.

Then, too, the colors of the copies were not incorporated into the wood, but could be scratched off. On antique pieces, where layer after layer of paint has been applied, the colors have soaked right into the wood. On new figures the green is whitish, whereas on old ones it has acquired the appearance of malachite. On old pieces the white painted sections would have taken on an ivory tint. In general, the effects wrought by nature during centuries cannot be achieved quickly by even the most skilled craftsmen.

These wooden figures fetched fairly modest prices, even when sold as original Ming or Sung pieces, but it is when one comes to the high-priced objects that the ingenuity of the counterfeiter comes into full play, as in the story of the confidence trick engineered by a "curio" dealer in Peking, with a modest little business which suddenly blossomed into an imposing well-stocked shop on a main street.

The man boasted to his colleagues about the method by which he had suddenly acquired his wealth. For about twenty years he had employed workmen to copy old stone carvings. He was very patient, and would not be satisfied with anything less than perfection. He disposed of these copies as he could, and continued to experiment over the years. When he was completely satisfied, he had his statues placed in different temples outside the city, and waited until a buyer for a large museum came to Peking. Then one day a Chinese monk presented himself at the hotel where the buyer was staying and told him about the priceless ancient stone statues that could still be found in certain temples.

Of course, the monk pointed out, they were not for sale, but he would like to show them to someone who would know how to appreciate their beauty. The buyer was delighted with the statues and wanted to know if there was any way he could acquire them, but the monk insisted that such a transaction would be altogether too risky.

After several visits, and when he had completely won the buyer's confidence, the self-styled monk said he thought he could arrange to have the statues stolen at night, but that he would have to pay very high bribes to the persons in charge of the various temples. He also pointed out that, once the theft was accomplished, he and everybody else concerned would have to disappear from Peking, so that it must be made worth their while. The ruse worked perfectly, and the stone statues were sold at a tremendously high figure. They are beautifully made, and are still greatly admired.

Archaic bronzes are amongst the finest examples of Chinese art, and it is only within the present century that Shang and Chou bronzes have come into the market. Before the Chinese Revolution of 1912 it was a very serious matter to violate a tomb, and no systematic excavation could be carried on. When a piece was unearthed secretly by grave robbers, who knew they were liable to be beheaded if caught, it was quickly sold at a very high price.

Even in recent years it was only occasionally that a complete and beautiful specimen was found, and, when such a piece came to light, word quickly reached the big dealers who bid against each other for it.

The rarity of such pieces, and their great value, proved a challenge to the ingenuity of Chinese and Japanese traders who worked long and hard to make good imitations. They were fairly successful because few persons had handled enough bronzes to be readily able to detect the fraud. Unfortunately, even those who had studied them often relied chiefly on designs, inscriptions, etc. in determining period, and all these things could be copied by the forgers. What could not be imitated is the workmanship of the original artist's hand, or the beautiful patina acquired slowly throughout the centuries.

In Soochow there was a man who spent years perfecting the most handsome-looking imitations of old bronzes. They were so convincing that they found a ready market as soon as they were completed. The important dealers who were buying genuine pieces from Anyang and Loyang complained bitterly that this was unfair competition, and realized that the steady stream of fake pieces would eventually damage their business by undermining the confidence of the buyers. A group of them arrived at an arrangement by which they agreed to pay this man a large sum of money monthly for life if he would agree to stop making bronzes. The Soochow man kept his part of the bargain, but, as the Chinese who told us the story added: "Of course, he did not live long after that. Only a few months."

As bronzes became better known and collectors began to understand the difference between genuine patina twenty or thirty centuries old and the type of patina created by chemical means, the sale of fake bronzes became more difficult. Then a new type of fraud was practiced, and one that was much harder to detect. In the excavation of sites, large quantities of fragments and broken pieces would be unearthed. In themselves these had little value, except for the student, but, spurred on by the high prices paid for complete bronzes, counterfeiters exercised great skill and ingenuity in assembling and building up impressive bronze specimens out of this material.

Such bronzes had the right patina and perfect workmanship, and they were quickly sold. In one American museum, when an apparatus was purchased that could X-ray the pieces, it was discovered that over 80 per cent of the specimens, hitherto believed to be in perfect condition, had been constructed of assembled fragments. This particular type of deception can now be easily detected with the proper equipment.

It would, of course, be unwise for any amateur collector to purchase anything so costly as a Shang or Chou bronze without the advice and assistance of an expert who has the necessary apparatus to make a careful and thorough examination, or through a reliable dealer who would have already made all essential tests.

It is unlikely that the novice or the "tourist" would make a casual purchase of an art object of this type. Dealers in fakes depend for the bulk of their trade on the sale of copies of porcelains, jades, and ivories, and unless one has the good fortune to make purchases through an honest dealer there are only two ways to avoid being cheated.

The first is to study and compare until one has sufficient judgment and knowledge of the type of pieces one wishes to collect. The other is to buy only things which one really likes and wishes to have, and to pay such modest prices that they can be enjoyed even if they are not genuine antiques. On this basis one can never go wrong.

There is a certain type of collector, well known to serious students of art in China, who goes out without any knowledge and picks up a piece of porcelain or jade because he or she "has a hunch" that it is real. Time and again we have been shown a specimen and asked what we thought of it, and, after having given an honest opinion, been told indignantly: "I just know it is a genuine Ming or Ch'ien Lung, and you don't recognize a good thing when you see it." Frequently the owner would then turn to one of his Chinese servants and ask him to corroborate that it was a good piece.

There was a widespread belief among some Westerners who lived in China that every houseboy or cook was a judge of Chinese art. It was no use pointing out that they would not expect every Englishman or Frenchman to be an expert in the art of their country, or to explain that Chinese art has such a long history and has so many particularities that it takes years of study to have even a modest knowledge of it. The Chinese "boy" was still the final arbiter, and his decision was often favorable or otherwise according to whether or not the seller had given him a commission on the purchase.

Chapter III

DISTINGUISHING THE GENUINE
FROM THE FALSE ARTICLE

ALTHOUGH THERE IS no quick and ready-made substitute for years of experience and study of museum pieces, coupled with a natural aptitude, there are a few simple rules that make the detection of copies easier.

In buying jades, for instance, apart from the question of period, the unwary is liable to be sold substitutes—soapstone, jasper, green glass, or even celluloid. Quantities of such objects were being sold all the time under the name of jade. One method of detecting the difference is that jade is extremely cold, smooth, and hard to the touch, while the copies usually lack luster, feel softer, and quickly absorb the warmth of the hand. Glass can be recognized by the air bubbles it always has, and soapstone by its softness. Glass and soapstone can be marked with the point of a penknife, but real jade is too hard to be scratched. A drop of water on real jade will not spread, as it will on the other substances.

In the case of many fine pieces of jade, because of the hardness of the material it has taken years of work to complete the carving. The first thing to be looked for in an old piece is the quality of the workmanship, delicacy of execution, and softness of line. A good old piece of jade will have no hard corners, no protrusions. The modern piece, even when well worked, is liable to have sharp angles, hard protrusions, and coarser workmanship. In other words it will lack the velvety quality implied when a Chinese says that a thing is as smooth and fine to the touch as jade.

Even in buying new jade there are traps for the unwary. Because of the demand for jade of a deep green color, many pieces are artificially colored. This applies particularly to personal ornaments—brooches, pendants, necklaces, earrings, etc. Deep green jade should be translucent, and resemble, as closely as possible, an emerald. The faked pieces are too dark in color, and opaque.

Other hard stones, such as *rose quartz, amethyst, turquoise, malachite,* and *coral,* have often been artificially colored or have had their color enhanced by being soaked in special dyes. The Chinese have a product called "rose oil," in which pieces of crystal are soaked to make them resemble rose quartz, for which there has been such a great demand. Such artificial colors become paler as time passes and may eventually fade away.

Ivory pieces are another popular form of purchase. New ivories are dipped in tea and then smoked to give them the mellow tint of age. Ivory, however, like wood, is a sensitive material that does not readily lend itself to deception. There is some subtle quality lacking in the new work, a fineness which the old pieces have acquired through many years of handling. This is a field which presents slight danger for those who have even a modest acquaintanceship with the real spirit of Chinese art.

With *lacquer,* too, it is fairly difficult to make really convincing copies of old work. Quality of material, elegance of design, and type of decoration should be the first criteria. It is helpful, however, to know that modern lacquer is much heavier than old pieces, and old lacquer is harder, does not peel, and has a total absence of the odor found in modern pieces.

Great quantities of *enamels* and *cloisonné* pieces have continued to be made up to the present time. Part of this output was destined to be sold to the unwary as antique, but the bulk is a purely commercial product—often sold by weight. The older pieces can be distinguished from the modern by the softness of the color and the quality of the design. In the case of new dishes and bowls, the copper which serves as a base is bright in color, often reddish, and the edges are sharp. In old pieces the base is of light color, and the edges have been softened and patinated by age. Old pieces are lighter in weight than the new ones.

The white *porcelain* made in Fukien province, known as "Blanc de Chine," is a medium in which it is difficult for amateurs to detect modern copies because these kilns have been working in the same place, with the same materials, and from the same models, since early Ming times. There are some definite tests that can be made. For instance, the porcelain in the older pieces is so nearly perfect that it is smooth as silk, whereas modern imitations have a somewhat mottled (or orange skin) effect when examined with a good magnifying glass under a strong light. Also, when the earliest Ming "Blanc de Chine" pieces are held to a strong light they have a warm rosy glow, while Ch'ien Lung pieces will show a lighter cream color. Old pieces will never be of a cold, powder-white shade as are the new specimens. Then, too, in the new pieces the glaze which has run down into the folds of the draperies of figures, or at the base of any object, will show a slightly bluish white color which could never be seen in an old piece. Many of the modern Fukien porcelains are made in moulds, whereas the finer old specimens were carefully carved by hand.

The Chinese have a saying: "Judge porcelain by the foot of the vessel." And you will notice that when a connoisseur examines a piece of porcelain he turns it upside down. First of all one looks at the seal, if any. But the seal is not a sure test, for many later pieces bear early seals.

Then there are other revealing features. For instance, around the foot, Ming porcelains do not have the grooves that one sees in later wares, which show that they were intended to be placed on a wooden stand. Also the bottom of a Ming piece often shows radial lines under the glaze, and the heat turns the foot ring brown.

On larger objects the base is seldom glazed, as it frequently is on smaller pieces. When a mark (usually in underglaze blue) has been put on, it is always covered with glaze. The bases of Ming bowls are of the same conical shape as Sung ones, and not flat as they are on Ch'ing pieces. Hsüan Tê dishes and bowls have slightly undulating convex bases, while Ch'ing copies are flat inside and underneath.

Here again it is chiefly only after comparison of great numbers of pieces that the base can be safely used as a guide.

It is not only the Chinese who have engaged in the manufacture of imitations. There is no type of antiques that has not been forged or misrepresented by unscrupulous dealers, and attested by equally unscrupulous experts in every country. In China, as elsewhere, there are certain experts who will certify for a given fee that a piece is genuine. We knew one old Chinese expert, the soul of integrity, and quite a poor man, who was offered a considerable fee by a large dealer to give a certain museum director his guarantee that a Han piece of bronze was of the Shang period. He refused, but, as he wryly remarked to us: "It did not help at all, because the seller simply got another expert to do what he wanted."

While frauds are perpetrated in all parts of the world, the manufacture of imitations developed into such a widespread industry in China because of the skill in craftsmanship of the Chinese and also because, in many places, the work was still carried on at the same sites where it had started many centuries ago.

And, above all, we must blame the fact that purchasers of Chinese art objects insist on things being old, so that much of the overwhelming stream of creative energy of the Chinese artists and craftsmen was diverted into this morass of faking and copying instead of into the joys of original work. There has been little encouragement for the honest craftsman who wants to give expression to his own ideas.

In Shanghai, at the home of an inexperienced Chinese collector, we were shown a whole group of the most exquisite ceramic sculptures in Yi-hsing pottery ware. They were so beautiful that their maker deserved recognition for his work. Unfortunately the owner had purchased them under the impression that they were made in the Ming period, although they had none of the characteristics of the work of that time. As soon as it became known that the pieces were made by a living artist, the purchaser rejected them, and nobody else would even look at them.

One exception to this unhappy state of affairs is in the field of Kuangtung pottery sculpture. This may be because the older specimens of this ware are little known outside of South China, and hence the demand for "antique" figures has been less developed.

The most important of all the arts of China, and the least understood by the outside world, are those of *calligraphy* and *painting*. If the work of Chinese artists, and especially that of the later ones, were better known and appreciated there would be less deception than is now the case. That does not mean that there would be no copying of previous works. From the earliest times even the most famous Chinese artists have enjoyed making copies of the work of older masters. Frequently they have written on their pictures that this is a copy of the work of a master whose painting they greatly admired.

Alan Priest, the Curator of Far Eastern Art at the Metropolitan Museum of Art in New York, writes in an article on Chinese painting: "Confusion for Western critics often arises from the fact that . . . there have always been (and still are) the painters who quite honestly love to copy the admired painters of the past and the painters who are conscientious forgers." He notes that even modern painters make several copies of the same pictures and adds: "If the twentieth century does this, is it possible that Ma Yüan and Hsia Kuei did dozens and dozens of album leaves? Is it possible that, where Western students try to trace back to one original, they may, in fact, discover that the Sung masters repeated themselves." It seems not only possible but highly probable since the copying of pictures is so much a part of Chinese tradition, and usually with no thought of forgery or deception. On one occasion at the home of a leading Chinese artist in Soochow, we saw a picture hanging on the wall, and at first glance remarked: "Why, we thought that was in the States." "It is," the artist answered, "but I think it is so wonderful that I made a copy of it before it left China."

There was certainly no attempt at deception, for on looking closer we saw that he had written on the painting: "This is such a fine picture that I sat up all night to make a copy of it before it leaves our country for a foreign land."

Then again, at exhibitions of the work of modern painters that we have attended in various Chinese cities, well-known artists have sold not only the original picture, but have accepted orders for as many copies as intending purchasers wished to acquire. Each of these will some day be the original work of a famous old master.

Professor Paul Pelliot, the French sinologist, made the following interesting comments on this subject in an address before the Chinese Art Society of America in January 1945:

> Another point which in my mind requires further study is that of the original works of early Chinese painters. We want to have, or we wish to have, original works of the greatest Chinese painters of the past, but I think that by looking for authentic original paintings of very early Chinese painters, we are again misled by misconceptions of what Chinese painting has been in the first centuries. The first Chinese paintings were works of artisans, and, in many cases, illustrations of books; the point was to have the illustrations copied and reproduced exactly in the same way as the books themselves.
>
> Let me explain what I mean. For instance, in a catalogue of the Ninth Century we read about many painters from the Third to the Ninth Century. We are told that such a painter has painted such and such a painting and that those paintings "are still circulated in the world." What does that

mean? It means that just as a literary work is in existence as long as there is a copy of it, a work of art created by a certain man survives by being copied. The works of art listed in the catalogues of the Ninth Century are not supposed to be original paintings of the original painters, but simply faithful copies of them, and that is why the last of Hsieh Ho's "six principles" is to copy the works of the masters.

Unfortunately many Western collectors have felt that no Chinese painting made later than the Sung dynasty was worth collecting. Even the "tourist" with a few hours and a few dollars to spend expected to go into a "curio" shop and casually pick up a genuine Sung or T'ang picture. Such works are extremely rare, and they are all catalogued and known, so that in this field the "lucky find" is, to put it mildly, rather improbable. Nevertheless the tremendous demand has led to the production of "T'ang" and "Sung" pictures becoming a definite field of endeavor for many Chinese artists.

It is almost impossible for such copies to deceive anyone who is familiar with old Chinese paintings. Chinese art experts will tell you that the brush of the artist can always be recognized, just as a man's handwriting can be distinguished. One stroke of Rembrandt is as much Rembrandt as is a whole painting, say the best European experts. The Chinese experts say the same about their masters. One Chinese connoisseur assured us and gave us convincing proof that, by seeing only a small fragment of a painting, he could tell not only by whom it had been painted, but also whether the artist had executed the work in his youth, maturity, or old age.

The copy can only reproduce the lines, but the inspiration and touch of the artist is lacking. The notes may be played correctly, but there is no real music.

However, fakes are not prepared for the connoisseur. They are made for those who seek short cuts, and who expect to procure in every store treasures for which collectors have to search and wait for years.

One conviction, common among those who know little of Chinese painting, is that an "old" picture must be dirty. Actually a valuable painting will have been treated with the greatest care, carefully mounted on a silk scroll, kept rolled up, enveloped in a brocade covering, put into a metal container, and then laid in a chest, from which it will have been brought forth only on very rare occasions. Such pictures have not been subjected to the dust and glare and frequent handling from which many old European paintings have suffered. The Chinese collector will send a painting to be cleaned and remounted if he thinks it shows the least sign of wear or soil, and a picture that is not in perfect condition depreciates in value.

The novice ignores all that. He wants an antique painting to look old and worn. We have seen such persons stand looking at a fine old picture and insist that it must be new because it looks so clean. Paintings are, accordingly, prepared by the Chinese to suit the taste of such clients. Silk is dyed a deep brown color and, while the painting is still wet, it is rubbed with a hard brush to give it a tattered appearance. That is one reason why the amateur is always encouraged by dealers in spurious antiques to collect paintings on silk, which is more easily doctored than paper. Many of the finest old Chinese pictures were painted on paper, a medium better suited to delicate or strong brush strokes than the porous silk. The extreme ugliness of many fake paintings on silk explains the strange notions that often prevail in the Western world about Chinese art in general.

When we discussed this question with a group of Chinese dealers and artists, they maintained that it was not their fault that Europeans and Americans do not appreciate or understand real Chinese painting and only want to think that they have bought something that is very, very old. They pointed out that many fine authenticated Ming and Ch'ing paintings, which had been offered in the United States, had been returned unsold to China, where they were snapped up at high prices by Chinese collectors.

To a Chinese, a later copy of an early work is not necessarily an imitation or a forgery. Each generation of artists has copied or worked in the same school as earlier painters in order to perpetuate what was considered admirable, and it is only through later copies that we know what many of the earlier Chinese pictures looked like.

When we asked a young Chinese artist why he chose to paint the same subjects as former generations of artists had done he answered: "Does a singer have to keep making up new songs? I want to show how well I can sing an old song."

In examining paintings, museums now frequently use specially enlarged photographs, infra-red, ultraviolet, and X-Ray pictures. These will show whether any parts have been retouched or tampered with. That, in itself, does not mean that the picture is a fake, although such defects lessen the intrinsic value. These scientific means will also quickly dispose of crude imitations.

When one must identify a really well-executed copy, however, there is no mechanical substitute for the artistic appreciation and knowledge of Chinese art that endows one with the sixth sense which we have referred to earlier.

II: *THE ARTS OF THE BRUSH*

Chapter IV

CALLIGRAPHY AND PAINTING

THE APPROACH TO CHINESE PAINTING

THE CHINESE consider calligraphy and painting—the twin arts of the brush—as the supreme forms of art, but it is only very recently that the true greatness of Chinese painting has begun to be appreciated by the outside world.

When Chinese painting was first introduced to the Western world, it was judged by the academic standards prevalent at the time. Critics condemned the Chinese perspective, since they assumed that a picture must be painted as if the artist stood squarely in front of the scene. Modern art has accustomed us to the Chinese idea that an object or a view can be seen from any position.

The Chinese conception that a painting is intended to portray an inner reality rather than an outward likeness conforms to modern ideas of art. It is generally recognized that Oriental art first inspired the modern movement in European painting, but it was the colorful, decorative qualities of Japanese prints which first attracted Western painters, especially in France.

It was not until the present century that modern artists began to be conscious of the great monochrome art of China. Many European and American artists have told us of the tremendous impact that these paintings had on them.

Alfred H. Barr, Jr., in his comprehensive work on Matisse, *Matisse, His Art and His Public* (1951), writes that Roger Fry, the English art critic, as early as 1912 praised Matisse's decorative unity and rhythm of design which he suggested approached ancient Chinese aesthetics.

Later in the same book there is the statement: "Matisse during the 1940s seems to have come nearer the Chinese in his drawing than ever before. In the garden at Vence [France] and later in Nice he made scores of drawings of leaves, observing not only their endless variations of form and distribution on the branch within a given species but also the characteristic changes of shape caused by growth and withering. Thus, like the philosopher-poet-painters of the T'ang and Sung, he mastered essential forms and relationships in so far as Western individual sensibility can penetrate essentials discerned and defined in China by many centuries of cumulative knowledge."

40

As far as general understanding went, a formidable obstacle to genuine appreciation presented itself in the fact that no attempt was made at first to distinguish between good and bad art. Everything that came from the Far East was lumped together under the heading of Oriental—the commercial wallpaper designed for export, the little pictures on rice paper made for the tourists, the copies on smoked silk fabricated for those looking for "old" pictures, the mass of work by minor artists, and the pictures made by students and others for their own amusement. These were all put in one class, so that there was no distinction made, to use a European analogy, between the works of Leonardo da Vinci, Rembrandt, Constable, Cezanne, the calendar given away by the grocer, the poster advertising soap, the Christmas card, and the scribblings of children on the pages of their exercise books.

Works of art must be judged by the inspiration and purpose that lie behind their conception and by the quality of the technique with which they have been executed. And the art of any nation should be judged by the work of its finest artists. The leading Chinese "masters," such as Ku K'ai-chih, Wu Tao-tzŭ, Han Kan, Mi Fei, Li Lung-mien, T'ang Yin, Wu Li, and a host of others, are household words in China—probably more universally known in that country than are the great artists of Europe in the Western world. Yet they have been almost entirely unknown outside China.

This has resulted in pictures being considered only as representing periods, so that people talk of a "Sung" or a "Ming," without even specifying the artist who painted it. That is as if one spoke of having seen a painting made in the sixteenth or eighteenth century. Such a statement conveys nothing in the field of art.

The great Chinese artists were—as are men of genius in all lands—men of strong personality, great individualists; and many of them played important roles in the life of their country. They had very definite ideas about painting and its aims; they wrote many books and treatises on the subject, and engaged in heated controversies with each other and with the critics. Nowhere in the world was art taken more seriously.

Although collections of old Chinese pictures can be seen in many museums in America and Europe, visitors seldom know what qualities indicate whether the paintings are the works of great masters, or are merely decorative. In China there was no confusion or misunderstanding, for there are definitely clear tenets as to what consitutes a fine picture. Chinese art has not been so subject to fashion and whim as has our own, and tastes did not differ so completely as in the West. There has never been such a radical break in Chinese standards of painting as there has been in the West within the last century.

Most Chinese artists have painted subjects that are the common heritage of men in all periods—mountains and streams, the changing seasons, trees and flowers, birds, beasts, and insects. When buildings appear in paintings, the type most commonly seen is the scholar's little hut or retreat, which is as simple as the dwelling of the poorest people. Figures are dressed in the classical Chinese garments and do not change from period to period, so that the paintings never become outmoded.

What the Chinese really aim to depict in their paintings is the whole sweep and continuity of life. They are not as interested in depicting man as an individual, as his existence in relation to the vast scheme of things in our universe.

We often hear the criticism that Chinese art does not reflect the passing events of that nation's history. Actually, of course, this is one of its great virtues. Chinese artists want to paint pictures that will have the same meaning for future generations as for themselves.

Once during a conversation with one of the most prominent contemporary Chinese artists, he showed us a picture he had just completed of a mountain scene, with a girl in the foreground dressed in ancient Chinese costume. We asked him why he could not have dressed the girl in the type of clothes worn by Chinese women today. "If I did that," he replied, "the style would change and in a few years the picture would look old-fashioned and ridiculous. My pictures are not painted for people of today only, but for those who will look at them during a thousand years."

One of our misconceptions about China has been the impression that the people are too much preoccupied with the past and with death. Actually it is just the contrary. The Chinese make no great distinction between the past and the present because they believe, as they have always done, that life and death are continuous, that there is no sudden break and ending.

In the past when a Chinese was buried, his family interred with him all the vessels and objects that he might need in a future life. The idea was that he was not going to disappear, but would continue his life in some other form or sphere. It was a gesture to their belief in eternity.

We see great evidence of this preoccupation with life—and rejection of death—in their painting. The Chinese artist depicts life in movement. He paints birds flying in the air, fish leaping in water, flowers growing in the field. Chinese have frequently asked us why Western artists give the name of "still life" to pictures of dead birds, or dead fish on plates, and cut flowers in vases. "Should not such things be called 'still death'?" they ask.

The art that the Chinese call the "highest" must be connected with the continual ebb and flow of life and the constant renewal of nature—the procession of the seasons with their comforting assurance of continuity and immortality.

Chinese painting was not intended to create doubt and confusion. It is an art of affirmation. One of the famous artists of the Sung dynasty, Kuo Hsi, explains the spirit of Chinese painting in this way: "Unless I dwell in peace and sit at leisure . . . ten thousand worries drowned and subdued, I am not able to get at the mood and meaning of beautiful lines, think excellent thoughts, and imagine the subtle feeling described in them. The same thing is true of painting. When I am responsive, and at one with my surroundings, and have achieved perfect coordination of mind and hand, then I start to paint freely and expertly as the proper standard of art demands."

Such painting was an act of faith in the eternal verities. When the "ten thousand worries have been drowned and subdued," the artist reasserted that life still continued and renewed itself, that the cycle of the seasons would not change, that the flowers would still bloom, and the birds continue to sing.

That does not mean that the artists lived in a calm untroubled world. Many of them led very tragic and uncertain lives, but what they brought to their painting was the quietude in the deepest core of their souls, like the calm spot in the very heart of a whirlpool.

As for the question of timelessness, the Chinese consider all time as a repeated renewal like human life. In studying Chinese history we are constantly reminded of the way in which events repeat themselves, of the similarities between persons and happenings in all periods. Certain themes form a regularly recurring pattern. We repeatedly find the empire splitting up into parts and being reunited, the country being occupied by foreign invaders and then being freed, the destruction of cities and art treasures, the building up of new cities and the creation of new works of art, the conflicts between opposing political and philosophical schools, and the feuds between art critics.

What we find in reading these records is the constant ebb and flow, great periods in history and art succeeded by a pause, then again a spell of preparation and sowing and growth succeeded by another time of fruition. And through it all runs the golden thread of Chinese art from the earliest time to the present, sometimes brighter and sometimes dimmer, but never entirely absent.

Chinese painting is never purely representational. The artist does not work directly from a model, or from nature. He makes a close study of his subject, and paints from memory only what he considers the essential elements, using the fewest possible strokes.

The Chinese say that a picture should not tell a story, but it should represent an idea . . . an individual thought of the artist. A painting does not aim at being "beautiful." In nature there is no good or bad, ugly or beautiful. There is only the static and the changing. All real art must contain the elements of movement, growth, and conflict. It is not by chance that many Chinese have preferred to paint gnarled and twisted old trees, and old men, for these portray the effect of growth.

A famous Sung poet, artist, and statesman, Su Tung-p'o, said in regard to some of the old masters he had studied:

"The most prominent among the ancient writers did not ask for praise or fame; the greatest among the painters did not seek for honors or success. They said: 'I write in order to express my heart, I paint in order to comfort my mind. I may wear rough clothes and eat coarse food, but I would not ask support from others.'"

Great Chinese paintings speak to us in a manner as direct as do those words. In a world of confusion and doubt, it is to the art of China, itself in the midst of a great upheaval, that we can turn for affirmation and assurance of the continuance and the essential truth and meaning of life.

CALLIGRAPHY

Chinese painting is intimately connected with calligraphy. The brush strokes used in writing are the same as in painting, and the same instruments are used—brush and ink.

Chinese calligraphy was conceived as a series of pictographs, or ideograms; and, once a man had devised a symbol that would sufficiently resemble a man, or a horse, or a house, to enable others to know what he meant, it might be said that he was already drawing. In fact much of the stylization and economy of line in Chinese painting is doubtless due to this tradition of suggesting an idea with as few lines as possible.

Calligraphy is far more than writing. We value the art of writing for the thoughts it communicates, but Chinese calligraphy has an intrinsic value and appeal quite apart from its message. The Chinese admire it as a purely abstract art, and, when we study modern forms of nonobjective painting, it is with the realization that the Chinese have enjoyed this form of art for well over four thousand years in the form of calligraphy. It is for the beauty, the spirit and movement of the pattern, the contrast, balance, spacing and life of the composition—not for what the characters mean—that the Chinese, even the millions who have been unable to read, have admired and treasured examples of calligraphy. Many men have become famous as calligraphers throughout the course of Chinese history, just as many as for painting. Their fame did not rest on the meaning of the words they wrote, but on their handling of the brush.

Wang Hsi-chih, who lived from 321 to 379, is considered the greatest calligraphist of all time, his calligraphy being described as "delicate as floating clouds, violent as a startled dragon."

The basic idea in calligraphy is that each character fits into an imaginary square space. It must not be static or be made with straight lines. It should have flowing rhythm and convey a sense of suspended motion, just as a painting is supposed to do. It must not be too smooth and perfect, for life is not perfect, and fine calligraphy must suggest life, movement, and continuity. Thus, within each imaginary square there is scope for a fine small-scale abstract rendering.

THE SIX CANONS OF PAINTING

In the latter part of the fifth century, there lived in Nanking a famous artist and critic, Hsieh Ho, who formulated six principles, usually called the Six Canons, which have been used ever since as a criterion for judging Chinese paintings.

Hsieh Ho said himself that he did not invent anything new, but merely put into concrete form the basic ideas for the judgment of pictures which had always been the essential foundations of art. He introduced the principles with the following remarks:

"Pictures must be classified according to their merits and their faults. Every picture has some influence, either for good or for evil. When we look at a painting, the silent records of past generations are unrolled before us. Although the Six Canons have long existed there have been few artists who have been able to meet them all, but many have excelled in one or more of them. . . . There have always been good and bad pictures, because art in itself remains the same—whether it is ancient or modern."

At the time when these canons were drawn up by Hsieh Ho, landscape painting had not yet attained its full maturity, but as schools of painting changed and developed, these principles maintained their validity, and they have, to a great extent, been adhered to and adapted by all succeeding generations of artists. As the Chinese point out, it is the "technique," and not the subject, that is judged by these standards.

The Six Canons have been translated, and interpreted, in various ways by different writers, but one can sum them up briefly as follows:

1. Rhythmic vitality (inspiration which gives spiritual meaning and harmony to the whole).
2. Structure by means of brush strokes (technique).
3. Depiction of subject according to its nature.
4. Appropriate coloring.
5. Composition, spacing, and perspective.
6. Study and copying of old masterpieces.

The first canon states that the prime essential of a work of art is the spiritual force or inspiration behind it. A Chinese art critic of the ninth century, Chang Yen-yüan, summed up this idea by saying: "To carefully plan and set about painting a picture is to entirely misunderstand the art of painting; on the other hand, the artist who is suddenly impelled to paint a picture understands the meaning of art. His hands will not tire, and his heart will not grow cold; without realizing why he does it he will achieve his aim."

This teaching is inherent in all the different philosophies of China—to understand a thing fully one must forget oneself, and become as much like what one is studying as possible. A famous Chinese artist who had been studying insects once cried out: "Am I a man, or am I an insect? I don't know the difference any more."

However the first canon would be useless without the second. No compelling drive could enable an artist to paint a fine picture unless he were able to command the necessary technical ability. There is no working over, or retouching, a Chinese painting. Once the strokes are set down on paper, or silk, they are there to stay, so they must be swift and sure. When Ingres said: "Drawing is the probity of art" he might have been referring to the Chinese artist, for the drawing—the brush stroke—is the essential element.

The third canon, which refers to the depiction of the subject, is fairly obvious, but it should be remembered that the artist did not seek to portray the exact outer likeness, but aimed at seizing the inner essence. Thus one thing was intended to represent all things of its kind. It was not necessary to paint a horse exactly like any one particular horse, but the picture should contain elements common to all horses.

The fourth canon, which refers to color, needs no special explanation, except that it refers not only to color, but also to the different gradations of black ink. The artist mixes more or less water with his black ink so that he can obtain a wide range of shades from jet to palest gray.

The fifth canon refers to composition, spacing, and perspective. The most important part of a Chinese composition is the blank space. The next thing to be considered is the relation of different objects to each other (if more than one is to be painted) so that the most important draws the eye first. There must be balance and harmony in the composition, but it must not be static. There must be life and movement.

And there must be no excess, no unnecessary strokes. Every picture must give the impression that the artist has "the skill to do more, with the will to refrain."

The sixth canon refers to the copying and studying of old masters. The students were to be inspired by the works of the past and encouraged to analyze them so as to understand what had made them great. The intention was less that the young artist should make exact copies than that he should nourish his artistic inspirations at the source, and work along the lines laid down by past masters until he was proficient enough to start out on a new trail by himself.

At the same time, there is no doubt that the Chinese students did acquire great skill in copying old paintings, and that it was considered a laudable and important thing to undertake such work. Had it not been for the vast number of copies executed by generation after generation of artists, our whole knowledge of early Chinese painting would be considerably less than it now is. Copies were ordered, in just the same way that additional editions of books are published, so that a wider audience could enjoy and study the pictures.

The Six Canons have been criticized and debated for centuries but they still hold their own. One of the most modern of Chinese painters, who studied in Paris and who says he has no use for traditional painting, went with us recently to a show of pictures by a contemporary Chinese painter. The pictures were not very good, and suddenly our Chinese artist friend erupted: "Look at them," he burst out. "By what standards does that man call himself a painter? Where is the rhythmic vitality? Where is the life force? Look at the weakness and lack of spirit in the brush strokes!"

We realized once more that the Six Canons are still as much alive today as they were fourteen hundred years ago.

THE EQUIPMENT OF THE ARTIST

The studio of the traditional Chinese artist is quite unlike that of the Western painter. There are no easels, no models, no paint-bespattered palettes. The room is usually neat and rather bare, with perhaps one or two hanging scroll pictures, and a few examples of calligraphy. For the surroundings and equipment of the Chinese painter are the same as those of the scholar.

The equipment is usually neatly arranged on a long rectangular table. There among other things, one will find the following objects:

1. A conical shaped brush pot, made of carved wood, ivory, jade, or porcelain.
2. This brush pot will contain an assortment of brushes. These are usually made of wood, and sometimes tipped with silver, ivory, crystal, or jade. The bristles are made of the hair of various animals, such as fox, sheep, sable, and, most frequently, rabbit. They come in different sizes. An artist will not allow anyone else to handle his brushes for, as one of them said to us, "It is a personal thing, like an extension of my own arm."
3. Ink blocks. The ink comes in a solid form, moulded in different shapes and sizes. The ink is ground fresh each time, and only as much as is required is rubbed off.
4. Ink slabs. These must present a flat surface on which a little water is poured, so that the ink stick can be ground on it. They are usually made of stone, but are also made of other substances such as pottery, quartz or jade.
In the Ch'ing dynasty (1644-1912) ink stones were designed in the most varied and elaborate forms, sometimes like a lotus flower, a peach, or a fish.
5. A collection of seals. Some artists cut a new seal for nearly every picture, and each of these seals is a little work of art in itself.
6. A tiny box of vermilion paste into which the seal is dipped to obtain the scarlet impression.
7. A small water container, usually of pottery or porcelain.
8. A small dish divided into partitions (like a miniature blue plate), which serves as a palette, since it enables the painter to prepare his black ink in a gradation of shades by adding more or less water to the ink in each section.
9. Then there will frequently be what is called a writing wrist rest. This enables the hand of the artist to make his strokes with greater ease and sureness.

The four main necessities of the artist are: the brush, the ink block, the ink slab, and paper. These are known as "The Four Treasures of the Room of Literature."

The artist most frequently works on paper which was already in use in the second century, but sometimes he paints on silk, which was invented even earlier. The paper used in Chinese painting is of a rather absorbent nature, and this makes it essential that the artist be sure of his strokes. Once a stroke is made it cannot be erased or corrected. To quote a Chinese maxim: "One should draw as if engraving a slab of rock crystal with a diamond point."

Before choosing his paper the artist must decide what form a painting will take. The one most commonly used is what is called a "hanging scroll" (Chinese "chou," Japanese "kakemono"). Many artists, however, prefer to paint long horizontal pictures called "hand scrolls" (Chinese "chüan," Japanese "make-mono").

The horizontal scroll was the earlier form, and it is painted on a long roll (sometimes many yards long) of thin silk or paper. It may show a river scene or a large stretch of landscape. This type of work was particularly popular with artists of the T'ang dynasty, and they painted many long roll pictures colored with blue and green and gold.

Once completed, the delicate picture is sent to a special "picture mounting shop" where it is backed with strong paper, then perhaps mounted on brocade, and provided with handles, or rollers, of wood, ivory, jade, or porcelain.

When the picture is ready it is rolled up and tied with ribbons. It must be looked at flat on a table, a few inches being unrolled at a time, so that one follows the panorama slowly as though reading a book page by page.

At the end of a horizontal picture of this type, there will be left a strip of blank silk or paper, and on this the artist puts his seals and signatures, and adds a poem or any comments about the picture. Then, his artist and connoisseur friends and patrons will each add a few lines of appreciation, and so will subsequent owners and collectors. In this way it is often possible to trace the history of a famous painting back through the centuries.

The long hanging scroll is backed and mounted in the same manner, and also provided with rollers which give it weight and enable it to hang straight or be rolled up when not in use.

A Chinese artist may also decide to paint a small album picture which can be circular, square, or fan shaped.

The one thing that certain artists might have in their studio and that the scholar does not need is a set of paints. The use of color is not even mentioned in Chinese writings until some five hundred years after the first records of painting, and many scholar-artists have felt that true painting requires only gradations of black ink handled with such skill that it suggests all variations of color.

In spite of that, there has been a tremendous amount of color painting in China, and that is the type of work that has, until very recently, been best known in the outside world. Chinese colors are not mixed or blended, but must be applied in their original state. The art lies in taking just the right quantity and thickness of paint on the brush so that, as a Chinese painter expressed it, each petal of a flower takes the right form, with all the proper shadings and shadows, at one stroke. Nothing must be added afterward.

Many of the scholar-artists are also collectors of pictures, and they take the greatest care of their treasures. In the Hua p'in, a book of art appreciation written in the late eleventh or early twelfth century, the author Li Chih writes: "No more than three or four pictures by eminent artists should ever be hung in one room. After these have been enjoyed for four or five days, others should be substituted. Every picture should occasionally be taken out into the open air, and they must never be exposed to smoke or damp. If they are constantly changed they will not collect dust or dirt, and, what is more, you will not get tired of seeing them. Great care must always be exercised in unrolling and rolling the pictures, and, whenever they are opened, they should be lightly dusted with a horsetail or a silk flapper."

THE BEGINNING OF CHINESE PAINTING

The origins and beginning of Chinese painting extend so far back into antiquity that no precise knowledge is available. The legendary story runs that a method of visual communication was miraculously revealed to Fu Hsi, the first of the primeval emperors of China, when he saw, on the back of a tortoise which arose from the waters, the diagram that we know as the Eight Trigrams, or the Pa Kua. This Pa Kua formed the basis of the ancient book "I Ching," or "Book of Changes," which has been used ever since in divination and fortunetelling. From this pattern the emperor is said to have invented a method of keeping records by means of knotted cords, and Chinese writing and painting are said to have been derived from this revelation of the Eight Trigrams.

Many centuries later, in the reign of the Yellow Emperor (circa 2697-2597 B.C.), we are told that one of his ministers "observed the shapes of things in Heaven; the forms of things on earth; and the footprints of birds upon the sands." When he thought upon what he had seen he conceived the idea of writing.

The first pictograms used in writing represented simple natural objects such as the sun, the moon, a man, a tree, a bird, or a horse. As the desire for communication increased, someone must have realized that not only objects but also ideas could be expressed in graphic form by combining different characters. For instance, the word "peace" was expressed by combining a woman and a roof, "good" by coupling a woman with a child, and "friend" by drawing two right hands joined. The sun coming up behind a tree indicated "east," "disaster" was expressed by flames and flood, and "sorrow" by a heart and autumn.

But the art of painting appears to have developed even earlier than the art of writing. Obviously, in order to invent a character, one had to be able to draw something that looked like a man or a horse or whatever one had in mind. Hence we read that this same Yellow Emperor ordered a portrait of his enemy Ch'ih Yu to be painted so that it might serve as a horrible warning to his people!

The earliest form of painting recorded was that of portraiture, and, during the Shang dynasty (1766-1122 B.C.*) the Viceroy I-Yin is said to have presented to the Emperor T'ang an immense panorama of the Nine Famous Emperors, painted by himself, and to have expressed the hope that his artistic skill would merit the increased confidence of his royal master.

While these early records of painting refer to portraits, a study of the designs on Shang bronzes shows that the drawing of animals and of various symbols was already in a highly advanced state.

* Traditional dates.

49

The earliest pictures in China (apart from decorations on pottery, lacquer, and bronzes) were wall paintings decorating palaces, official buildings, and temples of religion, and these considerably antedated the invention and widespread use of silk, and even more that of paper.

We learn from Chinese records that, as early as the Chou dynasty (1122-221 B.C.*), the walls of official buildings were covered with pictures, and that, apart from portraits, the motifs most frequently used were the dragon and the tiger—the tiger representing dignity and sternness, and the dragon symbolizing vigilance and protection. The tiger also watches over earth and mountains, while the dragon, guardian of sky and water, promotes fertility by sending the much-needed rain.

PORTRAIT AND FIGURE PAINTING

After these early references to painting, it is not until the time of Confucius (551-479 B.C.) that we find more than a passing reference to the art. It is recorded that Confucius visited a palace at Loyang, in 517 B.C., and there saw painted on the walls of the Hall of Audience portraits of Yao and Shun (those ancient model rulers of China), as well as many other princes and notables. This, he pointed out, was the main purpose of painting—to preserve the features of great men as stimulating and ennobling examples to successive generations.

Although portrait and figure painting was the form in which pictorial art first reached its fullest maturity, China never experienced anything like the Greek glorification of the human body. The Chinese artist did not consider it necessary to study anatomy, for he was not concerned with the bones and organs, but only aimed at depicting how the sitter appeared to those who saw him. What was considered important was to reveal character by the expression of the eyes and mouth, and to convey the line and movement of the body as it appeared to the onlooker.

In the series of books on the art of painting, known as the "Mustard Seed Garden" (which were published early in the seventeenth century, but were based on the teachings of the ancient masters), there are some interesting comments on the art of figure painting, in the section Jên-wu (Men and Things):

"The different types of men included in a landscape must not be too detailed, nor must they be too sketchy. They must be related to the landscape; the man must appear to look at the mountain, the mountain appear to be bending over to see the man. . . . The spectator should feel regret that he cannot enter into the picture to change places with the person there depicted. Otherwise the mountain remains merely a mountain, and the man a man . . ."

As far as more formal portraits were concerned, there were certain traditions that had to be observed—for instance, an emperor must look dignified, a lady gentle, a general bold, and a farmer rustic—but these rules seldom prevented even the artisan-painter (and all the early painters were artisan-painters) from expressing his opinion of the character of the sitter in his pictures.

* Traditional dates.

50

Hu Ch'üan, a writer on art who died in 1172, wrote: "There is no branch of painting so difficult as making portraits. It is not so hard to depict the features, but the problem is to show what is hidden in the heart. The face of a great man may resemble that of a mean man, but their hearts will be quite different. Thus a man cannot be regarded as having skill as a portrait-painter unless he can show plainly the character of the person he is painting."

Leonardo da Vinci expressed the same idea when he said: "A good painter has two chief objects to paint—Man and the intention of his soul."

THE GOLDEN MEAN

Confucius never attempted to found a religion or even a cult. He was content to be a learned scholar and teacher—a transmitter of knowledge—who did not seek personal power. He remained a poor man who, for a great part of his life, was unable to obtain any employment whatever, but wandered from state to state with a few chosen pupils and friends.

His life was as gentle as his teachings, which were always of a moderate nature and based on the Golden Mean, as developed in his work the Chung Yung, or Doctrine of the Mean. He advocated a love of learning and knowledge so that one might become a "superior man." Such a man would love moderation in everything—never too much or too little, but just enough.

Confucius taught that every man was entitled to his own opinions and way of life, provided that this did not cause wrong or injury to others. It was chiefly in the relation of men to one another that he felt guidance to be necessary to enable life to run smoothly.

This tolerant, scholarly, and well-mannered approach to life exercised the most profound influence on Chinese thought and character. Even in the field of painting his influence was an important one. The Chinese painter followed the Doctrine of the Mean. Neither too much nor too little. No overcrowding of details. Not too many or too bright colors. Just enough to obtain the desired effect.

There is another way in which the Chinese painter followed the doctrines of Confucius. The artist had a completely tolerant approach to different religions and philosophies, and would paint Buddhist, Taoist, and Confucian pictures, and afterward Christian ones, with the utmost impartiality. One doctrine did not have to oust or supersede all others.

THE DESPOTISM OF THE CH'INS

The Confucian way of life received a severe setback when, in 221 B.C., the first strong centralized government of China was established by the Ch'ins. Their leader proclaimed himself the "First Emperor," under the name of Shih Huang Ti (221-210 B.C.). Energetically he proceeded to inaugurate sweeping changes.

Until his time China had been split up into various feudal states, only loosely knit together, but Shih Huang Ti completely abolished feudalism, which was never to return, and created an empire in which a military governor ruled over each of his provinces but was directly responsible to the emperor. He maintained a large standing army and all his edicts were carried out by force.

There was great opposition, and the scholars complained of the lack of precedent for his methods of procedure. The emperor then decided that, since the bonds of tradition were hampering the spread of his new ideas, the solution would be to destroy all existing records.

This "burning of the books" was carried out with great thoroughness, and not only were countless treasures lost to future generations but many gaps were left in the continuity of history, including the history of art.

The scholars, aghast at this sacrilege, managed to hide away many books, but Shih Huang Ti had numbers of them put to death with the greatest cruelty. Many other learned men were sent to join the hosts of slave laborers who were being forced, under the most frightful conditions, and with enormous loss of life, to build the Great Wall which he was erecting to protect the northern frontiers against the encroachments of the nomad peoples of the north.

The rule of Shih Huang Ti was a complete despotism, maintained by brutal force, but he ruled only eleven years, and, after his death, the whole structure of government that he had built up disintegrated. There was a period of chaos and confusion until the founding of a strong native dynasty, the Han, in 206 B.C.

THE HAN DYNASTY (206 B.C. TO A.D. 220)

The Hans ruled for four centuries, and their dynasty was one of the most stable and prosperous in the history of China. After the tyranny of the Ch'ins, the Chinese people were happy to find themselves again under a government which respected their ideals and traditions.

The Han dynasty was a time of great political and military strength, during which China firmly established itself as the leading power of the Far East. There was wide expansion and intercourse with other countries; and the famous caravan routes, called the Silk Route, which enabled traders to carry Chinese silks and other goods abroad, extended as far west as Rome.

After seventy years of Han rule, the famous historian, Ssŭ-ma Ch'ien wrote: "The Empire was at peace, grain burst from the overflowing granaries . . . the government treasuries held an excess of wealth . . . the streets were crowded with horses belonging to the people . . . the village elders ate meat and drank wine."

The Han dynasty was famous for its scholars and learning, and one of the first great tasks undertaken was the replacement of all the burned classical books of which any hidden copy could be found. The desire of the Confucian and Taoist scholars to accomplish this task as quickly as possible encouraged the discovery, improvement, and widespread use of all materials used in writing—brushes, ink, silk, paper. All the equipment used in painting reached its full development.

At this time painting began to be taken more seriously, and it was recognized that an artist could make a picture in accordance with his own inspiration rather than at the command of the emperor. Painting was no longer confined to artisans, but also began to be practiced by literary scholars. It continued to be used chiefly for wall decoration, and the Emperor Hsüan Ti ordered portraits of those generals and officials whom he wished to honor to be painted on the palace walls.

Painting in the later Han dynasty was not confined to portraits; and of one of the earliest artists mentioned by name, Liu Pao (second century), it was said: "His pictures of misty plains made men feel hot, while those swept by the north wind made them shiver."

THE HAN TOMBS

While no examples of the work of Han artists have survived, we do have actual evidence of the graphic arts of this period in the bas-reliefs found in tombs. The main groups of these have been found in Hsiao T'ang Shan (about first century) and Wu Liang Tz'ŭ (near Chia-hsiang-hsien), which are of a somewhat later date. Both groups are in Shantung province.

It is generally believed, and the theory is upheld by such an eminent authority on Chinese art and archaeology as the late Professor Paul Pelliot, that these bas-reliefs were copied from the paintings on the walls of the palaces in which the persons buried in the tombs had lived.

These bas-reliefs consist of rather tight compositions treated in a direct linear manner, obviously based on the calligraphic stroke. Of a simple—almost severe—nature, they have a remarkable sense of movement and of simultaneity. The drawings are stylized, and show certain conventions such as that of making personages of high rank larger than those around them. They are arranged in horizontal bands and show the life of the deceased in this world and in the spirit realm after his death.

There are three main groups of subjects:

1. Illustration of Confucian teachings.
2. Religious and fantastic scenes inspired by Taoism.
3. Scenes from the life of the deceased while alive—such as military and hunting expeditions and official successes.

The decoration was for the pleasure of the dead, since no live men could enter the tomb after it had been sealed.

These tomb decorations enable the student to appreciate the spirit and style of the Han artist. The work is by no means primitive. The general effect is one of sophistication, and this applies even more to the painted hollow bricks of the second and third centuries, which were taken from tombs in Loyang. The Museum of Fine Arts in Boston has some of these bricks in good condition. They show the aristocratic men and women of the Court, in the Imperial Gardens, watching a fight between animals.

Recently there have been extensive studies made of Han tomb art of the first and second centuries in West China. These bas-reliefs show even more freedom of spirit and movement than do those in the Hsiao T'ang Shan and Wu Liang tombs.

After more than three centuries of great achievement and prosperity, the Han dynasty began to deteriorate in accordance with the cycle so firmly maintained throughout Chinese history—or world history, for that matter. "Such is the everlasting law—prosperity followed by decay," wrote Ssŭ-ma Ch'ien. The final downfall of the House of Han came A.D. 220.

THREE KINGDOMS (220-280) AND SIX DYNASTIES (222-589)

There followed a period of internal chaos and strife, as well as foreign invasion by Mongols, Tartars, and other border tribes. The country was divided into various separate states under different rulers. But Chinese art continued undaunted, providing a much-needed source of refreshment for weary minds and souls. Figure and animal painting had already reached high levels of development, but it was during these turbulent centuries that landscape painting began to develop into the supreme art it was later to become.

THE INFLUENCE OF BUDDHISM

The most significant influence that came to Chinese painting from the world outside, or from the events of the time, was the establishment and development of Buddhism. This provided a new source of inspiration, and most of the famous artists of the time painted Buddhist subjects.

It is easy to overestimate the importance of this development because the western mind is apt to associate religion with art. Certainly it was Buddhism that inspired most Chinese sculpture, but that was because images were created for purposes of worship.

When Buddhism was introduced into China late in the Han dynasty, the Chinese intellectuals took art more seriously than they did religion. The scholars and artists had a great tradition of culture behind them, and their minds were already permeated with other philosophies and ideas—such as those of Confucius, Mencius, and Lao Tzŭ. Even when they painted Buddhist subjects, it was not in the same devotional spirit in which Europeans created Christian art. They believed in "art for art's sake," a medium of expression for the personality of the artist. Buddhist art aimed at teaching the people about Buddhism, and because it tried to "show something" it was not regarded as the highest form of art.

Buddhism first reached its high peak of popularity in the Wei dynasties, which conquered and ruled over large parts of China from 386 to 557. Thus early was started the trend that has persisted ever since of Buddhism being more ardently followed as a religion by the tribes bordering China than by the Chinese themselves. The latter regarded with equal tolerance all religions and philosophies; and perhaps the most important of them all, especially where art was concerned, was a Chinese philosophy dating from the beginnings of their history,

54

and based on the idea of counterbalance in order to obtain harmony—the idea expressed by the yang and yin.

There are written records of several artists who worked during the Three Kingdoms. The most outstanding one is Ts'ao Pu-hsing, who painted figures and animals.

Between 280 and 589, Chinese records show nearly 500 painters who achieved celebrity, in addition to those who specialized in religious subjects and were less highly regarded.

The foremost artist of this whole period was Ku K'ai-chih, who lived in the fourth century. He is of particular interest to the Western world because there is a fine example of his work now in the British Museum in London.

The picture is a roll painting on brown silk, 9¾ inches wide by 11 feet 4½ inches long. It illustrates a poem written in the third century, entitled: "Admonitions of the Imperial Preceptress to the Ladies of the Palace," and it shows a series of scenes of domestic life in the palace, each scene bearing an inscription which contains a moral precept.

This painting—one of the great landmarks in the history of art—was acquired in the most haphazard manner. At the time of the Boxer Uprising (1900), one of the concubines of the Imperial Palace came to an old English sea captain, Captain Johnson, who was living in Peking, and begged him to hide and protect her. He took her into his home where she stayed safely until things calmed down. On taking her leave, she gave the Johnsons a gift of a long scroll which she said she had taken away with her from the Palace.

Later, after Captain Johnson died, his widow came back to England and offered the scroll to the British Museum in London. They did not know exactly what it was, but it looked interesting, so they bought it from her for a nominal amount. At first it lay unrecognized among the innumerable treasures of the Museum. Then, in the light of increasing knowledge of Chinese art, it was thoroughly examined by experts and adjudged to be the famous Ku K'ai-chih picture (or a very early copy) and one of the oldest and most valuable paintings in the world.

As is the case with most early Chinese painting, bronze, or sculpture, the work is obviously the result of a long tradition of art development and is particularly remarkable for the strength and sweep of the brush strokes.

Ku K'ai-chih was the first Chinese artist to have painted landscape as a background to his figures, starting this new idea about eleven hundred years before landscape painting was introduced into Europe. He lived in a time of great interest in art and philosophy, and he was famous for his imagination and observation. It was said of him that he had a childlike nature, and that he was "the greatest wit, the greatest painter, and the greatest fool." He lived in a period of revolt against the conventions. Many artists and poets were inspired by the teachings of Lao Tzŭ, who advocated complete freedom for the individual, as opposed to the social laws of Confucius. The Taoist philosophy advised its followers to appear foolish with the apparent simplicity of the truly wise (in contrast to the know-it-allness of the small mind).

Hardly less famous was another artist of this period, Lu T'an-wei (fifth century). He was especially famed because he could paint a whole picture at one stroke, thus achieving the highly admired effect of spontaneity and immediacy.

The most important artist of the sixth century was Chang Sêng-yu, who is called one of the "Four Patriarchs" of Chinese painting. (The other three are Ku K'ai-chih, Lu T'an-wei, and Chan Tzŭ-ch'ien [sixth century].) His favored subjects were dragons and tigers, and he also painted Buddhist pictures. One of his best-known works, "A drunken Buddhist priest," has been much copied by later artists, and so, too, has his picture "Washing the Elephant."

Nothing now remains of his original work, for during these centuries of conflict there was enormous destruction of temples and palaces. And the danger did not always come from invading armies. It is recorded, for instance, that Yuan Ti (552-555), ruler of the Liang Kingdom, having gathered together a vast collection of pictures and written scrolls, felt he did not want them to pass into other hands, and so had them all burned.

SUI DYNASTY (589-618)

Toward the end of the sixth century, one general managed to triumph over the rulers of all the other states. The scattered fragments were again reassembled into one empire, under one ruler, who established the Sui dynasty.

This short period was one of marked encouragement and progress in all branches of art—and the number and fame of the recorded artists increased rapidly.

The first important name to emerge was that of Chan Tzŭ-ch'ien, who has been called the "Founder of T'ang Painting." He made pictures of buildings and temples, carriages and horses.

During this period Buddhist art received great encouragement because of the increasing power of Buddhism as a religion. New temples were built and old ones repaired, and they were embellished with paintings and sculpture. Most of this art was created by artisans whose names were not recorded.

The art of mural painting was widely practiced in these temples, the pictures being executed on a white prepared ground where the master painter drew the outlines, and his helpers filled in the colors. Practically all this art was destroyed during periods of persecution of Buddhism, so that the discovery of a large quantity of early Buddhist art, such as that found in the rock temples at Tun-huang, was of paramount importance to students of Chinese art.

THE TUN-HUANG CAVES

The walled oasis of Tun-huang is the last stopping place in Central Asia on the way to China, and the last outpost of China on the caravan route to Central Asia, India, and Iran. Here, situated in the province of Kansu on the borders of Turkestan, across a barren desert, are the famous Caves of the Thousand Buddhas.

There are nearly five hundred of these ancient Buddhist cave temples honeycombed in irregular tiers, which have had to be, and are still being, dug out of the sand and gravel of the river bank. They contain a vast wealth of Buddhist art in the form of wall paintings, as well as sculpture, pictures on silk and linen and paper, books, and woodcuts.

The art works in these grottoes cover nearly a thousand years. The earliest cave shrine was built A.D. 366, according to an inscribed stele of 689, and some of the rock shrines were maintained and painted right up to the Yüan dynasty (1280-1368).

In 1035, Tun-huang was invaded by Tartars, and it was probably then that more than twenty thousand rolls of manuscripts and many paintings and sutras were collected and deposited in a small chapel which was walled up. They were forgotten for nearly nine hundred years, and then accidentally discovered by a Taoist monk. The dryness of the desert air has perfectly preserved the contents of the sealed chamber. Among the ancient manuscripts found was the earliest known block printed book—the Diamond Sutra, printed in 868.

While there is variation in quality, many of the murals are of a grandeur not realized by those who have seen only the silk banners found in the sealed chamber. To compare the two is like comparing the murals in the Sistine Chapel with the colored religious images sold at the church door.

"GOLDEN ERA" OF THE T'ANG DYNASTY (618-907)

The extravagance, misconduct, and incompetence of the second Sui emperor brought about the downfall of the dynasty in 618. During its short sway it had united the country under one ruler, and prepared the way for the outpouring of creative energy which characterized the T'ang dynasty. The spirit of the time was to be one of strength, grandeur, and worldliness rather than of austerity and religious fervor.

As soon as he felt that peace was firmly established throughout the Empire, the Prince of T'ang, who founded the dynasty, handed the reins of government to his son, who ascended the throne in 627 under the title of Emperor T'ai Tsung.

To his capital, which had become a world center, the young emperor called the greatest thinkers of the time so that he might have the benefit of their knowledge and advice. Many of the leading scholars were also artists, and painting was soon accorded an even higher place of honor than it had held previously.

Artists engaged in every type of painting—religious pictures, landscapes, figure painting, genre painting, animals and birds and flowers. While most original T'ang paintings have been destroyed, there are still enough specimens available both in China and the West (as well as good early copies) to give us a fairly accurate idea of the art of the time.

With such delicate objects as pictures, the destruction and loss throughout the centuries has, of course, been tremendous. Wars, looting, floods, and sacking and burning of palaces have all taken their toll. In this connection it is interesting to read the life story of Li Ch'ing-ch'ao, who lived in the Sung dynasty and whom the Chinese consider their greatest woman poet. She describes how she and her husband were both ardent collectors of books and paintings, and other antique works of art. She tells of the joy they had in finding, acquiring, and studying their treasures. Then, with the coming of the Mongols to the capital, K'ai-fêng Fu, they had to escape, taking with them only as much as they could carry in their cargo boats.

What they had saved from their collection they locked in ten rooms in Ch'ing Chou, but, when they returned there, it was to find that the house had been burned down. The whole story is an account of how their treasures grew gradually less and less—by invasion, by fire, by pillage. Her husband died, and, finally, she had nothing left.

When her last books were stolen by a robber, leaving only a few incomplete writings behind, she said: "Suddenly, seeing these books, it was as if I saw my loved man . . . arranging slips on books, laying together ten volumes to fill a wrapper . . . as he did in the beginning . . . The handwriting was still fresh as new, yet, on his grave, trees already arched their boughs. Then I realized: 'To have the have, one must suffer the not have; those who rejoice in union must endure separation. This universal law is the Rule of Life. My slight record, from end to opening, is a warning to the learned, the accomplished, to all in this floating world who love ancient things.' I close." *

This poignant passage might have been written in almost any period of China's history, and, as we think of it, we find ourselves surprised, once more, that so many treasures have survived the many centuries of intermittent strife.

The early part of the T'ang dynasty was a flourishing period for Buddhist art, but it was not until this influence was about to wane that the foremost Buddhist painter appeared on the scene. There is a Chinese proverb: "When the sun is highest in the heaven it is beginning to sink," and the high noon of Buddhist art was reached with the work of Wu Tao-tzŭ, born in the eighth century.

The child of very poor parents, Wu Tao-tzŭ was early left an orphan, but he had already shown such marked ability as an artist that the emperor sent for him to come to the capital, and had him educated in the Academy of Fine Arts. He was renowned for his powerful imagination and originality, as well as for the plastic, three-dimensional quality of his pictures.

Wu Tao-tzŭ is said to have painted alternately like a man possessed by a demon and one guided by some divine hand. His most important work was the painting of more than three hundred frescoes on the walls of temples and palaces. At the end of the T'ang dynasty, China experienced one of its rare instances of religious persecution. In this case the movement was inspired more by fear of the growing political power of the Buddhists than because of their beliefs. This led to the destruction of most of the Buddhist temples, and the great wall

* Translated by Florence Ayscough.

paintings of Wu Tao-tzŭ were swept away. All that is left are the rubbings of a few engravings on stone, said to have been taken from his designs. These include the Kwan-yin (Goddess of Mercy), Confucius, and some animal designs. They are small testimony to the work of a man whose name has been familiar to the Chinese for over twelve centuries.

The whole story of Wu Tao-tzŭ is a mingling of history and fable. Even the account of his death is told in the form of a legend. The emperor is said to have commissioned him to decorate one of the palace walls. All the time he was working the painting was kept covered with a curtain. When the work was completed he revealed it to the emperor, who was overwhelmed by the beauty of the painted landscape—"the grandeur of the mountains, the depths of the forest."

"A spirit lives in the cave at the foot of the mountain" Wu told him and, as he clapped his hands, a painted door opened. Wu stepped inside the pictured door and it closed behind him. While the emperor watched, every trace of the painting vanished, and the wall was left blank. Wu Tao-tzŭ was never seen again.

Like all the myths that have grown up around the early artists of China, this one should be taken in the same spirit as a Chinese painting—not for its literal meaning, but for its inner significance. The story is symbolical of his life and work. Much was written of their splendor, but they have vanished without a trace.

There are innumerable legends told about famous Chinese artists—how their pictures moved and lived, how painted birds flew, fishes swam, babies cried, women sang, horses kicked. These stories, as originally told by the skeptical art critics, were certainly not intended to be taken literally, but were a tribute to the inspiration which endowed the works of genius with a living quality. In China, however, art was so intrinsic a part of the texture of life and artists were considered so important that these tales of famous painters, in a more and more distorted form, were told by succeeding generations of storytellers who traveled from village to village, and the impression was often created that these men of genius had supernatural powers.

Wu Tao-tzŭ was said to have changed the whole conception of landscape painting, using free bold strokes where formerly the artists had used their brush with meticulous delicacy.

There was another painter, Li Ssŭ-hsün, who worked in a most precise and careful manner and who was considered the finest colorist of his time. Because of the differences of technique between these two masters, the Emperor Hsüan Tsung (himself a noted artist, who is said to have invented the famous bamboo stroke) ordered them both to paint the same landscape for him. Li Ssŭ-hsün set to work at once, and worked hard and carefully for three months, using brilliant colors. Wu Tao-tzŭ, in the meantime, spent his time lying idly under pine trees, listening to the running streams, and observing the landscape until he felt he had completely mastered it. Then he rapidly and boldly executed a picture in monochrome in a few hours. The emperor decided that the paintings were both equally good, and rewarded them both in the same manner.

This story of the two schools of painting, and the emperor's decision, forms a prologue to the splitting up of Chinese painting into two schools—the Northern and the Southern. This split began to develop during the latter part of the T'ang dynasty, has persisted all through the history of Chinese painting, and still divides Chinese artists and art critics. The terms Northern and Southern had no geographical significance at the beginning, but, as time went on, the Southern school of painting did come to be more popular with the artists around Hangchow, Soochow, and Yangchow in the south, while the Peking artists favored the Northern, or Academic, school.

The founder of the Northern school was the same Li Ssŭ-hsün, and the emphasis was all on meticulous (kung-pi) brush strokes, realism, and a wide range of color, including brilliant green and gold.

The founder of the Southern school was Wang Wei (698-759). He used bold, free stroke (hsieh-pi) of the brush, and worked in black ink without added color. The work of this school was intended to leave free rein to the imagination, and was soon to be associated with "literary painting." It was of Wang Wei that it was first said: "His pictures are poems, and his poems are pictures."

He was the first artist to paint landscapes in a broad expressionistic manner, and he excelled at reproducing atmospheric changes and effects. His love for nature and solitude, an attitude typical of the sensitive scholars of the time, is expressed in this poem by the leading poet of the period, Li Tai-po (circa 701-762):

> Why do I live among the green mountains?
> I laugh and answer not. My soul is serene.
> It dwells in another heaven and earth belonging to no man.
> The peach trees are in flower, and the water flows on. . . .

One of the most important artists working during this period was Han Kan, considered to have been the supreme painter of horses. These animals were tremendously admired in China, and they were the subject of countless stories and fables extolling them as free, proud, noble creatures. A symbol of wealth and luxury, the Emperor Ming Huang—admirer of poets, painters, and beautiful women and a keen lover of horses—had over forty thousand thoroughbreds in his stable.

When Han Kan was called to the Court, about the middle of the eighth century, the emperor advised him to study the painting of horses under Ch'ên Hung, a contemporary Court painter. Han Kan ignored the suggestion, which was equivalent to a command. When the emperor scolded him, he replied: "I have been learning how to paint horses, and every one of the horses in the Imperial Stables has been my teacher."

His fame increased with the passage of time so that a later critic wrote: "When Han Kan painted horses he was truly a horse." This was the supreme compliment, as it meant that the artist had achieved such full identification that he was able to transmit the inner spirit of the horse.

Another painter of animals was T'ai Sung who excelled in painting water buffaloes.

Other outstanding artists were the two brothers Yen Li-pên and Yen Li-tê (latter part of seventh century), who were famous for their portraits, and Chang Hsüan, noted for his scenes of court life.

The whole period was one of vitality and creativeness. There was less imitation of old masters, and more creation of new styles than before. The finest contribution that the T'ang artists made to Chinese art was the recognition that the spirit of the artist himself, and not the thing that he depicted, was the essential element in a work of art. During this period artists became individualists, and started to sign their paintings. The signatures were very small and placed in some inconspicuous spot so as not to spoil the composition of the picture.

Many of the T'ang artists were famous for their poetry, writing, and wit, as well as for their skill as painters. Several started life very poor, but did not remain so, once their talents were recognized. The famous Han Kan, for instance, was a poor pot boy. Wang Wei, a keen connoisseur of art, recognized the boy's talent when he saw him drawing pictures in the dust outdoors, and gave him the money with which to acquire an education. Another great painter, Wu Tao-tzŭ, had once been a penniless orphan. Gifted artists were often given an official position if they desired it. If they did not care to assume such a post, they seldom failed to find a rich patron who released them from financial worries.

The middle period of the T'ang dynasty was staged against a background worthy of the brilliant statesmen, artists, poets, and philosophers who peopled it. The new flowering of genius was presided over by the Emperor Ming Huang ("The Illustrious Sovereign") (713-56). Himself an artist, Ming Huang was a great patron of every form of art and literature. In the Imperial Library there were more than 200,000 volumes, and the emperor insisted that there be a school in every village in the fifteen provinces of his empire.

Ming Huang, his love for the fascinating Yang Kuei-fei and the magnificence of the Court over which they both reigned have been an everlasting source of inspiration for Chinese poets and painters.

But Yang Kuei-fei, one of the four most famous beauties in Chinese history, was destined to play a disastrous role in the life of the empire. Greedy for pleasure and power, she dominated the blindly infatuated emperor and eventually caused his downfall. Before the end, the emperor's own army demanded that the beauty, whom they blamed for all the misfortunes that had befallen the country, be sacrificed. The emperor fought against the edict, but was finally forced to yield, and Yang Kuei-fei was ordered to hang herself from a pear tree with a silken scarf.

The Tartar rebels who had invaded the country, led by one of Yang Kuei-fei's lovers, were finally driven out, but not before the capital had been plundered and burned and most of its treasures lost. With this debacle the "golden" era ended.

Persons who have lived in China are familiar with the Chinese use of note paper decorated with designs which are often the work of famous artists. This type of note paper was inaugurated by a woman who lived in the T'ang dynasty, and whose name was Hsüeh T'ao. The way in which the past lives on into the present in China, especially in art, is illustrated by her story. She was born in the latter half of the eighth century, and was extremely poor, living by going from hamlet to hamlet and singing songs which she herself had composed. Her family was so poor that they eventually sold her to a sing-song house, but her fame as a poet was such that she was brought to Court and was greatly honored. One of her poems starts: "Time shot by like an arrow, and the days and months flew like the weaver's shuttle."

Not only her poems were famous, but the unique manner in which she decorated the paper on which she wrote them. So much so that today, over a thousand years later, when you walk into a stationer's shop in Peking, Shanghai, or Hankow to buy the kind of paper the Chinese use for their correspondence, you still ask for: "Hsüeh T'ao chien" (Hsüeh T'ao note paper).

This is one more example of the foreshortening and continuity of time of which one is always aware in China. The bridge of a thousand years of time has flown "like a weaver's shuttle," and the names of men and women who lived centuries earlier are casually introduced into everyday conversation, so that the whole nation has a strong sense of identity with its past.

THE TWILIGHT OF T'ANG (756-907)

During the period of decline, marked by border wars, general uncertainty, and waning imperial patronage, painting did not flourish as it had done in the preceding era of peace and expansion. However, the late T'ang era produced two artists who, while possibly not of the first rank, are nevertheless important in the history of art. One was Chou Fang, working in the latter part of the eighth century, who painted scenes of Court life, especially women and children. In 805, a large number of his paintings were acquired by a Korean who took them back to his country. It would appear that this collection had its influence on the art of Korea, and in turn on that of Japan which derived much of its art inspiration from Korea.

The other artist was Li Chên, a set of whose paintings of the Five Patriarchs of the Shingon sect of Buddhism was taken to Japan in 814. They are still in Kyoto; and, while only one of them is in fairly good condition, they show great skill in portraiture, revealing character with a minimum of strokes. These works had an important influence on the development of Japanese art, the T'ang period being the one most admired in that country. Such preference is shown not only in their art, but, right up to the present generation, in their dress, the women's coiffures, and much of their architecture and furnishings.

62

The complete collapse of the T'ang dynasty gave way to a period when five "little" dynasties succeeded one another rapidly within the course of fifty-four years. Not only did one ruler replace another, but various local rulers set up independent states.

The art of painting, which had declined after the end of the "golden" T'ang era, now began a new period of development in preparation for the fulfillment of the Sung dynasty.

Landscape painting continued to mature, and so did the painting of flowers, previously used almost solely for decorating religious pictures. Birds and insects also became popular subject matter. This intense love for the beauty of nature, as manifested not only in the grandeur of mountains but in all living things, even the smallest of insects, was an outgrowth of Taoism.

The first important painter to emerge at this time was Kuan-hsiu (832-912). His special forte was the painting of series of Lohans (disciples of Buddha) in temples all over China. He is said to have created the type of Lohans that is now familiar to students of Buddhist art—violent-looking old men, extremely un-Chinese, with very large eyes and long bushy eyebrows, emaciated bodies and haggard faces, seated on a rock or beneath a tree.

One of the first artists to paint the now well-known "landscape with figures" was Kuan T'ung (tenth century). In the famous Sung Catalogue of Imperial Paintings, the Hsüan Ho Hua P'u (1119-1126), we find the following comments on his work: "What he liked to paint most was mountains in the autumn after the leaves had fallen from the trees, dangerous passes . . . His paintings were like sketches—the simpler the picture, the deeper appeared the thought behind it."

An artist who rivals Kuan T'ung in fame was Ching Hao, a farmer who lived on what his own soil produced. He loved solitude and painted scenes of rugged nature. He wrote a pamphlet called the "Pi Fa Chi" ("Records of Brushwork"), in which he explained what was meant by expressing the "inner spirit." He set forth his theories in the form of a dialogue between an old sage and a young painter, part of which runs as follows:

"When the old sage met me in the forest, he asked: 'Do you know the method of painting?' To which I answered: 'You seem to be an old uncouth rustic; how can you know anything about brushwork?'

"But the old man said: 'How can you know what I carry in my bosom?' Then I listened and felt ashamed . . . I remarked: 'Painting is to make beautiful things; and the important point is to obtain their true likeness, is it not?'

"He answered: 'It is not. Painting is to paint, to estimate the shapes of things, to really grasp them; . . . to estimate the reality of things and to communicate it. One should not take outward beauty for reality. He who does not understand this mystery will not obtain truth, even though his picture may contain likeness.'

"I asked: 'What is likeness, and what is truth?' The old man said: 'Likeness can be obtained by shapes without spirit, but when truth is reached, both spirit and substance are fully expressed. He who tries to express spirit through ornamental beauty will make dead things.' "

In Chengtu (Szechüan) during this period, there arose an art school which treated flowers and birds as individual subjects, in a manner which influenced Chinese painters for a thousand years. The best-known artist of this school was Huang Ch'üan (tenth century). He depended more on color than on brush strokes and is said to have originated the "boneless method" of painting; in other words, washes of color without outlines. The other pioneer in painting flowers and vegetables was Hsü Hsi, who worked entirely from nature.

Chou Wên-chü, who also belonged to this period although he continued to work in the Sung dynasty, specialized in painting the ladies of the Court.

Without any marked change in the field of painting, the period came to an end when a general united most of the empire and became the founder of the Sung dynasty, under the title of Emperor T'ai Tsu (960-976).

NORTHERN SUNG DYNASTY (960-1127)

The Sung dynasty ushered in the modern age of Chinese painting. It was a purely Chinese period in art, for all foreign influences had been absorbed. Throughout the long course of Chinese history all outside influences, whether religious or secular, have been like tributaries of a river. They may have served to nourish, but they never really changed or diverted it from its main course.

Europe was still in the Dark Ages, but China at this time had reached a state of civilization perhaps higher than any other ever evolved—from both an intellectual and a material point of view. In writing about *Sung Culture and Ideals* the English Orientalist, L. Cranmer Byng, said: "Life centred around K'ai-fêng Fu, the capital of Northern Sung, and, after its capture, by the Nüchen Tartars, around Hangchow, was in some ways the nearest approach to Heaven on Earth the world has known as yet. A nation of artists and artisans, and nature worshippers, was drawn together by a common bond and a common aim in living creatively, each one intent on his own work, conscious of the joy that creation brings, yet greatly aware in his hours of leisure of the supreme happiness that can only be partaken in communion. . . .

"And . . . with the Chinese . . . communion is not with some small section of one's fellow worshippers . . . not even with humanity, but with life in every aspect; not with contemporary life alone, but with a living past and a future that widens its avenues and horizons to receive us."

The earliest Sung artists started their careers during the Five Dynasties and may be said to constitute a bridge between the two periods. Among these, besides Chou Wên-chü, mentioned before, was Shih K'o (tenth century), a man noted for his wit and eccentricity. He was famous for his Buddhist and Taoist subjects and for a series of unflattering portraits which might be called cartoons. In Tokyo, there are two fine pictures of monks which are attributed to him.

One of the first important painters of the dynasty was Li Ch'êng (latter part tenth century), who went to the Sung capital at K'ai-fêng Fu to work under the patronage of the emperor. He is said to have brought to perfection the Southern school of landscape painting, and is regarded as one of the classic masters of the literary man's (wên jên) school of painting, a new style developed in the early Sung period. The man whom other critics considered the master of landscape painting was Tung Yüan (late tenth century), who made actual sketches in the mountains, and then painted in a bold impressionistic manner which made it essential to view his work from a distance. Another name often classed with Li Ch'êng and Tung Yüan is that of the monk painter Chü Jan (late tenth century), who painted murals on the walls of official buildings.

Some critics say that it was with Fan K'uan (active circa 990-1030) that the Southern school of landscape painting attained its full stature. He was a man of generous and outgoing nature, who retired to the mountains and spent his days studying the effects of clouds, mists, rains, and winds, and watching the heavens. He is said to have been the first Chinese artist who really understood the construction of mountains. This he considered necessary in order to convey a true impression of their massive strength. We also read that "his works were on a great and heroic scale, and yet profound and mysterious as the gathering twilight."

The second Sung emperor, T'ai Tsung (976-997), was actively interested in art, as were all the succeeding Sung rulers. He ordered all the scholars to search for literary and artistic works, arranging for the compilation of a catalogue of the Imperial Collection of Paintings. He also founded the Academy of Painting. Huang Chü-ts'ai, painter of flowers and birds, became the first director, establishing a pattern which was followed by later generations of artists.

In connection with the Academy of Painting, Dr. A. G. Wenley, Director of the Freer Gallery of Art in Washington, makes some interesting comments. He says that, while the term is frequently used in Chinese books of art criticism, he has found few references to any school of painting inside the government in official Sung history. Dr. Wenley is right, of course, in his statement that the Academy was not a separate school where painting was taught. It was a government department, which might have been called the Department, or Ministry, of Painting, and was concerned with everything that pertained to that art. In 1110 it was put under the Han Lin Hüa T'u Chu, or Han Lin Academy, which had been established in 621 for all the leading intellectuals of the country.

Dr. Wenley also points out that men were not chosen for high government posts because they were good painters but because of their administrative ability. Painting a picture was one of the tests in the government civil service examinations, because every highly educated man was supposed to be able to paint a picture and write a poem, but nobody could become a government official unless he was highly proficient in all the other subjects.

When we refer to the Academy of Painting, it is not as an art school but as a Department of Painting, which engaged the special interest of the emperors who were all patrons of the arts.

Kuo Hsi (circa 1020-1090) was considered by his contemporaries to be the leading landscape painter of his day. He expressed the striving for freedom of thought and expression which was typical of Sung, and, famous as he was for his painting, he was even more widely known for the "Essay on Landscape Painting" ("Lin Chüan Kao Chih") in which his son wrote the thoughts and teachings of his father.

The essay explains that a painter should have complete mastery of his technique—be the master and not the servant of his brush. Then he gives some basic rules of Chinese landscape painting: "Water must flow or it is stagnant. Clouds which are not animated would be like frozen clouds. Mountains where there are not darker and lighter sections would be subject to neither sun nor shade. . . . A mountain without clouds or mists would be like a spring without flowers or grass. . . . A distant mountain has no ridges, distant water no waves. . . . When far away a man has no eyes. Not that they have none, but that they seem not to have any."

Discussing the technique of painting Kuo Hsi says that a picture "may be spread out in a large composition, and yet contain nothing superfluous," or be "condensed to a small scene and yet lack nothing."

Kuo Hsi's son quotes some of the poems his father used to recite as containing themes appropriate for painting. They express much of the spirit of a Sung landscape—a gentle mood of melancholy and nostalgia, combined with a realization of man's close relationship with nature:

> South of my house, north of my house,
>   the spring is in flood;
> Day after day I have seen only gulls.
>   (Tu Fu)
>
> I will walk till the stream ends
> And sit to watch the clouds rise.
>   (Wang Mo-ch'i)
>
> On the distant horizon an approaching
>   goose appears small;
> On the vast waters a departing ship seems forlorn.
>   (Yao Ho)
>
> Together we gazed on distant waters;
> Alone I sit in a lone boat.
>   (Chang Ku)

Although T'ang artists had written poems about their paintings, and Hsüeh T'ao had put her poems on paper on which she had painted appropriate designs, it was not until the Sung dynasty that it became the general custom to inscribe poems on paintings, and to link the two forms of art more closely together.

While magnificent landscapes were being produced, the artists considered nothing too small or insignificant to be studied and made the subject of a picture —a bird, a leaf, a blossom, or an insect. "To see the world in a grain of sand" might well have been the maxim of many a Sung painter.

The rise of the literary painters (wên jên), who wrote poems and painted pictures for their own intellectual pleasure, reached its high noon in the latter part of the eleventh century. A group of men of genius then rose to prominence, including the brilliant poet Su Tung-p'o (Su Shih) (1036-1101), who was equally renowned as philosopher, statesman, and artist; and such painters as Mi Fei (1051-1107); Wên T'ung (died 1079); Chao Ta-nien (active circa 1080-1100); Li Lung-mien (died 1106); the famous radical statesman and reformer Wang An-shih (1021-1086); the great historian Ssŭ-ma Kuang (1019-1086); and the statesman, art collector, and critic Ou-yang Hsiu (1007-1072).

Then men in their youth were all close friends, and formed a circle which met and discussed all aesthetic questions—painting and looking at pictures, reading and writing poems. At the same time they were all deeply involved in the affairs of state.

Mi Fei could perhaps be called the leader of this group, which worked in the Southern style, and disdained "Academic" painting because, they claimed, its exponents insisted on formal resemblance. He was a brilliant, caustic, arrogant man, critical not only of other schools of painting, but of all other artists and collectors.

Mi Fei was determined not only to be original in his work but to be "different" in everything. He always dressed in T'ang costume, and wherever he appeared, crowds would gather around him. He was too much of an individualist to succeed in his career as an official and, as a result, became a poor man later in life. In spite of this his modest home remained a center of pilgrimage for lovers of letters and art.

A passionate collector of pictures and examples of old calligraphy, Mi Fei, like many a Chinese connoisseur today, would never show his greatest treasures to those unable to appreciate them. He divided his collection into two parts, one consisting of pictures that could be shown to anybody; while the other—the secret one—was made up of works of art that could be shared only with his chosen friends and not with unthinking persons who might touch them with their fingers, or brush them with their sleeves.

Mi Fei, and the other artists of his group, considered that to understand a picture was almost as difficult and required almost as much natural talent as to be a painter. They considered that the appeal of great paintings was wholly spiritual and intellectual and that their qualities could not reveal themselves to the casual passerby. Once anyone entered into the spirit of one of these landscapes, he could never tire of it or take it for granted. The Taoist philosopher Chuang Tzŭ tells of two sages who, when they met, did not need to say a word to each other because their eyes revealed everything. There should be the same communion and understanding between the artist and the man who looks at his pictures.

One of this "company of friends," Su Tung-p'o, wrote the following poem about the reverence with which Chinese connoisseurs study fine paintings:

> Brocaded cases and rollers tipped with rhinoceros horn
> lie piled upon the ivory-mounted couch;

Forked sticks and sequent scrolls bring back to us
    the glories of the clouds.
As the hand unwinds the horizontal scroll,
    we feel a breeze arise;
And all day long, without haste, we spread
    the pictures out.
Our wandering souls are deeply stirred,
    our hearts are purified,
Our souls are lifted up by the beautiful scenes
    thus set before our eyes.

(Translated by Herbert A. Giles)

Mi Fei's best-known pictures are those showing mountains wreathed in clouds and mists. He piled up ink on ink, to achieve utterly new effects, made use of "ink splashes," and is called the originator of "pointillism," inventing what became known as the "Mi dot."

PAINTERS OF BAMBOOS

Wên T'ung, one of the best bamboo painters, thus explained his method: "When you decide to paint bamboos, you have to clearly visualize them in your mind. Then grasp your brush, and concentrate on your conception; begin at once, move your brush quickly, and then go straight ahead as a buzzard swoops as soon as the hare emerges. One moment of hesitation and the inspiration is gone."

Wên T'ung died at an early age, and Su Tung-p'o arranged to have one of his paintings of two bent bamboo trees engraved on stone "so that the sight of them . . . would lead connoisseurs to understand the nobility of heart of my regretted friend, who was also afflicted and bent, but never broken, just like the bamboo."

We read that the famous bamboo painter, Li K'an of the Yüan dynasty, spent ten years looking for a picture by Wên T'ung, and considered he had been greatly blessed by Heaven when he found one. He says Wên T'ung is in a class by himself . . . like a sun shining in the sky which dims the light of torches.

SU TUNG-P'O, POET, ARTIST, AND STATESMAN

Su Tung-p'o, born in the far west of China in the province of Szechüan, was a brilliant scholar who was able to pass the final civil service examinations at the early age of twenty-one. He quickly made a reputation for his poetry, wit, calligraphy and knowledge of public affairs, and was appointed to the highest offices in the state. He was extremely popular for his good nature, loyalty to his friends, and his complete integrity.

As far as painting was concerned he did a few landscapes, but, above all, he loved to paint bamboos and water, two subjects which united strength and resiliency.

His group, and the whole of the new school of literary painters aimed not only at self-expression but also at expressing the inner spirit (li) of the subject. In this connection Su Tung-p'o, in judging the work of a young artist, said: "Judging scholars' paintings is like judging horses. The professional artists often see only the skin and hair, the whips, the trough, and the hay. That is why the paintings of professional artists are lacking in spirit, and, after seeing a few such paintings one is bored."

To explain what is meant by this inner spirit (li) Lin Yutang in his book *The Gay Genius* tells about a poem that Su Tung-p'o wrote on a picture he had painted of a crane. He states that when a crane, standing in the marshes, sees a human being approach, he has prepared himself for flight even before moving a feather. When nobody is around, the bird has an air of complete relaxation. That is the inner spirit that Su Tung-p'o tried to set forth in his painting.

When his father died, Su Tung-p'o had to go home and remain there for a mourning period of three years. On his return to the capital the whole situation had changed because Wang An-shih, the social reformer, had managed to win the emperor over to his theories of government, and had been appointed prime minister. Although mentioned in the list of Sung painters, it is for his bold ideas as a statesman that Wang An-shih is known as one of the most important figures of the Sung period. He introduced a complete system of state socialism with strict government control of all commerce, industry, and agriculture. Prices and wages were fixed.

Wang An-shih insisted that all his reforms were strictly in accordance with the ideas of government laid down by Confucius, but his opponents also invoked Confucius to defend their own viewpoint. It was all a matter of interpretation.

Wang An-shih's great weakness, and the reason why he encountered such bitter opposition not only from other statesmen but from the people themselves, was that his schemes necessitated a strong centralized control and heavier taxation. This was completely at variance with the Chinese principle that the best form of government is the one of which they are least aware. They felt freer and more comfortable under the old, loosely knit form of empire, which required only modest taxes to be paid and in which an unsatisfactory governor of a province might always be replaced by a more popular one.

Su Tung-p'o and many of his group, including the historian Ssŭ-ma Kuang, were inexorably opposed to Wang An-shih's plans; and, because he felt that they were blocking his reforms, Wang An-shih had all his opponents, including some of his closest friends, banished from the capital.

When the people grew discontented, and the new ideas failed to bring about the desired results, the emperor lost confidence in Wang An-shih and recalled Su Tung-p'o. For many years the two parties alternated in power, the "outs" being temporarily exiled. Su Tung-p'o said he could never agree with his friend Wang An-shih on political matters "any more than ice could agree with burning charcoal."

Banished and recalled, again and again, to a Court which seemed to be unable to get along either with or without the poet statesman, Su Tung-p'o led a sad life for a man known in his youth as "The Gay Genius," and it is no wonder he wrote the following poem on the birth of one of his sons:

> Families, when a child is born
> Want it to be intelligent.
> I, through intelligence,
> Having wrecked my whole life,
> Only hope the baby will prove
> Ignorant and stupid.
> Then he will crown a tranquil life
> By becoming a Cabinet Minister.
> (Translated by Arthur Waley)

He was exiled again when he felt he could not agree with everything a new young emperor did, and on leaving, he gave the young emperor these words of advice: "The good government and peace of a country depend wholly upon the free communication between ruler and the ruled. During periods of ideal government, the humblest subject was free to make known to the emperor his wishes and his woes, but, when trouble and disorder prevailed, even the officer nearest to the emperor was denied the right to voice his complaints."

When he was finally recalled it was only two months before his death, and his last words were: "I have done no wrong in my life, and I need fear nothing after my death." There was widespread mourning throughout the empire on his death, and it was felt that one of the great glories of the country had passed away.

"PLAYING WITH INK"

It was during this period that the literary painters firmly established another branch of the Southern School of painting, called "playing with ink," and it was intended to convey the joy of expression through the medium of rhythmic brush strokes rapidly executed.

Su Tung-p'o says of his own practice of this art: "I realize that full mastery is not just license, but arises from the perfection of details. When my brush touches the paper, it goes as fast as the wind. My spirit sweeps all before it, before my brush has reached a point."

The four subjects most favored for this "ink play" were the prunus (or plum) blossom, the orchid, the bamboo, and the chrysanthemum, which came to be called "The Four Gentlemen." It is surprising to see the variety and beauty that can be found in the multitude of pictures of these subjects, each artist expressing his own personality and "li" in his method of presenting them.

These four growing things symbolized the qualities most beloved by scholars and artists and poets. The wild plum blossoms have courage because they are the first to brave the cold winds of winter. The bamboo and the plum trees together signify close friendship throughout life. The bamboo alone has a host of virtues —for instance, it is upright, faithful, its hollow body is capable of holding truth and reason, its robust knots show its spirit of endurance. The wild orchid symbolizes humility combined with beauty, modesty, and exquisite delicacy. The chrysanthemum, the last flower to bloom before the cold weather sets in, symbolizes the man who maintains his integrity in spite of temptation.

These subjects, however, were chosen less for their symbolism than because they afforded such play for the exercise of the art of "mao hsi"—"playing with ink."

The idea is to achieve a free-flowing stroke which looks almost careless but which is the result of long years of practice in the use of the brush. Not only the brush stroke but also the subject has to be studied for years, so that eventually the picture can be executed rapidly and "with an air of the utmost ease."

One criticism often leveled at the scholar-painters is that they lacked originality in the choice of subjects. The Chinese point out that nobody objects to the fact that many Western poets write about love and spring. It is the manner of execution, and not the subject, which is important.

Another criticism frequently voiced in the West is that these scholar-painters lived a life of escape. Yet, a perfect example of the wên jên is Su Tung-p'o, all of whose sufferings were caused by his sincere efforts to do what he felt best for the welfare of the people.

Most of the other scholars who indulged in "ink play" were officials, too, and men who had great cares and burdens. Their art was a relaxation—and more than that. Although not a religious people in the Western sense, the Chinese, in their art, have found what others seek in religion, a deep communion with the spiritual values of life. As the Mohammedan, at certain hours of the day, forgets his work and preoccupations, and "turns to the East to pray," so the Chinese wên jên would sit down at his desk, cleanse his mind of all worldly thoughts, take up his brush, and immerse himself in painting a picture.

LI LUNG-MIEN (DIED 1106)

Among the "group of friends" was one who surpassed all the others as a painter. Li Lung-mien said that, during his thirty years as an official, he could never for one moment forget the beauties of the mountains and forests of his native province of Anhui, and he felt compelled to paint "the scenes ever present in his mind."

In the capital he never visited rich or influential people or tried to advance his career, but enjoyed excursions into the country with his chosen friends, among whom were Mi Fei, Wang An-shih, and Su Tung-p'o. They enjoyed an intellectual companionship which had not yet been threatened by the conflict of political ideas. It was during that time that the custom of making cooperative paintings was originated. A group of scholars would meet in a pavilion in a bamboo grove, or a hut on a mountain ledge, drink wine, and then, in a mood of poetic conviviality, recite verses and compose pictures together.

Li Lung-mien painted a picture of one such outing, which is known as the "Gathering of Scholars in the Western Garden" and has been repeatedly copied.

He painted an almost unlimited variety of subjects—Buddhist pictures, pictures depicting the stories of Confucian and Taoist lore, landscapes, architecture, horses, portraits, Court scenes, genre pictures—and in all fields he was superlatively successful.

He so completely identified himself with his subject that when he painted horses his friends jokingly warned him against becoming too much like a horse. He created a new type of Kwan Yin (Goddess of Mercy), making her still more graceful and feminine with flowing robes, and he discarded the strange ugly types of Lohans conceived by Kuan-hsiu. Instead he painted them in a humorous, playful manner, more in the spirit of the Taoist immortals.

Most of his work was in monochrome, painted on thin transparent paper, in a fine calligraphic style. His brushwork was said to resemble "floating clouds" and "running water."

PAINTERS OF THE IMPERIAL ACADEMY

The members of the Imperial Academy of Painters formed another important group of artists. Although the scholar-painters attacked the Academicians for lacking individuality, many of the leading artists, such as Kuo Hsi and Chao Ta-nien, were connected with the Academy, and some of the leading members were among the forerunners of the Ch'an (Zen) school of art, which was soon to be an important factor in Chinese painting.

Most of the members specialized in painting flowers and vegetables, birds and insects. Among the most prominent were Chao Ch'ang (active about 1000); Ts'ui Po and his brother Ts'ui Ko (late eleventh century), who specialized in "feathers and fur" (birds and small animals); Ma Fên (late eleventh century), to whom is attributed "The Hundred Wild Geese" painting in Honolulu; I Yüan-chi (late eleventh century), famed for painting monkeys; and Ai Hsüan, painter of birds, flowers, and vegetables.

THE EMPEROR HUI TSUNG (1101-1125), ARTIST AND ART PATRON

The last emperor of the Northern Sung dynasty was Hui Tsung, another great connoisseur and patron of arts and painter of birds, flowers, animals, and landscapes. He founded a museum and searched everywhere throughout the country for fine paintings and art objects. A catalogue was drawn up, classifying and describing the objects in his possession. This was completed and published in twenty volumes in 1120.

The section of this catalogue that referred to paintings was called the "Hsüan Ho Hua P'u" ("Collection of Paintings in the Hsüan Ho Palace"). It included the works of 231 painters and comprised 6192 pictures. All the works were divided into the ten following categories:

1. Tao Shih.   "Taoist and Buddhist" paintings.
2. Jên Wu.   "Human Figures." (A supplement to this section was devoted to professional portrait painters.)

72

3. Kung Shih.	"Palaces and buildings."	
	(This included ships, chariots, etc.)	
4. Fan Tsu.	"Barbarian Tribes" (Foreigners).	
5. Lung Yü.	"Dragons and Fishes."	
6. Shan Shui.	"Landscapes."	
7. Ch'u Shou.	"Domestic Animals and Wild Beasts."	
8. Hua Niao.	"Flowers and Birds."	
9. Mo Chu.	"Bamboos" in monochrome.	
10. Su Kuo.	"Vegetables and fruits."	

The literary painters of the Southern school entirely ignored the first four groups, and these groups declined in importance.

The Emperor Hui Tsung included the painting of a picture among the qualifications required of those competing in the civil service examinations for official posts. Often a line of poetry was chosen, and the artist had to interpret it in the most subtle manner. One year, for instance, the emperor asked for a picture to illustrate the couplet:

> I return from trampling on flowers
> And the hoofs of my horse are fragrant.

The winning picture showed a horse with two butterflies flying around its hoofs.

Another time the line chosen was:

> A monastery buried deep in the mountains.

The chosen picture showed no monastery, only mountains and a small figure of a monk fetching water from a stream.

Everything had to be shown by implication. Overemphasis was considered vulgar, and the artist was supposed to seek the most delicate and elusive way of making his point. The butterflies would not be attracted to the horse's hoofs unless they smelled of flowers, and the monk would not carry water unless there was a monastery in the vicinity.

Historical events followed a familiar pattern of destruction. The Nü-chên Tartars (Chins) invaded the country and, by 1125, had seized all the northern provinces, capturing the capital city of K'ai-fêng Fu. The emperor himself was carried off (with three thousand persons of the royal household), and he was held in captivity until his death in 1135. The palaces were sacked and the art treasures were all destroyed or dispersed.

The loss of the northern provinces, however, did not mark the end of the Sung dynasty. The capital moved south, and, in the beautiful city of Hangchow, there was another great period of art before the weakened empire finally fell into the hands of the Mongol invaders.

SOUTHERN SUNG DYNASTY (1127-1279)

When the northern provinces of China fell before the invading hordes, one of the emperor's sons managed to escape. After some years of wandering, he established the Southern Sung dynasty with Hangchow as its capital, and ascended the throne under the title of Emperor Kao Tsung. He managed to bring together many of the artists who had worked around his father and who had taken flight, and he re-established an Imperial Academy of Painting.

Hangchow was one of the loveliest cities in the world. Even today, although its handsome palaces and buildings have long since vanished, one realizes, as one admires the lovely lake with its graceful arched bridges and drooping willows, why the natives proudly chant:

> Above is Heaven;
> Below are Hangchow and Soochow.

When the artists arrived in this idyllic setting, they settled down to work at what the Chinese considered the most important and enduring purpose of life—the creation of art. The artists painted their pictures, the artisans worked at their crafts, and there was an atmosphere of serenity and permanence. Despite this, the artists were not indifferent to the loss of the northern provinces. We are told that when the birds flew over Hangchow on their way south, they would call out: "What news do you bring from our northern capital?" And, sometimes, when they painted a flock of birds in their pictures, they would say: "They are taking our thoughts back to the north."

THE IMPERIAL ACADEMY OF PAINTING IN HANGCHOW

The man whom the emperor appointed director of the new Academy was Li T'ang (circa 1049-1130). Previously he had worked in the northern capital, painting landscapes in a precise "Northern" manner. When he came to Hangchow he was already seventy-five years old, yet he abandoned the academic method, and worked in a fresh, bold, and free style. It is chiefly on the original and humorous genre pictures of this later period that his fame rests.

Among the artists from K'ai-fêng Fu who now worked with him in Hangchow were Chao Po-chü and his younger brother Chao Po-su. The elder was the more famous, and he painted portraits and historical scenes. Other artists were Su Han-ch'ên (circa 1115-1170), known for his genre pictures of women and children, Liu Sung-nien (active circa 1190-1230), who painted a series of pictures showing scenes of agriculture and sericulture which have been much copied by later artists (as well as used in series of woodcuts), and Li Sung (twelfth century), who is another example of the poor boy whose talents were recognized. Li Sung started life as a carpenter and was adopted by an artist who admired his work. Known for his genre pictures and illustrated folk tales, his technique was most individual when he painted the sea. He evolved an original and highly effective method of indicating swirling waves by a series of fine concentric lines.

74

TWO GREAT LANDSCAPE PAINTERS, HSIA KUEI AND MA YÜAN

The spirit of Sung landscape painting is revealed in the works of two outstanding masters—Hsia Kuei and Ma Yüan. Many Western and Japanese art critics have considered them the most important of all landscape painters, but Chinese art critics feel that this art did not reach its apex until the Yüan dynasty.

They were the leading Academicians of their period, both working at the same time (late twelfth and early thirteenth centuries) and in a somewhat similar manner. These two artists have for so long been classed together that it becomes difficult to write about them separately. Hsia Kuei is usually considered to be the greater painter, with his austere yet delicate brush strokes and bold shadows, while Ma Yüan, with his strong and vigorous brush and nostalgic evocation of far-off horizons, is called the greater poet. His pictures were "all pushed in one corner," the composition consisting of trees or hills on one side with most of the remaining space left blank.

While many Chinese critics dismiss them as "too romantic," the artists themselves would have rejected the term scornfully, claiming that they were trying to reach the very heart of reality.

COMPETITIVE CIVIL SERVICE EXAMINATIONS

The Chinese method of selecting government officials by public competitive examinations was instituted in 165 B.C., during the Western Han dynasty (206 B.C.-A.D. 65). In the Southern Sung dynasty, the philosopher Chu Hsi (1131-1200) revised the precepts of Confucius, giving his philosophy a new form called Neo-Confucianism, and his interpretation of the Classics became an essential part of the literary civil service examinations until 1903 when the whole system was abolished. For vague Buddhist mysticism and superstition, he substituted a doctrine of rationalism. Each individual was called on to take responsibility for his own morality and conduct.

The idea of having all government officials chosen in competitive examinations created an aristocracy of intelligence, since intelligence and education completely superseded birth and wealth. The examination was open to boys of all classes and extended to every remote corner of the empire. Each village sent its most gifted candidate to the examination, which was held annually in every town. Not more than one in a hundred won the coveted degree. The winners could compete again the following year. The top candidates were eligible for the third-degree contest in the capital. The tiny percentage of chosen scholars who headed the list were then considered ready to start their official careers and to become members of the ruling class—the mandarins.

A successful candidate brought such great honor to his native town and to the whole province that, if any poor boy was especially gifted, a way would be found to procure him a teacher and give him a chance to become a candidate. Since there was no age or time limit, candidates often presented themselves year after year, and it would sometimes happen that a grandfather, father, and son all competed at the same time. Some arrived at the coveted goal only when seventy or eighty years old.

The system completely eliminated hereditary aristocracy from Chinese life, and it also increased the Chinese respect and admiration for learning, so that the scholar was put highest in evaluating the different classes of society. Criticism in modern times was directed not at the system itself, but at the fact that the requirements had remained too classical and cultural in nature and were not adapted to changing world conditions.

Some of the artists were officials who had won high places in the examinations where painting was one of the required subjects. Many pictures show a successful scholar returning in triumph to his home town; and other pictures, painted as congratulatory scrolls for parents of sons, carried the symbolic wish that the son might one day win a high place in the official examinations.

THE CH'AN SCHOOL OF PAINTING

There has been a tendency to overestimate the significance of Buddhism in Chinese art mainly because many of the few remaining specimens of the art of the early periods—such as the murals in the Tun-huang caves—are of this type. The main basis of Chinese art was Confucianism, and the rationalistic and deterministic interpretation of Confucius' teachings by Chu Hsi found ready acceptance. But, in addition to these practical doctrines, there was the craving for a more idealistic way of thought, and this was supplied by the teachings of Lao Tzŭ, which had a great deal of influence at this time.

It was feared that if Buddhism maintained too strong a hold over the people, it would degenerate into pure superstition and ritualism as it did later in Tibet and Mongolia. But as Buddhism declined, one of its branches—that of the Ch'an sect (Japanese Zen)—was steadily growing in importance, especially in the field of art. *Ch'an* means "contemplation," and the sect was originally introduced from India A.D. 526 when Bodhidharma, called the first Chinese patriarch, landed from India. It was not, however, until the Sung period that its influence on painting developed.

The Ch'an school was less a form of Buddhism than a revolt against it. Buddhist art was almost entirely devoted to representations of Buddha and his disciples and other subjects of a religious nature, while the Ch'an teachings opposed the making, or use, of religious symbols. They maintained that there is more religion in the study of a flower, or an insect, than in all the images of Buddhist deities or pictures of the tortures of hell.

The whole school of thought was deeply grounded in the purely Chinese philosophy of Taoism. Lao Tzŭ believed in the importance of the individual, and he preached complete liberty. He believed in withdrawing from the world and shunning public office. His teachings encouraged the desire that many Chinese artists and scholars have had through the ages to go and live in a hut on a mountainside and lead a life free of all worldly obligations or conventional restraints.

Lao Tzŭ did not advocate any active steps. Everything existed in the mind. Live according to your nature, he preached, and do not struggle to reach high places. Water seeks low levels, but it penetrates everywhere. It is soft and weak but can dissolve things which are hard and strong.

Such were the Taoist teachings, and they had little to learn from the Ch'an sect of Buddhism. The two merged as easily as water poured from two spouts into one cup.

The Ch'an sect held that the important thing was to develop self-mastery and will power. It was felt that perfect discipline of the body released the spirit for higher things, and one must shake off all preoccupation with worldly matters.

There was no real conflict among the artists of the time. One of the Ch'an masters said: "Buddha is Tao, Tao is Ch'an" to show the unity of all schools of religion. Eventually all the schools were reconciled, and not only did Ch'an combine with Buddhism and Taoism, but it also merged with Confucianism, forming a new stream of inspiration in the main body of Chinese art. This merging of schools of art ushered in many important changes. During the Sung dynasty, balance was substituted for symmetry because Nature was not symmetrical. According to Lao Tzŭ, completion or perfection means the end of growth and, therefore, death. The artists insisted on the asymmetrical, the imperfect, the incomplete. Always the little less, rather than the one stroke too much.

Lao Tzŭ scorned the use of color, saying that "color blinds the human eye"; while the Ch'an teachers said: "Illusion is color, and color is illusion." All insisted on the importance of blank spaces. They worked mostly in monochrome, and the artist was expected to paint "as if a whirlwind possessed his hand."

This method of working feverishly and only under strong compulsion was one of the main principles of the Ch'an school, and even more so of all Taoist thought. Lao Tzŭ wrote: "A violent wind does not outlast the morning; a squall of rain does not outlast the day. Such is the course of Nature. And if Nature herself cannot sustain her efforts long, how much less can man!"

Each picture consisted of a few strokes or ink splashes and was filled with hidden meanings and symbols. That is why Chinese literary critics are cold to this school of painting. As one Chinese critic expressed it: "Ch'an painting, like Western painting, was intended to show something. The true artist wants to express only his own personality."

One of the foremost painters of the school was Mu-ch'i, who came to Hang-chow in 1215 to found a Ch'an monastery. Another was Liang K'ai (first half of thirteenth century), who started life as a member of the Academy, won the highest honors, and then suddenly retired to a Ch'an monastery in the hills. One of his best-known pictures, now in Tokyo, shows one of the Ch'an patriarchs tearing up Buddhist sutras to show the uselessness of studying sacred scripts, since truth and inspiration come only from within the soul.

Then there was Ch'ên Jung (worked circa 1235-1255), a capable administrator and governor of a province in Fukien where he worked at land reclamation with considerable energy. Besides being a gifted artist, he was a poet and literary man, and noted for the austerity of his life. After having read the above account of his life in Chinese records, it is with astonishment that we read further and find: "He was admired for his habits as a confirmed drunkard. He made clouds by splashing ink on his pictures, for mists he spat out water . . ."

He specialized in painting dragons, and there are magnificent examples of his work in the Museum of Fine Arts in Boston, the Metropolitan Museum of Art in New York, and the William Rockhill Nelson Collection in Kansas City.

END OF THE SUNG DYNASTY

The Chins (Nü-chên Tartars), who invaded and occupied North China, are said to have first discovered art when they captured Peking in 1122. Their first emperor visited the Imperial Gallery of Paintings, and, never having seen pictures before, asked what was the use of such things. Told that they had been put there for the pleasure of the emperor, he said: "If that is what they are good for, they had better be enjoyed by many people rather than one." He then ordered the pictures to be distributed among various tea houses.

When the Chins had lived long enough among the Chinese, they learned the importance of art, and later Chin emperors became patrons of the arts in the manner of the Chinese emperors. The artists who worked for them appear to have painted the subjects that were of interest to this nomad race—horses and horsemen, hunters and hunting scenes. Little of their work has survived because the Mongols swept down from the north and destroyed the city of Peking.

In 1264, Kublai Khan rebuilt Peking into an even more magnificent city, and established himself there, taking the Chinese name Yüan as a title for his dynasty. In 1271, he began to plan his campaign of attack upon the Chinese.

It was with some satisfaction that the Chinese had first heard of the defeat of their old enemies, the Chins. They felt safe with the natural barrier of the broad Yangtze River between them and their enemies, for the Mongols—a desert tribe—knew nothing of ships and navigation. But neither the stretch of water nor the Lao Tzŭ doctrine that "if a man does not fight, none can fight with him" were of any avail against the powerful armies of Kublai Khan.

Hangchow fell in 1276, but the Chinese did not capitulate. They fought desperately, retreating to the south, for the Sung dynasty, which had done so much in social reform and in the development of the arts and philosophy, meant much to the Chinese people.

In 1279 the young emperor and his mother were captured by the Mongols, but the generals still tried to save the Sung dynasty by fleeing still farther south with one of the boy princes whom they named emperor. Finally, beyond Canton, they made a last stand. With a hundred thousand corpses in the water around him, the commander took the infant prince on his back, and, with his family at his side, they all walked into the sea rather than surrender. The idealistic age of Sung had been wiped out.

YÜAN DYNASTY (1280-1368)

In 1280 the whole of China became part of the Mongol empire that extended from the Yellow Sea in the east to the Black Sea in the west, and from northern Mongolia to Tonkin in the south.

When Kublai Khan conquered China he was greatly impressed by the Sung civilization. Once installed with all possible pomp and ceremony, and with incalculable wealth and treasure at his disposal, Kublai Khan wanted to emulate the Chinese emperors in every respect. He took all the arts under his patronage and invited noted scholars and artists to come to the Court in Peking.

CHAO MÊNG-FU (1254-1322)

The first important artist to come to the Court was Chao Mêng-fu, a man of great learning, known as "The Sage of Pines and Snow." After the Mongol conquest, he had retired into private life, but, in 1286, he and twenty other leading intellectuals succumbed to the emperor's appeal. He became a great favorite and achieved notable success as an administrator in addition to his fame as an artist.

It was natural that a nomad warlike tribe, much as they admired Sung art, should really prefer something less subtle, delicate, and intellectual, so Chao Mêng-fu founded the Chao School of Painting, which returned to the more virile T'ang tradition. The Mongols particularly admired historic and military pictures and, above all, paintings of horses. Hence it is not surprising that Chao Mêng-fu, and many other artists of the time, specialized in pictures of horses and horsemen.

In addition to this type of work, he also painted landscapes, bamboos, orchids, and rocks in monochrome in the Sung style.

His beloved young wife, known as the Lady Kuan Tao-shêng, also as Lady Kuan Tao-jên (1262-1319), was a famous painter in her own right, but she adhered to the themes of the Sung literary artists, painting bamboos and plum blossoms, orchids and rocks, all in black ink. She wrote a treatise on "The Bamboo in Monochrome" which is still a standard work. She was a most popular figure at Court, and we learn from her husband's writings that she was beautiful, talented, charming, exquisite, a capable housekeeper, a faithful daughter, and a most devoted wife. In addition she was the mother of nine children.

The Lady Kuan is the most famous woman painter, but in each dynasty there were other women artists, most of whom specialized in painting flowers.

Another prominent official who painted horses in the T'ang style was Jên Jên-fa. Then there was Kung K'ai, noted painter of horses who refused to enter the service of the Mongols. He painted a picture called "The Emaciated Horse" symbolizing the fate of those artists who refused to work for the Mongols. He also painted devils and spirits of the underworld.

FAMOUS PAINTERS OF BAMBOOS

Some of the leading Chinese painters of bamboos worked during this period, and outstanding among them were Kao K'o-kung, Li K'an (called the "King of

Bamboo"), Ku An (active circa 1333), and Ko Chiu-ssŭ (1312-1365). There was a great vogue for painting bamboos because it was a way of expressing disgust with the Mongol regime. The gallant bamboos, bent under the force of rude winds, symbolized the cultured Chinese scholars forced to submit to the barbaric nomad tribes.

LIFE UNDER THE MONGOLS

The country prospered, and great public works were undertaken. Communications were established by road and water throughout China, and a postal system was organized with relays of 200,000 fast horses. There was peace throughout the land and constant intercourse with the outside world, but the Chinese resented the presence of the Mongol military governors and began to form secret groups with the purpose of ridding the country of the invaders.

Marco Polo from Venice, who lived in China during this period, wrote much about the outward civilization and prosperity, the orderliness, and beauty of the cities, but he says nothing of what the Chinese thought or felt. He understood nothing of their bitter resentment against the alien conquerors. His sympathies were with the Mongols, in whose service he worked, and he saw everything from their point of view, even using the Mongol names such as Cambaluc (Peking), Quinsay (Hangchow) and Cathay (China).

He described at great length the magnificence of the palace of the emperor ". . . the walls covered with gold and silver . . . the hall so large that it could easily dine 6000 people . . . the gold, silver, gems, pearls, and gold plate . . . the guard of 12,000 horsemen, the robes of beaten gold. . . ." Dazzled by such opulence, he never even mentioned, and perhaps never even noticed, the restrained simplicity of Chinese paintings.

RELIGIONS AND RELIGIOUS PAINTERS

Large groups of Mohammedans and Jews now entered China and settled in Hangchow, Ningpo, and other centers. They had considerable political power not only in China but also in Mongolia and Tibet. The Mongols, who feared the hostility of the Chinese scholars, suspended for thirty years the civil service examinations and gave preference in filling higher official posts to Mohammedans, Tartars, Jews, Christians, and others; hence these minority groups found themselves in a position of special privilege.

Christian missionaries came too. Jean de Mont-Corvin, a Franciscan from the Kingdom of Naples, arrived in Peking in 1293 and stayed for about forty years. He is said to have made 30,000 converts. He organized, and had built, numerous Christian churches which were decorated by Chinese painters. This type of painting, however, was not considered of sufficient importance for the names of the artists to be recorded.

All religions and philosophies were allowed to flourish without interference—Buddhism, Confucianism, Christianity, and Mohammedanism. The one religion which had to suffer a certain amount of persecution was Taoism, and there were large-scale burnings of Taoist books. The Taoists had always been individualists who would not respect any form of imposed authority. It was because of their independent attitude that the Mongols (and later the Mings, and the Manchus) persecuted them. That, too, is why the important movements in painting led by Taoist monks had their centers far removed from the Court.

Although the Mongols tried not to interfere with the native Chinese culture, it was inevitable that their virility and organizing ability should bring about certain changes in viewpoint and a more energetic outlook. Mystic paintings, such as those of the Ch'an (Zen) sect, began to lose their appeal, and this school of art moved over to Japan, where it long continued to exercise an enormous influence.

One noted artist of the Ch'an type was Jen-hui (thirteenth-fourteenth centuries), who made humorous studies of devils and figures of the underworld. Most of his work is in Japan.

Tibetan art came under the influence of the Chinese at that time through Kublai Khan, who favored Lamaism as a religion for his soldiers.

Although China was still far ahead of Europe in art and civilization, the gulf was no longer quite so wide. Europe was about to experience a Renaissance of culture, and it is interesting to speculate whether the marvelous tales of the returning travelers from China and the treasures they brought from that land may not have added a spark to the flame that was finally to consume the Dark Ages.

CH'IEN HSÜAN (1235-CIRCA 1290)

The greater number of Chinese artists refused to work for the Mongols. Ch'ien Hsüan, an artist who had been a follower of Chao Mêng-fu before the invasion, could not forgive him for taking office under the enemy. He himself would have nothing to do with the conquerors but spent the rest of his life, far from the capital, as a wandering poet and painter, who was called "Man of the Jade Pool and the Roaring Torrent." He painted delicate studies of birds and flowers, giving away his pictures to anyone who admired them.

THE "FOUR MASTERS" OF THE YÜAN DYNASTY

The artists who are known as the "Four Masters" are:

Ni Tsan	(1301-1374)
Huang Kung-wang	(1269-1354)
Wang Mêng	(circa 1325-1385)
Wu Chên	(1280-1354)

They lived far removed from the capital, completely ignoring the Mongols and having neither official nor any other patronage. They were greatly admired for their independence, as well as for their work, which represents the highest culmination of the Southern school of landscape painting.

Ni Tsan (1301-1374) is considered the ideal painter, both for his work, and for the purity of his life and character. The son of a wealthy family, he distributed all his wealth and chose to live a life of obscure poverty. He traveled in fishermen's boats among the lakes and rivers of Kiangsu, and lived in Buddhist temples. His art, he asserted, was an expression of the "poetry of loneliness." He never put any figures into his landscapes, which frequently reveal the melancholy of autumn and winter scenes.

His pictures were painted with a dry free brush and give an effect of spontaneous simplicity. The brushwork has harmony and softness and yet is very virile. The Chinese say "his strokes which appear so delicate are capable of carrying iron tripods; stronger than those of any previous artist."

Ni Tsan gave away his pictures freely to his friends but refused to sell any. To a rich man who offered to pay him lavishly, he said: "I have never painted for the vulgar and ostentatious. I am no paid artisan."

Huang Kung-wang gave up an official career in order to devote his life to painting. He wandered about as "the guest of lakes and mountains" and suffered great hardships, often lacking food because he was so generous, but his ink painting was characterized by a serenity which revealed his contentment with life.

Wu Chên was another hermit-painter who scorned official patronage. He was more poet than painter, and his poems were an integral part of his compositions. He lived austerely and painted landscapes with gnarled old trees, bare hills, and rugged rocks, as well as fishing boats and bamboos in the wind. He worked with a dry brush, using mosslike dots, and was a master of light and shade.

These "hermit-painters" all withdrew from the world of affairs "as the birds fly into the woods and the fishes dive into deep water, not merely to follow their natural inclinations, but in order to escape the peril of arrows and nets."

Wang Mêng was a literary painter of the same school but was unlike the other three in his character and work. He painted an astounding volume of landscapes in "ten different manners," all of them entirely distinctive.

He painted large landscapes with emphasis on structure. His compositions are massive and crowded, but built up in perfect harmony like a symphony. His mountains tower layer above layer but are firmly rooted to the ground, and his paths wind and wind, and yet one can follow them to their conclusion. They are worked out with mathematical precision, achieve complete balance of masses, and have great strength and unity.

THE END OF THE MONGOL OCCUPATION

Despite certain cultural advances during this period—there was never a moment when the Chinese did not plan for the overthrow of the Mongols. The later emperors, having none of the finer qualities of Kublai Khan, quickly degenerated as a result of the overluxurious life they led in the capital.

The growing anger of the people for a long while had to confine itself to the formation of secret societies and to local disturbances; but, as soon as a leader arose, the whole country was ready to follow him. Such a leader was Chu Yüan-chang, son of a poor laborer, who had been left a penniless orphan.

After twelve years of fighting he drove out the hated Mongols, and was acclaimed emperor under the title of Hung Wu, inaugurating the Ming ("Radiant") dynasty in 1368. All traces of the foreign occupation were soon wiped out.

MING DYNASTY (1368-1644)

With the Mongols at last liquidated, the first reaction was a wave of ardent nationalism throughout China. The attempt to exclude all foreigners may have been partly responsible for the unpopularity of the Ming period in the Western world, and so may the fact that the period lacked the wistful idealism which gave such charm to the Sung.

In *A Short History of the Chinese People,* Professor L. Carrington Goodrich says: "The Ming has had a bad press. Actually this period was noteworthy for reconstruction in many fields . . . public works, government, law, colonization, literature and the fine arts . . ."

The art of the Ming dynasty, covering nearly three hundred years, was extremely rich and varied. As Lawrence Binyon stated: "If no paintings had survived earlier than the 14th century, we should mark the Ming dynasty as a great period for art."

The Chinese themselves fully appreciate the Ming masters, but in the world outside there has until very recently been a marked tendency to judge paintings only by age. A Chinese saying runs: "Out of every ten Sung pictures, eleven are imitation," but some Western collectors will go into ecstacies over a poor imitation of a Sung picture, while dismissing as unworthy of attention a genuine masterpiece by a Ming artist.

PAINTING AT THE COURT OF HUNG WU (1368-1398)

The first Ming emperor, Hung Wu, invited prominent artists to come to his Court at Nanking, where he gave them official rank and an income which enabled them to devote all their energies to their efforts with the brush.

At first the artists felt that their lean days were over, but they soon found that painters did not have the same standing as under the Sung emperors. They were expected to decorate buildings, paint imperial portraits, and be completely subservient to the emperor, who—although a capable and far-sighted ruler—was a ruthless and violent man. He would brook no reflections on his artistic judgment, and many artists actually lost their lives or were imprisoned or exiled. The great Wang Mêng died in prison, and his friend Ch'ên Ju-yen was beheaded.

THE HERMIT TAOIST PAINTERS

The more important trends in painting were a continuation of those inaugurated by the Four Masters of the preceding dynasty; and, even though a native dynasty had been restored, many of the best artists still preferred to live far from the Court.

Among the artists who had lived on from the Yüan dynasty were Tsou Fu-lei (fourteenth century), and Wang Mien (1335-1407). They both specialized in painting branches of prunus blossom, which carry a message of courage and hope and have always been particularly popular as a subject for pictures when China has been in enemy hands, as they imply that the day will come when the invaders will be driven out.

ACHIEVEMENTS UNDER THE EARLY MING EMPERORS

During the fourteenth and fifteenth centuries, the tendency to return to the virile T'ang school in art continued. Painters aimed at a wider audience than did those of the Sung dynasty. The trend was definitely toward native culture and practical rather than metaphysical ideas. Buddhism was considered foreign and fell out of favor, as it usually did in purely native dynasties. Confucianism again was the dominant philosophy. Rationalism was emphasized, and, in the Confucian temples, tablets replaced images so that they would not be looked upon as places of worship.

In many fields there were bold and imaginative innovations. Foreign trade was encouraged, important public works were undertaken, and there were great achievements in architecture. Schools and libraries were instituted in every town and village.

PAINTERS OF THE YUNG-LO PERIOD (1403-1424)

Among the best landscape painters was Wang Fu (1362-1416), who continued the tradition of the Yüan hermit-painters. He traveled around the country, making pictures and composing and singing ballads and poems. He painted towering mountains and cliffs, open stretches of water, and bamboos. It was said that "his bosom was rich in hills and valleys." He followed the Ming custom of introducing more than one figure into his landscapes, but he kept them very small.

A typical Court painter was Pien Wên-chin, a man of great culture who was considered the most successful painter of flowers and birds since the Sung dynasty. It was said that "his flowers smile sweetly, his birds fly and sing, his leaves rustle in the breeze, and his buds open."

TAI CHIN AND THE CHÊ SCHOOL

The next emperor Hsüan Tê (1426-1435) was himself an outstanding poet, calligrapher, and artist, who painted with great sensitiveness and delicacy. His preferred subjects were animals—cats, goats, monkeys, and dogs. He summoned many artists to Court and took great interest in their work, but he was easily influenced by the flattery and insinuation of those around him. The artists were completely subject to his whims and moods.

The emperor persuaded Tai Chin (active first part of fifteenth century), an extremely original and independent artist, to come to his Court and warmly praised his work. This aroused the jealousy of the Academic painters; and, when Tai Chin painted a fisherman in a deep red coat, they convinced Hsüan Tê that this was intended to show disrespect since red was the color of state robes. Tai Chin was dismissed from the Court, and he returned to his home where he lived and died in great poverty. He was a professional painter and turned out a tremendous volume of work on a great variety of subjects, but it was only after his death that he was recognized as "the foremost of all Ming painters" of the Northern school. He founded the Chekiang (Chê) School of Painting, in which landscapes were no longer painted for their own sake, but as a background for a story or a group of persons. These pictures were objective, decorative, and made use of bright colors.

A new development in Ming painting was the increasing importance given to human beings as subject matter. Also, during the sixteenth and seventeenth centuries, many Chinese artists returned to the painting of historical subjects and legends, drawing upon their memory, knowledge, and observation rather than upon their inner spirit for their subjects. For this reason Ming pictures often appear less "modern" and less "universal" than the older ones.

While Tai Chin is regarded as the founder of the Chê School of Painting, his name is bracketed in that respect with another artist, Wu Wei, who also had unhappy connections with the Court. Wu Wei (1458-1508) was known for his artistic temperament and peculiar manners. When the emperor sent for him, he would come into the imperial presence with a dirty face and uncombed hair, so drunk that he had to be supported by two eunuchs. But when he knelt down and painted a picture, the clouds and landscapes emerged with such strength and sureness of line that the emperor would congratulate him on having the "brush of an immortal."

Wu Wei despised the courtiers, and, as a consequence, they spread such evil reports about him that he was finally dismissed from the Court. He died from overindulgence in drink.

SHÊN CHOU—AND THE WU SCHOOL

An important and more fortunate painter than Tai Chin was Shên Chou (1427-1509), the best fifteenth-century representative of the Southern school of landscape painting. He never had to accept any official position or go to Court, yet he never lacked recognition because he painted in the manner preferred by the literary critics, who wrote that "his genius diffused a radiance over the age in which he lived."

Shên Chou was the founder of the Wu School at Soochow, and he gathered around him a group of devoted pupils and admirers. He was a learned and kind-hearted man, always generous in giving money to those who needed help. He not only gave his pictures and poems to those who cared for them, but even consented to sign his name to a copy someone else had made of one of his pictures so that they could sell it for a good price.

In commenting on an album of landscapes and poems by Shên Chou, acquired by the Museum of Fine Arts, Boston, Kojiro Tomita and A. Kaiming Chiu write: "As Shên Chou's fame spread, to his Abode among the Bamboos came callers from all walks of life . . . Nevertheless, he was at heart a recluse. His personality is clearly reflected in his own words: 'One flower and one bamboo, one lamp and one small table, books of poems and volumes of classics,—with them I pass the rest of my years. My friends are elderly farmers, my conversations are with the mountains, my life is devoted to gardening. News of worldly affairs does not enter my gate. Should it intrude, the breeze in the pines would waft it away.' "

The most famous follower of Shên Chou was Wên Chêng-ming (1470-1559), who became one of the "Four Great Masters" of the Ming dynasty. He was famed for his gentle and lovable disposition, his high ethical standards, and his simple manner of life. He loved to wander through the countryside around his home and paint the scenes most familiar to him. Whenever he noticed a house with no smoke coming from the chimney, he would feel that the occupants had nothing to cook and would send food over to them.

A Chinese critic said that for rhythm and tonal values "he walked alone in his generation." He painted large landscapes in a bold, free manner, and smaller pictures in a refined meticulous style. Although his work was highly valued, he remained a poor man because he gave away his pictures to those in want. The recipients would have "thousands of copies" made, so that genuine and imitation pictures by Wên Chêng-ming were well mixed in private collections and in the stocks of dealers. That did not trouble him, for, he said, "those with keen eyes will be able to distinguish the fishes' eyes from the shining pearls."

THE JAPANESE PAINTER SESSHU (BORN 1420)

One of the few foreign painters included in the Chinese lists of great painters is Sesshu, a Japanese. When in his forties, and already one of the foremost artists of Japan, he decided to visit China in order to study art at its source. His first idea had been to work under Chinese teachers, but he soon decided to seek "enlightenment" directly from the "noble waters and mountains of China."

The Chinese praised his originality and the vigor of his brush strokes, and many Chinese artists and critics called him "the best painter now working in China." He stayed nearly three years, and his work was equally admired by the literary painters and the Court artists. Sesshu painted thousands of pictures in China, and all this mass of new material gave a tremendous impetus to Japanese art, and to the Sesshu School which he founded.

T'ANG YIN (1470-1523)

T'ang Yin, like his master, Shên Chou, was another of the "Four Great Masters" of the Ming dynasty. (The other two were Wên Chêng-ming and Tung Ch'i-ch'ang). T'ang Yin was not only one of the outstanding artists of his time but was also one of the most beloved characters. On one occasion, when we were in Shanghai, there were two different Chinese movies being shown in different theaters, both depicting episodes of his life. He was a contemporary of Raphael, and his life in some respects resembled that of the Italian painters of the Renaissance. He was handsome, gay, witty, and unconventional. He loved women, wine, and poetry, and got into many scrapes. His house was besieged by crowds of persons coming to order his paintings.

When, as a youth, T'ang Yin sat for his final state examination, he came out at the head of the list, but then it was discovered that a friend, with whom he had traveled to the capital, had bribed the servant of the chief examiner to show him the examination questions. T'ang Yin was involved and, although never proved guilty, lost many honors. He was offered a post as a minor official which he refused. His whole life was affected by this incident, and he alternated between bouts of wild indulgence and periods of profound melancholy. The uneven quality of his pictures testifies to his way of life.

T'ang Yin had a great friend Chou Ch'ên, an established painter of landscapes, who flourished around 1500-1535. Although he was not much older than T'ang Yin he was often called his teacher, and when, because of dissipation or laziness, T'ang Yin was unable to fill his orders he would get Chou Ch'ên to paint pictures for him, which he then signed.

Remarkable for its versatility, T'ang Yin's work includes fine impressionistic studies, gay genre pictures, and studies of beautiful young women alternating with the most somber of landscapes.

As T'ang Yin grew older, the moods of sadness outweighed all others and eventually he sought peace in a Ch'an monastery where he changed his name to Liu-ju, which means "Six Likes"—and is taken from a passage in the Diamond Sutra which describes life as "like a dream, like a vision, like a bubble, like a shadow, like dew, like lightning."

CH'IU YING (WORKED FIRST HALF OF SIXTEENTH CENTURY)

Ch'iu Ying was born into a very humble family, and he served as a painter's apprentice, until Chou Ch'ên saw some of his drawings and took him as a pupil. There is no trace of Ch'iu Ying's origins in either his work, which is distinguished by its delicacy and refinement, or in his subjects, for he loved to paint gay men and women of the Court, dressed in brilliantly colored costumes with gold touches, and genre pictures.

Although he enjoyed tremendous popularity, many critics considered his work altogether too detailed, and it was said that "when he painted a snake he could not refrain from adding feet." His pictures depict clearly, and in great detail, residences, gardens, furniture, costumes, games, musical instruments and other objects which provide valuable documentation on the life of the period.

Apart from his services as a historian, however, Ch'iu Ying's main contribution to the art of painting was of rather doubtful value. He originated the school of decorative and highly colored paintings, which was much practiced in the later Ming and in the Ch'ing periods by many Northern artists and by hosts of copyists. It was just this type of picture—conventional, brightly-colored, detailed—that pleased the Westerners who visited China, and the outside world was thus given a completely false conception of Chinese art.

Among these were a few artists of genius, such as Lin Liang, who excelled in painting wild birds in monochrome. His pictures of eagles, cormorants, wild geese and other birds are powerful and full of movement. In complete contrast was Lü Chi, who painted calm, colored pictures of ducks floating on ponds or birds nesting in trees.

Liu Chün (active circa 1500), a Taoist, specialized in large lively figures, and Hsü Lin (early sixteenth century) painted landscapes with figures in a romantic manner.

TUNG CH'I-CH'ANG (1555-1636)

The man who dominates the whole latter part of the Ming dynasty is Tung Ch'i-ch'ang. As already mentioned he was one of the "Four Great Masters" and, according to many Chinese critics, the most gifted landscape painter of his time. He was also a statesman, calligrapher, poet, aesthete, writer, and collector.

With all these accomplishments, his chief claim to fame is as a leading art connoisseur and critic, whose views on art not only influenced painting and art criticism up to the present day but also caused all existing pictures by old masters to be evaluated in accordance with his standards. Even in the Western world—among persons interested in Chinese painting—the name of Tung Ch'i-ch'ang still has power to excite the most violent arguments, pro and con. A great Ming patriot, he fared badly in the public records when the Manchus came into power, but he continued to have ever-increasing fame and influence with literary painters.

Tung held the strongest views about the division of painting into Northern and Southern schools. The classification had long existed, and, in the Sung dynasty, Su Tung-p'o had written: "To judge a picture by its resemblance is to have the critical faculty of a child." This saying embodies the main thesis of the Southern school, yet nobody had ever gone as far as Tung and his followers, who had nothing but contempt for the work of the Northern school.

Tung held that the purpose of art is pure self-expression. He was instrumental in placing the Four Masters of the Yüan dynasty to whom "the spirit was everything" in the first rank of Chinese painters—thus increasing the influence they exercised over succeeding generations of artists. He has been criticized by some Western writers for defending the painting of the wên jên (literary artists), but what he worked for was a revolt against academic restrictions of freedom. Artists of the Southern school, both before and after Tung, were ready to live in poverty and give up all Court protection and financial security in order to paint as they pleased.

Tung Ch'i-ch'ang blazed new trails and fought for the creative freedom of the artist.

In 1949, an exhibition of important Ming and Ch'ing paintings was held, for the first time, in New York. Reviewing this show in the *Art News*, Henry A. La Farge stated: "Far from showing decadence, these later schools show new trends equal in significance to what was accomplished in the west by Velasquez, Chardin, and Cézanne . . . the radical departure seen in the works of Tung Ch'i-ch'ang represented by an album of eight leaves . . . showing studies of rocks and trees. . . . A completely new vision is created, and a new ideal of painting, in his serious analysis of form and structure."

WOMEN ARTISTS

The names of thirty-four women artists are recorded in the official list of artists of the Ming dynasty. One of these, Wên Shu (1595-1634), ranks second only to Lady Kuan Tao-shêng of the Yüan dynasty. She specialized in making small delicate pictures of rare flowers and plants, insects, and butterflies on album leaves.

PAINTERS OF CHIA-HSING AND CHIA-TING, NEAR SHANGHAI (CHEKIANG)

There was a group of artists in Chia-hsing who were greatly influenced by the ideas of Tung Ch'i-ch'ang. Outstanding among them was Hsiang Shêng-mo (1597-1658), the grandson of the famous art critic and collector Hsiang Yüan-p'ien, who loved to paint branches of trees bright with blossoms or heavy with fruit. Two older artists were Li Jih-hua (1565-1635) and Ku Ning-yüan (middle seventeenth century). Both wrote illuminating books on the technique of painting. Ku Ning-yüan maintained that the great essentials are simplicity and freshness. Students, he believed, are frequently hampered by all the rules they have learned, but often children, who are completely natural and unself-conscious, succeed in fully expressing themselves in a way not possible to the learned and accomplished artist. They have not erected any barriers to "divine inspiration."

Among the leading artists in Chia-ting was Li Liu-fang (1575-1629). His small album pictures were pure examples of "thought writing" (hsieh i), the character of which, it was said, revealed that "his spirit was free." Another well-known artist, who lived at Kashing, between Shanghai and Hangchow, was Lu Tê Chih (seventeenth century), one of the leading bamboo painters of the period. His specialty was black bamboos moving in the wind. In his later years paralysis of his right arm forced him to paint with his left hand.

HSÜ WEI (WÊN-CH'ING)—(1521-1593)

An artist who does not fit into any special school or category, and whose violent and tragic life brings to mind Van Gogh, was Hsü Wei of Chekiang. When he was only ten years old he wrote an "Essay on Slander" which attracted much attention. He passed his examinations brilliantly, and soon became known as an artist, calligrapher, writer, and poet.

Not only was Hsü Wei a man of wild and reckless nature, but he drank heavily and, when inebriate, his violence knew no bounds. He held his official position only because he happened to be a great favorite of the governor of the province, who protected him from the consequences of his disorderly conduct and failure to perform his normal duties. When, owing to a political upheaval, the governor was thrown into prison, Hsü, in order to avoid sharing his fate, feigned madness. He took a sharp awl and pierced his ear, and then smashed his testicles with a hammer. In actual fact, to say that he feigned madness must be considered an understatement, for all his acts prove that he was always on the borderline between genius and madness. In a fit of frenzy he killed his wife and was then taken to prison.

Later, when he was released from confinement, Hsü Wei refused to allow anyone to enter his home, and this still further increased his unpopularity. Forced to live off the meager sale of his paintings, he was reduced to extreme poverty. As might be expected, as an artist he had great originality and worked in a vehement manner, with coarse, strong strokes which expressed his untamed nature. There are many fine examples of his work in private collections in China.

FOREIGN INFLUENCES

While the early Ming emperors had extended the borders of their empire, and had sought trade relations far afield, yet they strove to keep outsiders from again penetrating into China, and for about two centuries they succeeded.

The first missionary who actually landed in China during the Ming dynasty was the Jesuit priest, François Xavier, who, in 1552, spent a few weeks on an island south of Canton. However the first notable mission was established thirty years later by the Jesuits at Macao, under the leadership of Matteo Ricci.

About 1600, Matteo Ricci went to Peking and appears to have been one of the first persons to interest the Chinese court in European ideas. He had studied the Chinese language, and he impressed the emperor with his knowledge of Western mathematics, astronomy, and other sciences. Having come to make converts to Christianity and to convince the Chinese of European superiority in all things, including painting, he tried first to win over the intellectuals. It appears, however, that he had no more understanding of Chinese art than Marco Polo had had three centuries earlier. But there was a notable difference in the attitude of the two men. While Marco Polo, coming from the Dark Ages in Europe, by comparison found himself in a wonderland, Matteo Ricci had come from Renaissance Europe, flowering in all fields of art and learning. He was deeply rooted in his own religion and a devotee of the new European culture. Already printing had been introduced by Gutenberg; Shakespeare, Dante, Milton, and Cervantes had made their contributions to world literature, while Raphael, Leonardo da Vinci, Michelangelo, Titian, Botticelli and Benvenuto Cellini had raised European art to its highest level.

Part of Matteo Ricci's program was to organize a small school of painting, bringing religious pictures and engravings from Italy; but these, like his teachings, were never regarded as anything but a novelty. The Chinese courtiers enjoyed his ideas on painting, just as the Europeans were later to be amused by "chinoiserie." Thus, he had no influence on serious Chinese art.

90

THE END OF THE MING ERA

Once more China entered a downward cycle. A gradual weakening of the inner structure of the government was accompanied by attacks and assaults from the outside world.

Conditions grew steadily worse throughout the country, and millions died through famines. Relief measures inaugurated by the government did little to alleviate the suffering. Growing discontent flared up into open agrarian revolts, and the Mongols, Manchus, Turkis, and other border tribes, seeing the whole country torn with civil war, seized the opportunity to make repeated attacks.

While the government troops were fighting the Manchus in the north, Li Tzŭ-ch'êng, a native of Shensi, united and led the various rebel Chinese forces. He took city after city, proclaimed himself emperor, and reached the gates of Peking so quickly that the government was taken completely by surprise. The last Ming emperor, Ch'ung Chêng (1628-1643), abandoned by his generals and eunuchs, went to the top of Coal Hill in Peking and saw the rebels burning and pillaging the city. In despair he hanged himself.

When the generals in charge of the troops defending the Great Wall learned what had happened, they made a truce with the Manchus and asked them to join forces with the Chinese to drive out the upstart rebel leader. Together, they succeeded in defeating the rebels, but, once within the walls of Peking, the Manchus refused to go away again. Without any organized opposition, they took over the whole vast empire, brought a six-year-old prince to Peking and proclaimed him emperor under the name of Shun Chih (1644-1661). Thus the Manchus established the Ch'ing dynasty which was to rule over China until the Revolution of 1912.

It should be noted that toward the end of the Ming dynasty an entirely new movement in Chinese painting was created by the hermit-painters—Taoist and Ch'an monks—who led isolated lives in the mountains.

One of the pioneers of this group had been Shên Hao, whose last known picture was dated 1640. He was a Buddhist monk who wrote two books on the history of painting that have been frequently reprinted. He asserted that the simplest pictures are best—"ordinary painters make their pictures too complicated in order to hide their shortcomings." His pictures and writings were an expression of a creative revival in painting which continued well into the Ch'ing dynasty.

Many "monk" painters worked at that time, each one painting individually and in a different place. They did not know each other, and yet all seemed to be working and thinking along the same lines—evolving a new type of expressionism, using bold free strokes, working in a spontaneous rapid manner, and turning out the most original pictures which had an incalculable effect on the Chinese artists who followed them.

Even in the bitter winter of defeat and foreign domination, the emergence of the "monk" painters again bore witness to the eternal renewal of nature and of art.

CH'ING DYNASTY (1644-1912)

The Manchus, like the Mongols, were admirers of Chinese culture and wanted art to continue in the old tradition. And, again, as during the Yüan dynasty, many artists refused to cooperate with or take office under the invaders.

Having seized the capital by subterfuge, the Manchus claimed that they represented a legitimate Chinese dynasty, and were not alien conquerors. But, although they claimed that there had been no military conquest, they placed in all the provincial capitals Manchu garrisons, which were a thorn in the flesh of the Chinese. Even more galling was the order that all Chinese men must wear their hair in the Manchu style, shaving the front of the head and wearing the back hair in a long queue.

The feeling against the Manchus was particularly marked among the wên jên (the intellectuals) and the artists, and this may have accounted for the bad press that "literary" artists received in official writings as compared to the academic painters who worked for the Court in Peking.

THE "MONK-PAINTERS"

Prominent among those who refused official honors were the large group of "monk-painters," who were the outstanding artists of the dynasty.

Perhaps the most famous of them all was Pa Ta Shan Jên (1626-1705), also known as Chu Ta. He was a descendent of the Ming imperial family and, when China was conquered by the Manchus, he became a Buddhist priest, living a solitary life in the mountains. He said that he preferred the cool air of the hills to holding public office.

Pa Ta Shan Jên used a form of signature on his paintings which can be read either as "Laughing at it" or "Crying at it" and which was intended to show his grief at the fall of the Ming dynasty. A great individualist, he worked in a more free and original manner than any of his predecessors, and his forceful brush expressed his solitary and original nature.

With a minimum of strokes and a minimum of ink, he made rapid sketches that are masterpieces of suggestiveness—giving a vivid impression of depth and distance, liveliness and, in the case of his birds, for instance, a decided touch of humor. He interpreted familiar subjects in an entirely new way.

Another Ch'an monk who was equally famous was Shih-t'ao (circa 1640-1704). He, too, was a descendent of one of the Ming princes and called himself "The Monk of the Bitter Melon." His genius was best expressed in his small studies of flowers, vegetables, bamboos, and birds.

He complained that "people are so infatuated with the old masters that they find it difficult to appreciate original and individualistic work." He pointed out that the old masters had to invent their own styles and had no one to follow. "The perfect method of painting," he wrote, "is to follow no method."

A "monk-artist" who equaled the two just mentioned was K'un-ts'an, active between 1650 and 1675. He was frank, fearless, and consequently, had few friends. Sometimes he spent many days in complete silence. He painted large landscapes which showed the vastness and wildness of nature, and also such subjects as hermits fishing.

These "monk-painters" were important landmarks in the history of Chinese art. They were great creative artists who painted to express their own feelings, and Chinese critics characterize them as "Revolutionists" because they broke so completely with past tradition.

They made no sharp distinctions between the real and the imaginary, between the subjective and the objective in their paintings. The trees and scenes they painted may have existed only in their imagination, but they convey an impression of reality. On the other hand, some of their pictures of distant mountains and floating clouds, deep ravines and lofty cliffs look incredible yet represent actual scenes.

THE "FOUR WANGS"

At the same time another and entirely different group of artists, known as the "Six Greatest Masters" of the Ch'ing dynasty, were also giving evidence of the vitality of Chinese painting.

Among these six masters were the artists known as the "Four Wangs" because they all had that surname. Not all, however, were related. The "Four Wangs" were:

Wang Shih-min	(born near Shanghai)	1592-1680
Wang Chien	(born near Soochow)	1598-1677
Wang Hui	(born near Soochow)	1632-1717
Wang Yüan-ch'i	(born near Soochow)	1642-1715

The leader of this group was Wang Shih-min, an admirer of the works and ideas of Tung Ch'i-ch'ang. He was said to have possessed remarkable ability even as a child and was noted for his sensitiveness and imagination.

The type of landscapes which are associated with the Four Wangs—structurally strong pictures remarkable for their composition, spacing, and atmospheric effects—are frequently compared by Chinese critics to musical compositions. They were usually painted in monochrome.

Wang Chien was a well-known art critic as well as a painter. He and Wang Shih-min were close friends and they were instrumental in guiding the whole course of Southern school painting during the Ch'ing dynasty. Both were always ready to help and advise young artists. Their most famous pupil, Wang Hui, came of a family of painters, but his people were very poor. Once when Wang Chien visited the town where he lived, Wang Hui sent him a specimen of his work. The older artist was much impressed with it and both he and Wang Shih-min agreed to help the young artist develop his talent fully. The two elder Wangs worked with and encouraged Wang Hui for over twenty years, by which time Wang Shih-min said that Wang Hui was capable of being the teacher rather than the pupil.

Wang Hui brought to his work deeper imagination, greater variety, and more purely individual touches than the others and is renowned for the purity and elegance of his brush work. In one of his writings he said that "proper consideration must be given to light and shade, for these are like the two wings of a bird—both are equally essential and they must be in proper proportion." He warned against pictures painted in too great detail. "Both repetition and over-crowding must be avoided, and there must always be room to move about with ease."

The last of the Wangs was Wang Yüan-ch'i, grandson of Wang Shih-min. He was only an infant at the time of the Manchu conquest, so he, unlike the other Wangs, had no scruples about taking an official post. He was a great favorite of the Emperor K'ang Hsi, who put him in charge of a commission which was to prepare for publication an Imperial Encyclopaedia of Calligraphy and Painting.

He worked hard in a very painstaking manner, building up his complicated stylized compositions, layer by layer, with a vast range of ink tones and brush strokes. He would work for weeks on a single picture. Although his paintings lack spontaneity, Chinese connoisseurs nevertheless consider that his technique attained the highest perfection, and it is for that reason that his work is so much valued.

During his lifetime Wang Yüan-chi's landscapes also commanded high prices. He would work only when offered a very substantial payment, which, of course, meant that only the richest collectors were his patrons. Often he had his pupils paint pictures and then put his name and seal on them. Wang Yüan-ch'i was always anxious to accumulate wealth, and is one of the few artists recorded as having had that attitude toward his art.

To the present day the paintings of all the Four Wangs continue to fetch amazingly high prices. Few of their original works have been seen outside China, since few foreigners would pay the fantastic sums offered by Chinese collectors.

YUN SHOU-P'ING (1633-1690)

Another of the Six Great Masters was Yün Shou-p'ing. He started by painting landscapes, but, when he saw Wang Hui's work, he was so overcome with admiration that he said: "I must leave this branch of art to you, for I would not want to go down to fame as the second landscape painter of China." And so it was as a flower painter that he succeeded in being the first.

Yün Shou-p'ing was born into a wealthy family, but his father was one of those who refused to submit to the Manchus. He fled south to Canton, and when, in 1653, the city was taken by the enemy, he entered a Buddhist monastery. Yün Shou-p'ing, who showed great talent from his early youth, was brought up and educated by good friends of his father.

He was a most fastidious and discriminating man who would often work for a whole month on one of his beautiful, meticulously executed flower studies, and then give the picture away to a friend. If he did not like a man he would refuse to sell him a drawing of "a single leaf or blossom." He said that he regarded offers of large sums of money "as lightly as a grain of mustard seed."

Naturally, with such an attitude toward money, unlike Wang Yüan-Ch'i, he always remained poor. He led a very happy life, painting for his own pleasure, and writing and exchanging poems with all the notables of his time. When he died his family could not raise enough money to bury him with suitable ceremonies. It was his great friend, Wang Hui, who paid the funeral expenses.

Definitely of the Northern school, he did not like impressionistic and mystic painting but was a pioneer among Chinese artists in painting directly from nature. He painted many large compositions in which the flowers were far larger than in nature, and achieved some wonderful effects of form, pattern, and color. He often used the "boneless" style—washes of color without outlines (Mo-ku hua)—achieving the desired effect by using color tones of varying depths and shades.

His daughter, Yün P'ing, was also a popular flower painter.

WU LI (1643-1708)

The sixth of the Great Masters, and the one considered by many to be the finest of all, was Wu Li (1643-1708).

His story is dramatic and unexpected. Born in the Ming dynasty, he led the life of a hermit, stayed with the Portuguese Jesuits in Macao, was said to have traveled in Europe, became a Christian, and, finally, ended his days as a Jesuit priest. He was buried in a Catholic cemetery at Ziccawei, which is just outside Shanghai.

Wu Li refused to take any position at Court, saying he had natural leanings toward a life of solitude and contemplation. He was therefore obliged to depend on his brush for a living, and his pictures were eagerly sought after by purchasers.

Although it was never proved that Wu Li went to Europe, he did stay several months in a Catholic monastery in Macao where he had an opportunity to study certain Western paintings. In a book called *Remarks on the Masterpieces of Chinese Painting* there is the statement: "Since Wu Li came back from Macao his brush has been more bold and natural. This may be because of his observations of the influence of open nature—mountains and seas."

Wu Li himself wrote: "In Macao many things are influenced by the Western world. I find Western paintings quite different from mine. They emphasize form, light and perspective in an effort to secure exact likeness. But we do not care for conventional style and outward form. What we try to express is inner rhythm and freedom. We are more interested in the spiritual content than in the bodily likeness."

He also adds: "They sign their pictures at the bottom, we sign them at the top. With us writing is composed of dots and strokes and the sound is incidental, but with them the sound is the most important and the written signs are secondary. We write in vertical lines and they write in horizontal lines. We use our brushes in quite a different way."

Wu Li's deep love of nature was one of his outstanding qualities. It shows not only in his landscapes, but also in the poems which he inscribed on them. On one of his paintings in a private collection in Shanghai, the following poem appears:

One can still rejoice as one looks at the winter moon. But, alas, the poet suffers too much from the cold. The clear light enables me to see, and it is not often that one can contemplate the scene of a year that is drawing to its close.

The cold penetrates the vast white spaces. The clarity of the moonlight passes through the trees bare of all foliage, and falls directly on the snow-covered branches. She has already filled with poetic inspiration the heart of the painter and poet.

As we look at each other, the moon and I, I think of our separation last autumn.

Without sleep, I suffer during the long, long night. Suddenly I start breathing on my frozen brush to soften it up. It seems to me that it will be difficult to show in my picture the shadow left by the moon.

To celebrate the winter moon

Wu Li's integrity, high purpose, and the nobility of his life make him a good example of the Chinese contention that "only a good man can be a really good artist."

INDEPENDENT GROUPS OF PAINTERS

The important painters of the dynasty are usually divided into groups such as the Four Great Masters of Anhui, the Eight Masters of Nanking, the Ten Saints, the Eight Wonders of Yangchow and the Five Gentlemen.

The leader of the Eight Masters of Nanking was Kung Hsien (circa 1635-1700). Eccentric in character, he lived in a little hut in Nanking, where he welcomed only visitors who shared his loyalty to the defeated Ming dynasty. He loved to paint somber and tragic scenes of desolation and loneliness. He said that human beings did not exist for him, and they do not appear in his pictures.

His pupil Wang Kai was a very different type of painter. He was one of the chief compilers of the Chieh Tzü Yüan Hua Chuan (the Mustard Seed Garden), a famous series of books, illustrated with woodcuts, which deal with the theory and practice of painting. The first five volumes were published in 1679 and met with such success that additional volumes were published, and new editions have appeared right up to the present century.

Another similar series of books, called the Shih Chu Chai Shu Hua P'u (the Ten Bamboo Studio Books on Painting), had appeared in the Ming dynasty. This, too, was intended for the use of students of painting and calligraphy and showed all stages in the drawing of flowers, birds, fruits, bamboos, rocks, and other subjects.

In both series the woodcuts in the early editions were most beautifully drawn and colored.

The aim and purpose of these books of painting has frequently been misunderstood. The idea was not that all painters should work to exact models, but that the hand of the artist should acquire such facility in handling his brush that his mind and hand would be left free to express his thoughts. These models provided an alphabet of drawing, and only after the artist had complete mastery of his brush could he do original work. The Chinese theory was that "Freedom grows inside law, not outside."

WOMEN PAINTERS

During the Ch'ing dynasty there were many notable women painters. A number of them were professional artists who worked to earn their living. One of the best known was Ch'ên Shu (1660-1736) from Chekiang. She was a talented and versatile painter of landscapes (in the style of Wang Yüan-ch'i), figures, Buddhist subjects, flowers, birds, trees, grasses, and insects. Twenty-three of her pictures are listed in the Imperial Catalogue of Paintings. She had three sons and one daughter. Because her husband's official duties kept him away from his home, she took charge of their education. She also handled the affairs of the family most efficiently and energetically and supplemented their income by the sale of her pictures. As a result of the fine education the children received, they were all very successful both in official life and as poets and painters. Ch'ên Shu is renowned too as the teacher of many outstanding artists and writers of her day.

Li Yin, also from Chekiang, who died in 1675 when she was over seventy, was another noted woman artist. She was the wife of a high official and well-known artist, Ko Chêng-ch'i, and was famous for her landscapes, but she excelled in the freshness and charm of her flower pictures. Her husband once remarked: "I surpass her in painting landscapes, but I am not her equal when it comes to painting flowers."

Chin Yüeh, born near Soochow, was a talented painter of landscapes and flowers. In 1667 she became the concubine of a famous poet, Mao Pi-chiang. Then there was Ma Ch'üan from Kiangsu, active in the eighteenth century. Her husband was also an artist and the two worked together. When they found it impossible to earn a living in their native town, they moved to Peking where they enjoyed considerable success—particularly Ma Ch'üan, whose work was far above that of her husband. Her husband died while she was still young, but she then returned to her home, and lived in retirement for the rest of her eighty years, in the traditional manner of a virtuous Chinese widow.

COURT PAINTERS

While many of the finest artists refused to recognize the Manchu invaders, other gifted artists became Court painters and turned out a large number of pictures of varying quality.

The second Ch'ing emperor, K'ang Hsi (1662-1722), was an enlightened and powerful man. He and his grandson, the Emperor Ch'ien Lung (1736-1795), were two of the finest administrators that China had known. They restored the former boundaries of the Chinese empire, conquering Mongolia, eastern Turkestan and Tibet, and received tribute from Burma, Nepal, Laos, Siam, Annam, and Korea. For the most part, however, they devoted their energies and abilities to government, industry, and the arts of peace.

The Imperial Bureau of Painting was developed and enlarged, but it became a government department for recording and classifying pictures and for the supervision of art works ordered by the emperor.

In 1705 the Emperor K'ang Hsi ordered a commission of eleven scholars and artists, under the supervision of Wang Yüan-ch'i, to compile an Imperial Encyclopædia of Calligraphy and Painting (the Shu-hua-p'u). Although somewhat slanted to conform to the imperial point of view, this monumental work (which comprises one hundred sections bound in sixty-four volumes) remains one of the most important sources of information on the history of Chinese painting.

THE JESUITS AT THE CHINESE COURT

Jesuit priests were now welcomed at the Chinese Court and given official rank. The Emperor K'ang Hsi was much impressed by their knowledge of geometry, mathematics, and science, and they looked after the mechanical toys, the astronomical instruments, and the clocks that had been brought from Europe, which they alone knew how to operate.

As far as Chinese painting is concerned, the most important of these Jesuits was Père Giuseppe Castiglione, who arrived in Peking in 1715, and lived there until his death in 1766. He had studied art in Italy and, when they first came to China, he and the other Jesuit priests painted in oils in the Western manner. They soon realized, however, that the Chinese did not appreciate their work, and they learned to paint in Chinese style with the Chinese brush and ink and water colors.

The work of Giuseppe Castiglione (who adopted the Chinese name of Lang Shih-ning) was in turn much admired by the Emperors K'ang Hsi, Yung Chêng, and Ch'ien Lung, who liked the idea of having a foreign painter at the Court. Fifty-six of his pictures, painted in the Chinese manner, are included in the catalogue of the Imperial Collection. He used a considerable amount of architecture in his pictures, and, in fact, his main talent lay in the direction of drawing exact plans and historical documents, rather than in creating original works.

Two other Jesuit painters who also worked in the Chinese style were Père Ignatius Sichelbarth (1708-1780), and Père Denis Attiret (1708-1768). These fathers, as well as Giuseppe Castiglione, worked with the Augustinian friar, Jean Damascène, by order of the Emperor Ch'ien Lung, on the preparation of a series of sixteen drawings to commemorate the conquest of Turkestan. The drawings were sent to France to be engraved on copper.

In both taste and outlook on life there was more similarity between the Chinese and European Courts during the eighteenth century than ever before or since. The temper of the time, both in the East and in the West, was gay, extravagant, and worldly, and yet permeated with a spirit of tolerance, skepticism, rationalism, and intellectual curiosity. But, although the West enjoyed playing with their make-believe Chinese world, in the form of *chinoiserie*, they entirely failed to understand the true Chinese conception of art.

The Jesuit priests in Peking complained of the "simplicity" of Chinese painting, characterizing in this way the spontaneity, directness, and reliance on line and space, rather than detail, of the creative Chinese artist. They could **not** understand the Chinese ideal of selecting only the essential points to convey **the** inner vision. On the other hand, the Chinese art historian of the period, **Chang Kêng**, wrote that Western painting consists in "copying every single hair" **and** adds that "the result is neither refined nor convincing."

Unfortunately the Emperor Ch'ien Lung was interested in painting as a pastime rather than as a means of intellectual expression. He therefore encouraged the spread of an inferior form of academic art among both the native and foreign Court painters—the type of art despised by Chinese art critics.

When the "Chinese" craze died out in Europe, the impression remained that Chinese art consisted of meticulous, brightly colored, amusing pictures, while the tremendous output of splendid austere monochrome paintings was to remain completely unknown for another century and a half.

As late as 1842 the British artist Benjamin Robert Haydon, writing the article on "Painting" in the seventh edition of the Encyclopaedia Britannica, stated that the art of the Chinese from the earliest ages and ever since has been "miserable and wretched." This sweeping statement from a man who had not seen a single example of the work of any outstanding Chinese painter is typical of the complete ignorance of Chinese art which prevailed in the Western world.

KAO CH'I-P'EI AND THE ART OF FINGER PAINTING

There was an artist named K'ao Ch'i-p'ei, a Manchu from Mukden (1672-1734), who rose to great prominence. He excelled in a special type of work known as "finger painting."

Finger painting had been practiced much earlier in China, and there is a record that an eighth-century artist, Chang Tsao, invented this manner of smearing the color on the silk with his hands. But, although many artists painted with their fingers, Kao Ch'i-p'ei was the first to win renown for his work in this medium.

In China, finger painting is not used, as now in the West, as an easy form of self-expression for children, or for its therapeutic value. It is regarded as a highly skilled accomplishment. An artist first had to attain skill in painting with a brush, and then he discarded the brush because he wanted a more direct method of expression.

Kao Ch'i-p'ei first became famous for his brush paintings, but it is his later works—finger paintings—which are the more notable for their boldness and originality.

THE PAINTING OF PORTRAITS

From the Sung dynasty onward, portrait painting had fallen into disrepute, and even the portraits painted by such famous artists as Shih K'o and Liang K'ai inclined toward caricature rather than depiction. With a few bold strokes the artist emphasized what he considered the most striking feature of his subject. A high forehead would be vastly exaggerated, as in the well-known pictures of

Confucius, a thin man would be shown as emaciated, and a stout one as a mountain of fat.

In the Ming dynasty there was an increased interest in figure and portrait painting, which continued through the Ch'ing dynasty, but most Chinese artists still looked on portraiture as an amalgamation of picture making and character delineation.

The only type of Chinese portrait that was painted directly from a model was the traditional ancestor portrait, or the Ta Shou as they are called. These were usually painted when the subject was already advanced in age, on his death bed, or else immediately after his death.

They are all very much alike in treatment. The subject is seated on a chair, squarely facing the painter, the feet resting on a footstool, and hands on lap. A woman wears her red bridal dress or a robe denoting her husband's official rank. There is often fine character portrayal in these faces, for the artisan-painter would usually have been familiar with the sitter's way of life and his reputation. The faces of the old women in these portraits are very revealing of character, showing strength, stubbornness, cruelty or else, perhaps, wisdom and benevolence. They are in decided contrast to the doll, or flowerlike, faces, completely devoid of expression, which are used in portraying girls and young women.

Ancestor portraits were made by artisans whose names have never been recorded, but some of them were highly gifted artists. Nevertheless the Chinese do not consider such portraits as works of art, and they do not form part of their collections. They are regarded simply as necessary items in the ceremonies of ancestral reverence. The portraits were hung directly over the coffin during the funeral ceremonies, and were afterward stored in the private ancestral hall. Traditionally they were not supposed to be brought out again except during the first six days of the New Year celebrations.

At present the whole art of portraiture is at a very low ebb. Even the artisan-painters are dying out, and few if any young men seem ready to take their places. The camera is replacing the brush in this particular field.

TRADE RELATIONS BETWEEN CHINA AND THE WEST

The reigns of the Emperors K'ang Hsi, Yung Chêng, and Ch'ien Lung were periods of extraordinary prosperity and internal order. During the reign of Ch'ien Lung, the country was so wealthy that all land taxes were remitted for several years in succession.

There was increasing communication and trade between China and the outside world, but it was always the West which took the initiative, for China was still almost completely self-sufficient. There was little in the way of foreign merchandise that the Chinese had any desire to acquire, and they were extremely wary about permitting foreign traders to travel freely about their country.

There was just one port in China which foreign vessels could enter and where dealers could load the merchandise they sought—porcelains, silks, ivory, spices, tea, wallpaper, and other items. That was the port of Canton in the south,

Ink-squeeze of 3rd century B.C. from Loyang tomb tile. Warrior, armed with sword and shield, in the attitude of attacking a monster.

Courtiers in the Imperial gardens, watching a fight between animals. Tile painted in color. Loyang. Han Dynasty.

Right: Buddhist wall painting of Kwan Yin (10th century?) discovered underneath a 12th century painting from temple near Shansi-Hopei border. Water color on clay. Formerly collection C. T. Loo. *Bottom:* Detail of silk hand scroll, "Portraits of Thirteen Emperors," attributed to Yen Li-pên (d. A.D. 673). T'ang Dynasty.

Below: Detail, lady having hair dressed, from hand scroll attributed to Ku K'ai-chih (4th century). "Admonitions of the Imperial Preceptress."

William Rockhill Nelson Gallery of Art, Kansas City

Opposite page, top: Detail of silk hand scroll, "Scholars of the Northern Ch'i Dynasty collating classic texts." Ca. 10th century. Sung Dynasty. *Bottom:* "Silk beaters — beating, winding and ironing," by Hui Tsung (1082-1135). Sung Dynasty. After a painting by Chang Hsüan (fl. ca. 713-742).

British Museum

Museum of Fine Arts, Boston

"Realms of the Immortals," attributed to Li Lung-mien (Li Kung-lin) (ca. A.D. 1040-1106).

"Mountains in Snow," by Fan K'uan (fl. ca. A.D. 990-1030).

Detail of scroll, "Spring Morning
in Palace," attributed to Chou
Wên-chü (fl. second half of 10th
century) but probably a later
adaptation.

Right:
"Blue Hills of Spring." Unknown
artist. Sung Dynasty. A. W. Bahr
Collection.

Detail of scroll "Fishing in a Mountain Stream," by Hsü Tao-ning. Early 11th century.

"Lady Before a Mirror in a Garden," by Su Han-ch'ên. (ca. A.D. 1115-1170).

106

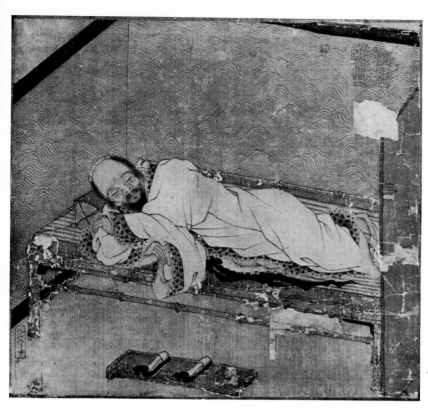

"The Sleeping Man." Unknown artist. Sung Dynasty. A. W. Bahr Collection.

Detail of hand scroll of "Emperor and Musicians" attributed to Chou Wên-chü (fl. second half 10th century). Sung Dynasty (?).

Detail of hand scroll "Yellow Roses and Bees—Pink Roses and Wasps," attributed to Chao Ch'ang (fl. ca. 1000). A. W. Bahr Collection.

Detail from hand scroll (four scenes) "Mountain and Lake Landscape," by Hsia Kuei (fl. 1180-1230).

Opposite:
"Magpie on a Flowering Branch." Unknown artist. Sung Dynasty.

Detail of hand scroll "The Hundred Geese." Sung Dynasty. Signed Ma Fên (second half of 11th century).

"Bare Willows and Distant Mountains," by Ma Yüan (fl. late 12th—early 13th centuries).

Below: "A Boat on a Stormy Sea," by Li Sung (fl. ca. 1190-1225). Southern Sung.

Opposite page: "Women bathing and dressing children." Unknown artist. Sung Dynasty fan.

"Mountains in Clouds," by Kao K'o Kung (active second half of 13th century).

Peking Palace Museum

Detail of hand scroll "Gathering of Philosophers," by Kung K'ai (late 13th century).

Metropolitan Museum of Art

Detail of hand scroll "Chung K'uei, the Demon-Queller on His Travels," by Kung K'ai (late 13th century). *Below:* Detail from Nine Dragon Scroll "Dragons Among Clouds and Waves," by Ch'ên Jung (middle 13th century).

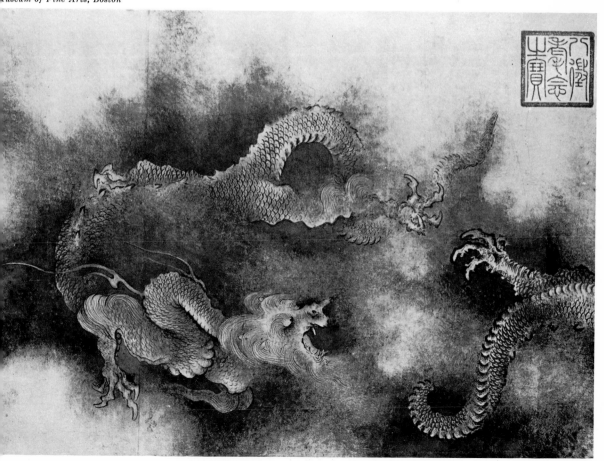

"A Goat and a Sheep," by Chao Mêng-fu (1254-1322)

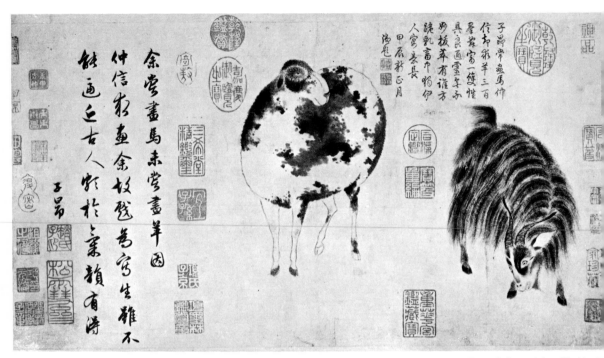

"Bamboo Study," by Kuan Tao-shêng (wife of Chao Mêng-fu).

"Ink Bamboo (detail), by Li K'an (fl. 1260-1310).

"A Horse and a Groom in a Red Coat," by Chao
Yung (son of Chao Mêng-fu). Dated 1347.

Private Collection, China

"A Winding Stream," by T'ang Yin (1470-1523).

Below: "Album of Eight Landscapes and Poems," by Shên Chou (1427-1509). Landscape accompanied by the poem:

"Slowly and alone I stroll at the sunset hour,
This old man filled with poetry;
Green hills for miles are mirrored in my silver hair;
None in the dusty town may know such joy."
(Trans. by Kojiro Tomita and A. Kaiming Chiu)

Section of a long hand scroll, "Clear Wind in the Hill-locked Valley," by Hsia Chang, (ca. 1450).

Honolulu Academy of Arts

Metropolitan Museum of Art

Spring Play in a T'ang Garden," attributed to the Emperor Hsüan Tsung (Hsüan Tê) (1426-1435). A. W. Bahr Collection.

Private Collection, China

"Landscape," by Wu Li (1632-
1718).

Above: Album picture "Bird," by Pa Ta Shan Jên (Chu Ta) (1626-ca. 1705).

Opposite page, top right: Sketch from album of twenty sketches by Tung Ch'i-ch'ang (1555-1636).

Opposite page, lower right: "Flower Study," by Yün Shou-p'ing (1633-1690).

Opposite:
"Ode to the Pomegranate," by
Shên Chou (1427-1509).

"Two Ducks," by Kao Ch'i-p'ei
(1672-1734). Finger painting. Inscription: "A friend brought me
a pair of ducks. They look like
loving birds, so I decided to paint
them."

有人
之浦来
赠
以鸭经
其又素
动静像
草
筆意炯真
也節見者
吴囡和圖

"Black Bamboos Moving in the
Wind," by Lu Tê Chih (17th
century).

"Landscape," by Wang Hui
(1632-1720), painted in his old
age.

Landscape by Wang Shih-min (1592-1680).

"Mountain scene," by Wang Yüan-ch'i (1642-1715).

Landscape by Wang Shih-min (1592-1680).

where, as early as 1720, the Co-hong system was established. A group of thirteen of the leading Chinese merchants of the city attended to all commerce with the foreigners and were held responsible for the good behavior of the "barbarians."

The foreign traders had to live in buildings called "factories" or "hongs," built along the river front, and they could stay only until their business was transacted. They were not allowed to enter the native city, and no women were permitted to set foot on land. The Westerners chafed under these restrictions, but they acknowledged that the Co-hongs treated them with scrupulous honesty in word and deed, and this early period of the Canton trade remains one of the brightest episodes in the history of relations between China and the West.

There is one artist of repute, George Chinnery (1774-1852), whose name is associated with the China trade. He was born in London and achieved early success as an artist. At the age of twenty-eight, he left the British Isles for the Far East and never returned. First he settled in India where he made an unfortunate marriage to a wife whom he called "the ugliest woman I ever saw in the whole course of my life." Then he suddenly disappeared, and turned up in Macao, which was then known as the "paradise of debtors," apparently with the double aim of escaping from his creditors and his wife. When his wife threatened to join him, he packed up and left for Canton where she could not follow him.

Eventually he returned to Macao, where he turned out many excellent oil paintings and numbers of fine pen and pencil sketches. He painted portraits of many of the leading figures of the time in South China—in Canton, Macao, and Hong Kong.

George Chinnery did not experiment in any Chinese techniques, but he gathered pupils around him, notably Lam Qua, a Chinese, whose work was exhibited at the Royal Academy in London. Because of the long-continued Portuguese occupation of Macao, the Chinese in that center were more familiar with foreign methods of painting than in other parts of China. For this reason George Chinnery and his pupils were able to influence the Chinese more than did Castiglione and other priests in Peking. In both Macao and Canton, schools were established for the teaching of foreign-style paintings in oil.

THE DETERIORATION AND OVERTHROW OF THE MANCHUS

In 1796, Ch'ien Lung, having ruled for sixty years, and not wishing his reign to be of longer duration than that of his revered grandfather K'ang Hsi, abdicated in favor of his son Chia Ch'ing (1796-1820). The sun of China's fortunes had by then reached its zenith, and the rest of the Ch'ing period is a tale of decline in art as in all else.

As soon as the rulers became weak and incompetent, secret societies began to be formed with the aim of overthrowing the dynasty. Growing discontent and conspiracy, combined with pressure and attacks from the outside world, gradually reduced the whole country to a state of disunity and chaos, which culminated in 1850 in a vast uprising where revolutionary ideas mingled with Christian doctrines.

The T'ai P'ing rebellion (called by the inappropriate name of Great Peace) aimed at driving out the Manchu dynasty. It was led by a Christian convert whose program had many good features such as the abolition of slavery, infanticide, murder, adultery, foot binding, and opium smoking. At first, most of the British and American missionaries and residents sided with the rebels. However, after some years of considerable military success, the rebel leaders lost sight of their early ideals and lived in luxury in Nanking, surrounded by beautiful concubines. There was abominable cruelty and treachery on both sides, and finally the foreign powers switched over and helped the Manchu government to restore peace in 1864.

By that time twenty million Chinese had lost their lives, six hundred towns and cities had been completely destroyed, and numbers of artists had been killed. The world had been deprived of quantities of irreplaceable treasures—old paintings, sculptures and other art objects, books, manuscripts, and records.

From that time until the downfall of the Manchu dynasty in 1912, the empire was ruled, for all but the last four years, by a woman, Tzŭ Hsi, known as the Empress Dowager (died 1908). She was an ambitious, cunning, and unscrupulous woman who was little interested either in the welfare of the people or in encouraging art.

A disastrous war with Japan was followed in 1900 by the Boxer uprisings, which were anti-foreign. Again palaces and temples were burned and looted by the Chinese and by the forces of the United States, Britain, France, Russia, Japan, and Germany. Numbers of art objects were taken from the famous collection of the Emperor Ch'ien Lung.

When the Revolution led by Dr. Sun Yat-Sen finally overthrew the Manchu dynasty in 1912, still more treasures were stolen from the Palace. Even after the revolution there was no strong central government. Paintings in temples continued to be defaced and destroyed, and dealers cut off and sold the heads of fine sculptured figures.

Further tremendous loss and devastation occurred during the war with Japan which started in 1937, and the Civil War which followed. The miracle is that there had been such an outpouring of works of art through the centuries that, even with this repeated destruction, so much still remains.

CONTEMPORARY PAINTING

Appalled by the growing deterioration of conditions in China, the thoughts of many Chinese turned toward the philosophy and the art of the West, and, in spite of all the confusion, agony, and fighting, the last three decades have witnessed a new burst of creative energy and an amazing revival of interest in art. There has been a passion for experimentation, and for weighing the new ideas from the West against the traditional Chinese techniques. Outstanding artists have worked in every part of China, producing pictures that testify to the eternal creative vitality of the Chinese.

III: *THE ARTS OF THE POTTER*

Chapter V

POTTERY AND PORCELAIN

CHINESE POTTERY and porcelain have provided the strongest and most widespread links between the culture of China and that of the rest of the world. Bernard Rackham wrote in his monograph on ceramics: "Of all the branches of Chinese Art ... pottery is that which provides for the student the fullest and most readily procurable material in tangible form for following the changing phases of Chinese thought ..."

This does not imply that the arts of the potter rank highest in the cultural history of China. As stated earlier, the only great arts recognized by the Chinese are those of calligraphy and painting. The making of pottery and porcelain is regarded as a craft, and is accorded the same position in the field of art as it is in Western countries.

The art of the Chinese potter does, however, assume tremendous significance because of its long continued history from the dawn of recorded time to the present day and because of its universal appeal.

When we say that the potter was regarded as a craftsman, we should add that the painter, too, in the early history of China, was a craftsman, and that the cleavage between arts and crafts has been less marked than in other countries. The finest Chinese sculptures and bronzes were also the work of artisans.

The early work of the Chinese potter was given added dignity because it was undertaken solely in order to meet some definite need, and yet the material was so well utilized and the forms conceived were so right that it has been difficult to improve upon them.

Eric Gill says: "The things that men have made are the best witnesses to them and the life they lived. They tell us who are their gods, and what their material civilisation and culture mean." The study of Chinese ceramic wares provides a key to the understanding of the Chinese people. A survey of the early pottery, with its simplicity, strength, and boldness of form and its utilization of simple material so that it may best serve the purpose for which it was intended, provides the clue to the true ideal of the Chinese artist and artisan.

Despite the fact that Chinese pottery and porcelain have been more appreciated and better understood by Western collectors than any other form of Chinese art, this has contributed to many misconceptions as to the nature of Chinese aesthetic standards. The early Western collectors knew only the later (Ch'ing dynasty) porcelains. They admired the perfection of the technique, the brilliant colors and the skillful designs, but they did not realize that such things (often pretty rather than beautiful) represented only one temporary manifestation of Chinese ceramic art, and that the true lasting art of the country was strong, simple, bold, and austere.

In early books written by Western connoisseurs of Chinese art, everything earlier than Ming is regarded as "primitive" or even merely "legendary." Ming wares are described as "coarse . . . poor in quality, shape and coloring . . . thick, heavy, not worth collecting." Then, early in the present century, the pendulum swung the other way.

As we know, from the earliest times, the Chinese buried replicas with their dead. The tombs were then sealed and it was forbidden to open them up. The punishment for such violation was death. However, during the course of the construction of railroads, starting in the nineteenth century, many tombs were accidentally opened and vast quantities of porcelain and pottery utensils, figures, animals, and other treasures were revealed. Not only did this throw much new light on the ancient history of China—showing how the people lived and worked —but it gave a new direction to collecting.

Collectors avidly sought Han, T'ang, and Sung pieces, discarding all later ones. Previously most collectors had sought the polished perfection of the Palace type of porcelain, considering that Chinese art consisted of things costly, elaborate, and highly colored. Now they discovered the charm of simple pottery—the art of the people and of the scholar.

The Ming pieces which had been regarded as too archaic for the early collectors were called "too modern" by the later ones. So this period, one of the richest and most typically Chinese, and one of the most highly appreciated by the Chinese connoisseurs, was again neglected and misunderstood. Around the rim of some large, well-moulded water pots of the Wan Li period (Ming), we found inscribed the following: "Harmonize your ware by making simple articles decorative." Those words might have served not only as a defense of Ming ceramics, but also as a motto for most Chinese potters throughout Chinese history.

THE ORIGINS OF POTTERY IN CHINA

The origins of pottery making are traced back in legend to the remotest periods, and this seems entirely logical since one can scarcely conceive of a people who would not have contrived some form of clay or earthenware vessels to hold water and food.

In talking of the past in China it has been difficult to judge where the line should be drawn between legend and history. The Chinese have kept chronological records from a very remote past; and, as Herrlee Glessner Creel points

128

out in his book *The Birth of China,* from 1500 B.C. onward existing records are confirmed by facts.

In spite of this there has been a tendency in the West to look upon much early Chinese history as "legendary"—perhaps because it dates so very far back, and also because much Chinese writing is couched in poetic and symbolical language. But, in one case after another, the Chinese records have proved to be correct. For instance, it is now generally conceded that authentic Chinese history begins with the foundation of the Hsia dynasty (circa 2205 B.C.*), although, at the beginning of this century, Chinese accounts of the Shang dynasty (1766-1122 B.C.*) were considered mythical. When archaeological excavations are resumed on a wide scale these boundaries will doubtless be pushed still further back.

We read that the Yellow Emperor Huang Ti (circa 2697 B.C.) taught the people how to make utensils of wood, pottery, and metal. The Chinese claim to have been the first to use the potter's wheel, attributing its invention to the director of pottery attached to the Court of this emperor.

In the reign of another emperor, Chin T'ien (around 2597 B.C.), pottery was said to have been made by pounding clay into shape. It is recorded that, under the Emperor Yao (around 2357 B.C.) different colored clays were used in making pottery, and the Emperor Shun (circa 2255-2205 B.C.) is credited with having greatly improved the methods of pottery-making. The Emperor Yao is said to have insisted on simplicity, and had his sacrificial vessels made of plain yellow earthenware, while the Emperor Shun was the first to have them glazed.

NEOLITHIC POTTERY

Many of these early accounts of history and of pottery making were confirmed when, in 1921, Dr. J. G. Andersson of the Geological Survey of China found, in the course of excavations on the site of a prehistoric village called Yang Shao, in Honan province, neolithic implements and pottery, some plain and some decorated with fine painted designs, dating back to about 3000-2500 B.C.

A year later Dr. Andersson found implements and pottery of the same culture in the Hsi-ning area in Chinghai, and then in the province of Kansu came upon a whole series of richly painted mortuary urns and other pieces of tomb pottery near the skeletons of the bodies with which they had been buried. Dr. Andersson called this "the finest ceramic ware of its kind in existence."

Similar neolithic pottery has been found on various sites in the valleys and plains of the Yellow River where the provinces of Shensi, Shansi, Honan, and Shantung now lie. Also found, besides pottery, were jade rings, jade bracelets, and stone implements of the same design as were made later in bronze and iron, and similar to those still in use today. Shards also prove that, in addition to painted and unpainted pottery, the prehistoric Chinese made glazed earthenware—showing that this invention is a thousand years older than had been previously believed.

* Traditional dates.

The neolithic pottery ware is made of fine-grained reddish buff clay. It was not turned on a potter's wheel but was apparently built up from a circular base entirely by hand which makes the perfection of form and finish even more remarkable. After being fired, the pieces were decorated with geometrical designs in rhythmical patterns in two colors—usually black and dark reddish brown (almost purple). Many of the vessels have handles. In Honan and Shantung, coarse thick gray pottery of an even earlier neolithic period has been found.

BLACK POTTERY CULTURE

These discoveries, which opened up new horizons to students of Chinese art, were followed by the discovery of the Black Pottery Culture of the latest Neolithic (or Stone Age) period in China. The first site was excavated in 1929, east of Tsinan-fu in Shantung, and the second in 1935 near Hangchow, in Chekiang province.

In the course of one single month nearly 25,000 artifacts were taken out of the Shantung excavation, including objects made of bone, horn and shell, jade, stone, and, above all, black pottery.

This Black Pottery Culture provides the missing link between the earlier neolithic cultures and the highly advanced material culture of the Shang dynasty. The oracle bones, the fine stone articles, the jade ornaments, and, especially, the black pottery were the direct forerunners of the bronzes and other objects made by the artisans of the Shang period.

The black pottery is thin, finely made, glazed, and highly polished. There is a great similarity between the forms of these vessels and some of those of the Shang bronzes—especially marked in the stem cups which are similar to the libation vessels of the Shang, Chou, and other early dynasties. The pieces are not all of the same quality, some being much finer than others. The finest specimens appear to have been turned on the wheel, are very thin—as thin as the eggshell porcelain of the eighteenth century, and are almost of the consistency of lacquer.

It was first assumed that these objects had been made to serve useful domestic purposes, and there was much discussion in China at the time of their discovery because most of them had been made in such a way that they could not be of any use at all. Some pieces could not stand upright, others had large holes pierced right through them, or had been filled in so that they could not hold food or liquid.

The explanation seems to us to be that these black pottery vessels were found in tombs and obviously had been made specifically to be buried. Confucius, most of whose teachings covered earlier periods than the one in which he lived, said that vessels made for serving the dead must not be such as could be actually used. They had to be fashioned so as to be useless. The earthenware vessels must be so constructed that they could not be used for washing, the lutes must be unevenly strung, the pipes must be out of tune, and the bells made without stands. "They are called vessels to the eye of imagination," the instructions run. "The dead are thus treated as though they are spiritual intelligences." The purpose behind this teaching was that the dead were not to be treated as dead, for that would hurt their feelings and show a lack of affection, but they could not be treated as if they were living for that would show lack of wisdom. The happy mean was to make objects that were nominally practical but unusable.

An additional reason might be that, in those very early days, grave objects were much finer than those in general use, and, by rendering them useless, all temptation to dig them up and use them was removed.

In later dynasties this principle appears to have been abandoned, and we find vessels that are capable of being used.

THE DYNASTIES OF SHANG-YIN AND OF CHOU

The Black Pottery Culture of the Hsia dynasty (about 4000 years ago) was followed by the dynasties of Shang-Yin (1766-1122 B.C.*) and that of Chou (1122-221 B.C.*). The Chinese considered their records of these periods to be correct, and they are confirmed by the writings of the Shang-Yin dynasty which were found engraved on the oracle pieces of bone and tortoise shell.

These were used for religious purposes. Whenever a problem arose, general or personal, questions were scratched on pieces of bone or shell, to be answered by departed ancestors or divinities. A hot metal rod was applied to one side, and the answer was worked out in accordance with the pattern of the cracks which appeared on the other side. The reply was inscribed on the bone too. Some of these bones and shell pieces bear a chronological record of the different rulers, so that sacrificial rites could be duly performed to each ancestor.

Chinese accounts of the Shang period and the records found on oracle bones and shells were borne out when, within the last quarter of a century, excavations at the site of the ancient Shang capital of Yin, now Anyang in Honan, brought to light quantities of oracle bones as well as bronzes, jades, ivories, marbles, pottery vessels, and shards, revealing a civilization in which art had already attained a degree of technical perfection and sophistication which proved that it must have been the culmination of centuries of development. That there had already been a long history of art is confirmed by the reference which Confucius made to the ministers of the Yin dynasty who had made great efforts to collect antiquities and rare and valuable objects.

Most of the pottery first found in the course of these excavations was broken (perhaps not more than ten whole pieces turned up), and about a hundred vessels were reconstructed from the broken pieces. Larger quantities of the more common types (broken and whole) were dug up later.

In addition to black pottery utensils and more painted and unpainted pottery, there were specimens of glazed thin white earthenware with bands of incised decoration. These Shang-Yin white jars were remarkable not only for their quality and elegance of form and decoration, but also because they came so close to being porcelaneous that they began to provide some basis for the Chinese claim

* Traditional dates.

131

that they had invented porcelain thousands of years ago. In fact, had they been fired at a higher temperature, these jars would have answered our definition of true porcelain.

Some of the Shang pottery had been turned on the wheel and some had been made by hand. The pieces were of different quality and varied greatly in size from very small to three feet high by eighteen inches wide. The pottery had been made in the bronze shapes, or perhaps one should say that the bronzes were shaped like the pottery vessels that had been created earlier. The finest pieces were of the white porcelaneous ware, and these were found in royal tombs. The designs—geometrical and stylized—were carved in the wet clay, and resembled the decorations on the Shang bronzes.

The clay for these white vessels came from the region of Tz'ŭ Chou, seventeen miles north of Anyang. The name Tz'ŭ Chou might be rendered as "pottery ware district." White pottery was made there in the T'ang dynasty (618-907), and has continued to be made there ever since.

The Shang-Yin dynasty—a period of sophisticated elegance mingled with violence—ended when the armies of the state of Chou inflicted on it a crushing defeat and set up a new dynasty—the Chou. The capital of Yin was destroyed and a new capital was established at Chang-an, with a subsidiary capital at Loyang.

The Chous were a more primitive people than the Shangs, and they established a feudal state with rulers who, at first, were mainly interested in hunting and fighting. However the bulk of the population continued to be farmers as they have throughout Chinese history.

The Chou dynasty had no traditional culture of its own, but, as has happened again and again in the history of China, the invaders took over the culture they found in existence.

In the field of pottery there were no important developments, but it is recorded that the founder of the Chou dynasty sought in marriage for his eldest daughter a lineal descendant of the Emperor Shun because of his skill in pottery making. This son-in-law was made the first director of pottery.

The "Ritual of the Chou" (which is included in the ancient Five classics) mentions the government potters of the period under two headings: "T'ao jên" —potters who worked on the wheel—and "Fang jên"—moulders of pottery.

The cooking utensils and sacrificial vessels that these potters turned out were sold in the market under certain official regulations. Excavations at Loyang show that the pottery was usually of a hard gray unpainted clay, but other specimens were made of a reddish clay. Some finer pieces—similar to bronze shapes— were made with carved geometrical decoration and had covers, legs, and handles.

At Loyang, in a Chou tomb site, beautiful colored glass buttons and beads and remains of glass vases were found.

The Chou dynasty, one of the longest in Chinese history and lasting nearly nine centuries, saw the birth of Confucius, who gave China its great codes of morality, and Lao Tzŭ (father of Taoism), also born in the sixth century B.C., who gave China its popular mystical philosophy of Nature. Mencius, who, as a philosopher and intellectual leader, ranked second only to Confucius, was born in 372 B.C. Because of these outstanding men it may be said that it was the Chou dynasty which charted the course for Chinese conduct and philosophy throughout the subsequent centuries.

THE HAN DYNASTY (206 B.C. TO A.D. 220)

During this period of great external expansion and internal progress, advances were made in all fields of art. Some glazed pottery has been found in the Shang tombs, and some pieces date from the time of The Warring States, but it was in the Han dynasty that the glazing of pottery appears to have become a common practice. The pottery was usually of either red or slate-gray earthenware, and it was enameled with an enamel of a grayish yellow color made of lead stained with copper oxide. On the red clay this produced a green color, which varies in intensity according to the thickness of the glaze. Most of the Han pottery now in existence has been found in tombs, and the action of the earth has oxidized this green enamel (when it has not worn it off altogether) to a fine gold, or silver, iridescence covered with minute cracks.

The decoration was made by using moulds or by stamping and carving and was applied before enameling. The motifs used were usually similar to those on contemporary bronzes—birds, dragons, hunting scenes, fishes in waves, lozenge ornaments, and the like.

The custom of marking earthenware dates back to the Han dynasty. The mark was engraved on the base, but such marked pieces are very rare.

When the Han pottery was not enameled, the pieces were covered with white clay and painted with unglazed colors—usually red or black. The designs are similar to those on textiles of the same period. Many of the Han vases are large and bold, modeled in bronze forms and often with elaborate designs in relief around them. One type of vessel that became popular was the hill incense burner. These had covers shaped like a hilly island with the sea washing around its base. Perforations in the cover allowed the incense fumes to escape.

Chinese writings mention that the potteries of the Emperor Wu Ti (140-86 B.C.) were located at Chang-nan in the province of Kiangsi. This is the same site where the famous pottery and porcelain center of Ching-tê Chên, which is still in operation, was established in the Sung dynasty.

The Chinese consider as porcelain a thin ceramic ware of a hardness that cannot be scratched with a knife and that is covered with a transparent coat of glaze which gives it a shining smooth appearance. It should produce a musical resonance when struck sharply with a fingernail. This Chinese definition of porcelain has led to much controversy. Some Chinese claim that porcelain dates back to the Shang thin white pottery, which has all these qualities, and others claim that it dates back to the Han dynasty. Western connoisseurs, however, insist that the body of the porcelain must be white and translucent, so they contend that real porcelain was not invented until the seventh century and give the name of proto-porcelain, or porcelaneous stoneware, to these earlier products.

Generally speaking, porcelain is a term denoting all pottery to which an incipient vitrification has been imparted by firing. The body of Chinese porcelain consists of two elements—white China clay, or kaolin, which gives plasticity to the paste, and petuntse, the feldspathic stone which is fusible at a high temperature and which gives transparency or translucency to the porcelain. The actual point at which proto-porcelain can be called true porcelain remains a subject for discussion by experts.

Following the decline of the Han dynasty China was divided up among several, and rapidly changing, rulers. There were The Three Kingdoms (220-280), the rule of the Wei Tartars (386-557), and the Six Dynasties (222-589). It was during this unsettled period that Buddhism was established in China. There was little new influence on the ceramic arts although certain technical advances are noted. Porcelaneous vases and bowls, with a thin green glaze, were made on the potter's wheel, fashioned from gray stoneware clay with a fairly high proportion of kaolin.

The whole country was reunited under the first emperor of the Sui dynasty (589-618), whose capital was at Chang-an in Shensi. Pottery shared in the great forward movement in all the arts and crafts, and new glazes were prepared. We read that the emperor formed a great and valuable collection and subsidized the potteries from his own pocket. The Sui dynasty lasted only a short time, but it paved the way for the foundation of the "Golden T'ang" era.

THE T'ANG DYNASTY (618-907)

After three hundred years of chaos, the T'ang dynasty carried forward and brought to a new level of achievement the era of peace and prosperity which had been ushered in by the brief Sui dynasty. There was an outpouring of creative energy in literature, painting, and all the arts.

The emperors extended the frontiers of China as far as Turkestan, they stormed the chief town of India, then Pataliputra, and their junks sailed the Persian Gulf. The capital of China became a world center to which pilgrims, scholars, and merchants flocked from other lands. Many of them—including large numbers of Arabs, Persians, Indians, and Jews—settled down and were absorbed into the life of the country. The presence of these foreign elements is evident in the shapes, ornaments, and figurines of the ceramic ware of the period.

The greater part of the still-existing pottery ware of the T'ang era was made for burial purposes. As early as the Han dynasty the earlier practice had been reversed, and vessels made to be placed in graves were less fine than those made for use. For this reason it is only in the tombs of important personages that pieces of fine quality and skilled workmanship have been found.

But even the general run of the excavated pottery shows advances in technique. For the first time the potters used polychrome painted enamel decoration, producing clearly defined patterns in color. This was done by means of channels cut in the clay, outlining the design, which served to prevent the different colored glazes from running into each other.

The typical T'ang pottery was of a whitish, grayish, or pinkish clay, of a consistency varying from soft earthenware to stoneware, and covered with thin lead glazes, often in a single color—green, yellow, or blue. There was also irregular splashing and flecking of colored glazes—green, amber, and blue on a yellowish ground. The glazes stopped short of the foot. Green, blue, and amber-yellow in clear bright colors were so greatly favored over all other shades that one wonders if there was any connection with the "blue and green and gold" for which many T'ang paintings were so renowned. Sometimes dark and light clays were mixed to produce marbled effects.

The wheel appears to have been in constant use, and the forms show a sureness of balance and proportion which are a tribute to the skill of the potter. The bases are flat and, usually, without foot rims. The pottery includes large vessels with covers, pilgrim bottles, ewers and wine jars with double handles terminating in dragon or serpent heads, elaborate funeral vases with figures in applied relief encircling the elongated necks, and incised decoration around the body, covered with opaque greenish gray glaze. Many of the handled wine jars show decided Greek and Persian influence. In addition there were, of course, many round bowls—some in flowerlike shapes—saucers, wine cups, objects for birdcages, flower vases, and so forth.

The ornamentation was usually moulded and applied in relief, but designs were also carved or tooled into the clay, and sometimes they were painted. The motifs included circular lines, palm leaves, flowers, tigers, horses, fishes, birds, and scenes from Confucian, Taoist, and Buddhist lore. The horse was a great favorite in the decoration of pottery, as it was in every form of T'ang art, symbolizing all that was free, proud, and noble.

The Tz'ŭ Chou potteries made white ware, decorated with fine freehand designs in brown and black both over and under the thin transparent glaze. They also turned out some plain and some engraved pieces.

In addition to the grave pottery, there are records of the production of finer ceramic works and of true porcelain. While pieces which were not buried were less likely to survive throughout the centuries, certain specimens are still to be found in Chinese and other collections.

An official record on "Porcelain Administration," first published in 1270, states that, according to local tradition, the ceramic works at Hsin-p'ing (the ancient name for Fou-liang) were founded in the Han dynasty and had been in constant operation. The celebrated superintendent of the Imperial potteries, T'ang Ying, appointed in 1728, confirms this, and he writes in his autobiography that his researches show that porcelain was first made at Chang-nan (Ching-tê Chên) in the district of Fou-liang (now Kiangsi province). This is the site where porcelain has been made ever since.

At the beginning of the T'ang dynasty a native of the above district is said to have presented the emperor with a quantity of porcelain, which he called "imitation jade." An order was issued that the Imperial Palace be furnished with a regular supply of this porcelain.

The ideal of the early porcelain maker was to imitate jade—white or green jade—to equal its hardness, purity of color, translucency, luster, and resonance. In the Han dynasty the large pottery jars with dark green and brown glaze were made as a cheaper substitute for bronze and copper, but when it came to finer porcelain the ideal was jade.

In the eighth century the poet Tu Fu (712-770) wrote in regard to the white porcelain being made in Szechüan:

> The porcelain of the Ta-yi kilns is light and yet strong.
> It rings with a low jade note and is famed throughout the city.
> The fine white bowls surpass hoar frost and snow.

Porcelain and pottery were made in various parts of the country—the quality varying according to the types of clay available and the standards of workmanship in different regions. In the Ch'a Ching, the "Tea Classic," written by Lü Yü in the middle eighth century, the author discusses the different glazes. He expresses his preference for the pale blue cups from Yüeh-chou (Chekiang), because of the greenish tint they impart to the yellow liquid, whereas the white ware of Hsing-chou gave the tea a reddish tinge. These blue bowls of Yüeh Chou and the white bowls of Hsing-chou from Chihli were also valued because of their clear musical note, and they were said to have been used by musicians, in sets of ten, to make chimes.

Other poets compare T'ang wine cups to "tilted lotus leaves floating downstream" (probably those with celadon glaze), and "discs of thinnest ice" (which might refer to those with white or pale blue glazes).

All this evidence of the existence of hard-fired translucent porcelain comes from Chinese sources, but Western connoisseurs were inclined to regard with skepticism all Chinese statements in regard to their own history and achievements, even when these have been confirmed, again and again, by written records and by tangible evidence. We might thus be forced to concede that all this fine porcelain existed only in the imagination of poets but for the existence of the following documents.

In his memoirs, a pilgrim, I Tsing, who came back from India in the seventh century, described true porcelain which he said had not hitherto been seen in India. Again, in 851, the Arab merchant Soleyman wrote, as quoted in *The Beginnings of Porcelain* by Berthold Laufer: "There is in China a very fine clay from which are made vases having the transparency of glass bottles; water in these vases is visible through them and yet they are made of clay."

The most convincing, if somewhat belated, proof came in the course of excavations made in the early part of this century. Pieces of hard, shell-like, high-fired Chinese porcelain, translucent and with an almost white body that could not be scratched with a knife, were found on the site of the city of Samarra, on the Tigris, which had been abandoned in 883. These fragments appear to conform to the description of the Hsing-chou ware from Chihli.

136

TOMB POTTERY FIGURES

In very early times it was the custom in China, as in other parts of the world, for actual sacrifices to be made when men were buried. These may have included wives, concubines, servants, horses, and other animals. This was part of the belief held by the Chinese that death was not an ending but another phase of existence and that a person would need to have with him in his new life the people and things that had been essential to him in this one.

We know that as early as the first millenium B.C. this practice had been discontinued, and, during the lifetime of Confucius, it was the custom to substitute effigies made of wood, paper, or other materials. Confucius not only condemned human or animal sacrifices but even objected to the burial of life-size wooden effigies because they too closely resembled human beings. Gradually it became the accepted rule to make replicas of clay.

Among the earliest known examples of this tomb art are the small figures recently found at Hui-hsien in North Honan, dated circa 450 B.C. Of these clay figures of kneeling chanters, Gustav Ecke writes: "What is to become psychology and dramatic movement in mature Han painting, more than half a millenium later, is here the impersonal, spell-bound vehemence of ritual dance and rhythmic litany." Unlike the tomb figures, made in the Han and later dynasties, many of which were made in moulds, these figurines are examples of original sculpture, covered, after firing, with coats of lacquer.

On the death of the despot Shih Huang Ti, in accordance with his wishes the barbarous custom of immolation had its final revival. As a part of the general inhumanity of this brief period of tyranny, all the concubines of the imperial household who had not borne male children, and thousands of slaves who had worked on the creation of the colossal mausoleum, were buried alive within its walls.

From that time onward, throughout the Han, Wei, and T'ang dynasties, there was no more human sacrifice, and clay models were employed. The use of this medium, so cheap and readily available, meant that even the poorest persons could follow the same custom. Thus, within the graves of a whole people baked clay models of everything that made up the life of their time were buried.

When the Peking-Hankow Railway was being built in Honan, immense quantities of tomb figures and objects came to light. Dealers offered them to Western collectors, who eagerly purchased them as quickly as graves were opened up in Honan, Shensi, Shansi, Shantung, and various other parts of China.

Many of these clay models date back to the Han dynasty and earlier. They include not only men, women, and animals, but also completely modeled miniature farms with dwellings, granary towers, urns, wells with tiny buckets on the rim, cooking ranges and cooking utensils, bread steamers, millstones for grinding flour, geese, fowls and goats. These household objects were buried with women, apparently so that they could continue to keep house. Most of these things were made of gray pottery, covered with white slip, and with traces of red and black pigment. They look surprisingly like the things which are in general use in China at the present time.

For the men there were horses—stocky little horses—attendants, hunters with falcons on their wrists, and huntings dogs. The men on the horses—both men and horses protected by armor—look like European Crusaders. Then, too, there were carts, chariots, buffaloes, elephants, camels with two humps and perhaps with a rider wearing a pointed cap, and wild boars.

Also found in the Han tombs were ladles, spoons, bowls, and jars of all types, usually in bronze shapes. These had been covered with green glaze and, because of oxidation, are now iridescent with soft golden or silvery sheen.

The grave objects made in the Wei dynasty, also in dark gray pottery with traces of color on unfired pigment, are more elongated, stylized, and less realistic.

It is the T'ang tombs, however, that contained the finest pieces. These clay figures were baked in moulds, the larger ones being hollow inside. T'ang grave figures are frequently enameled on a white slip with the usual T'ang glazes—green, yellow, and brown, and sometimes blue and black. Some of them are glazed all over with a monochrome neutral glaze which gives them a greenish or yellowish tinge. The faces are usually not enameled.

These figurines are of amazing variety—dignitaries, priests, warriors, actors, servants, mourners, jugglers, wrestlers, merchants, and supernatural images. There are many feminine figures, too—tall, stately women with high waists, wide skirts, elaborate coiffures, flowing sleeves, necklaces, and turned-up shoes; graceful dancing girls in different postures; female musicians—standing and sitting. Because of the wide influx of foreigners into China during the T'ang dynasty these clay figures include men of different races—curly haired African wrestlers, Semitic traders with sacks on their backs, men of Western type, and numerous other characters.

Most important—and sometimes the most beautifully modeled of all—are the T'ang horses. There are few tombs where a model of at least one beloved steed was not buried with its owner. These were not the stocky Mongolian ponies of the Han dynasty or of the present day. They were thoroughbred horses of Arabian pedigree, with arched necks and flowing manes—probably of the type presented to the Chinese emperors as tribute by the Circassian and Caucasian tribes. The horses are richly saddled, tassels often adorning the saddlecloth. Many are mounted by both men and women, the women riding astride, for this was a period when women enjoyed great freedom. In some cases the horse is led by a groom.

The tomb horses were made in such numbers that they are not of equal artistic value. Among the potters there were always some who excelled and who modeled the spirited noble animals that have won such admiration.

Among the grave figures we must not overlook the models of supernatural beings. Some were beneficent and some malignant. There were guardians, earth spirits with human heads to protect the tombs from intruders, and other strange creatures. Then, too, because Buddhism had made great inroads in the early part of the dynasty, we find figures of Lohans in many tombs.

There were fewer figures buried in the Sung dynasty, and these were often made of wood. The grave objects that have been excavated consist for the most part of utensils.

According to Chinese records the grave furnishings of the Yüan dynasty were usually made of paper and burned at the funeral. The practice of burying clay models was revived in the Ming dynasty, as were so many other customs of the Han and T'ang periods. In the Ch'ing dynasty the clay models were again replaced, as under the Mongols, by paper effigies. Just as in the early dynasties, everything that might be desired by the dead was prepared, and carried to the place of burial where it was burned to ashes.

When we were in China we frequently witnessed long funeral processions where life-sized paper bicycles or automobiles took the place of horses and chariots. There is an intriguing Han tomb group of two men playing a game, with an attendant watching. This we saw matched in modern China by a mah-jong table, all complete with three paper partners so that the game could be played at any time in the world beyond.

THE TWILIGHT OF T'ANG (756-907) AND THE FIVE DYNASTIES (907-960)

There are two important types of porcelain which are usually associated with the period of half a century called the Five Dynasties, although they were known already to be in existence during the T'ang dynasty. One is the Yüeh Chou ware, called Pi-sé (secret color). This is a type of porcelain similar to celadon, with an olive-green glaze and an underglaze decoration—often of leaves and flowers—finely incised in the paste. This was made at Yü-yao Hsien, near Shao-hsing Fu (formerly Yüeh Chou) in northern Chekiang. From A.D. 907 to 976 the output of this ware was reserved for the exclusive use of the princes of Wu and Yüeh. Because it could not generally be used it was given the name of "secret color," and it is for this reason also that it is especially connected with this particular period, although it had been made long before and continued to be made long afterward throughout the Sung dynasty.

The other type of porcelain is the famous Ch'ai ware, subject of much legend and debate, which was said to have been made for the exclusive use of the Emperor Shih Tsung (954-959). This Ch'ai porcelain was reputed to have been "blue as the sky after rain, as clear as a mirror, as thin as paper, and as resonant as a musical stone of jade." Ch'ai ware was so rare that it has even been stated that it never really existed. It appears improbable, however, that poems would be written to describe a nonexistent type of porcelain. Furthermore there is one type of porcelain of which a certain amount was made during the T'ang dynasty, and the Five Dynasties, the very finest specimens of which have all the above mentioned qualities. The existence of this ware has been known only a few years, since it was found in excavated tombs. For want of a better name, it is called by the dealer's term of "ying ch'ing," which means "shadowy blue." It is "sky-blue in color, of rich luster and delicate beauty, with a finely crackled glaze. It has often coarse yellow clay on the rim of the foot." This is exactly the way Ch'ai ware is described in old Chinese writings.

Ying ch'ing ware appears to have been made in various parts of China, and the T'ang specimens are often modeled in Grecian forms. It continued to be made throughout the Sung dynasty, varying greatly in quality, color, thinness, and resonance. It is possible that the emperor reserved for his own exclusive use the very finest and most delicate pieces of this ware, and that, because of its very fragile and brittle nature, few specimens (except those buried in tombs) survived the repeated pattern of conquest, pillage, revolution, and counterrevolution. More will be said about ying ch'ing ware a little further on.

SUNG DYNASTY (960-1279)

The art of the Sung period, whether it be in the form of a painting, a piece of jade, or porcelain, communicates a feeling of serenity and harmony. This, despite the fact that the country was in a weak and insecure state, both from a military and an economic point of view. China was surrounded by aggressive and envious semi-barbarous states, which were constantly threatening attack and making forays. In time the Northern Tartars (known as the "Chin" or "Golden Hordes" invaded the country and forced the government to evacuate the capital at K'ai-fêng Fu in order to move south of the Yangtze River. Finally the Mongols conquered the whole country.

Just as in Sung philosophy outward events were considered of less importance than inner feelings, so throughout the country wars and invasions had the minimum effect on the individual creative spirit. Outer turmoil could be ignored for it was only the harmony and tranquility of mind and soul that counted. This state of mind could not be called one of "escape," for it was deliberate and could be attained only by the constant and systematic self-discipline practiced by literary men and creative artists and craftsmen. They would have said that they were not attempting to "escape" from life but to enter more fully into it—to penetrate its deepest mysteries and understand it in all its varying manifestations.

The Sung emperors were great patrons of all forms of artistic expression, but it was the scholars and philosophers who set the standards. The grandeur and lavish ostentation of the T'ang emperors and courtiers gave way to a Court where sobriety was the supreme luxury. This was a unique culture where art was expressed by simplicity of form and refinement of color.

In ceramics, admiration was given to the material itself—both in its appeal to the eye and to the touch. The skill of the potter aimed at developing the hardness, durability, musical resonance, translucency, and even the color of jade. But porcelain was not looked upon merely as a substitute for jade. Decoration was subordinated to harmony, and color was kept delicate and monochromatic.

This was a time when not only artists but also artisans knew that they could express their love of beauty in the serene certainty that their efforts would be appreciated. And the love of beauty was not confined to certain classes of the

140

population, for excavations show that high-grade, well-proportioned ceramic wares were used by all classes.

The feeling for simplicity, rather than for luxury, is expressed in the following lines by a Sung poet:

Laugh not at a countryman's old earthenware pots.
They have been filled with wine for generations of sons and grandsons.
Pouring from silver vessels and cups of jade only dazzles the eyes.
So let us drink merrily together and sleep beneath the bamboos.

Most of the kilns that produced Sung pottery and porcelain had already been in operation during the preceding dynasties, but they now attained their high point of beauty and quality. The perfect balance and harmony in form, color, and such slight decoration as was used have given Sung porcelains such a sense of rightness that they still set the standards for modern students of ceramic art.

Sung porcelain was practically unknown outside China half a century ago. There have always been examples of Sung porcelains in the collections of Chinese connoisseurs, but, as in the case of Shang and Chou bronzes, it has been the accepted custom to scoff at Chinese attributions. It was only with the grave excavations and the opening up of the Chinese palace collections to the public after the Chinese Revolution that the Western world began to realize the importance and nature of Sung art.

Today, so far from considering it as "primitive," as suggested by earlier Western books, we know that the Sung dynasty was a time of great sophistication—one of the periods when man reached the highest levels of cultural, philosophical, and idealistic achievements.

In regard to porcelain, the demand for decoration in many-colored glazes that had arisen in the T'ang era was discontinued. All ornamentation was restrained. Such decoration as appears on Sung pieces was engraved or impressed in the paste before glazing, and there was only one firing.

In spite of the insistence upon simplicity, porcelain was, for the first time, prized for its artistic perfection rather than solely for its utility. Porcelain came into its own as a medium of expression whereas previously it had been regarded chiefly as a cheaper substitute for bronze and jade.

The Sung emperors and the courtiers became enthusiastic patrons and collectors of ceramic wares. The Emperor Ching-tê (1004-1007) changed the name of the great pottery center at Chang-nan in Kiangsi to Ching-tê Chên, and he ordered all official porcelain to be stamped with the "nien-hao," or name of the reigning monarch. (This was not the emperor's own name, but the name given to him at the time he ascended the throne.) These seals were incised and then glazed, but pieces with such marks are rare owing to the periodic sacking and burning of palaces.

Ching-tê Chên had already been in existence for centuries, as we have mentioned, and it has remained to this day the leading ceramic center of the world. It had all the elements necessary for the production and distribution of great quantities of pottery and porcelain—vast natural deposits of china stone (pe-tuntse), said to make "the flesh," and of white clay (kaolin) to make "the bones." Also available are all the other essential materials, such as fire clay for the sag-gers, and cobaltiferrous ore for painting in blue. Ching-tê Chên was connected by water and land with the great trade routes. The river provided it with water power for its mills and wheels, and there was ample wood in the forests for heat-ing the furnaces.

But this great ceramic district was only one of the many pottery-producing centers of China during the Sung dynasty. Actually, whenever and wherever there were large settlements, some form of pottery making for the everyday needs of the people was started. However, it was the kilns which produced the finest porcelain for the use of the Court, which, with one or two exceptions, became the most widely known. Such pieces were included in collections, were buried in royal tombs, and were written about in verses, books, and catalogues.

CELADON, OR LUNG-CH'ÜAN YAO

Probably the type of Sung ware with which the outside world is most famil-iar is that known in the West as "celadon." In China it is called Lung-ch'üan yao ("yao" means "pottery"), after the town of Lung-ch'üan, in the province of Chekiang, where it was chiefly made.

The Western name of "celadon" has been attributed to two different sources. One story runs that its green color was similar to that of the costume worn by the shepherd Céladon, in a pastoral play L'Astrée by d'Urfé, first produced in Paris in 1610. The other explanation is that it refers to the Sultan Saladin the Great, who is said always to have used celadon ware cups because of the legend that they would change color if the wine was poisoned. This same Sultan sent forty pieces of celadon ware to Nur-ed-din in Damascus in 1171.

Celadon ware was widely exported throughout the Far and Near East during the T'ang dynasty, and the trade continued right through the Sung, Yüan, and Ming periods. The "Warham Bowl," mounted in Tudor silver-gilt and be-queathed in 1530 by Archbishop Warham to New College, Oxford, is the first piece known to have reached England, although the ware had reached other parts of Europe a century earlier.

The export ware was heavy and coarse, and many pieces were modeled in the bronze forms for which they were meant to be substitutes. The finer speci-mens made for Chinese use during the Sung dynasty were intended to suggest jade rather than bronze.

The body of the celadon pieces was of a whitish or stone gray paste; but, where exposed to heat without the protection of glaze, it turned red owing to the presence of iron in the clay. The glaze—olive-green or sea green in color—was applied to the clay in many successive layers, the use of insufflation being alternated with the use of a brush. This gave uniformity of tone although the actual color depended on the baking. The decoration was mostly carved or en-graved.

The reason that the export ware was coarse, heavy, and durable is obvious, since it had to survive the hazards of travel by sea and caravan. Then, too, these goods were sold for use, and there were few persons outside China who fully appreciated or desired to collect fine porcelains. Throughout their history the Chinese appear to have exported only the coarser and heavier types of porcelain and pottery, since they enjoyed the finer specimens too much themselves to wish to part with them.

Celadon wares were made in various parts of China. Although they are generally known as Lung-ch'üan yao, there is no doubt that they were previously made elsewhere, probably in Honan and other Northern centers. For instance, the so-called Northern celadons, which are among the finest examples of this type of ware, have been found in various places in Honan and other parts of North China. The name "Northern celadon" implies not only that the ware was made in North China but also that it was made before the Sung emperors were driven south by the Tartars.

This Northern celadon has a gray porcelaneous body, finer than the export wares, and the glaze is usually of an olive-green shade. The delicacy of the material, the skill in the potting, and the remarkably well-drawn decoration—which often consists of a formal pattern of petals, leaves, and allied motifs—either carved or incised, has led to the assumption that these celadons were made for the use of the Northern Imperial Court.

The specimens found consist chiefly of conical bowls, circular covered boxes, saucers, a few spouted ewers, and high-shouldered vases. The spirit in which the Sung craftsmen worked is well illustrated by this inscription, which appears on a tall covered vase of Northern celadon, dated 1080, in the collection of Sir Percival David: "I have baked this first-class urn, in the hope that it may hold fragrant wine for thousands and myriads of years; that after a hundred years, it may be handed down to my descendants; that I may have a thousand sons and ten thousand grandsons; that they may have wealth and occupy high positions in the government continually; that they may live long and enjoy good fortune and unlimited happiness, and that the world may be at peace."

This joy in creation is a thread running through Chinese art, so that it is quite usual to find on paintings, whether of the Sung dynasty, or those painted ten years ago, such inscriptions as "This is a lovely thing" or "This will be admired for a thousand years to come."

In the latter part of the Sung dynasty, two brothers named Chang set up factories at a place about twenty miles from Lung-ch'üan in Chekiang province. (This is the province in which Hangchow, the capital of Southern Sung, was situated.) The younger of these Chang brothers manufactured the celadon wares which have since been called Lung-ch'üan yao. While continuing to make the heavy durable celadon wares for export, he became best known for the thin, delicate, translucent porcelain with a smooth jadelike glaze varying in color from light green to light bluish gray which is the delight of Chinese collectors.

The most prized specimens are of a soft blue color and are often called "kinuta" (Japanese for "mallet"), after a celebrated mallet-shaped vase in a Japanese collection. The vase has a tall straight neck and two handles.

The fine porcelain is made of the same material as the heavier celadon ware, and the whitish or grayish paste also turns red when exposed to heat. Most of the pieces existing are rather small (unlike the export ware), and consist of plates, dishes, vases, bowls, and articles for the scholar's table such as brush rests, water droppers, and ink stones. They are decorated in the following ways:

1. Carving, or etching, on body before applying the glaze.
2. Decoration in relief by pressing the soft paste into a mould before glazing.
3. Mould decoration which is left unglazed so that it will turn red with the heat. This results in the green celadon dishes with red fishes, dragons, or flower sprays, in relief.
4. Brown patches caused more or less accidentally by flaws in the glaze or by excess of iron in certain places. This "spotted" celadon is highly valued.

Finally, perhaps in deference to the Sung love of simplicity, the very finest pieces—like the blue kinuta vases, and others of the most delicate vases and dishes—are frequently left without any other decorative appeal but perfection of form and softness of color and texture.

KO YAO

At the same time the elder brother Chang was making a type of porcelain which is known as Ko yao, or Ko ware. This name is derived from the term "ko ko," which means "elder brother." This Ko ware is now rare and fine pieces are most eagerly sought by collectors. It is made of a dark-colored clay from around Hangchow, and the glazes are thick and unctuous, varying in color from stone-gray to greenish gray. Sometimes they even have a soft white or yellowish tone. The glaze is moist looking and glassy, with bubbles in the depths, and it is always crackled with a close and regular mesh. This crackle is the outstanding feature of Ko ware, and red or black pigments were sometimes rubbed into the cracks to make the crackle stand out more clearly.

Like most Sung porcelains, with the exception of the Chün and the Tz'ŭ Chou wares, the Ko pieces we have seen are usually small, and consist of small bowls, vases, covered boxes, and, again, the usual objects for the scholar's table. There are sometimes oval spur marks—like small seed—on the base.

KUAN YAO

Ko yao is usually associated with and compared with kuan yao, a ware which it resembles. "Kuan yao" means "imperial porcelain" and was the name given to the ware especially made for the use of the imperial household.

The kilns were first established in the capital city of K'ai-fêng Fu, early in the twelfth century. Only a few years later, the Sung Court was driven south by the Tartar invasion, and another producing center was established in the new capital of Hangchow to supply the Imperial Palace.

The designation Kuan yao continued to be used for all porcelains made especially for imperial use right up to the fall of the Chinese empire in 1912, but the name Kuan yao, used alone, specifically indicates a certain type of Sung ware.

The Kuan yao in Northern Sung was very thin, crackled all over, and in white, clair de lune, pale bluish green, and dark green. Specimens of Hangchow Kuan are more readily available, and they consist of a fine dark gray to reddish paste covered with a brilliant smooth glaze, in colors ranging from pale blue to emerald green, and also gray and white. They are usually crackled, but with a larger and less regular, less well-defined crackle than the Ko wares. We read in old Chinese records that these pieces have "iron colored feet and brown mouths," which shows that, like celadon, the iron in the clay turned reddish when not completely protected by glaze. The bowls were placed upside down in the kiln, and, frequently, the glaze ran off the edges. Sometimes these Kuan pieces were covered with rims of metal to hide this "brown mouth." Some of the small Southern Kuan pieces, made in ancient bronze forms, are of extreme delicacy, with a very thin body.

Kuan yao and Ko yao were very seldom decorated. The Chinese write that they were admired because they were "perfectly moulded, and decorated with a clear transparent glaze."

TING CHOU YAO

When the Court or the head of a large household went into mourning, all the dishes and vases used had to be white in color. Those who have lived in China find white the appropriate color to associate with death since, even in the West, ghosts, spirits, angels, and other symbols of departed persons are usually described as garbed in white. Because white is the Chinese color for mourning, in each dynasty there have been factories which turned out quantities of white ware.

The bulk of the Ting Chou ware was intended for this purpose. It was made at Ting Chou, in Chihli province, throughout the T'ang dynasty; and a T'ang pharmacopoeia, compiled about 650, recommends a powder prepared from the "white ware of Ting Chou" as a remedy for certain ailments. It goes on to mention that kaolin is "now used for painter's work and rarely enters into medical prescriptions." This would seem to prove that kaolin—the basis of true porcelain—was in common use early in the seventh century, and perhaps it also proves an understanding of the dangers of calcium deficiency.

The Northern Ting Chou ware made in the Sung dynasty is considered by many collectors to be the finest of all porcelains. It is of a pure white color, velvety smooth, and as translucent as the white jade it was made to resemble. The glaze was thin and clear, and the decoration was very restrained. Floral designs, fishes in waves, ducks, phoenixes are typical of the designs found on the finest pieces. The drawing is free and is made with a minimum of bold strokes of the etching tool in accordance with Sung taste.

Less admired are those pieces with moulded or stamped designs. These are more formal and crowded—perhaps presenting a formalized design of flowers and leaves with a border of fret decoration. As is the case with other Sung porcelains, some of the most valued pieces have no decoration at all.

Most of the Ting Chou pieces that have survived are bowls with a wide mouth and narrow base. The rims often remained unglazed because the pieces were placed upside down in firing and the glaze ran down, forming teardrops toward the foot. These teardrops are not considered a flaw, but are highly prized and taken as a proof of authenticity. To cover up the unglazed mouth, the rims were often bound with a thin band of copper or silver.

When the Court fled south, the making of Ting Chou ware was transferred to Ching-tê Chên, but there is reason to believe that this ware also continued to be made in the North under Tartar occupation.

There is some controversy as to whether the Ting porcelain made in the south was actually made at Ching-tê Chên, or somewhere else in the vicinity. There was a somewhat similar, but coarser, ware called Chi Chou, which was also made in Kiangsi province. However, the development of the Ting Chou white porcelain into the pure white porcelain made in early Ming seems evidence enough that the manufacture of Ting ware was carried on at Ching-tê Chên.

Some of the Southern Ting ware is just as fine as, and almost indistinguishable from, the Northern Ting. The fine white pieces were called "pai Ting" (white Ting) or "fên Ting" (flour-color Ting), while the yellower, coarser, more opaque ware was given the name of "t'u Ting" (earth-colored Ting).

Ting ware was also made in color, but to a much lesser extent. We have seen black pieces and purple pieces; and, according to the records, the ware was made in other colors too. Few specimens of this fragile porcelain have survived except those found in graves, which may explain the great preponderance of the white pieces over those of all other colors.

There is an old story about Ting ware which well illustrates the Chinese feeling about the art of making copies. A famous potter of Ching-tê Chên called Chou Tan-ch'üan visited T'ang, the president of the sacrifices, and said he would like to examine carefully an ancient tripod vessel of Ting porcelain which was one of the gems of his collection. He took the exact measurements of the piece with his hand and made an impression of the moulded decoration with a paper he had hidden in his sleeve. Then the potter returned to Ching-tê Chên.

Six months later he went to see T'ang again. This time he took a tripod vessel out of his sleeve, and said: "Your Excellency owns a tripod censer of white Ting porcelain. Here is its fellow which belongs to me."

T'ang was amazed. He compared it with his own piece and could not find any difference. He measured the feet against those on his own censer. He exchanged covers and found that they fitted perfectly. Then he asked Chou where he had found this wonderful thing.

"A few months ago" Chou answered, "I asked your permission to examine your tripod. I then took all the measurements with my hand. I assure you that this is a copy of your piece, and that I have no desire to deceive you."

The president of the sacrifices bought the tripod for forty ounces of silver and placed it in his collection beside the original.

Another collector, who had seen T'ang's censer, was seized with an overwhelming desire to possess it. In the course of time he managed, through intermediaries, to persuade T'ang to sell it to him for a thousand ounces of silver. He was delighted to acquire the imitation made by Chou, and doubtless T'ang was equally happy to have made such a profitable transaction and still be in possession of the original.

This took place in the Ming dynasty, in the reign of Wan Li, but there were few potters as skilled as Chou, and it is usually possible to distinguish between Sung porcelains and later copies.

JU CHOU YAO

Another important type of Sung porcelain is the Ju yao, which was made for imperial use by special potters transferred from Ju Chou in Honan to the Palace precincts at K'ai-fêng Fu, only a few years before the Tartar invasion. Ju yao has a buff porcelaneous body and is covered with glazes in lavender-gray, blue-gray, greenish blue, and fine clear blue. Sometimes it has a crackle which is made for the purpose of ornament. The foot rim is splayed, the foot covered with glaze, and there are frequently small oval spur marks left on the base by the stilts on which it rested in the kiln.

Since this kiln was in operation such a short time, few specimens have survived. Like the Kuan yao and the fine celadon porcelains, its chief beauty lies in the rich smooth quality of the glaze.

YING CH'ING WARE

Another type of fine translucent porcelain, mentioned earlier, and about which little has been known until very recently, is the pale blue ware named ying ch'ing ("shadowy blue"). Like the Ting ware this is so brittle and delicate that it disappeared and was found again only in opened tombs and through the discovery of old cities, like Chü-lu, which had been inundated by the rising of the Yellow River in the Sung dynasty. The porcelains excavated there were mainly of the Tz'ŭ Chou, Ting, and ying ch'ing types, and showed that the ordinary people of China used vessels that were exquisite in taste, even if the finest output had been reserved for the Imperial Courts.

Ying ch'ing ware had been made in the Five Dynasties, and, as we have already explained, there is good reason to assume that the finest specimens may have been the celebrated Ch'ai ware, especially since so much of it was found in the Honan tombs. This ware came closest to what is considered true porcelain in the Western world. It has a translucent white body and a thin pale-blue to greenish blue glaze. It appears to have been made in widely scattered parts of China and to have varied greatly in quality so that it could be used by all classes of the population.

Like the Ting ware, the bowls were fired upside down and the bare rims where the glaze had run down were often covered with a metal rim. Many of the pieces are plain, but some are incised and others have moulded decoration.

THE CHIEN YAO TEA BOWLS OF FUKIEN

In the Sung dynasty, writers such as Ts'ai Hsiang, who wrote the "Ch'a Lu" ("Description of Tea") in the eleventh century, preferred the "black cups mottled like hare's fur from Chien-an (Chien-chou), because they preserved the best trace of the whitish tea dust in the bottom of the cup."

This ware consisted chiefly of tea bowls, and it was in great demand for the competitive tea-tasting games which were the vogue in the Sung dynasty. The trace of tea was more easily visible when poured into black cups. Another reason for the popularity of this ware was its thickness which retained the heat well.

These bowls were originally made at Chien-an (then Chien-yang) and at various other villages in Fukien province—a great tea growing center. The Fukien kilns date back to Northern Sung, and they continued to operate throughout the Yüan dynasty and probably considerably later.

The Fukien bowls have a heavy dark brown or gray porcelaneous stoneware body, in which the heat turned the iron red as in other Sung wares. They are covered with a thick lustrous dark glaze—usually black or brown—with varying streaks and splashes produced by the use of metallic oxides—terminating in large drops about an inch from the base. In some cases the splashes were made into designs through use of stencils. The best known, however, are those with thick streaked markings, known as hare's fur, partridge pattern, lizard skin, and those with silvery oil spots. The glaze runs thick at the bottom so that it forms deep lustrous pools inside the bowls, which are conical in form with tapering sides. The largest bowls were about eight inches in diameter, but most of them just fit the hand. Some of them were dark green and some were dark blue, but both of these types are rare.

The tea-tasting games were accompanied by elaborate ceremonies, and these were introduced into Japan, where formal tea ceremonies still take place. The Japanese prize Chien yao bowls above all others for this purpose, giving them the name of "temmoku" (from the Chinese "T'ien mu"), because they are said to have been brought to Japan in the Sung dynasty by priests who had studied at the Zen (Ch'an) Buddhist monastery, on the T'ien-mu Mountains.

The same type of bowls were made in other parts of China, notably in Honan, where the body was made of light buff stoneware, and also in Kiangsi.

A Japanese connoisseur told us that he believes the reason that the output of Fukien Chien ware consisted almost entirely of bowls is that they were made especially for Buddhist priests, who used them to offer tea to Buddha.

A local story tells how the production of these bowls ceased. Only one village had the right to make the ebony black glossy bowls for imperial use. When a second village started to copy them, the first one complained to the emperor, who at once sent an army to annihilate the offending village. Then a third village began to fight the first one, and, eventually, all the villages fought each other till the manufacture of these bowls came to an end altogether.

It is only quite recently that interest in these Chien yao bowls has revived in the West. Expeditions have been made to the original kilns, where there are hills—one a hundred feet high and two hundred feet long—which are a solid mass of broken bowls. The hills resulted from the great number that were broken in firing. This amounted to over 95 per cent. The bowls were made in a heavy sagger, in the bottom of which was placed a round lump of clay. Then the bowl was placed on this lump of clay. Often the glaze dripped down, and it became impossible to detach the bowl without breaking it. Consequently, although there are few whole pieces left, there are still enormous supplies of broken and damaged specimens—even though the people of the districts in which they were made have been piecing them together and using them for centuries.

The Chien yao bowls can be called the last group of "scholars' wares" of the Sung dynasty, having achieved this position because of their popularity in the tea-tasting competitions.

CHÜN CHOU WARES

Another important group of Sung porcelains is the ware made at a kiln established at the beginning of the Sung dynasty at Chün Chou, in the province of Honan, near K'ai-fêng Fu.

One type of this ware has a fine, smooth, whitish gray body, and the other a yellowish coarse thick paste. The enamel was put on very heavily, and is found in the widest and most magnificent range of colors—shading at times from clear light blue or lavender to deep blue, rich crimson, and purple. The glaze ends near the base with large teardrops or a thick roll. The surface is full of air bubbles and pin holes. The base is coated with a clear color enamel such as gray, green or blue, and often shows the stilt marks left by the baking stand. Many pieces are numbered one to ten, the figure indicating the size of the stilt used. The inside of the bowls is usually deep or light blue.

The output of the Chün kilns was almost entirely devoted to useful domestic receptacles like flower pots with holes for drainage, bulb bowls, and wine pots.

Although these Chün pieces are greatly admired by Western collectors, they were less prized by Sung connoisseurs because the body is thick and heavy, and they are too highly colored. One old Chinese book ("Po-wu-yao-lan") refers to them in this way: "There are also incense urns and boxes of Chün Chou porcelain, but they are made of coarse yellow clay and are not good." Another old Chinese book, the "T'ao Shuo" ("Description of Pottery by Chu Yen," published in 1774), states that specimens with uniform colors are the finest. These remarks are in harmony with the insistence of the Sung scholars on purity and simplicity. There was a revulsion against bright colors by the Ch'an priests, and by the Taoists who quoted Lao Tzǔ as saying "color blinded the human eye."

While the austere scholars held this opinion, it is possible that some artisans revolted against it. Because the factory at Chün Chou turned out objects for household use, it did not have to conform too closely to the artistic canons of the time. It is often said in Western books that the gorgeous colors of the Chün wares were achieved by "accident." Anyone who has visited Chinese kilns and seen the enormous amount of breakage which they take for granted and the high hills of broken shards that grow up around them would realize that if the potter were not pleased with the result of a firing he would simply discard the pieces. It seems more likely that the wide range of colors was the deliberate result of experimentation.

Perhaps some of the Sung potters felt that they had had enough of the green glaze "like cool water" and the clair-de-lune and the white "like ice," and they yearned to reproduce the varied colors of a sunset—shading from light blue and green to deep crimson and purple. In any event, that is exactly the result achieved by many of the Chün yao glazes. However, just as in nature the glowing colors of a sunset do not last as long as the cool green of the far-off hills, or the clear blue of the evening sky, or the silvery radiance of the moon, so it may have been the innate Chinese sense of rightness that confined the burst of sunset colors to just one type of ceramic ware, and one that was not intended primarily for the pleasure of scholars and aesthetes.

When the Tartars overran the North, some of the Chün Chou potters went and worked in Hangchow, while others appear to have fled south to Kuangtung, where they continued to apply the same type of varicolored glazes over the dark gray stoneware of the region where pottery had been made since the T'ang dynasty.

Other potters apparently went to Yi-hsing in Kiangsi province where their descendants turned out pottery of red stoneware covered with glazes similar to those made at Chün Chou.

TZ'Ŭ CHOU WARE

The last important group of Sung ceramic wares is that known as Tz'ŭ Chou yao, and it represents the art of the people. These kilns have worked continuously from the Sui dynasty (589-618) to the present day, first in Honan, and later in Chihli province (now Hopei), turning out objects for general domestic use: large heavy vases for storing wine and oil and vinegar, bowls, plates and kitchen utensils, flower pots and vases, pillows—for the Chinese like hard pottery pillows better than soft down ones, especially in hot weather—and images of the Kwan Yin, the Lohans, the Taoist Immortals, and all the other figures of Buddhist, Taoist, Confucianist and other folklore, which the people liked to have in their houses as ornaments or household gods.

While such things were in general use, they were not designed to be held in the hands of a connoisseur or to be put on the scholar's table, but were made to meet the everyday needs of all the people. And it is a great tribute to the taste of the Chinese that these Tz'ŭ Chou pieces are a pleasure to the eye.

Tz'ŭ Chou ware is a hard porcelaneous stoneware, grayish white, sometimes yellowish. A coat of white slip was applied, then a transparent film of glaze, and the freehand decoration in brown or black shiny paint was applied afterward with a brush. The technique used was that favored in painting—a bold and free brush with a minimum of strokes. For instance, on a large piece, each petal and each leaf had to be made with one stroke of the brush.

150

There was also overglaze painting in red and green, which carried on the T'ang tradition of multicolor decoration, and which was the forerunner of the overglaze painting in colored enamels which became so popular in the Ming dynasty. Among the few Sung grave figures found are small images of men and women and children and small Kwan Yins. Made of this ware, they were covered with white slip and decorated in red and green and black. At the end of the dynasty a clear blue or green glaze was sometimes applied over the painted decoration.

Another type of decoration was of the sgraffito type, where the white slip was scratched away around the decoration so that its whiteness under the glaze contrasted with the grayish color of the biscuit. The subjects chosen were varied —ranging from designs of flowers and leaves, fishes in waves, dragons, phoenixes, and tigers to line drawings of familiar tales of folklore, history, and legend. Not only did the subjects of decoration have an almost endless variety, but the ware itself assumed a wide range of styles. There are monochrome pieces that closely resemble Ting yao, and there are dark brown pieces with hare's fur markings that are like Chien yao. The potters gave free rein to their inventive powers in form, type, and decoration, and they could do so all the more readily because they did not have to conform to the strict prevailing canons of taste.

These potters have continued to work to the present time, but the later brown and black pigments have not been as good, lustrous, or durable as those used in the early periods. The result is that it is often remarked that the older the piece the fresher and newer it looks.

The types of ware described above are the best-known groups, and most of the Sung ceramic wares made in kilns in various parts of the country fall into one or another of the above categories.

Whereas, not so very long ago, pieces were designated merely as "Sung," much is now known about the sites of the kilns and the different types of wares. Some groups are still not completely identified, but there is every reason to assume that, with the resumption of archaeological exploration, more complete information about the wares already known will come to light, as well as knowledge of additional types made in different parts of the country.

One of the great fascinations of the study of Chinese art is that our knowledge is never static, but is always being modified and enlarged.

YÜAN DYNASTY (1280-1368)

Marco Polo, who visited the city of Soochow in China in the latter part of the thirteenth century, wrote: "Indeed if the men of this city . . . and the rest of the country . . . had but the spirit of soldiers they would conquer the world; but they are no soldiers at all, only accomplished traders and most skillful craftsmen. There are also in this city many philosophers. . . ."

As Marco Polo understood, the Chinese excelled in the arts of the mind rather than in the arts of war, and, in spite of the heroic resistance they put up, the whole of China was absorbed into the vast Mongol empire in 1280. The conqueror, Kublai Khan, grandson of Genghis Khan, set up a new dynasty in China, to which he gave the name of Yüan. Although he was cruel and ruthless while the actual fighting was in progress, Kublai Khan was a man of some education, and he was much impressed by Sung art and culture. He admired the beautiful city of Hangchow so much that he gave orders that it was to be left intact. There is a story that when he and his wife saw the lovely art treasures of the city they were overcome, and the woman burst into tears, saying: "I have a premonition that our vast Mongol empire will be conquered like this one day."

The pottery and porcelain kilns continued to operate during the Yüan dynasty, but their production did not come up to the Sung standard. The celadons and other porcelains are coarser and appear to have suffered from the fact that the courtiers and nobles of the new regime were no longer able to appreciate the fine features of the work.

Perhaps for this very reason, however, there was much experimentation. The potteries did not have to supply so much fine porcelain for imperial use— the Mongols preferring vessels of gold and silver—so the potters were free to make use of this period to try out new ideas.

It was during the Yüan dynasty that the technique of painting white vessels with underglaze blue, which had been experimented with late in the Sung dynasty, was further developed. Overglaze painting in transparent enamels was also being tried out, and Ting wares were gradually being transformed into the fine clear white substance known in the West as porcelain.

"SHU FU" PORCELAIN

There was a type of ware made at Ching-tê Chên in the Yüan dynasty that was spoken of as resembling jade and was ordered for official use. These dishes, which included rounded flat-bottomed plates, bowls, and cups, were marked "Shu fu" ("Privy Council"). This ware is considered to be the transition between Ting yao and the fine, thin, translucent Ming porcelain (t'o-t'ai) made later, in the Yung Lo period.

Few "Shu fu" pieces have survived, and most of these were taken from graves. However, A. D. Brankston records in his book *The Early Ming Wares of Chingtehchen* that he found many shards and that the glaze was opaque and had a pale blue or greenish blue tinge. From this description the "Shu fu" ware appears to have been linked up with the delicate ying ch'ing as well as with Ting yao.

By the time the Mongol dynasty was overthrown, the Chinese potters were all set for the great renaissance of the porcelain industry which came to full flower in the Ming dynasty.

MING DYNASTY (1368-1644)

The early years of the Ming ("Radiant") dynasty were marked by sporadic fighting and unrest, but Yung Lo, a son of the first emperor, Hung Wu (who

152

had overthrown the Mongols), was a strong and determined ruler who brought an end to all hostilities. In the reign of the next emperor, Hsüan-tê, the empire was prosperous and peaceful, the people were contented, and the officials capable and loyal. A Chinese writer (Shên Tê-fu) says that at that time "potters were inspired by Heaven to produce works of subtle meaning and supreme artistry."

The Ming dynasty produced the fullest flowering of ceramic art of all time. The joy of liberation from alien invaders is seen in the bold opulent forms and glowing colors of Ming porcelains. There is no more of the restraint of the Sung connoisseurs. The porcelains and potteries of the period are symbols of a time of great prosperity. There was no more fear of realism, no dread of bright colors, or of painted decoration, no dread of overstepping the strict canons of refined taste of the hermit-scholar.

Ceramic wares in the Sung dynasty had largely consisted of small objects for table use and for the scholar's desk, but under the Ming emperors the rage for porcelain broke all bounds. The most enormous pieces were made—vases five and six feet high, large fish bowls in which children could stand, huge dishes three and four feet in diameter, baths and barrel garden seats, as well as tall statues of deities, larger than life size. All of these must have required the utmost skill of the potters to bring them from the furnace unbroken. Besides this, houses were covered with porcelain roof tiles, and pagodas were concocted entirely of porcelain and stoneware. Yet, at the same time, the finest and most delicate of tiny cups and boxes no bigger than a coin were turned out. In the time of Wan Li, the potters claimed that there was nothing that could not be made of porcelain. People put porcelain on their walls and on their beds; they slept on porcelain pillows; they sat on porcelain seats. They used porcelain for cooking and for eating, for ritual purposes and for entertainment.

When Hung Wu (1368-1398), moved the capital south to Nanking, he started a new imperial factory at Ching-tê Chên in 1369. Under this imperial patronage, Ching-tê Chên became the undisputed ceramic center, turning out about 80 to 90 per cent of all the wares produced in the empire. Actually, the imperial factories themselves accounted for only a small proportion of the output of the ceramic kilns. Père d'Entrecolles, a French missionary, who visited Ching-tê Chên in 1712, wrote in a letter that a million persons lived in Ching-tê Chên, and that all were connected in some way or other with the porcelain industry. He added: "They tell me that a piece of porcelain, when it comes out from the kiln, has passed through the hands of 70 workmen, . . . and I can well believe it, from what I myself have seen, as their huge workshops have often been for me a kind of Areophagus, where I have proclaimed Him who created the first man out of clay, and from whose hands we proceed to become vessels, either of glory or of shame."

In the year 1544, among a very long list of other things, the imperial household alone ordered 26,350 bowls with 30,500 saucers to match, 6000 ewers with 6900 wine cups, 680 large garden fish bowls, and 1340 table services of 27 pieces each. This gives some idea of what the output must have been for the whole of China, and for the export trade all over the world.

It is often said that in the Ming dynasty there was a return to the glory of T'ang, but, as far as porcelain was concerned, that was only true in relation to color and realism, for porcelain had made great strides forward. While the making of celadon and Tz'ŭ Chou wares continued, there was an eager demand for every type of innovation. The potters no longer aimed only at copying white or green jade—they also gloried in producing the pure white translucent material identified as porcelain in the Western world.

The word "porcelain" derives from "porcellana," which was the Italian word for cowrie shells and other hard shiny substances. (The word meant "little pig" because it was thought that the back of a cowrie shell somewhat resembled that animal.) Marco Polo first used this word to describe the Chinese ceramic ware, since he appears to have believed it was made of crushed shells. He used the word for other substances, too, and it was not until the sixteenth century that the word was used solely for porcelain.

While there is not much porcelain of the Hung Wu period in existence, the "Ko-ku Yao Lun" ("A discussion of the Essential Criteria of Antiquities"), first published in 1388, says: "At the present time the best porcelain made in Ching-tê Chên is white and brilliant. There are also wares with blue-black or golden decoration, winepots and cups, greatly admired."

YUNG LO PORCELAINS

When we come to the reign of Yung Lo (1403-1424), we find the delicate pure white dishes, including the famous "ya shou pei" cups, so elegantly designed to fit the hand. Evolved from the Sung Ting wares, these white dishes are translucent and ring with a musical note when struck. Because they are so thin, appearing to consist only of two transparent layers of glaze, they are called "t'o-t'ai," meaning "bodiless." In spite of this, they frequently bear an incised design, and sometimes an inscription, which had to be added when the piece was in a semiplastic state before glazing or firing. The design can barely be seen until the bowl, or saucer, is held to the light, and for this reason it is called "an hua" or "secret design." Floral designs, dragons catching a pearl, phoenixes and lotus leaves are common motifs. Some pieces bear seals on the base indicating that they were "Made in the reign of Yung Lo of the great Ming dynasty."

In contrast to these delicate bowls was the Nanking Porcelain Pagoda, erected 1412-1431, by order of the Emperor Yung Lo in memory of his mother, shortly after he had transferred the capital of his empire to Peking. This building was about three hundred feet high, and consisted of nine stories. The lowest was made of white porcelain tiles, and the others of glazed stoneware. Each story had a projecting balcony with a light balustrade of green porcelain. The pagoda was destroyed in 1854, during the T'ai P'ing Rebellion. All that remains are a few separate tiles on display in various museums.

In addition to the "bodiless" ware previously mentioned there were other cups and bowls of varying sizes and shapes, painted with designs in underglaze

154

blue, both on the inside and outside. The Chinese had experimented with underglaze blue decoration from the latter part of the Sung period, but the Sung shards, and the Yüan pieces of this type that we have seen, do not approach the Ming standard. The porcelain is grayish, and the blue is muddy and dark.

It appears that early in the Ming dynasty vast new strata of fine clay were discovered, and this stimulated the development of fine porcelains. In order to paint successfully in underglaze blue it was necessary first to have a fine hard paste white body. At first the native cobalts had had a grayish tinge, but, by the reign of Hsüan Tê (1426-1435), the Chinese began importing a fine cobalt, known as "Mohammedan blue," from the Near East. This was very expensive (it was said to have been worth twice its weight in gold), and it had to be mixed with the native blue in just the proper proportion to obtain the desired effect.

PORCELAINS IN THE REIGN OF THE EMPEROR HSÜAN TÊ

All these problems seem to have been solved by the reign of Hsüan Tê, and it was then that white porcelain decorated in underglaze blue (known in the West as "blue-and-white") reached its greatest perfection. We find the drawing bold and free, its rhythmic vitality revealing the hand of a skilled artist. The forms are finely balanced, and the blue is deep and brilliant. The Chinese also describe the ware as being "thickly heaped and piled." The design appears to swim under the glaze rather than to be attached to the body. The latter effect was achieved by the vessel being covered with a thin, glazelike slip before it was painted, and being reglazed afterward, the decoration in blue lying between two layers of glaze. The final glaze is very rich and thick. The decoration of these pieces usually consists of the familiar dragons in waves or phoenixes (the dragon and the phoenix being the symbols of the emperor and the empress), birds on branches, medallions of flowers and fruits, children at play, five lions (denoting five generations under one roof), and the Three Friends—a combination of pine, plum, and bamboo trees, all of which are hardy enough to bloom in winter.

At the same time, work was also being done in underglaze copper red, notably in stem cups with red underglaze fishes, or with red peaches. Underglaze colors had to be able to stand the intense heat required to fuse the feldspathic glaze, and it was found possible to do this with copper, which gives underglaze red, as well as with the cobalt, giving blue.

As stated previously all the porcelain intended for the use of the imperial palaces was called "Kuan yao," and, from the reign of Hsüan Tê onward, it was marked with the dynasty and the name used by the ruling monarch (the nien hao). The seal, however, cannot be taken as a conclusive sign of a piece being genuine, since later copies often bore marks of early reigns. Imperial porcelain was not always the finest of its kind. Often such low prices were paid by the imperial household that an inferior quality was supplied, and some of the most precious and perfect porcelains frequently went to private collectors and connoisseurs.

EXPORT TRADE

A large export trade developed in blue-and-white porcelain, first with the Near East, and then with Europe, where its popularity spread. By the sixteenth century, when production was at its height, there was already direct regular trade with Europe in tea and silk as well as porcelain. The porcelain trade consisted almost entirely of coarse, strong blue-and-whites and of heavy celadons. Specimens of the multicolored Ming porcelains rarely reached Europe until around the beginning of the present century, and it was considerably later before there was any knowledge of the existence of the fine delicate Ming bowls and cups. Yet even these inferior blue-and-white products made a tremendous impression. In 1487, the sultan of Egypt sent a gift of porcelains to Lorenzo di Medici in Florence, Italy, which were so admired that determined efforts were made to copy them. The result was the so-called "Porcelain de Medici" type of blue-and-white ware, made at the end of the sixteenth century.

The potters of Delft in Holland, and of Nevers and Rouen in France, also made faience copies of Chinese "blue-and-whites," which became equally famous in the West.

As the trade expanded, the Chinese accepted orders for pieces of foreign shape and decoration, and, sometimes, with foreign inscriptions. These are often referred to as showing "foreign influence," but it is to be noted that there was never any influence at all on the wares that the Chinese made for their own use. For instance, later, after the vast East India trade developed, they turned out quantities of cups with handles for export, but the Chinese still used only handleless cups; they filled orders for thousands of sets of tableware, including plates with flat rims (for condiments), but they still used rounded dishes themselves—putting their condiments on tiny special saucers. In accordance with European orders they made oblong tureens with two handles, but they went on using their own large round handleless dishes for serving their food. In other words, all these objects made for the foreign trade had no more effect on the Chinese taste in porcelain than the paintings of the Jesuit fathers in Peking had on Chinese painting.

PORCELAINS OF THE REIGN OF CH'ÊNG HUA (1465-1487)

The reign of Ch'êng Hua ranks with that of Hsüan Tê for the quality of its porcelains, especially those with polychrome decoration. The porcelain was noted for its fragile quality, much of it being of the egg-shell type, and it was also famed for the beauty of the decoration. Often the best-known Court artists prepared the designs, which were made in bold, free strokes, in the style called "following the will of the brush." Only the most skilled artisan-painters, with the surest brush, were entrusted with the task of transferring these designs to the porcelains.

The "Po wu yao lan" (published in the Ming dynasty) states: "In the highest class of porcelain of the reign of Ch'êng Hua there is nothing to excel the stemmed wine cups with shallow bowls and swelling rims decorated in five colors with grapes. . . . Next to these come the wedding cups decorated in colors with flowers and insects, or with a hen and chicken, the wine cups of the shape of a lotus nut painted with figure scenes, the shallow cups decorated with the five sacrificial utensils, the tiny cups with flowering plants and butterflies, and the blue-and-white wine cups that are as thin as paper."

There is also mention of "Dragon Boat Cups" with boats racing in the annual Dragon Festival, the "Famous Scholar Cups," and the "Wa-wa cups" with five little boys playing together, the name indicating the speech of babies.

These little cups were highly valued in the Ming dynasty, and we read that, in the reign of Wan Li, "tiny cups decorated with fighting cocks could not be bought for less than five hundred ounces of the purest silver, being valued far more highly than the most precious jade." They are finely made, cream-white, the glaze perfectly smooth and glossy. The enamels are pale and transparent— only the red being brilliant. The outlines are painted in underglaze blue, and, after glazing, the colors are applied in washes. The enamels used are blue, apple green, scarlet, pink, aubergine (eggplant), and yellow. These are known as tou ts'ai ("clashing colors").

Until quite recently Western connoisseurs could not believe that these delicate little cups were made in the Ch'êng Hua period but believed them to be of the Ch'ing dynasty. Now that it is firmly established that many of these pieces are originals, and not copies, it completely changes our whole conception of Ming porcelains.

The production of blue-and-white porcelain continued throughout the dynasty, the quality of the blue decoration varying according to the absence, or arrival, of supplies of Mohammedan blue. In the reign of Chêng-tê (1506-1521) the scarce and precious cobalt was reserved for use by the imperial factory, and severe regulations were set up to prevent workmen stealing it and selling it to private potters.

Evidence of the amount of blue-and-white ware manufactured is afforded by the fact that, when we were in Peking, it was a common sight to see street vendors selling cold drinks from Ming bowls, or sweetmeats and noodles from very large Ming round platters. These had invariably been broken and riveted together, but they were of the Ming period, and had probably been in the family since that time.

MING WARES WITH MULTICOLOR ENAMELS; THE SAN TS'AI —THREE-COLOR DECORATION

Better known than the Ch'êng Hua porcelains during the last half century have been the Ming wares with multicolor decoration, known as the "san ts'ai" (three-color) and the "wu ts'ai" (five color).

The first type—san ts'ai—appears on pottery and stoneware as well as on porcelain, and it was used in many places besides Ching-tê Chên for garden seats, fish ponds, and large (often larger than life size) figures of deities in temples and grottoes. This three-color decoration was sometimes applied directly on the biscuit, giving the piece a soft and rather crackled effect which is known as "fa hua."

Three-color decoration was applied by outlining the designs in threads of clay, carving or moulding in relief, cutting in openwork, or tracing the outlines with a sharp point as had been done in the T'ang dynasty, with a technique similar to that used in making cloisonné. The object of all these devices was the same—to keep the various glazes from running into each other.

The term "three-color" is not quite literal, since it includes two, three, or four of the following—green, aubergine, deep yellow, turquoise, white, and black. These enamel colors are glassy compounds tinted with mineral oxides—copper for green and turquoise, iron or antimony for yellow, iron for red, and manganese for purple. Sometimes they were applied to the glazed surface and sometimes to the unglazed but fired body. The latter process is called "painting on the biscuit." Then they were put in a cooler part of the kiln. Gilding, when used, necessitated another firing at a still lower temperature.

Three-color decoration was often used over a slip of one color, such as purple, turquoise, or green; sometimes it was also used over a white glazed slip. This last method is frequently seen on the many fine Ming porcelain figures. In these, the face and hands were left white.

ROOF TILES AND ROOF TILE FIGURES

The roof tiles and the roof tile figures, which were so important a branch of the Ming ceramic industry, were nearly always decorated in the san ts'ai enamels.

The roof is the most important decorative feature of a Chinese building—both in itself for its graceful lines, and also because it afforded an obvious place for ornamentation. The roof tile figures were not merely added at random, but formed an integral part of the building, in addition to being charged with the responsibility of guarding the house, and its inmates, against evil spirits and hostile influences.

In early times, roof figures were carved of wood; but, from the latter part of the Han dynasty, pottery tiles—first unglazed and then glazed—were used. Great quantities of these tiles were made in the Ming dynasty, and numbers of them can still be found—as well as later ones and new copies. They were very popular with foreign Peking residents who used them as book ends and door stops.

The tiles were made of hard earthenware, glazed to make them waterproof. The finer ones were modeled entirely by hand, but the bulk were made in moulds. The roof-tile figures were glazed either in monochrome or in several of the san ts'ai colors—yellow, green, blue, purple, and black. Yellow was reserved for imperial roofs, and green for the houses of officials. These roof tiles usually range from about six to eighteen inches high, but some specimens run to more than four feet.

Traditionally, the row of figures on a roof begins with a man riding astride a cock into the dawn. Other figures may include various animals, real and mythical, fishes, dragons, phoenixes, tigers, lions, Fo dogs to defend the house against robbers, various Taoist and Buddhist figures, Kuan Ti * (God of War and of Literature), heroes on horseback, and fierce devils in the attitude of prize fighters designed to frighten away marauding spirits.

These roof figures at their best were modeled variously with great intensity of emotion, serene calm, or with much humor. They are among the most vigorous and expressive manifestations of the potter's art.

MING PORCELAINS WITH WU TS'AI (FIVE-COLOR) DECORATION

One of the great advances in technique of the Ming potters was the decoration of porcelain with vitreous multicolor glazes, which achieved brilliant, jewel-like effects. Known as wu ts'ai, or five-color, this technique really included all colors, and was combined with underglaze blue and underglaze red. The porcelain was first painted in blue or, in some cases, in red. It was then coated with a colorless glaze and fired. Afterward, it was painted with a brush with vitreous colored enamels in liquid form and was then fired again in a cooler part of the kiln.

The painting in colored enamels was done with great care, often by several different artists, each one specializing separately, in the painting of flowers, birds, animals, landscapes, or people. Popular subjects were historical scenes; tales from Buddhist, Taoist and Confucian lore; folktales; the usual dragons, lions, tigers, horses and sea-horses in waves; pictures of children playing, reading, or burning incense; family scenes; flowers and trees. The intricate border patterns were taken from ancient silk brocades, textiles, and bronzes. All the decoration conveys a message to the Chinese eye.

MONOCHROME GLAZES

Besides the five-color and three-color wares, there were also many pieces decorated with two colors, sometimes combining under- and overglaze decoration in red and green, blue and yellow, green and gold, and other two-color combinations.

While there was this great admiration for translucent white porcelain— plain, incised, or decorated in underglaze or overglaze colors—there was still a continued demand for monochromes. Yellow, used over a coat of colorless glaze, was reserved for imperial use and was sometimes combined with underglaze blue and red. Then there was turquoise blue, dark blue, sky blue, green, brown, red, and mirror-black. An incised design was used under the glaze on many of these monochrome porcelains.

The color used in porcelains often had an important association. For instance, in Peking, the sacrificial vessels used for the Temple of Heaven were

* A famous figure of the time of the Three Kingdoms, who helped to consolidate a China left in chaos after the collapse of the Han dynasty.

glazed blue (as were the roof tiles of the temple) to represent the deep blue of the evening sky. The vessels used at the Altar of Earth and for the worship of the God of Agriculture and the Goddess of Silk were yellow, the color of earth and of fields of grain. Red was used for the vessels at the Altar of the Sun, and white for the Altar of the Year-Star, and, of course, at times of mourning.

OTHER TYPES OF DECORATION

Besides painting, other processes of decoration were used on porcelain, including embossing, chiseling, and openwork carving. In the latter part of the dynasty, a very fine type of fretwork carving, which was designed to show off the great skill of the potter, was given the name of "kuei kung" or devil's work.

CHIA CHING (1522-1566), LUNG CH'ING (1567-1572), AND WAN LI (1573-1619)

These reigns were notable for the vast output and quality of all the types of porcelain previously manufactured. In the latter reigns, however, it began to be difficult to find supplies of good clay, with the result that the surface of some pieces is less smooth and has a somewhat pitted effect.

The whole period is especially famous for the combination of blue and red underglaze painting combined with five-color overglaze decoration. The Chia Ching blue had a deep violet tone, while in the Wan Li pieces the blue is soft and silvery.

During these reigns there were evidently protests against the extravagant purchases of porcelains, and we read that on one occasion, the president of the Censorate suggested that the installments of fifteen thousand pieces for Palace use should be changed from monthly to yearly.

It was in the reign of Wan Li that Chou Tan-ch'üan, the famous imitator of old porcelain and the maker of the Ting censer already described, flourished.

Still more famous was another potter of the same period, Hao Shih-chiu. He made delicate, tiny wine cups, which people thronged from all parts of the empire to buy. These eggshell cups of pure translucent white were so thin that they could float upon water with nothing but the rim at the base submerged. Hao Shih-chiu lived poorly from choice, but was an educated man who exchanged verses with other poets. He was equally famed for his pale celadon teapots, and he gave himself the sobriquet "The old man hidden in the teapots," which he used as a seal, meaning that he had put the best of himself into his work, and that all who acquired one of his pieces would find that he, himself, was embodied in it.

BLANC DE CHINE

While Ching-tê Chên remained the undisputed center of the ceramic industry, the making of pottery and porcelain were still carried on in various other parts of China.

Held in high esteem throughout the Ming dynasty was the porcelain turned out at Tê-hua, in the province of Fukien, which became known in the West as "Blanc de Chine" because of its special appeal to the French. This is a smooth paste, intensely vitrified, white porcelain, covered with a thick velvety white glaze which seems to blend until it forms one substance with the body. In the "T'ao Lu," the author of this work complains that it is "thick," yet it is just this solidity that gives it the appearance of ivory, which it was supposed to imitate. The quality of the porcelain is especially adapted to the modeling of figures with soft yet well-defined draperies and clearly integrated detail.

In regard to Tê-hua porcelains, W. B. Honey, Keeper of the Department of Ceramics in the Victoria and Albert Museum, London, writes: "Their material has been described as the most beautiful porcelain ever made." And in respect to the figures he says: "They are an object lesson in the principle that beauty in a porcelain figure depends absolutely upon beauty in the material of which it is made."

This porcelain continued to be made throughout the Ch'ing dynasty, and the potters were still turning out these white pieces when we were last in that area. Not only are the Ming specimens heavier, and more perfectly modeled than later ones, but they possess a greater rhythmic movement, and resemble ivory more closely. When held to the light the Ming ware shines with a rosy glow. This becomes a warm cream tone in the K'ang Hsi pieces, and a paler cream in the Ch'ien Lung ones. The modern pieces are chalky white.

Tê-hua pieces often have seal marks engraved under the glaze, either on the base or on the back of the figures. These usually represent shop marks, potter's marks, artist's seals, or perhaps some religious symbol. Many of the pieces bear inscriptions incised under the glaze. For instance, a fine, flat-sided Ming teapot of the sixteenth century bears an inscription on one side which, in translation, reads: "When one has drunk enough tea one feels one is floating on air," and on the other side: "When you drink from this pot the air seems refreshingly cool." A plain wine cup on three short feet, of the same period, bears the legend: "I, Tz'ŭ, fashioned this in the form of an imperial wine cup."

While few known pieces can, with certainty, be dated earlier than the Ming dynasty, the local people all insist that porcelain has been made in the district since Sung times, and quantities of shards of porcelain decorated in underglaze blue and of other types of Sung wares can be found in the vicinity of the kilns.

The finished perfection of the workmanship and the material of the earliest Ming specimens show that this Blanc de Chine must have developed from the work of generations of skilled and experienced potters. As frequently happens in the field of Chinese art, the earliest specimens are the finest, and it seems improbable that they suddenly evolved from nothing.

The Fukien white wares comprise libation cups, incense burners, goblets, teapots, wine pots, vases, boxes, plates, saucers, bowls, and other pieces, either plain or with decoration in relief. The decoration usually consists of sprays of prunus blossom or plants and deer. The most interesting part of the production, however, consists in the figures which are a triumph of the art of the modeler—

the lovely and compassionate figure of Kwan Yin, "who looketh down and hears the cries of the world"; the cheerful God of Contentment, Pu-tai (sometimes called The Laughing Buddha); the Eight Taoist Immortals; the fierce warrior Kuan Ti, and all the other legendary figures.

The export trade with the West led to orders for foreign figures, so that one finds many Western types, including a St. Anthony of Padua, a Dutch soldier dated 1610, and a seventeenth-century Dutch family. These Blanc de Chine porcelains excited so much admiration in Europe that they served as models for the potters of St. Cloud, Chantilly, Bow, Chelsea, and Meissen.

Before leaving the subject of the Tê-hua potteries, we would like to add that we learned from the local people the little-known fact that—in the Ch'ing dynasty —white teapots with twisted handles, straight spouts, and a strawberry knob on top of the lid were decorated there with *famille rose* flower designs in the style which has mistakenly been called "Lowestoft," for the European market. These pieces are distinguished from those painted in Canton by the absence of any gold decoration, and also by a generally softer appearance. This trade does not seem to have developed to the extent that the Canton export trade did, and no pieces have been thus decorated later than the reign of Ch'ien Lung.

THE TEAPOTS AND OTHER WARES OF YI-HSING

Not far from Shanghai, on the western shores of the Great Lake in Kiangsu province, lies Yi-hsing Hsien, famous for the stoneware known as Yi-hsing made from the different color clays found in the surrounding hills—red, chocolate brown, dark brown, white, black, and buff. The stoneware is almost as hard and as smooth as porcelain. In its preferred form it has been left undecorated and unglazed—although it acquires a natural sheen from rubbing and polishing so that the longer it is used the more lustrous it becomes. It depends for its appeal upon its simplicity, perfection of form, and fineness of potting.

Yi-hsing is especially famed for its teapots, which both the Chinese and the Japanese consider superior to all others for infusing the beverage and preserving its aroma and flavor. While some form of pottery has been made in this district from the Sung period onward, this particular type of stoneware—and especially the manufacture of the teapots—seems to have started in the reign of the Ming Emperor Chêng Tê (1506-1521), when the renowned potter Kung Ch'un designed and made what was considered to be the perfect type of vessel. He is said to have invented "the true form of the teapot," although small winepots in similar shapes were found to have been in general use in the Sung dynasty. What he did, apparently, was to improve upon existing shapes and render them more suitable for pouring tea and more pleasing to the eye and touch.

The origin of the custom of tea drinking is so remote that there is a legend that in 2700 B.C. the Emperor Shên Nung drank tea. In early times it was used only for medicinal purposes, but vague references to tea can be found in the writings of Confucius. The earliest definite and reliable reference to tea is contained in a Chinese dictionary dated about A.D. 350. During the fourth century,

162

Liu Kin, a general of the Chin dynasty, wrote that he felt old and depressed and needed to drink some good tea. By the fifth century, tea had become an article of trade, and during the sixth century it began to be generally regarded as a refreshing drink and not merely as a medicine. Undoubtedly its popularity may have been due, in part at least, to the fact that the custom of drinking boiled water (in the form of tea) rather than cold water must have prevented many internal diseases and epidemics.

The ancient method of making tea was by boiling the leaves in water, and the first appliance used was the primitive kettle. The Chinese soon found that they preferred tea made by infusion, boiling the water in a small kettle and then pouring it over the leaves which had been placed in a tall, vase-shaped, and spouted jug, similar to that used for pouring wine. The earliest known teapot of this type is mentioned in the "Ch'a Ching" by Lu Yu, the Treatise on Tea written in the eighth century.

The practical Chinese mind soon realized the unsuitability of a tall, slender jug as a container for scalding liquid, because it could so easily be overturned. Also the curved spout soon became clogged with tea leaves. It was only after a more functional type of pot, with a squat shape, firm base, and wide spout was designed that the use of the teapot became general.

In this regard it is interesting to note that in the tea-growing center of Fukien province, where enormous quantities of Chien yao tea bowls were made in the Sung dynasty, no Chien ware teapots have been found. This, we learned, was because these bowls were made especially for the Buddhist monks, each of whom had his own bowl. In the monasteries they were filled from a large common kettle.

The designs of Kung Ch'un in Yi-hsing ware appear to have met with instant success in Japan as well as in China, and the type of teapot attributed to him is as essential a part of the tea ceremony as are the Chien yao bowls. The perfect vessel for the ceremony is a small and shallow teapot with a cover that is concave inside and not flat. It must have a straight spout so that the tea can pour easily —the slightest curvature is fatal.

Kung Ch'un was one of the long line of well-known Yi-hsing potters who signed their works and whose names are remembered and recorded. The simpler pieces are the most highly prized, especially those inscribed with old poems or sayings in ancient seal or grass characters. The prices paid for some of these may seem astonishing to those who do not appreciate this art or realize that to be a master of this type of calligraphy requires twenty to thirty years of continuous practice.

In the seventeenth and eighteenth centuries, Yi-hsing teapots were sent to Europe, together with tea, as an article of export. They became known by the Portuguese name of "Buccaro" because, when they first arrived in Europe, they were confused with American Indian wares known by that name. These Yi-hsing pots served as models for the Brothers Elers in Staffordshire, Dwight in Fulham, and Böttger in Dresden. The Brothers Elers appear to have copied only the red stoneware models, but they did so most successfully, for we found one of their pieces in a collection of Yi-hsing teapots in the house of a collector in South China. The owner was astonished when we pointed out that it was an English piece, and he said it had never occurred to him that it was not made at Yi-hsing, or that such things could be made outside China.

Some of the later potters developed more elaborate wares, with moulded decoration, glazing, enameling in *famille rose* colors, which will be described later on, gilding, and other effects.

Toward the end of the Ming dynasty there was a potter named Ou Tzü-ming, who became famous for his imitations of the Sung glazes, such as those on the Ko yao, Chün yao, and other Sung imperial wares. His work was so skillful that, where the body was entirely covered with enamel, many experts were deceived and thought they were handling Sung wares.

Teapots were made in various shapes—in the form of flowers, birds, wheels, drums, clusters of bamboos, and other novel designs; but the simplest pieces have remained the most admired.

Less known outside China are the winepots made in Yi-hsing ware, as well as in many other types of pottery and porcelain. These date back even earlier than the teapots. A commonly used and practical form of winepot is the double pot. The larger outside part of this vessel is filled with hot water to keep the wine in the inner and smaller part warm, for the Chinese prefer drinking warm wine, using very tiny cups for this purpose. Other winepots are filled from a hole in the bottom, and these are modeled in such a way that the liquid is retained when they are turned right side up.

In addition to these pots, various other articles, such as flower vases and pots, bulb bowls, mirror frames, articles for the toilet table, tea table, and the scholar's writing table, were, and still are, being made. The miniature wares—tiny, doll-size tea sets, diminutive wine cups, toilet articles, boxes, beads, rings, ornaments, and toys—are particularly popular.

A fine group of Yi-hsing wares, which have not received the recognition they deserve, are the finely modeled figures that are equal to those made in Tê-hua or in Kuangtung. We have seen few of these outside China.

THE POTTERY WARES OF KUANGTUNG

In the province of Kuangtung there is another large ceramic center, where pottery has been made continuously since the Southern Sung dynasty, and even earlier. A poet-scholar, who was viceroy of the province of Kuangtung during the reign of the Emperor Ch'ien Lung, wrote a poem, part of which, in free translation, reads:

> Since the removal of the pottery kilns to Southern China,
> Though their products are less famous than porcelain,
>   they are of great value.
> One cannot compare this pottery with any other, for it is
>   so simple and ancient-looking.
> Yet it has no clear ringing note—it keeps its mouth shut.

The poet suggests that this Kuangtung pottery lacks one of the qualities that appeal so much to connoisseurs of fine porcelain—it gives forth no musical note when sharply struck.

The verses also refer to the fact that when the Tartars invaded North China many of the potters who made the Chün yao and other Sung porcelains fled south to Kuangtung, where there was still peace. For some time they experimented with the clays in different regions, but in the latter years of the Sung dynasty and through the Yüan dynasty the potteries were located at Yang Chiang. Once established there, these potters and their descendants directed all their efforts toward reproducing the wonderful color effects of the Chün ware—"the red like a rose, the dark violet as black as ink, the reddish brown as if burned by fire, the light green like a tender bamboo leaf, and the deep green color of the peacock's tail." We witnessed their success in achieving these results when, in other parts of China, we were present at hot arguments as to whether certain pieces of Chün ware had been made in the North or the South.

This particular type of Kuangtung ware is usually referred to in the West as Fatshan Chün, for the kilns were located at Fatshan for a short period, apparently having been removed from Yang Chiang when the supply of suitable clay became exhausted. Fatshan, a busy commercial town near Canton, has always been the center from which this pottery was marketed and distributed.

Early in the Ming dynasty the kilns were permanently established at the town of Shekwan (Shihwan), about twenty miles west of Canton. At the entrance to this town, where 50,000 persons are all dependent on the potteries for their living, stands a temple dedicated to the god, or inventor, of the art of pottery making. The town still remains essentially the same as in the Ming dynasty, with kilns of the same structure, where, almost every night, pottery is fired. There is not a piece of modern machinery in the town, and the same ancient processes are used as in the most remote days of the art of the potter's wheel.

It became easy to lose all sense of time in the course of research in this center. There were two young Chinese students, whose fathers were connoisseurs of ceramics, and we asked one of them if his father would spare us a little time in order to help us in verifying our information. He looked reflective, and then said that he thought his friend's father would be of much more help to us. "You see," he said, "my father is from the North, but his father is Cantonese, so he understands things that concern the South better."

When we asked how long his father had lived in Canton, he took out a notebook and started making lengthy calculations. Presently he stated, in a very matter-of-fact way: "It is about thirteen hundred years now since my ancestor incurred the wrath of the emperor and had to flee to the South. We are really a Northern family."

Most of the output of the Kuangtung potteries has consisted of articles for everyday use—receptacles for water, oil, vinegar and wine, rice bowls, cooking utensils, flower pots, teapots, tea bowls, roof tiles, winepots, incense burners, toys, pillows, garden seats, bulb bowls, and vases of all types.

But while the kilns have been engaged for centuries in supplying the daily needs of the local population and in making utilitarian wares for export, they have created much that is purely ornamental. For instance, there are the ducks of Wang Ping, the most famous potter of the last century. We talked with his descendant, who was modeling one of the pottery ducks for which he told us his family had been known for over five hundred years. Most of the potters come of a long family line that has been engaged in the same work, and we saw the children being trained in modeling figures and animals, so that they would be ready to carry on in their turn.

The figure modeling is exceptionally fine, and the older pieces, especially, are vigorous and expressive. Very important, however, is the work of Poon Yok Hsi, who died about 1930. He was the first pottery sculptor in Shekwan, and perhaps the first in China, to depart from depicting the traditional subjects of religious and legendary lore. He took his subjects from his own tragic life, using himself and his concubine among other models. Although his works were eagerly sought by buyers and are now much copied, he died in prison.

Kuangtung pottery is a stoneware. Although the modern pieces are often coarse and heavy, many of the oldest ones are as thin and fine as porcelain. The clay varies, with the result that the body may be light gray, buff, dark gray to black, and dark red to reddish brown. As to the glazes, there is an almost unlimited variety, probably exceeding in number those achieved at Ching-tê Chên. Attempts were made to reproduce the appearance of ancient bronze and ancient jade. There was an iron glaze. There were fine colors such as onion green, melon-skin green, pomegranate red, and eel yellow.

The celadon glazes were successfully copied, and so were the Ming and K'ang Hsi san ts'ai and wu ts'ai. Much admired are fine examples of spotted bamboo glaze, tiger skin glaze, and sapphire blue. The pieces that are best known abroad are those with the Chün type glaze and the *flambé* effects into which this glaze later developed.

One type of Shekwan ware that is most familiar in the West takes the form of trays, small figures, animals, bridges, pagodas, and other accessories that are used in the making of miniature gardens.

When Kuangtung pieces were marked, it was with the seals of the potter, the pottery house, and the household for which the pieces were ordered. No old pieces bore false marks, for it was considered a serious misdemeanor under the old guild rules of Shekwan to forge the name of a potter, or any other mark. Dynastic marks or names of emperors were not used. In fact, in the Kuangtung potteries, as in the other pottery-making districts which are far removed from the capital, little notice was taken of the rulers.

There is an old folk song, dated about 2500 B.C. which runs:

> When the sun rises, I work.
> When the sun sets, I rest.
> I dig the well to drink,
> I plough the field to eat.
> What has the Emperor to do with me?

and which sums up the attitude of the potters in these outlying provinces. A dynastic mark would be used (as in the case of some of the later Yi-hsing copies of Chün ware) only in order to make an imitation piece look more realistic.

THE CH'ING DYNASTY (1644-1912)

The Chinese do not believe in the steady upward march of progress but admit the fact that countries and dynasties—like everything else in nature—have their cycles of youth, maturity, decline, and rebirth. The latter part of the Ming dynasty showed a marked decline in the vigor and integrity of the government, with a corresponding decline in the creative arts. In the last decades it was mainly the large export trade with Western traders, who wanted to fill the holds of their ships with the heavy porcelain that would serve first as ballast and then as a profitable, and easily marketable, commodity, that absorbed most of the output of the ceramic centers. Since there was more interest in quantity and durability than in quality, the products of the kilns naturally tended to deteriorate.

As soon as the stability of the Ming regime was undermined by internal troubles and uprisings, it was menaced by invasion from the outside. By a combination of weakness, folly, and treachery, the whole Chinese empire again passed into the hands of alien rulers when the Manchus established the Ch'ing ("Pure") dynasty in 1644.

Although Peking and the northern provinces fell into the hands of the Manchus as an overripe plum falls from a tree, in other parts of the country there was fierce opposition to the invaders, and many of the finest artists and intellectuals committed suicide or lost their lives fighting in vain for the restoration of a Chinese dynasty.

EMPEROR K'ANG HSI (1662-1722)

Due to the unsettled conditions of the country there was little activity in the field of ceramics at the beginning of the Ch'ing dynasty. The second emperor, K'ang Hsi, ascended the throne at the age of nine. Later, by his administrative ability and also by the fact that he himself was the leader of a great revival of interest in all Chinese arts and crafts, he won the good will of all the people, including the intellectuals.

In 1680, K'ang Hsi established workshops in the Palace precincts for twenty-seven different handicrafts—including lacquer, jade, ivory, glass, and enamel. In the same year he sent an official of the imperial household to reside at the imperial factory in Ching-tê Chên. This had been destroyed in the course of a rebellion between 1673 and 1680, but the emperor ordered it to be rebuilt, and Ching-tê Chên now entered upon an era of the greatest prosperity and achievement.

From 1683 the superintendent of the imperial factory was Ts'ang Ying-hsüan, of whom it was said that: "When he was at work God guided his hand in designing, and also protected the porcelains in the kilns from any mishap." At the same time he was a good administrator, who greatly improved working conditions and raised wages. We read that oppression and exactions were stopped, and the workers were well cared for and contented.

This new sense of well being released a great flood of creative energy, so that the Chinese, and many Westerners, considered that the ceramic art reached its culmination in perfection of technique, quality of material, beauty of design, and brilliance of enamels during this reign. Former styles were developed and improved; many new shapes, colors, glazes, and types of decoration were introduced.

MONOCHROME GLAZES

Outstanding were the new monochrome glazes—apple green and ruby red—which were called Lang yao after Lang T'ing-tso, viceroy of the province of Kiangsi, who was put in charge of Ching-tê Chên, and who is said to have invented these new glazes. The red, derived from copper, is known in the West as *sang de boeuf* (ox-blood). The color varies from bright cherry red to crushed strawberry. The glaze does not lie on the piece evenly but tends to shade off and runs down from the neck, which remains nearly white. It usually stops short of the foot where a whitish rim again appears. The base is glazed either apple-green or white. The technique is similar in the apple-green Lang yao pieces, which also remain whitish around the neck and foot.

These glazes were used on various types of vases and bowls and boxes. To the same group belong the peach-bloom glazes, many of which were applied over a celadon glaze. These were used mostly on smaller pieces, for which collectors were willing to pay very high prices.

Attempts to reproduce these Lang yao glazes in the West have failed because the beauty of the coloring depends entirely on the piece being taken from the kiln at the exact instant.

In connection with this question of firing, Père d'Entrecolles in his famous letter explains: "So the Chinese, whose porcelain is so diversified, employ a methodically irregular furnace which allows them to execute, in the same firing, all the fantasies inspired by their special genius as porcelainiers. They are able, in fact, in one operation, thanks to the irregularity of their furnace, to fire successfully the crackles, which are of difficult fusibility, the flambé reds and the celadons, which require reducing flames, the blue under the glaze, the blacks which fuse so readily, as well as the series of turquoise, green, yellow and violet enamels,—while in Europe, with our furnaces of regular type, three or four different firings would be required to obtain the same results."

Other monochrome glazes were deep blue, peacock green, eel-skin yellow, powder blue (this glaze was blown on the vases in fine powder through gauze stretched over the mouth of a bamboo tube), dark coffee brown to pale gold (called Nanking yellow), mirror black (usually decorated with gold), green-black, apple-green, iron-red, tea dust, and iron dust.

The Palace services were yellow, green, and purple, and, of course, white

168

for mourning. They were decorated with five-claw dragons, usually incised into the paste under the monochrome glaze.

ENAMEL DECORATED PORCELAINS—FAMILLE VERTE, FAMILLE NOIRE, AND FAMILLE JAUNE

While the French terms *famille verte, famille noire,* and *famille jaune* have been generally accepted to describe certain K'ang Hsi porcelains, they are not altogether satisfactory because it is green which predominates in all of them. Even the black is covered with a thin green glaze, and the yellow has a greenish tinge.

These terms are used to describe two groups of porcelains. The *famille verte* group, which follows the five-color Ming porcelains, was painted on a white glazed surface in jewel-like enamels of green, eggplant, yellow, and violet-blue, as well as a pigment of coral red. The other groups—the *famille noire* and the *famille jaune*—are enameled directly on the biscuit and are the successors of the Ming three-color. These were fired without glaze, painted all over directly on the biscuit with transparent enamels in black-green or greenish yellow. This enamel served as a background for free-flowing natural tree and flower designs —such as those of the four seasons: blossoming prunus for winter, tree peony for spring, lotus for summer, and chrysanthemum for autumn—and other designs of the same type, as well as for Taoist and Buddhist symbols. While the colors were less vivid and gemlike, the softer effect was much admired; and these vases, which were often made in large sizes, have been among the costliest of Chinese porcelains. Whatever they may be called, one will find that green is the predominant color, as it is in most K'ang Hsi porcelain.

This same method of enameling on the biscuit was used for many delightful animals and figures, often modeled with charm and humor. The faces and hands were left white.

In the early part of the reign there was a continuation of the Ming tradition of combining enamels with underglaze blue. In the K'ang Hsi pieces there is much use of composite green-black enamel and of gold; the iron-red is thinner, the yellow lighter, and the Ming turquoise is replaced by a cobalt blue violet-toned enamel.

There was little copying of the work of any previous reigns, but only a natural continuation and transition. The K'ang Hsi vases can be distinguished from the Ming not only by the enamels but also by the greater elegance of the forms. This is accentuated in the later pieces where both the form and the drawing become less vigorous, while the enamels become thinner and more delicate.

This trend is very marked in the exquisite "birthday plates," also of the *famille verte,* which were made in the latter part of the reign and which were inscribed around the border with the imperial birthday greeting "Wan shou wu chiang" ("Ten thousand lives without end").

MARKS

A special edict was issued in 1677 by the district magistrate of Ching-tê Chên, forbidding the use of the emperor's name on material which was likely to be broken or defaced. For this reason one finds few pieces with K'ang Hsi seals. In some cases Ming seals were used; in others an artemisia leaf or other symbol, enclosed in a single or double circle, was painted on the base in underglaze blue. Many K'ang Hsi pieces have no mark whatever. Toward the end of the reign this prohibition seems to have fallen into abeyance.

K'ANG HSI BLUE-AND-WHITE

Until quite recently K'ang Hsi "blue-and-white" was considered superior to all others in its perfection of technique, beauty of design, and brilliance of coloring. However, the blue-and-white wares of the Hsüan Tê (Ming) period are now accorded first place because of their greater age, individuality of drawing, and combination of simplicity and strength. The main reason, of course, is that fashions change in collecting as in other things.

The K'ang Hsi blue-and-white owes the deep lustrous tone of its blue to the complete success of experiments in the purification of the native cobalt blue. The result is a dazzling combination of pure white body, clear lustrous glaze, and brilliant sapphire blue applied in graded washes which enhance the depth and movement of the designs. Except in the pieces made for export, they are sparsely decorated so that full value is given to the color and to the material.

One very popular type of the K'ang Hsi blue-and-white is the ovoid jar with cover, known as the prunus, or hawthorne, jar. This is also generally referred to as a ginger jar in the West, but it was made to contain a gift of tea to be presented at the New Year. The jar was considered so valuable that it was the custom to return it to the sender of the gift after the tea had been used up. It has a deep blue ground, broken up with a network of black lines, to suggest ice cracking over the blue water of spring. Lying on the ice are sprays of prunus blossom.

STEATITE OR "SOAPSTONE" PORCELAIN

Among the porcelain wares of the period are the creamy white pieces, called by the Chinese chiang t'ai (paste bodied). By many Western collectors, especially in the United States where they are very popular, they are erroneously designated as soft paste.

According to Père d'Entrecolles, the porcelain was made with a special ingredient, "hua shih" ("slippery stone"), believed to have been soapstone or steatite, so that it has been called steatitic porcelain. Certain experts now state that hua shih is actually pegmatite.

There are two varieties of this ware. In one the hua shih replaces the kaolin, and the porcelain is very light in weight and of fine grain. In the other the pieces are coated with this hua shih.

This type of porcelain is chiefly seen in small objects such as snuff bottles, tiny vases, water pots, and small plates. It was often left in the plain creamy white, with a slight crackle. Sometimes—especially on the larger plates and dishes —it was decorated in underglaze blue. The blue design on this medium has the softness of painting on vellum.

EMPEROR YUNG CHÊNG (1722-1735)

Toward the end of the previous reign (or much earlier according to certain authorities) a rose-pink derived from the use of precipitate of gold ("purple of Cassius") was successfully produced. This led to the introduction of a new type of decoration, in opaque and transparent enamels, in which pink—deepest crimson to palest pearl pink—replaced green as the dominant color, and which is known in the west as the *famille rose*.

The Chinese refer to these porcelains as yang ts'ai (foreign colors) or juan ts'ai (soft colors). It has been suggested that the reason for referring to this coloring as "foreign" is that it was similar to that used in Canton for enamel painting on metal—a process introduced from the West. T'ang Ying, director of the imperial factory from 1736 to 1749, for instance, calls this type of decoration "painting the white porcelain in enamels after the manner of the Western foreigners," and adds that the "colors are the same as those used for enameling on metal."

While pink was the dominant color, the *famille rose* decoration included pale green, yellow, blue, and mauve, with the addition of black, gold, and iron-red. Colors and designs were of a delicate type to suit the fine eggshell porcelain on which they were usually used.

Many of the plates of the Yung Chêng reign have identical decorations on both the back and front. In others the front has a spray of flowers, a single figure, or other restrained design, while the back is painted a deep pink. These are known as "ruby-backs."

THE MAKING OF GLASS AND KU YÜEH-HSÜAN TYPE PORCELAIN

There are only a few scattered references to the early making of glass in Chinese writings, and these usually occur in works concerning ceramics. This may be because in early times the most important use of glass was as the substance to glaze pottery.

Glass was imported into China during the Han dynasty, and in the "Wei Lu" (a work based on the records of the Wei division of the Three Kingdoms A.D. 220-265) we read that ten different colors of opaque glass (liu-li) were then imported from the Roman Empire. Clear glass was also imported.

Judging from the statements in two entirely different historical treatises— one written in North China and the other in South China—the Chinese in both parts of the country began to make glass themselves in the fifth century after Christ. It is claimed that, having found the necessary materials, they were able to make glass which was not only cheaper than the imported product but also of superior color and brilliancy.

171

However, there is reason to believe that actually glass production began much earlier in China, for there have been found in tombs in Loyang (dating back to the Han dynasty at the latest, and believed by some experts to date back to 400 B.C.) glass beads which contain barium, a substance not known to occur in Western or Near Eastern glass before the nineteenth century.

In addition several pieces of glass made in the same forms as Chinese jade tomb objects, including a pi, a cicada, and a fish-shaped girdle pendant, have also been found in the same tombs. These are of greenish or bluish color, and are now decayed and brittle. The glass had evidently been used as a cheaper substitute for jade.

The suggestion has been put forth that these things may have been fashioned of imported glass that had been melted down and then reworked by the Chinese. On the other hand, B. Laufer has remarked that liu-li (opaque glass) was the substance of which the pottery glaze used on Han pottery was made, and he further pointed out that "in the Han period we have accounts of objects wrought from liu-li by Chinese craftsmen." There is no evidence to show that any substantial quantity of glass was made, or whether its manufacture continued over an extended period.

A few interesting pieces of glass, assumed to be of the T'ang dynasty, have been found, and in the "T'ao Shuo" we read: "During the T'ang Dynasty [A.D. 618-907] cups were made of ruddy gold, white jade, engraved silver, rock-crystal and glass, beautifully carved and designed for drinking wine."

T'ang and Sung specimens of glass are still quite rare and difficult to date except by their general shape and type of decoration, as well as by the tomb, or other place, where they were found.

The Chinese did not accord the same standing to glass as they did to porcelain, and little is known about the manufacture of glass before the Ch'ing dynasty, when we find that there was a thriving center of glass manufacture at Po-shan Hsien in Shantung province. Here the production of all types and colors of glass was carried on, and probably had been for centuries past. Some glass was sent in a raw state to Peking, where it was worked up into shapes which were in accordance with the prevailing taste.

The Emperor K'ang Hsi had set up in the Palace precincts, about 1680, a glass atelier to supply the imperial needs. By the eighteenth century the Chinese were highly skilled in all glassmaking processes. They made beautiful semi-opaque glass of various colors, and they were able to imitate hard stones, such as jade, turquoise, onyx, and agate, in glass. They made many snuff bottles which copied those substances.

There was one famous director of this factory, named Hu, who flourished around 1730. He is said to have excelled at turning out opaque vessels in layers of different colored glass, which he carved with cameolike designs, and in painting with enamel colors on clear glass. He showed amazing skill in painting enameled designs inside snuff bottles and other small-mouthed vessels.

The story runs that the Emperor Yung Chêng greatly admired Hu's work, but regretted that such brilliant transparent effects could not be obtained in

Top left: Kansu funerary urn, Pan-shan type. Neolithic period, middle Yang-shao age (ca. 2000 B.C.). Reddish-brown pottery with painted ornament of saw-tooth pattern, spirals in red and black. Eugene Fuller Memorial Collection.

Above: Black pottery stem bowl, from Liang-chu, Chekiang. Burnished black, stem with parallel rings. Late neolithic period prior to 1500 B.C.

Left: Prehistoric pottery jar.

Soft white pottery jar, unglazed. Decorated with carved design in countersunk relief in two registers. Shang Dynasty (14th-12th century B.C.) from Anyang.

Black pottery jar with scroll ornaments in low relief. Chou Dynasty.

Round pottery box with cover. Traces of red pigment. Chou Dynasty.

Black pottery amphora from Szechüan (ca. 1500 B.C.). Bromberger Collection.

Two tomb figures, high-fired, lacquered black clay, from Hui Hsien, Honan province (type as yet unpublished). Late Chou (first half of 5th century B.C.).

High-fired large jar, glazed at top. Ca. 3rd century B.C.

Covered Tou (burnished black pottery painted in red pigment). Bronze shape. From Hui Hsien, Honan province. Late Chou period (5th-3rd century B.C.). Eugene Fuller Memorial Collection.

Pottery facsimile of a bronze bell, covered with black lacquer and cinnabar. Late Chou Dynasty (Warring States). Believed to be from Hui Hsien, Honan.

Detail of vase in shape of bronze Hu. Proto-porcelain, olive-green glaze covering upper body and portions of neck. Upper body ornamented with two bands of incised design of interlaced birds. Han Dynasty.

Honolulu Academy of Arts

Los Angeles County Museum

Pair of pottery horses. Wei or Six Dynasties.

Pottery horse. Wei Dynasty, ca. A.D. 550.

Camel and rider, pottery, yellow-brown, green, and white glazes. T'ang Dynasty.

Equestrienne dismounting, pottery. T'ang Dynasty.

Figures of female dancers and musicians. T'ang Dynasty.

Above: Covered jar, glazed. T'ang Dynasty.

Left: Merchant holding wine skin vessel. T'ang Dynasty.

Covered jar and small water pot, san ts'ai (three-color) type. Glazed and decorated in green, yellow, and blue. T'ang Dynasty.

Below: Dish on three legs. Glazed earthenware with buff body, stained green and orange. Technique similar to that later used on cloisonné enamel. T'ang Dynasty. Eumorfopoulos Collection.

Clay tomb figure of warrior. T'ang Dynasty.

Bowls of Chün yao ware. Sung Dynasty.

Vase, spotted Yüeh ware, probably from the Chiu-yen kilns. Gray stoneware, with greenish transparent glaze on upper portion. Blackish brown iron oxide spots on mouth. Six Dynasties (4th-6th century). Wright S. Ludington Collection.

Vase of Tz'ŭ Chou ware. Sung Dynasty.

Pottery dog. T'ang Dynasty.

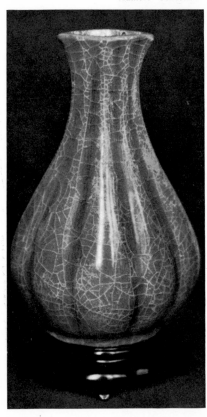

Left: Vase of Ying Ch'ing porcelain. Yellowish body, pale blue glaze. Late T'ang or early Sung Dynasty. *Above:* Lotus-shaped Southern kūan yao bottle. Sung Dynasty.

Honolulu Academy of Arts

Above: Ying Ch'ing ewer. Sung Dynasty.

Right: Vase. Tz'ǔ Chou ware. Sung Dynasty.

Below: Ju-i or cloud-shaped pillow. Tz'ǔ Chou ware. Sung Dynasty.

Cincinnati Art Museum

Los Angeles County Museum

Authors' Collection

Three articles in everyday use—a vase for a single
flower, a rice bowl, and a wine pot. Tz'ŭ Chou
ware. The bowl is painted in green and red which
have become oxidized. Sung Dynasty.

Los Angeles County Museum

Jar with cover. Tz'ŭ Chou ware. Sung Dynasty.

Left: Tall, wide-lipped vase. Tz'ŭ Chou ware.
Sung Dynasty.

Freer Gallery of Art, Washington

Above: Vase. Lung-ch'üan celadon. Sung Dynasty.

Right: Lung-ch'üan celadon vase. Sung Dynasty.

Below: Jar and bowls. Chien yao stoneware. Sung Dynasty. Herman and Paul Jaehne Collection.

Collection Mrs. Margot Holmes

Left to right: Tz'ǔ Chou pottery bowl with red and green decoration. Sung Dynasty. Black Chien yao bowl with silvery oil spots. Sung Dynasty. Shu Fu ware bowl, with incised floral decoration inside. Yüan Dynasty. Chün yao bowl with red and blue glaze. Sung Dynasty.

Honolulu Academy of Arts

Honolulu Academy of Arts

Above: Northern celadon bowl. Sung Dynasty.

Right: Kinuta shaped vase, Lung-ch'üan celadon ware. Blue glaze. Sung Dynasty.

Ivory-colored bowl of porcelaneous stoneware with lotus pattern incised. Southern Ting ware. Sung Dynasty. Herman and Paul Jaehne Collection.

Ko yao bowl. Sung Dynasty.

Blue and white vase, double gourd shape. Ming. Chia Ching period (1522-1566).

Brooklyn Museum

Right: White ewer, underglaze floral engraving. Ming Dynasty. Yung Lo period (1403-1424). Eli Lilly Collection.

John Herron Art Institute, Indianapolis

Above: Porcelain bowl with underglaze painting in cobalt blue. Ming. Mark and period of the reign of Hsüan Tê (1426-1435).

Porcelain cup stand, decorated in underglaze lavender. Late 14th century.

Honolulu Academy of Arts

189

Blue and white porcelain vase
with five-clawed dragon. Ming,
Hsüan Tê (1426-1435).

Blue and white porcelain bowl.
Ming. Chia Ching period and
mark (1522-1566).

...lue and white bowl. Ming. ...eign of Hsüan Tê (1426-1435).

...air of small bowls, eggshell por-...elain, decorated with chickens ...nd rockery in tou ts'ai colors. ...Ming. Reign of Ch'êng Hua ...1465-1487).

...ctagonal bowl, blue and white, ...ith reticulated ling lung ...pierced work) medallions. Ming. ...Mark and period of Chia Ching ...1522-1566). Roy Leventritt Col-...ection.

Beaker-shaped vase. Three-color decoration on yellow ground. Ming Dynasty. John L. Severance Collection.

Dish of Chinese blue-and-white porcelain of the Wan Li period (1573-1619), decorated with silvergilt mounts made in London about 1585.

Cleveland Museum of Art

Metropolitan Museum of Ar

City Art Museum of St. Louis

Freer Gallery of Art, Washington

Above: Yi-hsing fine stoneware fluted teapot of light brown unglazed clay by Ch'ên Ming-yüan (fl. 1573-1629). Ming.

Right: Tê Hua teapot. Blanc de chine. Ming dynasty. Samuel C. Davis Bequest.

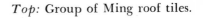

Top: Group of Ming roof tiles.

Center, left: Blue and white porcelain box with lid, showing children at play. Ming. Reign of Wan Li (1573-1619).

Center, right: Tê-hua porcelain stem cup (blanc de chine). 17th century.

On left: Large vase with figure of leaping carp. Ch'ien Lung. *On right:* Ming Dynasty vase. Both from Ching-tê Chên.

Left: Pottery figure of the poet Li Po made in the kilns at Shekwan (Kuangtung province). 18th century. *Right:* Shekwan pottery from Kuangtung. Pale yellow glazed bowl with green medallions. Ming Dynasty. *Below:* Porcelain, decorated in *famille verte* style. Ch'ing Dynasty, K'ang Hsi period (1662-1722). Eugene Fuller Memorial Collection.

Private Collection

Authors' Collection

Seattle Art Museum

City Art Museum of St. Louis

Above: Figure of Kwan Yin, Goddess of Mercy, decorated in *famille verte* colors. K'ang Hsi period (1662-1722). Samuel C. Davis Collection.

Right: Porcelain covered bowl. White design in reserve on dark blue ground. Mark and period of Yung Chêng (1722-1735).

Honolulu Academy of Arts

Three-color vase and cover, *famille noire*. Reign
of K'ang Hsi (1662-1722).

195

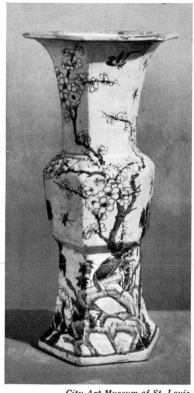

Top, left: Blue and white covered prunus jar with branches of prunus blossom reserved in white on ground of cracking ice in underglaze blue. Used as New Year gifts, filled with tea. Ch'ing Dynasty. K'ang Hsi period (1662-1722). *Above:* Tall vase, decorated in three-color enamels. Ch'ing Dynasty. Gift of Samuel C. Davis. *Below:* Bowl of transparent glass. Engraved. Probably Sung Dynasty.

Above, right: Ch'ien Lung glass bowl decorated in the Ku-yüeh Hsüan style. *Left:* Glass snuff bottle, Imperial Ku-yüeh Hsüan oval flask with black ground minutely flecked with gold. Decoration in *famille rose* colors. Six-character mark of reign in blue underfoot. Ch'ien Lung period (1736-1795).

196

porcelain. T'ang Ying, of the imperial porcelain factory, who was ready to meet every challenge, managed to produce small vessels of a vitreous porcelain of exceptional transparency, and painted them in a combination of brilliant *famille rose* and *famille verte* colors. Some of these pieces he inscribed: "Modeled on the pattern of the Ku Yüeh-hsüan."

The name Ku Yüeh-hsüan, which means "Ancient Moon Terrace," was a sobriquet derived from his own name by the glass-maker Hu. It has been objected that this same name is given to the maker of the glass, to his workshop, to the porcelain, and to the place where the finest enameled wares were stored. To the Chinese none of these things are contradictory. Most Chinese artists and craftsmen adopt a fancy name and call their studio or workshop by that name. Once a particular type of work had won special admiration, it would be considered natural that the Palace pavilion where the finest enameled porcelains were stored would be called by that name. As to the porcelain itself, this is not called Ku Yüeh-hsüan, but Fang Ku Yüeh Hsüan, which means "Copy of the Ancient Moon Terrace work," or else "In the style of" or "Modeled after" Ku Yüeh-hsüan.

The best artists in the Palace made pictures for these brilliant glasslike porcelains, including the Jesuit Court painters, who contributed designs with foreign motifs and figures.

On some pieces there is inscribed a verse signed with red seals and, on the base, the reign mark appears in blue enamel.

Ku Yüeh-hsüan pieces, whether in glass or in porcelain, are very rare and extremely costly. Alfred E. Hippisley, who was a Commissioner in the Imperial Maritime Customs Service of China, and who was probably the first to bring this type of ware to the attention of the Western world, writes: ". . . under the auspices of T'ang Ying, all the artistic and technical skill of the government factory was lavished upon these little gems, which are certainly among the masterpieces, if not *the* masterpieces, of ceramic art in China . . ."

SNUFF BOTTLES

T'ang Ying inspired a great number of new types of snuff bottles. These little bottles, with a small spoon attached to the stopper, were originally made to hold aromatics or medicines and were called "yao p'ing" (medicine bottles). The early ones, specimens of which date back to the Sung dynasty and earlier, were usually simple in shape and without decoration.

They apparently began to be used for snuff late in the Ming dynasty, and from that time onward they were made in endless variety and were used as a medium for displaying creative imagination and exquisite workmanship. In the reigns of Yung Chêng and Ch'ien Lung they were made of cameo carved glass, silver, jade, crystal, onyx, turquoise, amber, coral, agate, cloisonné enamel, painted enamel, *burgautée* lacquer, cinnabar lacquer, bronze, tortoise shell, ivory, and mother-of-pearl, as well as in porcelain which imitated all the above-mentioned materials. Snuff bottles were also made in the various types of pottery and porcelain.

They were turned out in every shape and color—in the form of all types of small vessels, and shaped as fruits, flowers, insects, butterflies, men, women, children, animals, gourds, leaves, ears of corn, boats, birds, Taoist deities, and famous beauties.

Many important collections have consisted only of medicine and snuff bottles, and the majority of the specimens date from the Ch'ing dynasty.

THE INFLUENCE OF T'ANG YING, THE FAMOUS DIRECTOR OF THE IMPERIAL KILNS

There were three kiln directors who dominated the history of porcelain making during the Ch'ing dynasty. The first was Ts'ang Ying-hsüan who worked in the reign of K'ang Hsi. He was followed by Nien Hsi-yao, whose works were known as Nien yao (Nien wares). His porcelains were chiefly of the monochrome type (occasionally decorated with flowers in white and gold on a black ground). The colors he used most were white, clair-de-lune, pale green, lavender, peach-bloom, soft pink, and also egg-yellow, emerald-green, and bright ruby-red.

The most famous director of them all, however, was T'ang Ying, who worked at Ching-tê Chên from 1727 to 1749. He wrote a most clear and detailed account of his term of office, and of all the processes of porcelain making, which is an invaluable guide to students of that subject. He explains that, for the first three years, he always had his meals with the workmen, and he slept in the same room with them. In this way he was able to familiarize himself with every detail of his craft. He further improved the living standards of the workers, looking after them "in cases of disease and trouble"; and the artisans responded by doing their best work for him.

In the reign of Yung Chêng there was a great vogue for reproducing old glazes and forms. Sung and Ming porcelains were sent from the Palace in Peking and were copied with the greatest attention to detail. The emperor ordered them as he might order a new edition of an old classic, with no intent to deceive, and they usually bore his own seals.

Much of the success in copying these old pieces was due to T'ang Ying. It was he, too, who succeeded in making, and decorating with *famille rose* colors, the huge fish bowls used in the Imperial Gardens which occupied a whole kiln and took fourteen days to fire. At some time in the Ming dynasty the potters had found themselves unable to make any more of these very large pieces. Under his direction there was also much skillful work done in repairing damaged old pieces.

T'ang Ying continued to work right into the next reign (that of Ch'ien Lung), making the finest of eggshell porcelain, the daintiest snuff bottles, and delicate, translucent hexagonal lanterns with pierced panels, decorated in *famille rose* enamels. He was able to control completely the flambé glaze effects, which

198

had previously proved so unpredictable. This was a glaze of copper-red type, in which the red was streaked with purples, blues, grays, and other shades.

He felt so completely in command of all the processes of porcelain making and all the vagaries of the furnaces, that he was always seeking new ways to display his skill. He liked to make porcelains which copied other materials—gold, silver, bronze, jade, grained wood, lacquer, and enamel. He made vases and snuff bottles coated with black enamel with inlaid designs of mother-of-pearl (lac *burgautée*), and was the first to use silver as a decoration.

OTHER PORCELAINS OF THE YUNG CHÊNG PERIOD

In addition to the copying of old porcelains, many fresh ideas in both color and decoration were introduced. The new monochrome glazes included cloisonné blue and purple, enameled silver, and line painting on the glaze in black and sepia which looks like Chinese black-and-white scroll painting. Gold was used, but with great restraint, and, in some pieces, red and gold, and black and gold, were effectively combined.

Another type of decoration which was revived was the tou ts'ai enameling of the Ch'êng Hua period. While the same technique—drawing the designs in underglaze blue and then filling them in with thin, softly colored enamels—was used, the designs were quite different. They usually consisted of a natural looking spray of blossom, a single flower, or a bird on a branch. Decoration was kept to a minimum. There was no crowding and no elaborate border.

The blue-and-white porcelains were not remarkable except for the excellent copies of Ming pieces.

EMPEROR CH'IEN LUNG (1736-1795)

The reigns of K'ang Hsi, Yung Chêng, and Ch'ien Lung covered a period of internal stability, peace, and progress. There were reform in government, increased opportunities for education, and encouragement of all the arts.

Most of the decorated porcelains were of the *famille rose* type. New monochrome enamels and variations of existing colors were introduced. These included a dark purplish blue, brown, aubergine, yellowish green, opaque ruby-pink, robin's egg, turquoise, crackled brown and buff, camelia leaf-green, emerald-green, bronze-green, tea dust, and iron rust.

In decorating porcelains, the potters turned more and more to nature for their designs; and, in addition to such subjects as sprays of flowers, they made porcelains with the "Hundred Flower" design, usually on a gold background. The flowers were so perfectly blended that the effect achieved was like a well-designed brocade. Other designs that were skillfully used on porcelain were the "Hundred Horses" (from a famous painting by Han Kan) and the "Hundred Deer." The term "hundred" when applied to subjects of decoration is not mathematically accurate, but is often used merely to signify a large number.

There was a new type of bowl known by various names such as Peking, medallion, and "graviata" bowls. These were made of fine porcelain, covered with a monochrome enamel in different colors—iron-red, pink, green, blue, and yellow, often engraved all over with scrollwork (graviata) under the enamel. Four white medallions were left in reserve, and these were painted in *famille rose* colors with freely drawn designs of flowers and figures. Many of them had European figures. The bowls were made as imperial gifts, the ones with foreign figures being designed for presentation to foreigners. These bowls continued to be made throughout the reigns of Ch'ien Lung, Chia Ch'ing, and Tao Kuang.

Another type of porcelain decoration took the form of lacework. Patterns were deeply incised in the biscuit, and then covered and filled in with greenish white glaze. The so-called "rice grain" vessels belong to this group. Transparencies were formed by cutting out of the paste small pieces—about the size of a grain of rice—and then letting the glaze fill the perforations.

Among the most successful of the Ch'ien Lung porcelains are the charming figures enameled in *famille rose* colors. But above all the kilns were devoted to the production of flower vases and bowls in all shapes, sizes, and types. Over the years, an average Chinese household accumulated numbers of vases, and an appropriate one was selected for each kind of flower or occasion. A branch of prunus blossom, a single peony, a bunch of chrysanthemums, or a wild orchid, each would be placed in a different shaped vase. The "T'ao Shuo" ("A Description of Chinese Pottery"), published in 1774 and translated by S. W. Bushell, states:

> Large vases are preferred for the hall and reception room, small ones for the library. Copper and porcelain are esteemed above gold and silver, to cultivate simplicity; rings and pairs should be avoided, and rarity be the quality specially aimed at. The mouth should be small, the foot thick, so that the vase may stand firmly and not emit vapor. If the mouth be large, a tube of tin should be fitted inside, to hold the flowers upright.

The emperor himself was an enthusiastic collector of porcelain, and, when he handled his beloved pieces, he was often inspired to write poems about them. These were inscribed in facsimile on the pieces, which were then reglazed. It is recorded that there were 195 pieces in the palace which had such poems engraved on them.

In regard to the porcelains produced during these reigns, Alfred E. Hippisley, wrote in 1887: "During the 75 years between 1698 and 1773, the manufacture and decoration of porcelain in China attained a degree of excellence, which, in my opinion, has never been reached either before or since."

Ch'ing porcelains are of particular interest to Western collectors because they make up the great bulk of the fine ceramic pieces to be found in homes, collections, or in the stocks of dealers. They are distinguished not only because of their delicacy, color, and beauty, but also because they provided the models for most European porcelain and pottery. The time when they were made was contemporaneous with the periods in decoration best known to us—Louis XIV, Louis XV, Louis XVI, and the Directoire (1643-1799), and most pieces of Ch'ing porcelain fit into one or another of those settings. In fact, many art historians agree that without the important influence of Chinese artistic skill, there would not have been the baroque and rococo periods in France and the rest of Europe.

THE IMPACT ON THE WEST

In *Civilization on Trial,* Arnold J. Toynbee writes:

> The Empire over which he [Ch'ien Lung] ruled was the oldest, most successful, and the most beneficent, of all living political institutions. Its foundation in the 3rd century B.C. had given a civilized world a civilized government conducted by a competitively recruited, and highly cultivated, Civil Service, in place of an international anarchy in which a number of parochial states, dominated by a hereditary feudal nobility had plagued mankind by waging perpetual war with one another. During the twenty intervening centuries, this carefully ordered world peace had occasionally lapsed, but such lapses had always been temporary, and, at the close of Ch'ien Lung's reign, the latest restoration of "the Middle Kingdom" was in its heyday.

These Ch'ing rulers had based their rule on the Chinese ideal that Heaven and Earth and Man were to live in harmony together, obeying the laws of God. The order and rhythm of Heaven were to flow through everything into the smallest details of human life, just as it flowed into the smallest bird and leaf, and moulded them after its pattern.

As more and more reports of this fabulous empire seeped through to the outside world, the vogue for all things Chinese increased. The Jesuit priests brought accounts of this faraway land to France, and many intellectuals there felt that the solution of the problems of Europe in the eighteenth century could be found by studying the philosophy and organization of China.

From the ideas and principles of China, many Europeans turned to an interest in what they considered to be the art of China, and this feeling snowballed until it became almost a "craze" for *chinoiserie.* In 1667 Louis XIV wore what was thought to be an Oriental costume at a Court ball, and this started a fashion which by 1725 had spread all over Europe. This was no short-lived fad but continued for well over a century, and we read that in 1756, at the suggestion of Madame La Pompadour, Louis XV guided a plough on the first day of spring, following the custom of the emperors of China.

A further impetus was given to this vogue in England in mid-eighteenth century when Sir William Chambers, a fashionable architect, who had visited Canton in his youth and had made sketches of the most ornate Chinese kiosks and pavilions, published a book of what he termed Chinese designs, based on these drawings. This was followed by Chippendale designing furniture, which he imagined to be in the Chinese style and which became known as Chinese Chippendale. Chinese pagodas were erected in Kew Gardens in London, at Het Loo in Holland, and on the property of the Duc de Choiseul in France.

The current mode in Europe was for the quaint and the exotic, for things that were ingenious and elaborate and "pretty"—in fact, for everything implied in the term "rococo." It mattered little that most of this European *chinoiserie* was based on fantastic notions of China and Chinese art. It suited the taste of the time.

And this taste was not so far removed from that of the Courts of the emperors K'ang Hsi and Ch'ien Lung as it might have been from either those of earlier Chinese rulers or from Chinese art centers remote from the Court. In China, too, the Court was seeking for things novel, colorful, intricate, and amusing. So Europe played with the toys of *chinoiserie* and, at the same time, respected and admired the Chinese philosophy and way of life.

The Chinese provided suitable porcelains, silks, and wallpapers for the people in the West, while in Peking the Jesuit priests painted pictures for the amusement of the emperor and his courtiers. The Landgrave of Kessel ordered a model Chinese village to be built where he and his entourage could play at being Chinese, and in Peking the Jesuits drew up plans for part of the Yüan Ming Yüan (the Summer Palace) to be laid out in the same manner as Versailles. When it was completed, the Chinese went there to fêtes, where they enjoyed fountain and firework displays in the French style, to the accompaniment of English and French music played by concealed orchestras.

Before the end of the eighteenth century the rage for *chinoiserie* in the Western world had at last begun to abate. It had done little to bring about a better understanding between the East and the West. The Europeans, judging China by their own efforts at *chinoiserie*, were left with the impression that Chinese art consisted of meticulous, quaint, highly colored pictures and objects. They remained in complete ignorance of the tremendous output of austere monochrome artists, who depended for their effects on nobility of line and the masterly use of blank spaces. They knew nothing of the strength or simplicity of Chinese pottery and porcelain that had been made to suit the Chinese taste. The Chinese, on the other hand, judged Western art by the elaborate and fussy clocks and watches which they had received as gifts and which the Emperor Ch'ien Lung described as "objects strange and ingenious."

THE CHINESE EXPORT TRADE

Portuguese navigators had arrived in Canton about 1514, and they were allowed to trade, enjoying a virtual monopoly until the Dutch East India Company was formed in 1602.

The English East India Company was established in the reign of Queen Elizabeth, but for a long time it was excluded from entering into trade relations with the Chinese by the Portuguese and the Dutch. In 1640 a British factory, or "hong," as the offices of foreign trading companies in China were called, was set up in Canton.

During the Ch'ing dynasty, East India companies were established in China by Spain, Portugal, Holland, England, France, Denmark, and Sweden, and an important export trade was carried on. At first it had been mostly celadon that was exported abroad, but in 1712 Père d'Entrecolles wrote that no type of porcelain but "blue-and-white" was sent to Europe. The same fact was reported by another French writer as late as 1747. This "blue-and-white" was the product of private potters and not of the imperial factory.

It was in the reign of K'ang Hsi that Ching-tê Chên first made porcelains in special forms and designs for the export trade. Among the first pieces especially made for Westerners were those known as "Jesuit China," which were said to have been designed by the Jesuits. These were usually blue-and-white, but painted with Catholic scenes, crucifixes, saints, clasped hands, and the like.

Another type of Jesuit porcelain was decorated with religious scenes drawn in black and sepia on a white background, which appear to have been copied from foreign religious engravings. Later, many of these Jesuit pieces were decorated in *famille rose* colors in Canton, in the same way as the other export porcelains.

But it was not only Jesuit China that was made for export in Ching-tê Chên. Quantities of blue-and-white porcelains were decorated according to designs sent from the agents in Canton, and these were made not only for all parts of Europe but also for the Near East.

The Dutch were among the chief importers of Chinese wares, and it is not surprising that many of these pieces were decorated with Dutch designs. The manufacture of Delft ware in Holland was, as we already know, greatly influenced by the first shipments of Chinese blue-and-white porcelains that arrived in their country, and their potters tried to imitate the Chinese pieces as closely as they could. At first they copied only the idea of making blue-and-white wares, using Dutch designs, but quite early they showed a preference for Chinese designs, and strove to make their products look as much like Chinese porcelain as the medium would permit.

One of the first to introduce these Chinese designs into the decoration of Delft faïence was Aelbrecht Cornelis de Keizer, who, from 1648, was made master of the Guild of St. Luke. His example was copied in other workshops and by about the year 1700 hardly any but Chinese designs were used.

Père d'Entrecolles complained that the porcelains ordered by European merchants were "often bizarre and difficult to manufacture properly." The foreign traders frequently wanted "quaint" and "grotesque" pieces; and, in order to please them, the potters would put several designs on the same piece—which made them confused and meaningless to the Chinese whose own simple decoration conveyed a clear message.

During the reign of K'ang Hsi the bulk of the decorated porcelain for the export trade was made at Ching-tê Chên, and then sent to Canton, from where it was shipped by the respective traders who were restricted to that one port. The armorial services made at Ching-tê Chên were decorated in underglaze blue and afterward with *famille verte* enamels, processes which could not be carried out elsewhere.

In the eighteenth century the idea gained ground that the orders for special decoration in the European taste might be more conveniently carried out in Canton, where the representatives of the export firms could supervise the painting of their own designs. The workshops of Canton were already engaged in the similar craft of painting in enamel colors on copper, and so it was arranged for the plain white glazed porcelain bodies to be shipped down from Ching-tê Chên to Canton where the "foreign colors" could be added.

This developed into a special type of work carried on only for the European and American markets. Many large dinner services were decorated with the armorial bearings of the European families for which they were destined.

A group of vases that was very popular with the Western traders was the one they called Mandarin porcelain. These were decorated all over in scrollwork in *famille rose* colors, with white panels left in reserve on which were painted Chinese figures in mandarin dress. These can be classed only as *Chinoiserie*.

Another type of porcelain which might come under the heading of *chinoiserie* is that with the blue-and-white willow pattern design. Thomas Turner of the Caughley Pottery works in England first made this design in 1780. The purely imaginary picture, which was not based upon any Chinese legend or story, was inspired by, but not copied from, the landscapes on Chinese blue-and-white porcelains.

The pattern became enormously popular. It was soon made by many other English pottery houses, and was then sent to China, where it was copied and exported to the West in large quantities. The Chinese even built up an elaborate story around the English drawn design, and explained that the name "willow pattern" derived from the fact that the incident it illustrated took place "when the willow tree was beginning to shed its leaves."

There has been an extraordinary amount of confusion and misunderstanding in regard to the Chinese export ware, especially in the United States. In 1863, William Chaffers, in his book *Marks and Monograms on Pottery and Porcelain,* classed Lowestoft ware as "hard paste porcelain," and mistakenly attributed all the Chinese export ware to the Lowestoft factory in England.

Since then the actual facts have been clearly demonstrated again and again. There was a small factory in Lowestoft, England, which manufactured a certain amount of soft paste porcelain between 1756 and 1807. Some of the articles were decorated with Chinese designs, and on others the decoration was similar to the English motifs on the export porcelains from China, destined for the British market. Most of the products of this factory, except for pieces which carried such inscriptions as "Made in Lowestoft" or "A Trifle from Lowestoft," bore marks that were imitations of those on the wares of other English factories or on Chinese pieces.

Nevertheless, an amazing amount of confusion still persists about this porcelain, and many persons continue to talk about "Chinese Lowestoft" and "Oriental Lowestoft," although the museums now call it by its correct name of Chinese Export porcelain.

The first American ship to engage in the China trade was the *Empress of China,* which went to Canton in 1785. The story of the China trade brings back to Americans thoughts of the time when the country was not yet industrialized, and when its people longed for the household goods and luxuries that they were unable to produce.

It brings to mind the young men (many of them hardly out of their teens) who sailed from the eastern ports of America to China. Their main difficulty at that time was that they had neither the money nor the goods which would enable them to pay for the Chinese wares. This led to a frantic search, with the young American sea captains scouring the northern waters for furs and the South Sea islands for products such as sandalwood, which the Chinese would be willing to accept as barter. Eventually, when many such sources of supplies appeared to be exhausted, the pleasing discovery was made that New England was able to grow a root called ginseng, which the Chinese highly valued for medicinal purposes, and of which they were willing to accept almost unlimited quantities in exchange for their goods.

This trade in Export porcelain between the United States and China was carried on for over a hundred years. Not only was it a highly profitable one for all parties concerned, but the Western traders learned that the Chinese merchants scrupulously fulfilled all obligations, and that their word meant more than any written contract.

Among the most sought-after patterns of Chinese Export porcelains in the United States are the pieces made for the Society of the Cincinnati, those with the American eagle design, and those with the arms of the states—such as New York and Pennsylvania.

THE LATER REIGNS OF THE CH'ING DYNASTY: CHIA CH'ING (1796-1820)

There is very little difference between Ch'ien Lung porcelains and those made in the early part of the reign of Chia Ch'ing. They were made by the same potters working in the same tradition, and are notable for their delicate finely drawn designs and perfection of technique. There was elaborate decoration in underglaze blue, with much overglaze gilding. In general, gold was used more lavishly than before. Among the best new monochrome glazes were a coral-red and an imperial yellow. However, even a practiced eye would find it difficult to distinguish between many of the pieces of this reign and those of Ch'ien Lung, except for the fact that they usually bear the seal of Chia Ch'ing.

Like his father, Chia Ch'ing liked writing poems to be inscribed on his favorite old pieces of porcelain. Such pieces are often more highly valued by the Chinese than those of Ch'ien Lung because they are much rarer.

Unfortunately Chia Ch'ing was a man given to dissipation who lacked the wisdom and administrative qualities of the earlier Ch'ing rulers, and his reign marked the beginning of the decline of the Manchu dynasty. In the later part of the reign the output of the porcelain factories deteriorated in quantity and quality.

TAO KUANG (1821-1850)

Again most of the porcelains closely followed those made earlier. Some of the most exquisite work of the period is seen on articles of general use, such as soup, rice and tea bowls, wine cups, and the medallion (or Peking) bowls already described.

There was great activity in the ceramic industry, including a revival of widespread copying of Ming, K'ang Hsi, and Ch'ien Lung pieces. Many new shapes and types of decoration were introduced. The *famille verte* colors were used as frequently as those of the *famille rose*, although decoration in brown and pink and gold remained very popular. There was a revival, too, of the Ch'êng Hua type of tou ts'ai decoration in clear enamels over designs of underglaze blue.

Tao Kuang made a sincere attempt to reform some of the abuses of his father's reign, but his efforts were foiled by the wars between China and both England and France, followed by the outbreak of the T'ai P'ing Rebellion.

HSIEN FÊNG (1851-1861)

It was in the midst of the T'ai P'ing Rebellion, with its unprecedented wiping out of millions of lives, its sacking of towns, its devastation of sixteen out of the eighteen provinces of the Chinese Empire, its burning of libraries, destruction of art treasures, and orgy of murder, looting, burning, and drowning, that the Emperor Hsien Fêng ascended the throne. In 1853, Ching-tê Chên was besieged and taken. The imperial potteries were burned to the ground, and the workers were massacred or driven away. Despite this, there exists a small quantity of fine porcelain with the mark of Hsien Fêng, which must have been made in the first years of his reign.

T'UNG CHIH (1862-1873)

The T'ai P'ing rebels were finally driven out of Kiangsi by Li Hung-chang, and in 1865 the imperial porcelain factory was rebuilt. The dinner and tea services made there are commonly described as "clean" and "pretty." There were some new colors and new combinations of colors—much pale green and pink and pale blue—and they are usually decorated with small patterned designs. Many of the bowls are lined inside with a pale green glaze.

KUANG HSÜ (1874-1908)

In this reign many pieces were painted with delicate designs in enamels in the Ku Yüeh-hsüan style. The colors of the *famille verte* were more used than those of the *famille rose*. Some porcelains were decorated with line drawings in black or sepia, sometimes with touches of color in enamels. A popular form of decoration consisted of butterflies or flowers drawn in black and white on a pale turquoise ground.

At first there was promise of a new era of progress in the ceramic industry, but it was short-lived. After the Boxer Uprising in 1900—another orgy of looting and destruction, when the great Han-lin Academy with its unique and vast collection of ancient literary works was burned—the Chinese Revolution of 1912 brought the Ch'ing dynasty to an end.

PORCELAINS OF THE CH'ING DYNASTY

The Chinese do not consider the Ch'ing dynasty a period of decadence in porcelain, but consider that in the reigns of the emperors K'ang Hsi, Yung Chêng, and Ch'ien Lung it reached the height of technical perfection.

Some westerners are often curiously eager to apply the word "decadence" to something as strong and vital and as fundamental to their culture as is Chinese art. And they apply the word with a curious lack of consistency. Some say that only the older Chinese pieces have merit, yet they find it a sign of "decadence" that the Chinese appreciate their own antiques enough to want to copy them or to continue working in the same tradition. Then, during the Ming and Ch'ing dynasties, when every effort was made to perfect the manufacture of porcelain, this was, of course, called a sign of "decadence" because the vessels produced were different from those which had preceded them. Having completely mastered all the techniques of the ceramic arts, the potters strove to show their skill by creating new things. This too was a proof of "decadence." When the *famille verte* enamels were superseded by the *famille rose* enamels, the pieces turned out were scoffed at as "too pretty" and hence, once more, "decadent." Even T'ang Ying's charming little porcelain creations done in the "rococo" spirit of the time, which resembled glass, jade, and other hard stones, are singled out by some Western writers as a sign of complete "decadence." If it was "decadent" to copy the old, it is, in some quarters, regarded as even more so to create new styles and designs.

As far as the later reigns of the Ch'ing dynasty are concerned, when we consider that for more than a century China has never known a stretch of even ten continuous years without foreign wars or internal uprisings and disturbances, it is almost incredible that such a quantity of fragile and beautiful porcelain was turned out, and that so much of it still survives.

The Chinese highly value fine specimens of Ch'ing porcelain—even those of the latest periods—for in the course of time they must inevitably become more and more rare, and they can never be replaced. There are millions of graves in all parts of China; and it is probable that, when excavations on a large scale are resumed, many new sources of Han, T'ang and Sung specimens will come to light. But there will be no new sources of Ch'ing porcelain to replace those that are destroyed.

The above is the Chinese point of view, but in China the love of old things is so widespread that matters relating to value are the subjects of much study and forethought. For instance, during the Japanese war, many Chinese put their money into antiques, saying: "Governments come and go, money goes up and down, but genuine antiques never lose their value."

Old porcelains and other antique pieces give the Chinese a real sense of security and permanence. It reassures them to feel that China has passed through so many vicissitudes since these things were fashioned, and yet they have survived triumphantly just as has the real spirit of China.

IV: *EARLY CHINESE CULTURE EXPRESSED IN BRONZE*

Chapter VI

BRONZES

SHANG-YIN DYNASTY (1525 B.C. TO 1028 B.C.*)

THE POWERFUL IMPACT of the earliest known Chinese bronzes—those of the Shang-Yin period—on people interested in Chinese art is due to their great age, the technical perfection of the casting, the grandeur of the shapes, the revealing ideas suggested by the motifs, and the amazing artistic skill with which those ideas have been translated into decorative designs. Above all, nothing about these bronzes is more impressive than the fact of their existence.

The Chinese themselves have known all along that there were Shang-Yin bronzes, and specimens have been included in Chinese collections; but, as we have repeatedly pointed out, many Western students have had no confidence in Chinese historical records. It is only within recent times that Western connoisseurs would even concede that the Chou period was a historical one. The Shang-Yin, and all preceding ones, were still called "legendary" at the time when the first Shang-Yin bronzes were excavated.

Scientific excavations which began in 1928 on the site of Anyang in northern Honan were continued, after several interruptions, in 1934. On this site, under the name of Yin, there had been one of the several capitals of the Shang-Yin dynasty from around 1300 to 1028 B.C. Dr. Karlgren points out, however, that the names Shang and Yin are interchangeable, and are both used for the capital, for the state, and for the royal house.

The results of these excavations threw startling light on the Western conception of ancient Chinese history and on the culture, religion, and way of life of the Shang-Yin people. The sheer perfection and sophistication of their art showed that there must have been earlier development over a long period.

The Chinese attribute the invention of all their arts and crafts to the three

---

* These dates follow the latest findings of Dr. Bernhard Karlgren, director of the East Asiatic Collections, The Museum of Far Eastern Antiquities, Stockholm, leading authority in the study of archaic bronzes. The traditional dates are 1766 B.C. to 1122 B.C.

great emperors—Fu Hsi, Shên Nung, and Huang Ti (the Yellow Emperor) whose reigns are traditionally given as from circa 2852-2597 B.C. They were not "legendary" because it is the fantastic tales that have grown up around them that are legendary, and not the fact that they existed. It was the last of these emperors—who is reputed to have laid down the foundations for Chinese civilization, religion, and ethics. It is also recorded that Huang Ti found a copper mine and conceived the idea of casting metal.

Emperor Yü, fifth in line of descent from the Yellow Emperor and founder of the Hsia dynasty, which began around 1994 B.C.,* is recorded as the first ruler to have had bronze vessels cast. The story runs that there was a Great Deluge (similar to the Biblical Flood), and that Yü, who understood the principles of irrigation control, was able to divert the waters from a large stretch of land, which he divided into nine provinces. Later, when each of these provinces brought him bronze as tribute, he had nine bronze three-legged cauldrons cast from the same metal. Each vessel was decorated with designs showing the special produce of the nine districts.

These tripods became the symbol of imperial power and were handed down from dynasty to dynasty. They were still in existence at the time of Confucius in the sixth century B.C., but the last Chou emperor, after suffering military defeat, had them thrown in the river to prevent them from falling into the hands of his enemy. The attempt of the emperor of the succeeding Ch'in dynasty (221 B.C.) to salvage one of these cauldrons from the river was a popular subject for pictures, and it is repeated four times in the Han bas-reliefs in the Wu Liang tombs in Shantung.

The constant stories of deluges in Chinese history lead to the assumption that many communities were completely engulfed by risings of the Yellow River and may explain why no bronzes earlier than those of Shang-Yin have yet been found, although in excavations of late neolithic cultures (3000-2500 B.C.) jade objects with bronze hafts and settings were unearthed. Scientific excavation in China had been carried on sporadically for less than ten years when the Sino-Japanese war broke out in 1937, and there must be many other historical treasure sites buried deep in the earth along both banks of the Yellow River awaiting the day of discovery.

Just as there is nothing primitive about the Shang bronzes, so there was nothing primitive about the people or their way of living. They had reached a high state of civilization, with an organized government, a social system, and a religion. They had cities with large public buildings and houses built much like those of the present time. They wrote books on wood and bamboo strips tied together with cords, they kept historical records, and they had a highly developed art, including bronzes and marble sculpture.

The Shang-Yin territory was only a small part of what we now know as China, and it was not a united empire. It consisted of several small states with a common religion, art, and culture, over which the Shang rulers—who were the

---

* Traditional date, 2205 B.C.

most powerful—exercised authority. Toward the end of the Shang-Yin period, the Court received as tribute from the surrounding states precious stones, silk, gold, silver, pearls, tortoises, musical stones, hemp, wood, hides, feathers, bears, foxes, fish, salt, varnish, and cinnabar.

The people were farmers—not a nomad pastoral people, but settled farmers who exercised the arts of husbandry, ploughing their fields as they have always done. Their emperor was the Son of Heaven, appointed by the Supreme Power to rule over them in order to assure their welfare. If he failed to carry out this mandate it was not only the right, but the duty, of someone else to lead a revolt, take his place, and rule for the good of all the population. The ruler was responsible for everything that happened—for wars, floods, droughts, plagues, failure of crops, poverty and other circumstances, both adverse and favorable. The first Shang-Yin ruler was said to have wrested the power from the Hsia rulers, when their sovereign, by his dissolute conduct, forfeited the protection of Heaven.

The emperor was also the high priest, whose duty it was to make sacrifices in order to assure the fertility of the land and the fecundity of the inhabitants.

There has been a general misconception to the effect that the Shang religion was confined to ancestor worship and nature worship. Actually the people worshiped a Supreme Power, but, because the Supreme Being was so far distant, it was left to lesser deities to protect and help man in his daily life. There were no idols and no temples, but an altar could be erected in any place at any time.

Because of the essential role that the forces of nature—sun, earth, rain, and the changing seasons—played in the lives of farmers, the lesser deities to whom sacrifices were made included the Sun-father and the Earth-mother. These represented the male and female elements—the yang and yin—which are such a basic part of Chinese philosophy and art. The times of sowing and harvesting were the times for their main religious festivals, as they have been, under different names, all over the world. Spring festivals and Autumn festivals are universal whether they are called Easter, Thanksgiving, or other names.

What we call ancestor worship was really part of the Chinese belief in filial piety. There was a sense of unity with the dead and an acceptance of the fact that birth, maturity, and death are a natural sequence. There was no complete ending. Life continued after death, and if one had to respect one's parents and grandparents in their lifetime, it was even more important to pay reverence to them after death. The dead, who were nearer to the Supreme Being, had greater power than the living and could exercise tremendous influence upon the fortunes of the family. It was, therefore, necessary to consult them and to propitiate them. Sacrifices made to the ancestors included food and drink and other things that might add to their pleasure and comfort and thus assure their good will toward those still on earth.

This is the basis of what has been termed ancestor worship, although the Chinese never actually worshiped their ancestors. This custom was also rooted in the necessity for fecundity and continuation—the importance of the family line could not be ignored. To neglect the ancestors was as bad as not having any descendants.

The nobility engaged in hunting. They hunted for furs and game, for horses and elephants; this they did not only for sport, furs, and food, but because they also had to supply the many sacrifices needed in the ceremonies of worship, which included cattle, sheep, pigs, and dogs, as well as fish and cereals.

The ritual bronzes were used in making these sacrificial offerings—not only to actual ancestors, but also to great men of the past who were chosen as "spiritual ancestors." The dead never ceased to be involved with the affairs of the living. Their advice was asked, by means of oracle bones, on matters of everyday life. Nobody would embark upon any important enterprise without consulting them, and the successful conclusion of such an undertaking might be signalized by the casting of a new bronze vessel dedicated to the ancestral shrine.

These bronze vessels were inscribed with events that added prestige to the family, such as royal favor, or the acquisition of property, and served as a perpetual reminder to ancestors as well as descendants. The inscriptions on Shang bronzes usually consist of only two, three, or four characters—the name of the ancestor and the nature of the happy event.

The position held by women in the Shang-Yin dynasty was one of equality, and women ancestors were revered and consulted in the same way as male ancestors.

In the tombs of persons of high standing numbers of fine bronze vessels, white pottery, and marble sculptures were buried. Also found in the graves were many bronze chariot fittings, battle axes, heads of spears and lances, warrior's helmets, bows, and arrows, agricultural and hand tools and musical instruments.

The Shang-Yin bronze vessels were used not only for religious and Court ceremonies but also for general domestic purposes. The number of vessels owned by a family was decided by its standing, and every bronze was highly esteemed for its mark of rank, the value of the metal, the perfection of the casting, its symbolic and ritual meaning, and also—perhaps most—for its inscriptions. In the Han dynasty, after so many ancient bronzes had been destroyed and lost, the discovery of an archaic bronze was considered of such importance that a town which found one in a river nearby had its name changed to Pao-ting (Precious Cauldron) to commemorate the event.

Bronze vessels were made in a great variety of forms, both large and small. Dishes, vases, cups, ewers, basins, and bells varied from three inches to two feet in height. When used for ritual and ceremonial purposes, different forms were prescribed for each type of offering. There were also special vessels for storing and cooking and serving food, wine, and water, both for ritualistic and for household purposes.

The following are some of the best-known types of bronze vessels used in the Shang-Yin and/or the Chou dynasties:

Li: A tripod vessel with three or four hollow legs (one of the most ancient pottery forms). Two upright loop handles through which a stick could be passed for lifting. Used for cooking meat.

Ting: Similar to the above, but with solid legs, also used for cooking meat. This is referred to in early Chinese dictionaries as "a sacred vessel for blending the Five Tastes" (acrid, sour, salt, bitter, and sweet), "a vessel for cooking food," or "a vessel for boiling well-cooked food."

Hsien: This is really two vessels. A steamer, formed like a Li, with an upper part consisting of a colander with handles. Used for cooking vegetables and cereals. One of these vessels bears the inscription: "for use while campaigning, while traveling, wherewith to make soup from rice and millet." *

Kuei (or Chiu): A bowl, with or without cover, sometimes with handles, resting on three or four feet, or else on a hollow base. Used as a container for grain.

Tou: A shallow dish with handles, on a round base and with a cover. The circular projection on the cover served as a foot when inverted. Used for offering fruit.

Fu: A rectangular covered dish with straight sloping sides, sometimes with four feet. The cover is almost a duplicate of the vessel. Used for cooked cereals.

Hsü: A shallow oval dish with handles and cover. Like a Tou, the projection on the cover served as a foot when inverted. This is not a ritual vessel. Many are inscribed "Traveling Hsü" and were used during expeditions.

I (also written Yi and Ih): A ewer from which water was poured—often shaped like a sauce boat. The name "I" is also used as a general term for "sacrificial vessels."

Kuang: A squat vessel, elongated from front to back, with a cover extending over open spout and with handle at back. Also shaped like a sauce boat but larger than an "I."

Hu: A large wine vessel with bulbous body and narrow neck. Usually with ring handles. Used for storing food.

Lei: A large vase, or jar, for wine. It is like a Hu, but with the widest part of the body just below the neck.

Tsun: A ceremonial wine vessel, rectangular, with flaring lip.

Chia: A round tripod, or square and four-legged, vessel with handle on one side and two uprights on lip. The legs are hollow so that, when the vessel is filled with wine or water and pushed down onto a glowing bed of coals, the maximum surface will be exposed to the heat.

Ku: A tall slender wine beaker with wide foot and trumpet mouth.

Chüeh (formerly written Chio): A tripod cup with handle and pointed lip.

Yü: A large, deep, covered vessel, with flaring lip, with or without handles, for storing wine or water.

P'an: A shallow basin (usually round) for washing. Used in ceremonial rites and in domestic life.

Chien (or Hsi): A large, deep basin with two handles, also used for washing.

Chung: A clapperless bell to be struck with a stick on the outside.

There were also many vessels made in the form of animals, notably tigers, elephants, goats, deer, and birds.

* Translated by Professor W. Perceval Yetts.

212

Tests made on a typical piece of bronze show that it was composed of 83 per cent copper and 17 per cent tin. Much of the casting was done by the cire-perdue (lost wax) method. An exact model was made of wax, around which a mould of clay was formed. A few holes were left in this so that the wax could be melted and drained out and the molten metal put in its place. When the bronze had hardened, the mould was broken off. Other specimens are thought to have been made in a mould devised of several pieces, which could be separated to remove the cast bronze and then used again to cast another piece.

Some of the bronze vessels were inlaid with black pigment, others were inlaid with gold and silver, and the very finest were gilded. Bronze weapons were of exquisite workmanship and were often inlaid with turquoise.

By whatever method the pieces were made, they were carefully finished off with special tools, and the final result was the most superb work in bronze casting that has ever been achieved. At the same time equally fine bronzes were being made in other parts of the country—for instance in West China.

Many pieces of Shang bronze are ornamented all over with geometric and animal designs, others have bands of decorative designs with the rest left blank. The symbolism of the decoration is chiefly connected with those two basic desires —fertility of the soil and procreation, but the animal and other forms are subordinated to the perfection of the design. Backgrounds are often made up of geometric patterns, wavy lines, spirals and whorls, or the thunder-and-cloud pattern. There are tigers which symbolize earth and mountains, and dragons which stand for sky and water and which cause the rain—so needed for fertility —to fall. There is the cicada which denotes harvest time because it appears when the crops are about to ripen. The bull, or water buffalo, represents male virility; while the curving lines of the snake are associated with flowing water, and hence suggest fertility. There are birds too—notably the pheasant, symbol of sun and light, and the owl which stands for night and darkness. These two together represent night and day—yin and yang. There are elephants and other animals, pupils of animals' eyes, fishes and silkworms. Also cowrie shells which are symbols of wealth and fertility.

One of the most frequently used motifs is a grotesque face, or mask, to which has been given the name T'ao-t'ieh. It usually consists of two eyes, eyebrows, nostrils, and upper lip. There has been much speculation as to its significance. It was once said to be a warning against gluttony. Some Chinese had advanced this opinion in the Sung dynasty—many centuries after the bronzes had been created, when most of them had long since disappeared and when much of their symbolism and purpose had been forgotten. The Sung period, unlike the lusty Shang and Chou dynasties, was a time of great delicacy and fastidiousness which looked with disfavor upon excesses in eating as in everything else.

This explanation, however, is no longer taken seriously. Even if there were not other sufficient reasons for discarding the idea, it would be inconceivable that the Chinese would have insulted their ancestors, their minor deities, or their guests at official banquets by warning them against eating or drinking too much.

There are theories to the effect that the mask represents a tiger, a bull, or other animal, but there is no conclusive evidence for any such assumption. It may have been intended to represent an animal head, but it is equally likely that it is a distortion of a human face—one of those half-devil, half-animal faces that the Chinese often gave to creatures of the underworld. The whole subject is still one of pure supposition. It is possible that it was meant to frighten away evil spirits, for the expression resembles that on the faces of some of the guardians later put in tombs or on the roofs of houses for that purpose. Whatever its meaning, it is a fine piece of decoration—strong, well-balanced, and impressive.

In addition to these T'ao-t'ieh masks, there are also various animal heads—feline and bovine—carved in the round, and with complete mouths.

Since it was once the recognized custom in the West to assume that all Chinese art must have been inspired by the West, the claim has frequently been made that these Chinese animal designs were derived from the Scythians, a people who lived in southern Russia and western Asia. But such theories have had to fall back before advancing knowledge, and as Dr. Herrlee Glessner Creel points out in his book, *The Birth of China:* "those who make this claim admittedly do so on the basis of Scythian materials not older than the 7th century B.C.: the Shang materials antedate them by at least four centuries. Furthermore the Scythian art has little resemblance to most of the early Chinese designs. . . . As a matter of fact, the data which are given by those who seek to prove that the Chinese borrowed their designs from the Scythians do much to indicate the exact opposite. It is pointed out that many Chinese articles are found in Scythian remains of the 6th and 5th centuries B.C., showing that there was much contact with China. They point out similarities between Scythian and Chinese art of that period. Since we know these indicated characteristics to be ancient possessions of the Chinese, the conclusion that it was the Scythians who borrowed is hard to avoid."

There are certain motifs in Chinese art decoration which are duplicated in various Pacific areas, but in none of them is there such a complete and continuous development of art as in China. It would be more logical to assume that China was the source from which other Pacific groups took certain ideas. Some years ago the eminent sinologist, Professor W. Perceval Yetts, suggested "the plausibility of a thesis that dwellers on the banks of the Yellow River, three thousand and more years ago, may have originated conceptions which were carried westward by many agencies and in many guises. Some may have returned to their land of origin, after having undergone modification."

Another possible conclusion is that, in a very dim past, the Chinese and the other peoples in the surrounding area derived certain art motifs from some common source and that it was the Chinese who fully absorbed, developed, and improved upon them. Certainly the early bronze art of China is the direct and pure expression of the feelings and artistic ideas of the Chinese people of that time.

When these Shang bronzes were found, after having been interred for thousands of years, the corrosion of the metal had caused them to be covered with a patina—a bluish green, yellowish, or reddish efflorescence—which is now greatly admired. Formerly the Chinese, when they discovered an archaic bronze, would rub off this patina, as they preferred the black polish which came as the result of centuries of handling.

THE CHOU DYNASTY (1027-222 B.C.*)

The Chous—described by the Chinese as a barbarian tribe from the north-west (in the region of what is now Shensi province)—had grown in military strength to a point where they were able to invade the Shang territory and defeat their army in a single decisive battle. Although these people had not reached the high stage of development of the Shangs, having no philosophy and only a primitive religion, they were of the same North Chinese stock. They eagerly adopted the Shang-Yin culture; and, before the end of the Chou dynasty (one of the longest in history, lasting nearly nine hundred years), such great strides had been made in political economy, philosophy, religion, and literature that this period became known as the Classical Age of China.

When the Chous first defeated the Shangs, the leaders divided up the territory among their relatives and friends. This created a feudal system similar to that of medieval Europe, the feudal lords all owing allegiance to the Chou emperor, and paying him tribute. These feudal lords formed a hereditary land-holding aristocracy, whose sons were trained as government officials and military officers. All the wealth was in land, and, in return for military protection, the farmers gave the nobles a share of the crops. One Chinese record fixes this share at 10 per cent.

The nobles lived much as did their counterparts in Europe many centuries later, engaging in archery contests, charioteering, hunting, fishing, and the arranging of elaborate ceremonies and banquets. They differed from the feudal lords of Europe in their love of books and learning, and they sought out men who understood the arts of government rather than those of war. The princes brought in scholars to teach their sons, and the sons grew to depend on the advice of these teachers.

The class system was less rigid than in Europe, and men of talent could rise to the aristocracy, while worthless sons of nobles could sink back into poverty. In order to show his kinship with the working farmers, the emperor engaged symbolically in tilling the soil in the religious ceremony in the spring. This custom was continued until the end of the Ch'ing dynasty. The merchants and artisans, who formed an intermediate class between the nobility and the farmers, appear to have been prosperous and to have lived well.

The family system was like the one which has prevailed ever since. The father was the head of the family, and all generations lived under the same roof. All propetty was held in common.

Much was written about the desirability of women being submissive, but this appears to have been a desperate male attempt to assert authority. Women exercised great power in every dynasty, as dowager empresses, beloved wives, or

* Traditional dates 1122-221 B.C.

favorite concubines. And in every home the oldest woman ruled despotically over the whole family. As early as the seventh century B.C. we find writings warning young men to beware of the evil power exercised by women, and pointing out that women had brought about the destruction of three previous dynasties.

CHOU BRONZES

Professor Bernhard Karlgren divides the Chou dynasty, as far as bronzes are concerned, into the following periods:

Early Chou. 1027-circa 900 B.C. Period of foundation and consolidation of the Chou empire.
Middle Chou. Circa 900-600 B.C. Confederation of powerful states. Feudal system.
Huai style (late Chou). Circa 600-256 B.C. Time of political disintegration.
Period of the Warring States. Circa 255-222 B.C.

These dates differ from those mentioned previously by him and by other experts, but, like every sincere pioneer worker, Professor Karlgren has always been ready to modify his former views in the light of new evidence. The study of Chinese bronzes by Western experts is such a comparatively new one that Professor Karlgren has been the first to point out that his findings are always subject to revision.

In the first century and a half, the Chou bronzes were copies of the Shang, so that it is quite difficult to distinguish between them, although there is a slight falling off in technical perfection. The designs tend to be overelaborate, as though, under their new conquerors, the workers lacked the divine spark.

In the Middle Chou period more definite changes took place. The vessels incline to be heavier, often being placed on a square foundation to add to the impression of weight. There is little use of the thunder-and-cloud and spiral patterns in the background, the handles and legs are decorated, and the relief stands out less sharply. The design is more decorative and less symbolic. While some of the same motifs—the T'ao-t'ieh mask and the dragon forms—appear, they are less forceful and impressive.

The straight legs of the Ting shaped vessels are curved, and many of the Shang forms—the Yü, Ku, Tsun, and Chüeh—are eliminated. On the other hand new forms—the I (sauce-boat shape), the Fu (low rectangular dish), and the spiral horn—appear. The bell (Chung) becomes more common. Fewer vessels are made in animal forms.

In the later Chou period (the so-called Huai style), which is also known as the style of the Warring States, many of the Shang-Yin motifs reappear, including snakes and protruding animal heads. The T'ao-t'ieh masks and dragons continue to be used with a ground pattern of spirals and elaborate hooked and dot patterns, but the religious fervor which characterized the Shang bronzes is lacking. The vessels are mainly intended to be decorative and elegant. They are intricate and delicate and suggest nervous restlessness rather than devotional calm. The relief is flatter and many pieces are inlaid with gold, silver, and copper.

Bronzes of the late Chou period include pole finials, axes, dagger hilts, chariot fittings, swords with turquoise inlaid handles, masks, realistic human and animal figures, plaques, spoons, and locks. There are also personal objects such as combs, pins, pendants, mirrors, and belt hooks.

In general, the Chou bronzes are not equal to the Shang ones in material, technique, design, or inspiration, but Chou bronzes are of the utmost interest to archaeologists and students of Chinese art because of the inscriptions they bear.

Some of these are simple statements, perhaps to the effect that so and so made this vessel at such a time. In many cases the bronze vessels were used to ensure that records would be safely handed down to posterity. The inscriptions record appointments, gifts, royal favors, treaties, delineations of property, solemn vows, criminal laws, and so forth. Above all they bear witness, as the Shang-Yin ones did, to every notable event that increased the prestige of the family. When a daughter of a noble family was married, she would be given a bronze vessel for sacrificial purposes as a marriage gift. It might bear an inscription expressing the hope that she "bear sons and daughters without limit."

The casting of a bronze vessel was an important event, and, if made for sacrificial purposes, the inscription would state just what was desired. One of the most common prayers was: "May my sons and grandsons forever treasure and use this vessel."

In contrast to those on the Shang-Yin bronzes, some of the Chou inscriptions were very long—running more than four hundred characters. Often a set of bronze vessels will reproduce the complete text of a book. Some of the inscriptions lack clearness because they concerned only the immediate family—living and dead. Accurate dating is difficult because dates were reckoned by local calendars, usually counting from the first year of some ruler who is not named.

It is mainly for these historical records that the Chinese now attach such importance to the bronzes, but even when they were first made they were considered among the greatest treasures of a state. Their value was such that there are recorded instances of bronze vessels being offered to invading armies to induce them to withdraw.

In about 770 B.C., after the collapse of the Chou state in the west, Loyang became the capital. This event inaugurated the great age of philosophy and literature when all the great classical books of China were written. These included the "I Ching" ("Book of Changes"), "Shang Shu" ("Document Classic"), "Shih Ching" ("Book of Poetry"), "I Li" ("Book of Etiquette and Ceremony"), and the "Kuo Yü" ("Discourses of the State"). Innumerable books were written on all subjects.

The fundamental elements of Chinese philosophy, laws, government, education, and ethics were formulated through the teachings of such philosophers as Confucius, Mencius, Lao Tzŭ who taught that "He who is content has enough," and Mo Ti, who went around distributing books written on bamboo tablets, preaching a doctrine of "peace among men, and of goodwill to all, even those outside the family."

The removal of the capital to Loyang also marked the beginning of the gradual weakening of the central imperial power. At first, it is said, there were over 1770 feudal states, but the number rapidly dwindled as the stronger feudal princes fought and absorbed their weaker neighbors. During this time of struggle the philosophers wandered from court to court expounding their theories of government and ethics.

Eventually there remained only four large states, each of which hoped some day to triumph over the others. This was the time known as the "Period of the Warring States" (255-222 B.C.*). Finally one of them—the state of Ch'in—grew powerful enough to defeat all the others, and its ruler made himself the emperor of China under the title of Ch'in Shih Huang Ti (The First Emperor).

CH'IN DYNASTY (221-206 B.C.)

The head of the Ch'in dynasty was the most oppressive and bloodthirsty ruler in Chinese history. Having given himself the title of First Emperor he set out to erase all evidence of there ever having been any previous ruler, or history, in China. Not only did he order all books to be burned, but he decreed the collection and melting down of all bronzes because of the historic inscriptions they bore. With the metal thus obtained he cast twelve huge statues, each fifty feet high, and it is recorded that, in the fourth century, the last two that remained were melted down for money. It is chiefly due to his wholesale destruction of bronze vessels that few archaic specimens have survived, except those later excavated or stolen from tombs.

On the other hand, Shih Huang Ti abolished feudalism for all time and, in the Ch'in dynasty, he opened up communications with other countries, with the result that the land under his sway was thenceforth known to the outside world as China. Yet no dynasty so hated or so completely at variance with all Chinese tradition as the Ch'in could long be tolerated by the people. There had been attempts to assassinate Shih Huang Ti, and one of them is illustrated in the bas-reliefs of the Wu Liang tombs. He died in 210 B.C. and the country rose up against his successor who, according to tradition, must share his guilt.

There is a historical record of how the leader of the rebels broke into the private chambers of the emperor, and said to him: "You have been guilty of unheard-of shamelessness. You have killed and massacred without regard to justice. The whole of China is in revolt against you. What are you going to do now?"

The emperor answered: "Can I consult my prime minister?"

"Impossible."

"Then let me be King of just one province."

"Impossible."

"Then let me be a noble with a retinue of ten thousand."

* These are Professor Karlgren's dates. The traditional dates are 481-222 B.C.

"Impossible."

"Let me renounce all rank and authority and live like a modest prince with my wife and family."

"Discussion is useless. I have my orders. You must die. The welfare of the empire demands your death. No more words."

The rebel leader ordered his soldiers to come forward and do their work. All the princes of the family were exterminated. The palaces, the houses, the whole magnificent capital was transformed into a furnace which smouldered for three months. The short-lived Ch'in tyranny had betrayed the mandate of Heaven and had been wiped out.

THE HAN DYNASTY (206 B.C. TO A.D. 220)

After a short period of chaos, Liu Pang, a general, founded the Han dynasty which ruled for four centuries over a strong and united empire. As Herrlee Glessner Creel says: "In the Han Dynasty, China came of age and stayed of age," for there were no Dark Ages in Chinese history.

Han bronzes were more severe and simple than those of the late Chou-Huai style. It was a period of realism, and there were few fantastic animal forms. The decoration often took the form of horizontal bands of conventionalized designs or naturalistic animal and human forms. Some of the animal forms are elongated. The horses have all four feet outstretched to give an exaggerated effect of movement. The process of inlays with gold and silver, with turquoise and malachite, which had begun earlier, increased considerably, and many pieces were gilded or silvered all over.

A new feeling for the material itself and a desire for simplicity led to the making of thin, completely undecorated bowls covered with silver. Some interesting toys were made in bronze, including the toy dove chariots (a dove riding in a small carriage drawn by another dove). About these there was a saying: "A boy of five delights in a dove chariot. A boy of seven prefers a hobby horse."

Many fine human and animal figures and vessels continued to be made in bronze during the succeeding dynasties, and the introduction of Buddhism into China led to the creation of numbers of gilt bronze images of Buddhas, Kwan Yins, and other Bodhisattvas. But these belonged to a different tradition, and it can be said that, with the Han dynasty, the great era of bronze casting came to an end.

BRONZE MIRRORS

Bronze mirrors appear to have been first made during the late Chou period, and they express the secular and decorative nature of the bronzes of that period.

They consist of a piece of bronze (usually round for heaven, but sometimes square for earth), one side of which is highly polished to give an accurate reflection, while the other side is decorated with varying designs. The back has a pierced central boss through which a ribbon or cord could be looped as a handle. Some of them are inlaid with gold and with turquoise.

While primarily intended to be used as mirrors by the living, and thus necessary for the toilet of the dead, they were also placed in graves—not only those of women—as a source of light.

It is on mirrors that the figures of the Taoist Immortals appear for the first time, and the Taoists considered that these mirrors were endowed with supernatural powers. In Taoist lore they were used as amulets to ward off evil spirits and diseases, and they were ground into a powder which was believed to cure the sick. A mirror with a concave face was used for kindling sacred fire from the sun's rays. They were also said to have prophetic power—for in them one could see the future as in a crystal ball.

Another quality ascribed to the bronze mirrors was that they acted as guardians of marital fidelity. There is a tale of a couple who, when forced to separate, broke a mirror and each kept half. The wife was unfaithful, whereupon her part of the mirror turned into a magpie which flew to her husband and told him what had happened. Many mirrors are decorated with magpies, apparently as a warning to fickle spouses.

Then there were the magic mirrors that reflected a person's inmost thoughts. The bloodthirsty Ch'in emperor would test his concubines with one of these and execute them if their thoughts were not to his liking.

In an ancient Chinese poem we read about a woman whose husband had gone away and who no longer cared about her appearance:

> Since my lord left—ah me, unhappy day!
> My mirror's dust has not been brushed away:
> My heart, like running water, knows no peace
> But bleeds and bleeds, forever without cease.

The Taoist monks, when they retired to their retreats in the mountains, hung a bright mirror on their backs in order to prevent ghosts from approaching them.

But it was not only the Taoists who were interested in mirrors. They are frequently mentioned in poetry and in proverbs, and there is a famous saying of Confucius: "Use history as a mirror in which to examine your conduct." Other sayings of the same type are: "The mirror of the mind should be polished up with books," and "The perfect man uses his mind as a mirror."

These mirrors form interesting collections because they continued to be made, and used, throughout the Ming dynasty, and they reflect the changing types of decoration.

In the late Chou dynasty, the decoration often showed fantastic animal and human shapes in motion—four-winged animals, birds flying, sprightly dragons, interwoven serpents with animal heads, and T'ao-t'ieh masks, usually against a background of thunder-and-cloud, or spiral, patterns. Another frequently seen design takes the form of slanting T's.

On Han mirrors the decoration is more crowded, the knob is heavier, and the surface tends to be more curved. The designs are symmetrical—of a geometrical or astronomical nature. Some show the symbolical animals representing

220

Bronze wine vessel, "Ku." Shang-Yin Dynasty.

Bronze covered jar, "Lei." Container for wine and sometimes water. Typical pottery shape translated into bronze. Shang-Yin Dynasty. Alfred F. Pillsbury Collection.

Bronze upright gong bell, "Chung." Shang-Yin Dynasty.

Bronze vessel, "Kuang." Shang-Yin Dynasty.

Bronze ceremonial wine vessel, "Chia." Shang-Yin Dynasty. J. Lionberger Davis Gift.

Bronze vessel, "Ting," with supporting animals in form of boldly modeled birds. Shang-Yin Dynasty. Alfred F. Pillsbury Collection.

222

Bronze ceremonial covered wine vessel of type "Huo," in form of elephant. Early Chou Dynasty or earlier.

Bronze ceremonial wine vessel of type "Fang Tsun." Early Chou Dynasty.

reer Gallery of Art, Washington

Minneapolis Institute of Arts

Bronze "P'an." Shang-Yin or Early Chou Dynasty. Alfred F. Pillsbury Collection.

Stout bronze wine beaker, "Tsun," inscribed: "The prince has made the precious vessel: may grandsons and sons forever use it." Early Chou. Alfred F. Pillsbury Collection.

Above: Bronze pole end. Mid Chou.

Left: Bronze "Kuei" on sta Provenance Si-an in Shensi. scription includes: "May fo myriad years sons and grands forever treasure it." Early Ch Alfred F. Pillsbury Collection

Opposite page, bottom l Bronze wine vessel in form owl or pheasant. Chou Dyna Eumorfopoulos Collection.

Minneapolis Institute of Arts

Bronze wine vessel, "Yi" (also written I and Ih). Inscription reads: "The T'ai-shi Tsi Ta for the eldest Lady Kiang has made the Yi to be brought along when married; with it may one pray for a vigorous old age; may sons and grandsons use it is a great treasure." Middle Chou. Alfred F. Pillsbury Collection.

Collection Mrs. Margot Holmes

Above: Bronze animal mask. Western Chou.

Victoria and Albert Museum, London

Bronze wine flask, "Hu," with hunting scenes. 481-205 B.C. Alfred F. Pillsbury Collection.

Large bronze "Chien." Late Chou (Warring States).

Right: Bronze vessel in shape of stag reclining. Late Chou.

Below: Bronze toilet box, "Lien," with three small feet in shape of bears. Han Dynasty. Alfred F. Pillsbury Collection.

Bronze lion, originally part of an altar set. A.D. 386-557. Gift of Mrs. John D. Rockefeller, Jr.

Seated figure of Buddha in bronze gilt. T'ang Dynasty.

Bronze mirrors of the Han and T'ang Dynasties.

the points of the compass: east, the Azure Dragon; north, the Black Serpent or Tortoise; south, the Scarlet Bird; and west, the White Tiger. In the Chinese compass there are five cardinal points, the center being symbolized by a Yellow Dragon. In the case of the mirrors the center is indicated by the boss on the back. This central knob symbolizes the center of earth, and also the dome of Heaven.

On Han mirrors one also finds the "eight-bows" decoration, a circular pattern intersected by eight arcs; the "swallows' wings," with radiating wing-like designs; and many other geometrical styles. There are some mirrors which show a pattern that looks like the letters *TVL,* and which Professor W. Perceval Yetts believed to be a representation of an ancient sundial.

Others show Taoist scenes with kneeling figures, deities, animals, and grotesque faces. Some mirrors bear inscriptions with the name of the owner together with wishes for long life, prosperity, and posterity.

In the period of upheaval of the Six Dynasties (A.D. 222-589) the serene simplicity of the Han designs was replaced by a sense of savagery and ruthlessness, which was expressed on bronze mirrors by writhing and twisting animal and human forms.

T'ang mirrors are heavier and larger, the relief is higher and more sculptural. They are round, six-foil, eight-foil, and, at times, square. Some have a gold wash and others have a silver lining. Mirrors were often presented to the emperor on his birthday by the courtiers.

The design is more sparsely used and is more graceful. It consists of squirrels and interlacing vines, animals playing among floral or grape tendrils, flowers, dragons, hunting scenes, phoenixes, floral medallions, mountains and trees with galloping animals, and mythological figures playing musical instruments. Some mirrors bear designs of seahorses, with and without wings, combined with grapes, and also some show animals (perhaps foxes) with grapes. It is thought that these may perhaps be derived from some direct or indirect Greek source since there was so much intercourse with other lands during this dynasty.

The making of bronze mirrors reached its culmination, but not its end, in the T'ang dynasty, and the last word on mirrors and on their power of revelation may be left to the renowned T'ang poet Li Po:

> My whitening hair would make a long, long rope,
> Yet could not fathom all my depth of woe;
> Though how it comes within a mirror's scope
> To sprinkle autumn frosts, I do not know.

V: *THE ARTS OF THE CARVER*

Chapter VII

SCULPTURE IN STONE AND WOOD

THE ARTS of the carver and moulder may be said to include most of the plastic arts—engraving on stone and metal, modeling in clay and earthenware, the casting of bronzes and iron, wood carving and engraving on wood, and the carving of jade and ivory and other substances.

In all these arts the Chinese have excelled from the dawn of their history. But to us sculpture usually brings to mind large human and animal figures hewn out of a block of stone or marble. Until very recently, there has been little evidence of this type of work in the earlier dynasties.

In the course of the excavations on the site of the Shang-Yin capital at Anyang, started in 1928, stone and marble sculptures came to light in the form of large carved masks, bears, owls, tortoises, dragons, and other mythical animals. There was also one human face. These pieces were carved with a finished technique and decorated with the same motifs as the Shang-Yin bronzes and white pottery. The largest of these pieces was only about three feet tall. Fragments were discovered, however, in antique shops which led to the assumption that large statues had existed and been carried off piecemeal by grave robbers. From 1934 to 1935, in the deepest tombs, pieces of large ornamental marble sculpture were discovered, including the head of an ox larger than life size, but no later specimens of this type of work have been found. This contributes to the other existing evidence that the Shang dynasty represented the culmination rather than the beginning of a great era in the history of Chinese art.

HAN SCULPTURE

The earliest large sculptures in the round which still exist date back to the Han dynasty (206 B.C. to A.D. 220), although, according to Chou records, long rows of large stone figures of retainers, animals, and chimeras, as well as carved grave pillars, were placed on either side of the long avenues leading to the tall flat-topped mounds of earth which were piled up to form the mausoleums for the imperial tombs. No trace of these Chou sculptures seems to have survived, but the same custom continued in the Han dynasty, and stone tomb statues of winged lions and fabulous monsters have been found in various parts of China —notably in Shantung, Honan, and Szechüan.

The best-known example is the statue of a horse, trampling on a defeated barbarian, which guards the tomb of the cavalry general Ho Chü-p'ing (dated 117 B.C.) in Shansi province. While not lacking in force, this statue, in common with the other Han stone tomb animals, shows a primitiveness in technique which is rarely met with in any Chinese work of art. The Shang art of fine marble sculpture seems to have ended with that dynasty.

The Han artisans were far more successful when it came to carving in either high or low relief. In the section on calligraphy and painting, we have already discussed the fine bas-reliefs such as those of the Wu Liang Tz'ü and Hsiao T'ang Shan tombs in Shantung province. These have no sculptural quality but are linear pictures on stone. They are copies of the paintings on the walls of the palaces where the buried personages once lived.

The deep relief carvings, such as those on the stone pillars of Ch'en in Szechüan, with their animated and naturalistic hunting scenes and animal subjects, also give evidence of a practiced hand and a sure, artistic sense, leading one to believe that the Han artisans had more complete mastery of the technique of carving and ornamenting surfaces than of making large sculptures in the round.

In general—and this applies right up to the present time—the Chinese have not regarded sculpture as a great art. Chinese art is intellectual rather than representational and seeks to express the mood of an individual rather than to communicate a theory to others. Hence calligraphy and painting ranked far higher than sculpture. The Chinese say, "Each stroke of the brush must contain a living thought." The hand of the artist is so trained, through long years of practice, that this thought can be expressed as soon as formulated.

In the case of sculpture, the hard physical labor involved renders impossible the immediate realization of a thought. Such work has to be done by craftsmen and not by artists, and few names of sculptors have been known, or have survived, unless they also had other claims to fame. Many of the artisan carvers were inspired by their material to do wonderful work, but they toiled for the joy of achievement rather than for fame, in the same spirit as the unknown artisans who carved miracles in stone and wood in the great cathedrals of Europe.

In the early days of Chinese history there were no idols. The people worshiped a Supreme Power to which they gave no outward form. Then, too, as we have also already observed, there was little interest in the human form and no desire to glorify it, as in Western art. Most sculpture was made for some utilitarian purpose and not merely as art. Art was the expression of an idea, not the depiction of an actual person or animal or deity. The artist sought to express his own personality, whereas the craftsman thought less of himself than of the nature of the material with which he was working.

Even the Shang-Yin sculptures are grotesque rather than beautiful and apparently were intended as architectural ornamentation. Sculpture in the Han dynasty was almost entirely confined to the making of tomb animals, and these must have represented the work of a specialized group of artisans.

BUDDHIST SCULPTURE

While the introduction of Buddhism into China opened up vast new fields for the arts of the sculptor in wood, stone, and bronze and greatly enlarged the scope and quality of the work of the artisan carvers, it did not change the feelings of the Chinese intellectuals toward the art of sculpture.

In the West, we greatly admire the Buddhist sculptures because they are in the tradition of European religious art, and we are familiar with visual religious imagery. But these steles and Buddhist images violated the canons of Chinese art and ethics because they were made for a definite purpose, according to fixed formulas which were not Chinese, to be set up in specified places, to be used for the purpose of making converts, to instill concrete images of deities in the minds of the people, and to enable the donors to endeavor to seek special favors from Heaven.

On a Buddhist statue, in the University of Pennsylvania Museum, Philadelphia, the following statement is engraved: "The shortage of religious teachers renders it necessary to spread the precepts of Buddhism by expository works. Sculpture is the means whereby the divine truths have been made manifest." And on a stele (dated 534), in the Metropolitan Museum of Art, New York, the inscription reads: "The Supreme is incorporeal, but by means of images it is brought before our eyes."

The Chinese, who had never previously had an iconography, who had never tried to convert anyone to any religion, and who felt that true art should never try to teach or demonstrate, considered that the introduction of Buddhist art, with its hagiolatry, was a retrogression from the purely intellectual conception of a Supreme Being and the ethical teachings of Confucius.

Such was, and is, the Chinese point of view, but it does not detract from the very real beauty and importance of many of the Buddhist sculptures. The artisans, either because they had embraced the new faith or because they were inspired by the materials and their own craftsmanship, frequently succeeded in endowing the images they turned out with true spiritual and artistic qualities. They improved on the original imported models and, with the Chinese sense of rightness, gave to many of these figures a dignity, restraint, and charm which were wholly indigenous.

The finest of these Buddhist sculptures nobly meet the tests of a work of art. They are impressive outside the limitations of time and space. We can admire them, removed from their setting, and without knowing which religion or which deity they were supposed to represent. They exist as masterpieces in their own right.

232

THE COMING OF BUDDHISM TO CHINA

Buddha, like Confucius and Lao Tzŭ, who lived at about the same time, was an ethical philosopher rather than a religious preacher. Born to great wealth and position, he was profoundly shocked at the realization that, while he led a life of pleasure and luxury, numbers of other men were living in extreme poverty and misery. He renounced all his possessions, left his beloved wife and child, and set out as a wandering monk to seek for some solution to this inequality and some reason for man's existence.

He came to the conclusion that suffering is due to selfishness and sensuality. He taught that until men renounced all desire for wealth and fame they would not be wise; and, without wisdom, they could not find peace. His message was a simple one and had much the same basis as the teachings of Christ and of Lao Tzŭ: "What shall it profit a man if he gain the whole world and lose his own soul?"

The sincerity and directness of his ideas proves that the last thing he would have wanted was what actually happened. The teachings of Buddha became enmeshed in all the superstitions of the Hindu and other earlier Indian religions: Buddha himself was made the chief figure in the most complicated system of iconolatry. As has so often been the case with ethical teachers in all parts of the world, Buddha's sincere desire to ease the sufferings of mankind became submerged in a welter of ritualism and superstition that have only added to mankind's difficulties and burdens.

The exact date when Buddhism was first introduced into China is not known, but there is every reason to believe that individuals and groups had been attracted to the new foreign religion from the beginning of the Christian era.

Buddhism was officially recognized in China A.D. 67, when, the legend runs, the Emperor Ming Ti saw, in a dream, a golden figure floating in a halo of light and was told by his advisers that it must have been an apparition of Buddha. He sent a mission to India, and the pilgrims returned, bearing with them Sanskrit books, which were translated, and pictures of Buddhist figures and scenes, which were copied on the walls of the Palace halls and the new temples which the emperor ordered to be erected.

The religion did not make any great headway until the Han empire collapsed and the people, in their confusion and distress, were looking for some hope of a future life which would console them for their sufferings on earth. Confucius, when asked about the hereafter, had replied: "When we know so little about life, why worry about what happens after death?" Nor had Lao Tzŭ made any but the vaguest references to any future life, but the Mahayana form of the Buddhist religion, which was the one adopted by the Chinese, held out the certainty of rebirth and complete happiness in Paradise. There seemed no reason to reject such a comforting prospect, and the Chinese flocked to add this new belief to the ones they already held.

BUDDHIST SCULPTURE IN THE WEI DYNASTIES (A.D. 386-557)

Buddhism has usually flourished most strongly when China was under foreign domination, so it is not surprising that it was under the Wei regime that it became firmly established as a state religion. The Weis were a Tartar tribe, from the region of Lake Baikal in Siberia, who first conquered the north, and then gradually extended their sway over an ever-widening area of Chinese territory. Their advent heralded the production of Buddhist art on a wide scale.

The Wei Tartars were a people particularly devoted to sculpture. Every male aspirant to the throne had first to cast a statue, and he could not choose an empress until she, too, had proved her skill as a sculptress.

When Buddhism had taken firm root, Chinese monks made pilgrimages to India. The best known is Fa Hsien, who returned to China in 411 with sacred texts and images of the Buddha and other deities of the Mahayana pantheon. He traveled by way of Turkestan, where there were Buddhist communities, so that the images he brought were inspired by Central Asia as much as by India. Since China had never made representations of any deity, the imported images had to serve as their models. However, the artisans soon adapted these foreign designs to conform to the aesthetic traditions of the Chinese, and great quantities of stone, wood, iron, and bronze images, stone steles, and votive shrines were turned out.

ROCK-CUT CAVE TEMPLES

The largest mass manifestations of Buddhist art can be seen in the rock-cut cave temples—the making of which was based on an Indian idea. The oldest of these would appear to be the ones at Tun Huang—the Caves of the Thousand Buddhas—in Kansu on the borders of Turkestan. This was started in 366, and there are records of many Buddhist figures having been made in the fourth century, but few of them have survived.

The most important group of Buddhist sculptures was found in the rock-cut grottoes of Yün Kang, situated near Ta Tung Fu, in Shansi, which became the first capital of the Northern Wei rulers about 380. Work on these temples was started in the middle of the fifth century. There are more than twenty caves hollowed out of a sandstone ridge, and the largest is about seventy feet deep. The walls of the caves are carved with figures of Buddhas (some of colossal size, the largest being fifty feet tall), scenes from the life of Buddha, Bodhisattvas, Lohans, angels, and Hindu gods, as well as decorative or symbolic floral and animal designs. It is believed that much of the work was done by carvers among the thirty thousand families from the Buddhist colony of Tun Huang, who were brought to Shensi in 439.

There are evidences that much of the Indian iconography, on which the earliest Buddhist art in China was based, had been the work of Greek artisans in Gandhara. Gandhara was one of the Greek settlements left behind in the wake of Alexander the Great's expedition into India, and the craftsmen continued to receive inspiration from both Greek and Roman sources. Some models had been made under Iranian and other Central Asian influences, with the result that, as is also clearly seen in the paintings at Tun Huang, the faces and figures of the Buddhist deities represent various racial types.

The best and most impressive of the sculptures were those made by Chinese artisans working in their own tradition. There is the Chinese insistence on linear style. The body is flat, and is not emphasized, all the attention being concentrated on the treatment of the folds of the garments. The figures may appear stiff in themselves, but the skillful treatment of the draperies, which turn up at the end in points, and the swaying pose give a sense of rhythm and movement. The figures have a spirituality, a charm, and a mysterious half smile that are wholly Chinese.

In 494 the Wei capital was removed to Loyang, in Honan, and soon afterward work was begun on the cave grottoes at Lung Mên. The sculpture here is technically superior to that at Yün Kang. Although the rock was harder to carve, there was more attention to detail. There was also frequent use of the low-relief carving in which the Chinese excel.

Unfortunately, great destruction and looting have taken place in these temples. Much of the sculpture has been carried away, and many of the remaining figures have had the heads broken off. Such heads could be seen for sale in antique shops all over China a few years ago. Only a small proportion of the work at Lung Mên remains intact, and this is particularly unfortunate because the sculpture there included the highest examples of Chinese Buddhist art.

The Northern Wei style of sculpture was still in force at Lung Mên. The Weis, like the other conquerors who have occupied China, were devoted to Chinese art. Indian and other influences were soon submerged in the indigenous work of the Chinese sculptors. The round sensuous figures of the Indian deities gave way to slender and spiritual forms. The strength of the Chinese calligraphic tradition is shown in the geometrical lines of the draperies and the formal, straight hair arrangement which replaces the curls and waves of the models. Austerity and elegance replace opulence and exuberance.

Many of the figures are placed in semicircular or three-sided shrines carved out of the rock.

Among the finest Wei sculptures in the Lung Mên and Yün Kang caves are the seated figures representing what is often called the Maitreya—the Buddha of the Future. (This figure is said by some experts to depict Avalokiteshvara, the God of Love and Mercy—the Chinese Kwan Yin.) The deity is usually depicted seated on a high throne with outspread knees and slender legs crossed at the ankles. The figure, wearing a transparent skirt pleated in regular folds, is reduced to an abstract linear pattern. On the head is a tall crown, and the hair falls in two plaits over the shoulders.

This Bodhisattva, although male, could easily be mistaken for a female, and, in the course of time, became merged with the feminine figure of Kwan Yin, the Chinese Goddess of Mercy.

If there appears to be confusion about the identity of some of these deities, it must be remembered that the Chinese carvers were working from foreign models, which often had no special meaning for them; and, at times, they may have been carried away by their own artistic impulses.

Another group of rock temples in North China is at T'ien Lung Shan in Shansi; and it is here that a period of transition which set in during the latter part of the sixth century, when there appears to have been a new influx of Indian influence, can best be observed. The figures begin to lose their flatness and to be three-dimensional; the draperies are less angular, appearing to cover a human body; arms and legs become cylindrical. Abstract deities are transformed into beneficent human creatures.

BUDDHIST PERSECUTION

It was not only the styles in sculpture that changed. The course of Buddhism did not run smoothly in China. At times it was a state religion to which all were ordered to conform; then again it would suddenly be proscribed and temples and images would be destroyed. As M. D'Ardenne de Tizac, who was Curator of the Musée Cernuschi in Paris, wrote: "Neither the religion nor the art fitted smoothly into Chinese principles or aesthetics."

In 444 there had been a persecution lasting eight years, and another one of these reverses occurred under Wu Ti (561-578), emperor of the Northern Chou dynasty. So great was the destruction at that time that, when China was reunited once more under the Sui dynasty (589-618), we read about the Sui emperor, a devout Buddhist, ordering 3792 new temples to be constructed, as well as 100,000 new Buddhist images in gold, bronze, stone, wood, lacquer, and ivory. In addition to all this, he ordered that a million and a half old images be restored and repaired. It was made a punishable offense to steal or damage a Buddhist image.

SUI DYNASTY (589-618)

Work in the rock-cut temples was resumed with renewed vigor in the Sui dynasty. While some of the sculpture continued to be made in the Wei tradition, side by side with this there evolved a new type of Buddhist sculpture in which the previously mentioned transition from the flat abstract deities to a greater realism became even more strongly apparent. The figures are still slender but more supple and human, with a long neck, and a rounder and more expressive face. They are less austere, wear more elaborate clothes, and have necklaces, rings, and other jewels. The draperies are softer and cling to the bodies which, if not modeled completely in the round, are in high relief and cylindrical rather than flat. There is a new freedom in the flowing skirts and the floating scarves and necklaces.

During this period of Buddhist domination, other rock-cut temples were started in many parts of China—including Szechüan, Yunnan and Shantung. Since work was continued during the five centuries of Buddhist power, and many of the votive offerings are dated, they afford the best means of studying the variations in sculptural style of different periods.

In addition to the work in the cave grottoes during the Six Dynasties, vast

Above: Chimera, stone. 4th-5th century.

Right: Colossal head of Buddha. Stone. Wei Dynasty.

Buddhist votive stele. Height 98
inches. First half of 6th century.
Wei Dynasty.

Black stone seated figure of
Maitreya from Lung Mên. A.D.
512.

Colossal stone head of a Bodhisattva. Probably 6th century.

Sakyamuni Buddha. Hopei marble (ca. A.D. 600).

Metropolitan Museum of A

William Rockhill Nelson Gallery of Art, Kansas City

Head of a Buddha, stone. Northern Wei (386-557).

Honolulu Academy of Arts

Group of four Bodhisattv
probably finial of a shrir
Carved wood. Sui Dynasty.

Opposite page, bottom left: Sto
statue of Guardian King. Fi
half 8th century.

Relief from the tomb of the Emperor T'ang T'ai Tsung, depicting his chestnut bay battle charger. Early 8th century.

One of a pair of Apsaras (Flying Angels) from the T'ien Lung Shan caves. T'ang Dynasty.

University Museum, Philadelphia

University Museum, Philadelphia

Head of a Bodhisattva, from the caves of T'ien Lung Shan. Stone. T'ang Dynasty. Gift of Mrs. John D. Rockefeller, Jr.

Metropolitan Museum of Art

Over life-size figure of Kwan Yin. Wood, with
color and gold leaf. 13th or 14th century.

Pottery figure of Lohan (life-size). Mottled green and brownish yellow glaze. One of a series from Eight Lohan Mountain, Chihli province. Ming Dynasty.

Carved and gilt wooden figures from Canton, South China. *Right and left:* Ming Dynasty. *Center:* Ch'ing Dynasty.

Metropolitan Museum of Art

numbers of Buddhist images were made in stone, wood, gilt bronze, and lacquer. Very few of them have survived. Most of the bronze ones were melted down for metal, and quantities of others were destroyed in times of Buddhist persecution.

What has survived are many fine Buddhist steles. These are stone (or metal) tablets, often 6 feet tall, 2½ by 3 feet wide, and a foot thick. They are carved in high or low relief with Buddhist figures and scenes enclosed in a niche surrounded by ornamental borders. The idea of these steles dates back to the time before paper was invented and Confucian classics had to be carved on stone and metal tablets.

These steles were paid for, as votive offerings, by groups of devout Buddhists, and figures of the donors are carved in bas-relief on the backs. At times the most important donors are drawn in a larger size and placed on the front, while the lesser ones are smaller and are placed on the sides and back. The Chinese usually added their own carved traditional symbols, such as dragons and lions, to these steles.

The Buddhist sculpture—like most other sculpture—was made for a definite purpose—to adorn a temple or a grave, to be fitted into a wayside shrine or the courtyard of a palace. The sculpture in wood and stone was highly colored, and the color was frequently renewed as a votive offering by donors. Actually, although we are used to thinking of sculpture in terms of pure uncolored marble and stone, most of the stone and wooden statues of the Western world were originally painted, too.

During the period of the Six Dynasties marked advances had been made in non-Buddhist sculpture, especially in the Liang dynasty (502-557). This was still largely confined to monumental tomb animals. Chimeras guarded the tombs of the emperors, and winged lions those of princes and dukes. The largest of these monsters are ten to twelve feet long. The vigor and vitality of these beasts show that sculpture had developed to a very high degree without the stimulus of Buddhism.

SCULPTURE IN THE T'ANG DYNASTY (618-907)

During the first century of T'ang rule, Buddhist art flourished. The Emperor T'ai Tsung (627-649), one of the best of all Chinese rulers, was a fine statesman, military leader, and patron of the arts and letters. The administrative reforms he inaugurated assured peace and prosperity for a hundred years after his death. He was an ardent follower of the teachings of Confucius. He did not think the country needed any other philosophy, for he maintained: "What water is to fishes, Confucius is to the Chinese." Nevertheless he in no way opposed the teachings of Buddhism in his realm. In fact, during this time of broadmindedness men of all religions—Nestorian Christians, Mohammedans, Jews, Manichaeans, Zoroastrians, and Buddhists—were allowed to worship freely and to proselytize.

Some of the best sculpture of the T'ang dynasty was of a non-Buddhist nature. Funerary sculpture reached its highest development in technique and powerful realism. Among the most superb examples of this art are the bas-reliefs of the six horses of the Emperor T'ai Tsung, two of which are now in the University of Pennsylvania Museum in Philadelphia. Because of his great affection for them, the emperor ordered carvings to be made of his six favorite chargers, which had died in battle, so that they could be placed around the base of his tomb near his capital at Ch'ang-an (City of Everlasting Peace).

Horses were held in high esteem at that time, and the designs for these carvings were drawn by Yen Li-pên, one of the foremost artists of the period. In their dignity, strength, reverence, and restraint, they are a tribute to the nobility and faithfulness not only of these particular chargers but of all horses.

There was some Taoist sculpture, but this consisted mainly of smaller figures and did not have any great development. The Taoist immortals have always been treated in a tolerant, half-humorous manner, and the stories about them are regarded as folklore. Taoism was a religion of nature worship, of solitude and individualism. Nobody made idols of Taoist immortals in order to worship them. The magic and witchcraft which grew up around Taoism was as contrary to its spirit as the whole hagiolatry of Buddhism was to the simple moral teachings of Buddha.

After the death of T'ai Tsung, the next Emperor, Kao Tsung (650-682), gave special protection to the Buddhist religion. The real ruler of the country was his wife, the Empress Wu, a devout Buddhist, and she continued her absolute domination for more than twenty years after his death.

This imperial encouragement, together with the greater intercourse with India which encouraged pilgrims to visit and return from that country with new Indian images, gave a fresh impetus to the creation of Buddhist figures. Numbers of additional sculptures were added to those already in existence in the caves of Lung Mên, Tun Huang, T'ien Lung Shan, and all the other rock temples.

The T'ang figures were modeled in the round. They are robust and worldly, mature and sophisticated, with little evidence of spirituality. They expressed the fullness of life of a period which had little use for asceticism.

There is evidence of Indian influence (Gupta School) in this work, but, as Alan Priest, in his book *Chinese Sculpture in the Metropolitan Museum of Art*, so aptly phrases it:

> It is well to say influences, for although the Chinese presented their Bodhisattvas with the skirts, the scarves, the jeweled chains and crowns of the Indian representations, they considered the voluptuous curves and loose-hipped antics of their models as highly unsuitable, and the Indian déhanchements are turned at once into dignified, matronly poise. As contrasted with Wei sculpture, the sweet smile gives way to a pout and then to stern, heavy lips. The tranquil gaze of the Wei Bodhisattvas changed to heavy-lidded contemplation. The necks shorten and become collared with folds of flesh. The linear quality is never lost but now there is a complete understanding of the body.

Many of these figures are admirable pieces of sculpture as far as technique is concerned; but the fact that these large massive figures, with their elaborate dress, heavy ornaments, and rather sullen faces, were turned out by the hundred and show a complete lack of spirituality or, in many cases, of individual inspiration makes it easy to understand why the Chinese connoisseurs rejected them as great art.

Because many of the artisans were also fine artists, however, certain figures stand out from the mass. Among the most interesting are the powerful statues of the Guardians of the Four Cardinal Points, which are wholly Chinese in concept.

In some of the caves the sculptors, apparently seeking expression for their creative abilities outside of the set models, would do secular figures and carve animals, floral designs, and other objects, which are often the most individual examples of their art.

There were many striking carvings of the Lohans. Later it became common to make temples with large numbers of these disciples of Buddha, sometimes as many as five hundred. Then there were many colossal statues of Buddha which, with their large obese forms and smooth, round, expressionless faces, looked more like typical eunuchs of North China than depictions of an Indian deity.

KWAN YIN, GODDESS OF MERCY

The most popular figure was Avalokiteshvara (Chinese: Kwan Yin), God of Love and Mercy, one of the Bodhisattvas of Mahayana Buddhism. The Bodhisattvas were beings who had lived such pure and virtuous lives that they were qualified to become Buddhas and enter nirvana. They renounced this privilege out of pity for suffering humanity, and preferred to be spiritual leaders (like the Christian saints), who would mediate between human beings and the deity until such time as all living things—human and animal—found salvation.

During the T'ang dynasty, this figure definitely assumed feminine form and became known as the Goddess of Mercy. The greatest painter of the period, Wu Tao-tzǔ, was said to have been the first to paint pictures and make designs for stone engravings, establishing the Kwan Yin as a woman, with long flowing draperies and a hood, standing on clouds or on waves. The reason for this metamorphosis may have been that the Chinese associated mercy, compassion and forgiveness more with woman—the mother—than with man.

The Chinese carvers and sculptors poured into their representations of the Kwan Yin their ideal of womanly beauty. They made images of her in stone, in wood, in porcelain and pottery, in jade, in ivory, and in lacquer. By the sixteenth century she appeared with a child in her arms or on her lap, which suggests that she was merged with the Christian Madonna as shown in the engravings of the Jesuit priests. This impression is further emphasized when, as is frequently the case, the beads around her neck end in the shape of a cross.

The cult of the Kwan Yin was widespread among Chinese of all faiths. Her image is to be found in Taoist temples as well as in Buddhist ones, in wayside shrines, and in many homes. The most beloved of all deities, the Chinese say of her: "The men love her, the children adore her, and the women chant her prayers." She has especial power over childbirth. In temples to this day one sees her image surrounded by little boy dolls in clay and porcelain, brought to her as votive offerings by pregnant and sterile women. She is also the one who secures forgiveness of sins and relief of suffering.

She is depicted standing on a rock, seated on an open lotus flower, rising from the waves—for she is also the Goddess of the Southern Seas—or riding on a mythological animal. In Sung wooden sculpture she is often shown in the position called "sitting at royal ease," with one knee drawn up and the hand resting on it.

The Kwan Yin is now considered a wholly Chinese deity, and it is probable that the mass of the people long ago forgot her Indian and male past. In fact, she has been provided with a pure Chinese genealogy in the legend which makes her the daughter of a sovereign of the Chou dynasty. The story runs that she was so devout that she wanted to become a nun and refused to marry. Because of her disobedience to his wishes, her father ordered her to be executed; but, when she arrived in hell, the flames were quenched and flowers began to bloom. She was then sent back to earth again in the heart of a lotus flower and showed the greatest filial piety toward her cruel father. This is part of a very involved story and only one of the many folk tales that have grown up around the Kwan Yin.

PERSECUTION OF BUDDHISM

By the beginning of the eighth century, when Buddhism was already losing ground as a religion, Han Yü (768-824), a leading statesman and literary figure, prepared a document setting forth his disgust at the state of degeneration into which Buddhism had fallen, with its superstition and worship of barbaric idols. His words had such influence on the thinking of the time that, in 845, an edict was issued against the religion. This led to the destruction of five thousand large and forty thousand small temples. A quarter of a million nuns and monks were forced to return to secular life. Many bronze images were melted down and thousands of others were burned or destroyed.

Although the edict was revoked in 848, Buddhism had been dealt a heavy blow. The religion did not die, but it survived mainly in its philosophical ideas —the emphasis being laid on love of nature, kindness, and consideration toward all living creatures. In that form it attracted many new followers. This period also witnessed the rise of the Ch'an (Zen) school of Buddhism, which combined the most subtle and delicate aspects of both Buddhism and Taoism. Images of the female Kwan Yin were placed in the Ch'an temples, but ritualism and idol worship were abolished. One of the best-known Ch'an paintings, by Liang K'ai, shows a monk tearing up Buddhist sutras because religion and philosophy must come from within and not from without.

The form of Buddhism called Lamaism, which is practiced in Tibet, Mongolia, and other countries surrounding China, shows the wisdom of Han Yü in his fears of what unchecked ritualism and idol and relic worship could degenerate into. In Peking this is clearly demonstrated when one compares the austere beauty and classic dignity of the Temple of Heaven with the ugliness of the Yellow Temple (Lamaist) and the Lama Temple there with their unforgettable smell, the tawdry painted banners, the hideous statues of fornicating Buddhas, the accumulation of piled up human bones, and the rows of open wooden boxes containing the bodies of dead Lamas in varying stages of disintegration.

THE SUNG ATTITUDE TOWARD SCULPTURE

In the Sung dynasty emphasis was on "art for art's sake." Art was a world apart and should not have to conform to set models as did religious sculpture. Intellectual idealism superseded religious ritualism, and rationalism displaced T'ang realism. The Sung artists found their true medium of expression in painting.

Nevertheless, throughout the Five Dynasties and the Northern Sung Dynasty, religious images did continue to be made. Stone and bronze were largely replaced by wood, clay, iron, and lacquer—usually brightly colored. Many religious carvings were influenced by Chinese paintings in the twelfth and thirteenth centuries, and figures were combined with rocky landscapes, buildings, and animals.

Some of the Sung wooden statues of the Kwan Yin are among the loveliest of Chinese sculptured figures. In this more easily worked medium, the artisan could ignore all iconography and carve his ideal of female beauty, striving to portray womanly tenderness and grace rather than religious asceticism or the heavy worldliness of T'ang.

In the cave temples, the carving of stone statues also went on, and these show the figures in more relaxed and natural positions, with more detailed modeling of hands and feet. Indian influences, such as in garments and headdresses, were discarded and the images are Chinese in every respect.

When the Tartars occupied the northern part of China there was renewed Buddhist fervor, and a quantity of wooden Buddhist sculpture was created, especially in Chihli and Shensi. In the Southern Sung capital of Hangchow religious sculpture was almost entirely confined to wooden figures of the Kwan Yin in Ch'an temples and wooden figures of the Lohans. These vary in artistic merit in accordance with the inspiration and talent of the sculptor who created them.

There must have been an enormous number of wooden statues carved during the Sung dynasty, as in the preceding ones. Probably the reason why so few early specimens have survived is that wood can so easily be burned. We have personally witnessed the wanton destruction wrought in temples by occupying soldiers. The number of wooden statues that must have been lost in the firing and pillaging of cities and temples throughout the centuries, as well as those that have been burned for fuel, is incalculable.

In Japan, a country with a damp climate, Chinese wooden figures of the T'ang dynasty still exist. These ancient wooden images could have been far better preserved in the dry climate of North China had it not been for the frequently recurring orgies of destruction.

SCULPTURE IN THE YÜAN DYNASTY

Under the Mongol conquerors, the art of sculpture seems to have continued in the Sung tradition. The official religion of the Mongols was Tibetan Lamaism, and the gilt-bronze figures of Tibetan or Nepalese type began to appear. The Chinese copied these in vast number, but most of them were destroyed in the reaction against the Mongols after they had been overthrown.

MING SCULPTURE

The Ming rulers were enthusiastic Confucians but they did not interfere with the creation of Buddhist sculpture. Much of it is in the T'ang style—heavy, worldly, mature Chinese figures. It is essential to remember, however, that in any period and in any country great artists are rare. While many of the Ming figures are lacking in individuality and vitality, being merely religious symbols, there are other Ming statues of the greatest beauty and charm—in both Buddhist and secular sculpture.

The colossal stone figures of animals and civil and military officials guarding the tombs of the Ming emperors are powerful but heavy and lacking in spirit. On the other hand, the larger than life-size glazed pottery figures of Lohans that were made in Ching-tê Chên are wonderfully perceptive studies of Chinese types and rank among the best examples of sculpture. Equally fine are the numerous smaller carvings of figures, scenes, and animals in wood, ivory, and jade, which are part of the great art of the Ming period.

The art of the Ming sculptors also found a wide field of expression in the richly carved marble balustrades and columns of the Forbidden City and the Imperial Palace, and on the terraces of the Temple and the Altar of Heaven, as well as in the masterly carving of the slabs of marble, called the "Spirit Road," over which the emperor's sedan chair was carried.

LATER SCULPTURE

While the output of large-scale stone sculpture rapidly declined in later centuries, the art of carving in all mediums continued and reached new heights. For instance, all over China, and especially in the south, one sees the most skillful and imaginative wooden carvings—usually lacquered and gilded—over the doorways of temples, shops, theaters, and restaurants. These are accorded little attention because they are part of familiar street scenes; and yet, if one carefully examines certain of these wood carvings, one is amazed at the tremendous talent of the artisan who created them.

Much of this work is from a hundred to two hundred years old; and the carving is in bas-relief, high relief, or completely in the round, often carved in several layers, showing scene after scene of some tale of historical, religious, or local lore.

In some of these wooden carvings the beauty of the background scenery, the perfection of spacing and grouping, and the way in which so much is expressed by the poise of a body or the droop of a hand show that there were many Chinese carvers who were able to best express their art when not confined to a prescribed set of religious images.

250

Chapter VIII

JADE

THE IMPORTANCE OF JADE

No OTHER PEOPLE have ever felt the same affinity for jade or have so completely absorbed it into their culture as have the Chinese. It is no exaggeration to say that jade is the most completely Chinese of all materials, even though much of it was imported from other countries.

Jade has represented an important element in the life of China from prehistoric times to the present day. An attempt to understand the Chinese reverence and feeling for the material throws a revealing light on the history and psychology of the Chinese people. The attitude toward jade has changed with the spirit of the times, but for at least five thousand years it has never ceased to be an integral part of Chinese culture.

"Jade is Heaven" says the "I Ching" ("The Book of Changes"). And in the "Li Chi" ("The Book of Rites") the following reasons are set forth as to why jade should be so highly honored:

> Benevolence lies in its gleaming surface;
> Knowledge in its luminous quality.
> Uprightness in its unyieldingness.
> Power in its harmlessness.
> Purity of soul in its rarity and immaculateness.
> Eternity in its durability.
> Moral leadership in the way in which it passes
>   from hand to hand and remains without a
>   blemish.

The ancient classics were revised by Confucius and his disciples in the Chou dynasty. Confucius himself, when asked if jade was valued above other stones because of its rarity, said that was not the reason. He explained that, since ancient times, men have found all virtues in jade. They have found it soft, smooth, and shining like benevolence; fine, compact, and strong like intelligence; its edges look sharp, but they do not cut, like justice; it hangs down toward the ground (referring to girdle pendants and necklaces) like humility; when struck it gives forth a clear prolonged musical note; it does not conceal flaws and these add to its beauty, like truthfulness; it is bright as heaven, and yet its firm substance, contained in hills and streams, is like earth. It is admired by all under the sky as a symbol of truth and duty.

The "Book of Poetry" also states: "When I think of a wise man he reminds me of jade."

These are some of the reasons why the Chinese revere jade, but many others have been given by different writers and scholars. From the earliest times jade was endowed with a divine quality. Although the Chinese did not worship the jade itself, it has figured for thousands of years in their religious ceremonies. The ruler, the Son of Heaven, was the only one permitted to make sacrifices to Heaven, and he used jade symbols because the material was considered to be a link between deity and man.

ARCHAIC JADES

Among the late neolithic objects, dating from 3000 B.C. to 2500 B.C., unearthed by Dr. J. G. Andersson and other archaeologists in Yang-shao (Honan) and various other sites in different parts of China, there were several large, plain, finely wrought heads of jade in bronze hafts and settings. These were probably used as ritual symbols rather than weapons.

The veneration for the special virtues and sacred quality of jade goes back to the earliest form of Chinese worship: the yang-yin principle of the two opposing, and yet combining, elements of life—the male and the female, the positive and the negative, light and darkness. It was felt that the use of jade emblems for religious, ceremonial, and personal use in the prescribed colors, sizes, and shapes would serve to maintain a perfect balance between these two elements.

Jade also had its role in nature worship. Most jade boulders and pebbles were excavated from mountains or found in the shallow beds of streams, and thus jade was said to have absorbed the very essence of the "hills and water" so beloved by the Chinese. It was felt that if a man handled jade and listened to its resonant note, he would acquire its qualities of nobility, serenity, purity, and faithfulness.

In the case of the archaic jades, the substance was not valued for its beauty, rarity, color or elaborate carving. Though beautifully wrought with extreme simplicity of design, it was honored for the noble virtues which it represented and not for its ornamental quality.

SHANG-YIN TOMB JADES

Between the late-neolithic jades and the Shang-Yin jades found in the course of the excavations at Anyang, and other sites, there is a gap of many centuries which will, doubtless, be bridged when large-scale excavations are resumed.

In the Anyang tombs there were many ceremonial and ritual weapons: jade daggers and knives about a foot long; axe heads and halberds; "ta kuei" (rectangular tablets with three holes that look like knives but were apparently made to be hung from the girdle); other ritual symbols, such as disks and geometric tablets; thumb rings worn by the nobility when they drew their bows; vigorous little figures carved in silhouette, such as crouching tigers, birds, hares, fishes, dragons, and other mythological creatures. Many of these are flat pendants of chisel-like projection.

There were also specimens of certain of the emblems of the six cosmic forces which controlled the life of the Chinese, and regarding which the "Book of Rites" states:

> With a sky-blue Pi worship is paid to Heaven.
> With a yellow Ts'ung to Earth.
> With a green Kuei to the East.
> With a red Ch'ang to the South.
> With a white Hu to the West.
> With a black Huang to the North.

Blue was the sky; yellow, the earth; green, wood and spring; red, fire; white, metal; and black, water.

These cosmic symbols were represented in the following forms:

1. The Pi. A flat circular disk with a hole in the center. This was the symbol of Heaven and belonged to the emperor.
2. The Ts'ung. Shaped like an upright rectangular block with a hollow cylinder inside. It was the symbol of Earth and was used in fertility cults. This was the property of the empress.
3. The Kuei. A long narrow tablet with a tapering point, given by the emperor to his bride as a talisman.
4. The Ch'ang. A semicircle.
5. The Hu. Thought to be a white plaque shaped like a tiger, or decorated with a tiger.
6. The Huang. A flat segment of jade, about a third of a circle. Sometimes shaped like a fish.

Since it was not always possible to procure jade of the prescribed colors, other shades were substituted. For instance the "pi" is often green, and the colors of the ritual emblems excavated cover a wide range—every shade of white, buff, gray, brown, dark green, purple, and black. The colors may have undergone changes in the course of the many centuries they lay buried in the earth. Some pieces have markings and spots, which give them the five colors that the Chinese treasure so highly when found in one piece. Others have the color and texture of old ivory or are calcined like chalk.

The early jades were very plain because the material itself was so highly regarded that the slight decoration usually served only to emphasize the markings. This decoration was of the same type as that used on bronzes. The size of these cosmic symbols varied.

These were not the only jade objects found in the tombs. Jade was also used to close the eyes and otherwise to fill the apertures of dead bodies. The piece of jade put in the mouth often took the form of a cicada. This insect, which had been endowed with many virtues, also symbolizes the hope of immortality since it emerges from its chrysalis to enjoy a new life every spring. The Chinese did not embalm their dead, but put all their faith in the commonly held belief that "Jade cannot prevent the living from dying but it can prevent the dead from decaying." Once a tomb was sealed it could not be opened again, so they had no way of knowing that the desired end had not been achieved.

Other pieces of jade in the form of stylized dragons, fishes, recumbent pigs, and other objects were used to hold the garments of the dead in their proper ritual folds. Excavated sets of these tomb jades are still eagerly purchased by the Chinese who enjoy the smooth surface and soft colors, and to whom these pieces still symbolize a hope for long life and immortality.

Tomb jades are known as Han yü, meaning "placed in the mouth," but the term came to be used for all jades found in the earth. This has sometimes led to the mistaken assumption that these things were made in the Han dynasty—but they may date from many centuries earlier or later.

The cosmic symbols and many of the other jade objects found in tombs were also used by the living—in fact, the objects buried were often inferior in size, quality, and workmanship to those used above ground. The living also used the precious jade tablets which, like the bronzes, were symbols of power. To the emperor alone belonged the big tablet (kuei), three feet long, which he wore suspended from his girdle, and the tablet of supreme protection which measured one and a half feet. He had other personal tablets—a round one which assured virtue; a pointed one which prevented vice; and one which he held when receiving the feudal lords.

Each feudal prince was entitled to jade tablets in accordance with his rank. The emperor alone could use a square writing tablet of polished jade. He wrote on this with a pointed bamboo stick dipped in black lacquer. The feudal princes used ivory tablets for the same purpose.

Although the "Book of Rites," which sets forth these rules, was revised in the Chou dynasty, it was supposed to cover also the ceremonial and religious rites of the Shang and Hsia dynasties. We know from Anyang records that the Shang people highly valued antique pieces of jade which had been made long before their time.

JADES OF THE CHOU DYNASTY

In the Chou dynasty there was a balance between religious austerity and sensual satisfaction. Without losing its exalted position—for a special official was put in charge of jade objects at Court—jade was also used for such utilitarian purposes as ornamenting chariots and furniture and making household vessels, as well as for articles of personal adornment. While still revered, jade was thus also considered accessible to mere mortals. The Chinese loved it for its tactile quality, comparing its coolness with morning dew and its softness with the skin of a small child.

MUSICAL JADES

As already mentioned, jade was appreciated for its clear musical note when struck. A set of jade chimes was used in imperial ceremonies and in Confucian rites. These consisted of sixteen pieces of graduated thickness, shaped like carpenter's squares. Suspended from a frame, they were struck with an ivory mallet.

It was the custom for Chou nobles to hang flat pendants (p'ei yü) from their girdles. These were cut in such forms as tigers, fishes, dragons, and twin figures and made musical sounds as they clinked against each other. Those on the right and left sounded different notes in the Chinese scale.

Even these musical pendants were made according to strict rules. The "Book of Rites" prescribes that the Son of Heaven is to wear white jade with green cords, a prince mountain green jade with red cords, a governor of a province water-green with black cords, and an heir-presumptive pale green with green cords.

The pleasant tinkle of the jades as the owner moved around was said to evoke thoughts of friendship and a desire to please. Confucius mentions that, when he went to pay his respects to the wife of one of the feudal lords, she greeted him from behind a curtain, bowing low so that he could hear the resonant sounds of her jade bracelets and pendants. In later dynasties when porcelain was made in imitation of green and white jade, the same quality of resonance was eagerly sought.

The use of these pendants was suppressed by an edict of the Ch'in Emperor Shih Huang Ti, who ordered that a sword be hung from the girdle in their place. In his passion to eliminate all objects that testified to a more civilized and peaceful era than his own, he destroyed innumerable pieces of jade; and the use of jade symbols in religious and ceremonial rituals ceased for many centuries.

JADES OF THE HUAI PERIOD

The late Chou jades (known as the Huai style, or style of the Warring States) show the same characteristics as do the bronzes of the period—a moving away from the tendency to regard the material with religious awe, and a desire to make use of its decorative qualities. The severity of the early pieces gave way to a spirit of movement and an expression of elegance and delicacy.

The pi (symbol of Heaven) found at Loyang, and now in Kansas City, presents a sharp contrast to the plain pis of earlier times.

THE GREAT JADE SEAL OF STATE

If the Ch'in emperor was responsible for the destruction of so many jades (with the exception, of course, of those that had been buried), he was well aware of the high esteem in which the people held that substance. In order to impress his subjects he ordered an official seal of state to be carved—a four-inch cube with a handle of five interlaced dragons. This became known as "The Seal that Transmits the State." It was believed to have been taken over by the Han rulers and by those of successive dynasties until the reign of the Emperor Ch'ien Lung.

In regard to such stories as this it is always difficult to draw the line between history and legend. Whether accurate or not, they have become an intrinsic part of the folklore of China; just as, regardless of their accuracy, the tales of King Arthur and his Knights of the Round Table, Dick Whittington and his cat, or Robin Hood and his Merry Men in the Forest of Sherwood are part of the national heritage of the English people and are handed down to each generation, in spite of all attempts to "debunk" them.

TYPES OF JADE

The Chinese word for jade is "yü" (signifying the five cardinal virtues—charity, modesty, courage, justice, and wisdom). Actually there is no such thing as jade, the term referring to various minerals of which the two main groups are nephrite and jadeite.

The Spanish conquerors of Mexico and Peru knew about this substance and called it "piedra de ijada" (stone of the loins). Through the French term *le jade* (a mistaken rendering of l'éjade) it became known as "jade." Jade was considered a remedy for internal disorders, and there was a Mexican superstition (similar to the Chinese one) that the drinking of water, shortly before death, in which powdered jade had been dissolved would prevent decomposition of the body.

Nephrite, too, was known as the kidney stone (Greek *nephrites*-"kidney") and was worn as a charm to protect that organ. It was under this name that Sir Walter Raleigh in 1595, on his return from his travels on the American continent, first brought this substance to the attention of the English. Jade was known and has been found in various parts of the world, but nowhere else was it prized as highly as it was in China.

It is only within the last century that Western scientists have analyzed these minerals, and it has been found that:

1. Nephrite is a silicate of calcium and magnesium, which would be pure white were it not that it also contains varying quantities of iron and other oxides which give it a wide variety of colors. It has a cold, oily feel, is very hard, cannot be scratched with a knife, but breaks into pieces if violently thrown down.

2. Jadeite, a pyroxene, is a sodium-aluminum silicate. This, too, would be pure white but for the presence of small quantities of iron, calcium, and magnesium which give it color. It is tougher, more glassy, and harder to the touch than nephrite. It is also more translucent, more granular, and has a somewhat vitreous luster when polished, whereas nephrite has a waxy sheen.

256

There are various other minerals that come under the heading of "jade" or "yü," but these are the two main groups. Certain Western experts complain that many of the minerals thus classified are not entitled to be called jade, but the Chinese did not study their favorite substance from a chemical or geological point of view. They were interested only in its symbolical virtues, its appearance, and its musical note.

WHERE JADE WAS FOUND

The archaic jades made before the Han dynasty were carved from native nephrite, quarried at various points along the Yellow River basin. About two thousand years ago the supply began to dwindle, and jade was brought by caravan route from Chinese Turkestan and Yarkand.

The early pieces were entirely different from what is conveyed to the Western mind by the word "jade." They were not translucent, and the artisans tried to get some light into them by cutting the mineral into very thin slices. Nor were they elaborately carved, but they were plain and geometrical in design. They were not bright green, but usually a neutral tone, such as cream, tan, brown, gray, or dull green. If a clear translucent piece was found it was considered a great treasure.

The jades that came from Turkestan were translucent, shining, and had an oilier feel. The colors commonly ranged from yellow to brown, and from light blue to bright green. Some were black and dark purple; other very highly valued pieces were pure white. The colors were given such names as ink black, snow white, kingfisher green, sea green, grass green, and vermilion red. The yellowish white jade, known as mutton-fat, was especially prized because of its heaviness and smoothness.

There were no brilliant jewel-green jades before the thirteenth century when jadeite began to be imported from Burma. This is the type that became best known outside China. It is not always green, but comes in a wide range of colors. The lavender jade, which looks like amethyst, and the pure white jade were particularly admired; most valued of all was a mottled green and white called "moss entangled in the melting snow."

Most of the jade worked in Canton came from Burma; while in Peking the bulk of the jade came by the same camel caravan route from Turkestan as it has for nearly two thousand years. The region from which it was brought was Mohammedan. The mineral was also transported by Mohammedans, and it is interesting that many of the dealers and workers in jade in Peking were of that faith.

HOW JADE WAS SOLD AND CARVED

Jadestones were brought into the Peking or Canton market in lumps of varying sizes. They were coated with brown earth from centuries of immersion and looked like ordinary boulders.

Each piece was laboriously bisected—an operation which took many hours of labor. Then one small section (about two by one inch) was polished, and the bidders had to take a chance when they offered a price. Even if a trace of good color appeared on the polished section it might be only on the surface. On the other hand, the buyer might be lucky, and the dullest-looking stone might prove to have a heart of pure translucent jade.

Jade has been worked in the same manner for centuries. First the material is roughly shaped with different types of saws and other tools, then it is smoothed down with polishing wheels before it is ready to be carved.

The lapidary works a treadle with his feet, and with his hands holds the piece against the tubular drill. The diamond drill pierces the jade, and a wire saw is used for fine fretwork. Throughout the whole process, use is made of hand-prepared abrasives. The final polishing is a prolonged process, requiring time, patience, and skill. It is essential that a well-carved piece of jade should have no sharp angles, and that "all lines be soft and fluent as if melted by the fire or sun." The finest examples of carving may represent the work of twenty years or more.

RESPECT FOR THE MATERIAL

When the piece of jade was acquired by the artisan he did not start work on it immediately. In archaic times the shape, dimensions, and decorations were strictly prescribed by ritual rules. However, if, in later times, the jade was no longer regarded as sacred, it was still the most honored of all stones, and the Chinese craftsman never lost his respect for the importance of the material. A piece of jade would be kept and studied for months or even years before a decision could be reached as to the best way in which to utilize it. Its form would be considered, its size, its color, and its markings. For instance, the shape of a white boulder might suggest a hill, and the green markings might be used to carve a grove of trees. One piece of jade might suggest the form of a Kwan Yin, another piece might be suitable for carving a bowl. On this a reddish streak might be used for carving a floral spray.

This respect for the material, and the dignity and meaning of fine craftsmanship are well illustrated in the following well-known story:

One of the Ming emperors, who had acquired a rough piece of white jade with green markings, suggested to his most skillful carver that it be made into a piece showing a dragon fighting two Fo dogs. The sculptor took the piece in his hands, studied it thoughtfully, and replied: "Your Majesty! Heaven has already shaped this piece of jade. It represents four carp swimming through the green weeds in the lake of the Celestial Palace."

The Emperor could see no such thing, and, although he commanded his courtiers to look at it steadily for an hour, none of them could see it either. The emperor then ordered the jade carver to prove the truth of his statement.

Two years later the carver returned and handed the emperor the piece of jade exquisitely carved and polished. The four silver carp swimming through the green weeds were now clearly apparent to everyone. The artisan then produced the jade dust he had removed in the course of the carving, and there was barely enough of it to cover a coin.

Because of this faith of the craftsman in his skill, his deep understanding of the material in which he worked, and his innate good taste, no two of the many thousands of carved jade pieces are exactly alike.

JADE THE EQUALIZER

Jade was the jewel that grants all desires in this world and the next; and it was for all the people, not only for the wealthy. In the first century, jade ornaments worn from the girdle would often indicate a person's occupation. For instance, farmers wore little ornaments like ploughshares, workmen wore axes, and married women wore such things as pins and needles. All through the centuries the workers as well as the aristocrats bought jade earrings, hairpins, or other ornaments for their wives, every Chinese woman wanting to possess at least one piece of jade.

The greater part of the cost of a piece of jade is accounted for by the long years of work that have gone into carving it. When a large piece is being worked, smaller pieces are cut off. Sometimes, too, a whole piece may be found unsuitable for carving. Thus we find pieces made up into ornaments at prices that vary with the quality of the material as well as the workmanship. Some of them may be worth more than emeralds, and others cost little more than glass. Yet even these latter ones are treasured, simply because they are jade.

JADES IN THE HAN DYNASTY

If, for the most part, the ritual uses and symbolism of the archaic jades had been forgotten or neglected by the time of the Han dynasty, the substance was still treasured for its decorative and noble qualities. We read of jade used in architecture, although such phrases as jade terraces, jade halls, and jade beds and doors presumably referred to things ornamented with jade. They might also have referred to objects made of pure white marble or stone, which could be said to resemble jade. Yet again, as the term "jade" was used to imply excellence or beauty, such descriptions may sometimes have been used in a purely complimentary sense.

Many jade symbols, including some of the same shapes as the archaic ones, were worn during the Han dynasty, but they were chosen for color, quality, and fine carving. There were rings which signified friendship without end, bells, axes, the fungus of immortality,* and the "Ju-i," a scepterlike object, the head of which is supposed to have been derived from the fungus. The "Ju-i," signifying "May all be according to your wishes," was presented to friends on birthdays,

---

* Fungus, the Plant of Immortality. This is ling-chih (Polyporus lucidus) which grows around the roots of trees. When dried it is very durable and the Taoists took it as a symbol of immortality and longevity.

New Year's, weddings, and other special occasions. This symbol was used by both Buddhists and Taoists.

Then there were all kinds of solid little animal charms in jade—dragons, tigers, phoenixes, elephants, tortoises, rats, frogs, two coupled fishes, cicadas, and unicorns (Ch'i lin), as well as little human figures carved in a free, natural style. The tiger symbolized manly courage; other animals stood for strength or male virility; the unicorn which protects the young, was given to boy babies.

The use of jade in ornamental sword and dagger hilts and scabbards, decorated with geometrical designs, carvings of dragons and T'ao-t'iehs, was further developed. There was widespread use of jade beads and bracelets, belt buckles and girdle hooks, hair ornaments, necklaces and pendants, as well as the large jade rings which had originally been made to protect the thumbs of archers but which were afterward worn for ornament. Those of pure white jade were reserved for the emperor. Mention is made of Han garments consisting of jade plaques joined by gold thread, like a coat of mail.

Besides these personal articles, there were fine large jade carvings of naturalistic horses and bears—the red bear and the jade green horse symbolizing a prosperous and peaceful reign. There is a very fine specimen of a carved horse's head of this period in the Victoria and Albert Museum, London.

With the introduction of Buddhism, carvings on a much larger scale became popular, and the work grew more depictional.

USE OF JADE IN THE T'ANG, SUNG, AND YÜAN DYNASTIES

Jade was lavishly used for ornamental purposes in the luxurious T'ang dynasty. We read about Yang Kuei-fei, the most famous of Chinese beauties, who had a skin white and smooth as jade, and who wore the most exquisite jade jewels and hair ornaments. Surrounded by objects made of this material, she slept in a jade bed and danced to music played on jade lutes.

As an art medium, however, jade was not considered of great importance until the Sung period, at which time carvers really began to reveal their taste and fine workmanship. Sung jade vessels excelled in solidity. Many of the archaic bronze ritual vessels were copied in this medium, and new forms were created. Sturdy and yet sensitive jade carvings of water buffaloes and other animals were made. There was no longer the T'ang tendency to overelaboration, and the carvers were able to use the restraint and strength which characterize all Sung art.

The wide range of colors in early jades did not appeal to the Sung connoisseurs. They admired only green and white jades, which were the colors the potters tried to emulate in the celadon and Ting porcelains.

In the Yüan dynasty jades were highly treasured by the Mongol rulers as vessels for serving food and wine. Friar Oderic, a missionary who traveled in China in 1318, describes a large jade bowl, or cistern, that he saw in the courtyard of the Palace of the Great Khan in Peking. He says he was told that "the price of the bowl was more than that of four large cities" and describes it as "all hooped around with gold, and in every corner thereof is a dragon . . . this jar

Plain "pi." Light green, shading to dark. Shang-Yin period. Eumorfopoulos Collection.

Jade mask of human face. Shang-Yin.

Ts'ung. Mottled grayish black and dark green. Probably middle Chou. Eumorfopoulos Collection.

Bird-dragon, white jade, calcified, with cinnabar. Middle Chou.

Pi. Spinach green jade, brown flecked. Late Chou.

Scabbard tip, brownish-white jade, calcinated. Late Chou. T. B. Walker Collection.

Green jade stags from Hsien
Chêng tomb in Honan. Chou
Dynasty.

Jade disk, type Pi. Nephrite.
Warring States.

Carved jade ornament. Late
Chou.

Art Institute of Chicago

Jade Dragon pendant, light green with brown markings. Late Eastern Chou. Bequest of Mrs. Edward Sonnenschein.

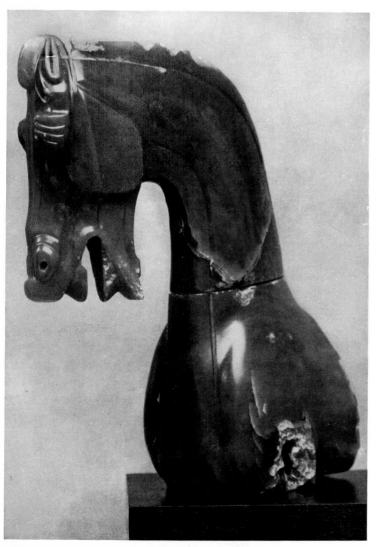

Horse's head, green jade. Han or third century. Eumorfopoulos Collection.

Victoria and Albert Museum, London

Pillow in form of baby, emerald green jadeite. Reign of K'ang Hsi. Bishop Collection.

Reclining water buffalo, dark green jade. Sung Dynasty. Bequest of Mrs. Edward Sonnenschein.

Nephrite screen, ivy green. Reign of Ch'ien Lung. Bishop Collection.

Greenish-white jade mountain carved from large boulder with figures of scholars meeting in a bamboo grove. Seals and period of Emperor Ch'ien Lung. T. B. Walker Collection.

Pair of jadeite cups, amethyst color, and green jade coupe in form of leaf gourd. Reign of Ch'ien Lung.

Dark green jade brush holder, deeply carved with Taoist figures in landscape. 18th-19th century.

Figure of a dignitary (late 15th—early 16th century) on dark ivory base, traces of green pigment; and figure of Shou Shing, God of Longevity, holding peach of immortality (late 15th century).

Three Buddhist female deities in heavily gilded ivory carving. Ming Dynasty.

Seated figure of Kuan Ti, dark ivory, partly painted black. Early 16th century.

Ceremonial cup of rhinoceros horn. Early 18th century. Gift of Mrs. Cutler Bonestell.

has also fringes of network of great pearls hanging therefrom. . . . Into these vessels drink is conveyed by conduits from the court of the Palace, and beside it are many golden goblets from which those drink who list."

This bowl disappeared after the fall of the Mongol dynasty in 1368, and it was not until the eighteenth century that it was found in the kitchen of a Buddhist monastery, stripped of its gold and jewels and serving as a receptacle for salted vegetables. The Emperor Ch'ien Lung purchased it for a few ounces of silver and had it carried into the Palace where he ordered a poem relating its whole history to be inscribed on it.

FURTHER IMPROVEMENTS IN TECHNIQUE DURING MING AND CH'ING DYNASTIES

One of the many arts of China which suffered no decline was the carving of jade. There are those who admire only the archaic jades because of their qualities of antiquity and austerity, but, as far as the technique of jade carving went, it improved from century to century, with the artisans working in the prevailing taste of the time. The jade objects made in the Ming dynasty were bold, dignified, and baroque. Some of the large imperial jade animals—recumbent buffaloes and horses—date from this period.

The Emperor K'ang Hsi established an atelier for the carving of jade in the Palace precincts, and here, throughout the Ch'ing dynasty, the lapidaries turned out quantities of jade pieces—large and small, elaborate and simple, strong and delicate. They made pieces based on the shapes of the ancient ritual vessels, and they created innumerable new designs. Jade was honored above all other materials, and the emperors themselves wrote poems which were engraved on many pieces.

During the reign of Ch'ien Lung, several very large blocks of jade were brought into Peking, and the emperor ordered that one of these, weighing about 640 pounds, be carved to represent a mountain landscape scene. This can now be seen in the Walker Art Gallery in Minneapolis, Minnesota. The largest known piece of jade in the United States, it is of a greenish white color, and is in the form of a mountain, with streams, trees, pavilions, and a bamboo grove peopled with literary scholars of the fourth century. The Emperor Ch'ien Lung wrote a poem about it which is engraved on the piece. The last couplet of this poem conveys the idea:

> When you look at this piece
> Who do you consider to be the man of jade?

The "man of jade" would, of course, be the man superior to all others in the group. The carving was completed in 1784.

There were other even larger mountain carvings in jade in Peking, as well as smaller ones, and many small brush rests shaped like little mountain ranges. Although the Emperor Ch'ien Lung ordered the large carvings to be made, his own personal taste favored small objects in pure white jade, delicately carved in low relief.

Jade was used in every conceivable manner. In the Forbidden City there were jade thrones and beds, jade pillows in such forms as tigers and children, jade screens of all sizes, jade dishes and chopsticks, jade teapots, plates, bowls, wine pots and cups. There were also jade books, with the writing inscribed in gold on jade plaques. These plaques were covered with brocade and kept in a sandalwood box.

The love for jade was not confined to the Palace. Jade Buddhas, Kwan Yins, Taoist Immortals, historical and literary figures, children, and animals were innumerable. So were jade snuff bottles, incense burners, vases, flower pots, bulb bowls, little carved trees and sprays of flowers, boxes for cosmetics, combs, and, of course, personal ornaments in the form of rings, necklaces, earrings, hair ornaments, bracelets, and belt buckles.

The period was also notable for jade chess sets, mahjong sets, fans, toys, opium pipes, and bowls. Then, too, one could find in jade all the requisites of the scholar's table—the arm rests, brush pots, ink slabs, water pots, jade-tipped brushes, jade seals, and all the exquisite paraphernalia with which the cultured scholar surrounded himself.

Other minerals, such as rock crystal, amber, turquoise, jasper, amethyst, coral, and lapis lazuli, were also carved by the Chinese craftsmen, but none of them was admired and revered in the same way as jade. Everything precious was likened to this favorite mineral and we find Chinese proverbs throughout the centuries abounding in such references as "It is better to be a piece of broken jade than a whole tile," or "A scholar should revere the truth as he reveres jade."

And yet, with all the reverence and affection shown to jade, it has some quality which will often elude even the Chinese. Apart from size, quality, and workmanship, there are all kinds of subtle distinctions, and these may include the person for whom the object was originally made, some special superstition or historical event connected with a particular piece, or even, perhaps, some rare feeling that it evokes when handled.

A friend of ours, an Englishman, who was well known as a connoisseur of Chinese art, was on his way to dinner in Peking one Christmas Eve. As he passed through Jade Street it occurred to him to buy a Christmas gift for his hostess, so he went into the Shop of the Ten Thousand Gems and asked to be shown some jade pendants. A tray was put before him, and, having only a few minutes to spare, he quickly selected a piece he thought suitable and asked the price.

"Fifty dollars," said the dealer.

"All right, I'll take it."

"How much you pay?" asked the dealer.

"Fifty dollars," was the answer.

The outraged dealer cried: "What do you mean? I said fifty dollars. Why do you say fifty dollars?"

"Look here," the customer answered, "I'm in a hurry, and don't want to stand here bargaining. Just put the thing in a box and let me have it."

270

"No can do," the dealer stated firmly. "I say fifty dollars. You say fifty dollars. How can I sell it to you?"

The dealer then went into an inner room, where our friend saw him excitedly telling the story while an ever-growing group of dealers from other stores gathered around him. They all studied the pendant, held it up to the light, and rubbed it between their hands.

At last the dealer came back to the impatient customer. "Tell me," he pleaded, "why did you say fifty dollars? What do you know about this piece of jade?"

After much argument our friend left, carrying the quite ordinary jade pendant in his pocket. The dealer, convinced that he had been cheated, was still muttering: "I said fifty dollars. He said fifty dollars. Why did he say fifty dollars?"

For months afterward Jade Street resounded with the story of the Englishman who had outwitted the dealers by finding a unique piece of jade which they had not recognized.

The moral of this story is that one simply did not buy a piece of jade or anything else in Peking without bargaining. That was a crude method of procedure, which entailed a loss of face all round. The seller felt that he had obviously asked too low a price, while the client had shown that he lacked a sense of decorum by his unbecoming haste in completing the purchase.

But that is only one side of the story. The important point is that, right on Jade Street in Peking, a group of dealers, trained to the trade from early childhood, still did not wholly trust their own judgment. They were convinced that the Westerner had discovered some rare property in the jade which had escaped them all, and he had been anxious to get the jade out of the store before they discovered it.

For jade is not just a stone whose value can be finally determined. It is the concentrated essence of hills and water, it is the pure thing, it is an essential element in Chinese art, philosophy, and religion; and it may always have some hidden virtue that escapes the eye of the keenest observer.

Chapter IX

THE CARVING OF IVORY

MORE LUXURIOUS than wood, ivory has ranked next to jade as a medium for fine carving. The Chinese have not endowed ivory with the supreme religious, mystical, philosophical, and poetic qualities of jade. They have, however, appreciated it for its intrinsic qualities of hardness and translucency, its soft warm tones, the ease with which it can be carved, and the beautiful polish it assumes.

The earliest-known examples of carved ivory are, once more, those found at Anyang. In the course of the Shang-Yin excavations at that site, exquisitely carved objects in bone, stone, and ivory, including little dragons, alligators, tortoises, and cowries, some elaborately inlaid with turquoise or cinnabar, came to light. As is the case with so many of the objects found at Anyang, the perfection of the technique makes it apparent that the art of ivory carving had already had a long period of development.

There is a legend that the last Shang emperor—referred to as a wicked and extravagant man—ordered chopsticks to be made of ivory, which was regarded as a sacrilegious act because ivory was used only for sacrificial and ceremonial purposes. Herrlee G. Creel, however, says that this story has been disproved by the inscriptions on the oracle bones, which show that the last Shang emperor was an able and efficient ruler, and also that chopsticks were not used until the Chou dynasty.

The Chous, to justify themselves for having attacked the Shangs without provocation, seem to have put out this propaganda to prove that the Shang-Yin emperor had forfeited the Mandate of Heaven by his own evil conduct. The arts of character assassination, and falsification of history, appear to have developed as early as did all the other arts.

Objects made of ivory were used for ritual and ceremonial purposes in the Shang-Yin dynasty, but it was under the Chous that this material began to be used extensively and for a great variety of purposes. There were the narrow

(See illustrations on pages 267 and 268.)

memoranda tablets, called Hu, which feudal princes and high officials held before the lower part of their faces with both hands while having audience with the emperor. These varied in shape according to rank and were not carved. With eyes fixed on the tablet, the official would address the emperor and then write down his replies.

It is believed that this custom originated because of the emperors' fear of assassination. It was realized that a man who had both his hands occupied, and in full view, could not suddenly draw forth a concealed weapon. It was also said that the officials' mouths had to be covered so that their breath could not give offense to the ruler.

Ivory was commonly used for decorating chariots, furniture, and the palanquins of officials. It was used for arm rests, brush holders, and fans; for combs, hairpins, and other ornaments; also for chopsticks and tips of bows. In the Metropolitan Museum of Art, New York, there is a small ivory piece, carved with a conventionalized animal's head and eye, ostensibly used for untying knots. Young men would wear these implements as a token of maturity for they symbolized an ability to solve difficult problems. The types of decoration used in ivory carving in the Chou dynasty were of the same angular, spiral, and geometrical type as is seen on the Shang pieces.

There is ample evidence that elephants once lived in a wild state in North China, and there are frequent references to captures of this animal on the Shang oracle bones found at Anyang. It is recorded, however, that by the sixth century B.C. the lavish use of ivory had led to the extermination of the elephant from the soil of China. There are many references, including those in the "Book of Odes," to ivory being offered as tribute by border tribes.

Gradually more and more ivory had to be imported from Siam, Burma, and India, as well as from Annam, where the tusks are described as short. The largest and heaviest tusks came from Africa. These were referred to as "great ivory" and were used only for the most important work. The ivory was most valuable when the tusks had been removed as soon as the animal was slain or found dead. If left too long after death, the ivory became dull and opaque.

Although the tusks of the elephant ranked highest, many other types of ivory were used. A trade in mammoth ivory was carried on with Siberian tribesmen in the Chou and Han dynasties (the mammoths being the extinct species which we see portrayed in the paintings by paleolithic man on cave walls in the Dordogne region of France). Some of these tusks, which may have lain buried in ice from ten thousand to fifty thousand years, remained in good condition, but much of this ivory was dull and opaque and it was chiefly used for furniture inlays.

From the same frozen regions as the mammoth came the ivory of the walrus and the narwhal, which the Chinese often refer to as "fish ivory." The tusks of the hippopotamus and the horns of the rhinoceros were also much used—the latter being of a rich, dark color which is particularly admired by certain Chinese connoisseurs.

Apart from the ivories found in the course of excavations of Shang and Chou sites, most of our knowledge of early ivory carving derives from literary references. For instance, we read about ivory chopsticks and delicately carved combs in the Han and T'ang dynasties, and also that ivory mats were made between the first and fifth centuries. These mats were made by cutting the ivory into thin threads, weaving them, and then dyeing them in different colors. Finally designs were etched on them so that the ivory color would show through.

Among other ivory pieces we saw a T'ang measuring ruler in a private collection in China. An ivory Buddha, which we did not see, was reported to have been found in a T'ang tomb.

In the Sung dynasty there is mention of ivory being used for sword and knife handles, chopsticks, carved figures, rollers at the end of painted scrolls, and fans.

In the Yüan dynasty, an imperial bureau for carving in ivory and rhinoceros horn was set up with an official in charge. Here a hundred and fifty workmen turned out couches, tables, and chairs, either made of or inlaid with ivory. They also made ornaments for girdles, objects for scholars' tables, and various other things for the use of the imperial household.

A few specimens of ivory carving attributed to the Yüan dynasty have been found, but as a general rule most of the now-existing examples of ivory carving date back no earlier than the Ming dynasty, which was the great period for work of this type.

In the Ming carvings, there is a mellowness and simplicity, a sureness of touch, and a great realization of the nature of the material which gives full value to the grain and curve of the ivory. Figures of all types were made, but more than half of them were of old men or men in their prime—deities, Immortals, Lohans, historical figures, scholars, farmers, sages, warriors, saints, and beggars.

The Chinese have always preferred to portray older persons, for as one of the outstanding Chinese painters, Ku K'ai-chih (fourth century), explained: "To paint a pretty young girl is like carving a portrait in silver. One has to concentrate on her clothes, and depend on a touch here, and a stroke there, to bring out her true beauty." Since the beauty of a young girl lies chiefly in her youth and freshness, it is felt that these qualities can be best expressed in a symbolic manner—perhaps by a branch of peach blossom—rather than by a direct likeness.

These Ming carvings of old men, their faces showing wisdom, tolerance, humor, and resignation, are among the most characteristic works of the Chinese craftsmen. Some of them were stained, painted, or lacquered, but those in which one can appreciate the deep natural tones of the old ivory are perhaps the most beautiful.

The ivory workers in China make their carvings all in one piece, following the shape and size of the material. There are no added arms and legs or other pieces, as is frequently the case in Japan and other countries. As with jade, the artisan planned his subject so as best to utilize his material, adding nothing and taking away as little as possible.

When, in 1680, the Ch'ing Emperor K'ang Hsi established ateliers for various crafts in the Palace precincts, he included ivory carving, and sent for Cantonese workers who were famed for their consummate skill in this type of work.

They could carve the most intricate patterns, make fans with the most delicate lacework, and make architectural models of all kinds of buildings. It is they who made the famous concentric revolving balls out of one solid block of ivory, carving from three to twenty balls one inside the other, showing different patterns as they turned. These were called "devil's work balls" because of the long, patient, and skillful labor that went into their creation. They are reputed to have been made first in the palace of the Sung emperors.

The Cantonese ivory was not colored, but in Peking ivory often continued to be stained, etched, or lacquered. The Cantonese artisans excelled in the delicacy, complexity, and ingenuity of their workmanship, but the works of the Peking carvers, who strove to express ideas, were on a higher plane of artistic expression.

The method of carving ivory and the tools used are very simple and have remained unchanged from the earliest times. The saw, scraper, and chisel are used for the cutting, and, when the piece has been carved, it is polished with pumice powder and a damp cloth.

In the Ch'ing dynasty the use of ivory became even more widespread, and it was used not only for chopsticks, fans, and handles, but also for arm rests, brush holders, writing brushes, all types of objects for the scholar's table and the woman's toilet table, cigarette holders, pipes for opium, snuff bottles, scent boxes, bird cages and cricket cages, hairpins, combs, card cases, picture frames, boxes of all types and sizes, trays, and games such as chess, mahjong, and checkers. Then, too, the ivory carvers would produce whole screens and inlays for screens, inlays for furniture of all kinds and for the decoration of buildings. There are beautiful carved panels depicting the flowers of the four seasons, the flowers of the twelve months, and all the other traditional subjects.

While turning out these objects for domestic use, as well as supplying ivories for the large export trade which had developed in the Ming and grown to greater proportions during the Ch'ing dynasties, the Chinese ivory carvers did not neglect their preferred medium of expression, and the one which was most appreciated by the connoisseurs of their art—the creation of ivory figures. They made innumerable figures of Buddhist deities, Taoist Immortals, and all the legendary, historical, and literary heroes and heroines. In addition to their representations of old men, still the most popular subject, they made many images of women, including the Kwan Yin and the famous beauties of China. Whole tusks—sometimes three feet long—were at times used in carving these figures, so that full value could be given to the grace of the figure and the flowing lines of the draperies.

While the Chinese did not usually carve nudes, they made an exception in the small recumbent ivory female figures which were made for the use of physicians. In the old days a male doctor could not examine a sick woman, so the little ivory figure was carried to the patient's bedside. She would put her hand through the bed curtains and indicate on the figure the exact spot where she felt pain. Then the doctor would feel her pulse, ask questions, and make his diagnosis.

Although the Ming pieces are considered more important as works of art, there was no deterioration in the quality of the work done during the Ch'ing dynasty. In fact the carving became more delicate, and technically more nearly perfect. Perhaps in ivory, as in other branches of Chinese art, we have a tendency to find Ch'ing works less satisfying because they are too completely realized. Nothing is left for the imagination to work on as in the earlier pieces. Everything has been done, and there is little or no room for improvement. This sense of total fulfillment is less exciting and appealing than is the promise of future development and realization.

VI: *OTHER EXPRESSIONS OF THE CRAFTSMAN*

Chapter X

ARCHITECTURE

"FROM AGES IMMEMORIAL, Man has seized the truth that he must live in harmony with the forces of Nature." This basic rule has governed architectural planning in China. The position, shape, and dimensions of every building, garden, bridge, or pagoda had to be in harmony with the surrounding landscape.

The principle of fêng-shui (wind and water) can be looked upon as a mere superstition, which is supposed to assure the propitious influences of wind, earth, water, and the spirits of the region. But, like many other superstitions, it was based on practical and aesthetic grounds. Each building was not only placed at the most suitable spot, but it was oriented to the cardinal points of the compass, and the rooms most used always faced south so that they would receive the most sun.

This principle applies to cities as well as to buildings. Peking, which was built on the same plan as Sian-fu, the ancient capital of the Han and T'ang dynasties, strictly conforms to the points of the compass. Its broad, long avenues run from north to south and from east to west, while all the important buildings, including the Imperial Palaces, face south. Its open altars are placed north, south, east, and west.

The average house is constructed according to the same basic plan as a city, a palace, or a temple. The fundamental design consists of a rectangular building (called t'ing) raised up on a stone platform, the entrance being placed in the center of the long side, which faces south. A Chinese homestead does not consist of a single building but of a compound containing a group of buildings, usually one story high—the important ones placed one behind the other with a courtyard between, and the lesser ones at the side. Main doors, facades, and gates face south.

This compound is surrounded by a wall. The Chinese word "ch'êng" means either a city or a wall. Thus the Chinese family home became a little walled city within a walled city, for most towns and villages were once surrounded by a crenelated wall with gates and watch towers.

The original plan adopted for dwellings and cities appears to have met with universal approval, for it remained practically unchanged from the earliest recorded history to the present century. In the course of the excavations on the Shang-Yin site, it was discovered that temples and palaces were built thirty-five centuries ago according to the same fundamental plan as houses are erected today.

The largest building foundation found was twenty-six feet wide, and ninety-two feet long. The raised platform, which provided the floor, was made of earth pounded down, layer by layer, inside a wooden frame. This technique was used in the neolithic Black Pottery era, and it is still used now. On this foundation a house was erected with a gabled roof, supported on three rows of pillars. The pillar bases were of rounded stone or bronze disks. The walls did not, and do not, support the roof, but served merely as screens. They may have been made of pounded earth too, but afterward they were constructed of bricks and wood.

A pictograph which appears on Shang oracle bones indicates that houses at that time resembled those still in use, with a roof of the same shape. Roofs were plastered and thatched, but afterward they were covered with bricks or clay tiles.

The massive roof with its curved edges—sometimes double or triple—dominates the Chinese building, as the overhanging branches of a tree in full bloom draw attention away from the trunk. This effect was further enhanced when, during the T'ang dynasty or earlier, it became the custom to cover the roof with brightly glazed tiles of yellow, blue, green, and sometimes other colors.

There has been much speculation about the origin of the Chinese roof. The theory has been advanced that it was based on the lines of a tent, but the Chinese were a settled agricultural people who considered the nomad tribes beyond their borders as people of an inferior culture. In an ancient poem about the building of a palace, there is a reference to the roof being "like the luxuriant head of a pine-tree." The Chinese love of trees, the feeling that the branches of a tree provided natural shelter from sun and rain, together with the stylized line of a pine tree branch as used in art suggest that this was the original model for the Chinese curved roof.

The connection between pine branches and roofs is borne out by the fact that, even in our time, the Chinese attached pine branches to the top of scaffolding poles when a new building was being erected. This was said to be done in order that evil spirits might be led to believe that they were passing over a forest, and would not be tempted to bring bad luck to the new house. That is the superstition, but the logical reason behind it was probably that the branches protected the workers from the direct rays of the sun.

The essential elements of the Chinese building were determined at least as early as the Shang dynasty. In the "Ritual of the Chou Dynasty" there is a chapter relating to building which explains that the angle of the roof near the ridge should be greater than near the eaves because the greater incline would enable the rainwater to run off more speedily, while the gentle upward slope at the base would throw the water away from the wall of the house. The projecting roof also shaded the house from the strong rays of the sun in summer.

278

With their insistence on combining the practical with the poetic, the Chinese also explain that the upturned curves of their roofs symbolize aspiration.

The supporting columns of important buildings were made of a variety of cedar called nan mu—the tallest and straightest of Chinese trees which preserves its aromatic odor for centuries, and the grain of which improves with age. The plan of architecture was essentially structural, based on the requirements of the material and the function of the building, with a well-planned system of sturdy cross beams and brackets below the eaves to support the heavy roof.

Once completed, however, the beams, pillars, and walls inside palaces, temples, and houses of important officials were decorated with paintings and with polychrome carvings, sometimes lacquered. The designs used would probably have been similar to those seen on bronzes, pottery, or fabrics of the same period.

By the T'ang dynasty the lines of the roof became more varied and more decorative. The top-heavy effect was lightened by skillfully curving the sides so as to give a sense of rhythm. It was the roof which gave character to a building and which determined its grandeur or simplicity, its strength or grace.

As already stated, the walls of buildings had no supporting function whatever, and it is possible that, in some cases, these may have been detachable, as they still are in many Japanese houses. This is quite likely, since the Japanese were so greatly and permanently influenced by Chinese architecture, as well as by all other aspects of Chinese art and culture—particularly of the T'ang dynasty. (The city of Kyoto was built on the model of the Chinese T'ang capital.)

The windows in homes, as in the palaces, consisted of narrow strips of wood which formed a lattice work. On the outside these were covered with specially prepared translucent white paper, which kept out the cold as effectually as glass, but which did not (like glass) keep out ultraviolet rays.

Sometimes the whole side of a wall would be covered with these windows, or there might be a series of windows of different shapes, such as a leaf, egg, urn, diamond, fan, bell, or sunflower. The lattices, too, were made in a great variety of patterns—thunder and cloud, spiral clouds, icicle, or meander. The great charm of these windows is enhanced by shadows of moving objects outside. There is a theory that the bamboo stroke, so popular with painters, originated when an artist traced the silhouettes of bamboos which the moonlight cast on the paper window.

Doorways in houses or in gardens vary as much as do the windows, and may be octagonal, or take the form of a moon (half or full), bell, lotus petal, gourd, Ju-i scepter, pear, or flower vase.

Many important Chinese buildings were constructed of wood, presumably because the Chinese preferred it to any other material. The Chinese did not lack stone, and they knew how to make bricks at least as early as the Ch'in dynasty. They built many stone bridges, including one in southern Hopei (made A.D. 600) which is still standing, and which, to quote Gustav Ecke, "in a very modern manner, modifies the construction of the compound Roman aqueduct."

Then, as early as the Chou dynasty (and possibly earlier) they built lofty stone towers, called t'ai. These were usually square in shape, sometimes as tall as three hundred feet, and were used as storehouses for treasures, as watch towers to follow the progress of the hunt, or as astronomical observatories.

In the Sung dynasty, Li Chieh (died A.D. 1110), the architect in charge of construction of temples and public buildings in the imperial capital wrote a treatise which gave specific rules for building all kinds of stone, wood, tile, and brick structures.

Yet, in spite of its perishable nature, the Chinese—with their love of trees—considered wood the most desirable of building materials. Cost was not a factor, since emperors would have procured whatever they wanted regardless of expense. Bricks and adobe were later used for more modest homes, but palaces continued to be made of wood.

The Chinese emperors had their mausoleums built of stone. They may have felt that living persons could put up new buildings but that the dead must be provided with resting places that would last forever.

Few old Chinese structures have survived except for some bridges, pagodas, mausoleums, and rock temples. When we say "old," we are using that word in the Chinese sense, for many buildings still exist which were erected early in the Ming dynasty, more than five centuries ago.

In regard to earlier buildings we have to rely on rare archaeological excavations, paintings, and written records. We read that in the Chou dynasty the Imperial Palace consisted of a vast enclosure, surrounded by high mud or brick walls, which contained the residences of the emperor and empress, the concubines, the children, and the servants. It contained the offices of the ministers, reception halls, temples, and workshops for the weaving of the silk and hemp needed by the Court; as well as treasuries for storing the imperial archives, documents, and valuables, and warehouses for stores and for all products necessary for the maintenance of life. The Imperial Palace was a complete walled city, and it has remained the model for all Chinese palaces that have been built since.

The Ch'in Emperor Shih Huang Ti was a great builder, who, in addition to building the fifteen-hundred-mile Great Wall—one of the architectural wonders of the world—constructed many palaces and a great mausoleum. The largest of these palaces was built on the banks of the river which flowed through the great hunting park of Shang Lin. This palace (completed in 212 B.C.) was constructed by 700,000 slave laborers. It was 500 feet long and 2500 feet wide; the great courtyard could hold 100,000 people, and 10,000 could be seated in the Central Court. Built according to Chou designs, it was lavishly decorated, the walls being covered with paintings, rich draperies, and works of art taken from conquered kingdoms.

It was connected with the 270 other imperial residences by covered roads bordered with walls. Each of these palaces included courtyards and was surrounded by magnificent gardens with terraces, pavilions, bridges, rare trees, lakes, fish pools, and galleries. The palaces and gardens that can still be seen in Peking conform to the same general pattern.

There are numerous records in prose and poetry of the splendid palaces built during the Han dynasty—the magnificent wooden carving which was

280

painted, gilded, and lacquered, the marble stairways, the large wall paintings, the carpets, the silk hangings, the gold and silver and jade, the bronze and lacquer. No trace of all this has survived, but the bas-reliefs in the Han tombs show that the architecture was basically the same as in the later dynasties, except that the roofs were less elaborately curved. We also know that the Forbidden City in Peking was built according to the earlier designs.

There is further tangible evidence of Han architecture in the tomb models of average Chinese homes of the second and third centuries, which can still be found in many parts of China.

Peking as it stands today is a Ming city, built in the fifteenth century. The Mongol capital, as described by Marco Polo, seems to have been built in the Chinese architectural style, except for the excess of gold and silver and of ornate decoration in the imperial palaces. It was considered "too barbaric" by the first Ming emperor, Hung Wu, and he set up his capital in Nanking on more austere lines.

The emperor Yung Lo rebuilt the city of Peking, using the plans and descriptions of the ancient capital of the Han and T'ang dynasties. Even though many of the buildings have since been destroyed by fire, they were rebuilt in exactly the same style.

Nowhere is the dignity, simplicity, and harmony of the Chinese style of architecture better seen than in the plan of the city of Peking. It consists of a series of rectangular cities, set one inside the other, each surrounded by its own walls. The central one is the (Purple) Forbidden City (the Imperial Palace), with its glistening yellow-tiled roofs, enclosed by walls once red but now subdued by time and weather to a deep mellow pink. Built around this is the Imperial City, which provided for all the needs of the Court. The Manchus created another oblong city, known as the Tartar City, which stretched around the Imperial City, enclosed by gray brick walls with twelve gateways.

Beyond this again is the Chinese City, also protected by gray brick walls—thick battlemented walls with high watchtowers. For the Chinese have always loved walls, from the Great Wall, which was rebuilt by the Ming emperors, to the little walls which enclose their own compounds.

When we last saw it Peking still seemed to be the loveliest of all cities, with its magnificent palaces and temples, its marble altars and stairways, its superb parks and gardens, lakes, bridges and courtyards. The curving roofs, with their yellow, green, and blue glazed tiles shining brightly in the northern sunlight, added an additional note of gaiety to an enchanting scene.

The Great Altar of Heaven (begun in 1420) remains one of the finest conceptions of a place of worship that man has realized. It consists of an immense white marble platform built in three tiers, each set back from the one below, and surrounded by a triple white marble balustrade. The gleaming white altar —austere and awe-inspiring—is set amid dark cypress trees, and its roof consists of the clear northern sky. The altar is surrounded by a wall three and a half miles long, enclosing grounds on which are numerous other temples dedicated to special ceremonies. The outstanding one is called the Hall of Prayers for Harvests (or Temple of Heaven), and it dominates the whole city with its high triple roof covered with deep blue tiles, built up on three tiers of white marble balustrades.

One could go on indefinitely describing the architectural landmarks in and outside Peking—the Ming tombs, the Summer Palace, the temples in the Western Hills, and the many other palaces and buildings erected in the Ming and Ch'ing dynasties.

There was one special aspect of the city of Peking which never lost its charm —the streets of the craftsmen and the vendors of art objects, which were called Lantern Street, Jade Street, Ivory Street, Brass Street, Big and Little Furniture streets, Silver Street, Flower Street, and other such names.

While most present-day Chinese architecture either adheres to the ancient models or discards them altogether in favor of Western-type buildings, there was a growing tendency in the bigger cities, such as Peking, Shanghai, and Canton, to erect a new type of building of steel and cement, with modern improvements, which retained the colored roof tiles, the latticed windows, the courtyards and other decorative features of traditional Chinese architecture.

PAGODAS

If the Chinese designed their palaces and dwellings on a horizontal plane, there is one distinctive type of Chinese architecture which soars up into the sky, often to a height of thirteen or fifteen stories. This is the pagoda. These familiar structures consist of little one-story buildings, each with its own roof, piled up one upon the other. They are usually seven or nine stories high, but may be any odd number. The walls are very thick at the base, and diminish as they ascend. They are round, hexagonal, or octagonal in shape, with a balcony on each story, and they are made of brick, stone, marble, cast iron, and sometimes of glazed pottery.

The first pagoda of which we have any record was built at Nanking about A.D. 250 on the same site as the famous Porcelain Pagoda, which was erected in the Ming dynasty. There still stands in Honan (at Sung Shan, one of the Five Sacred Mountains) a brick pagoda which was built in 523.

Pagodas can be seen in every part of China, as there are still over two thousand of them in existence. The tallest is the one at Ting Chou in Chihli, which reaches a height of over 360 feet.

There is a theory that these pagodas were suggested to the Chinese by the type of Indian monuments called stupas, which were erected to contain Buddhist relics. The weakness with all these theories of foreign influence is that it is difficult to know on how firm a basis they have been formulated.

The Chinese did not favor tall dwellings. In his *Lettres Edifiantes* (written 1749), Père Attiret relates how, when he showed the Emperor K'ang Hsi some plans of European houses, the emperor was moved to exclaim: "How small and poor Europe must be! There is not enough ground to build dwellings, and the

282

people are forced to live up in the air." However, the Chinese have always loved high towers and they are mentioned in the most ancient writings.

It is possible that the pagoda, a purely Chinese form of building, may have been developed from a combination of the tower and the Buddhist stupa. Contradicting this, however, is the fact that in various parts of China there are Buddhist stupas, including the famous white marble dagoba in Peking. These are quite different in shape and are not called pagodas. Then there is the additional fact that the pagoda is not used as a reliquary, and has no special connection with Buddhism.

Actually these buildings serve no utilitarian purpose, and the Chinese advance both poetic and fantastic reasons for their existence. The poets say that they symbolize "the breaking of the bonds which hold man down to earth," and the geomancers say that they bring good luck to any district where they are erected.

In choosing the sites for pagodas, the Chinese have well displayed their instinctive feeling for beauty and have placed them on the exact spot where they have harmonized most perfectly with, and best accented, the surrounding landscape. They may be built on a hilltop where their silhouette can be seen against the sky for miles around, or set in the center of a flat region where a high note is needed to break the monotony.

THE P'AI-LOU OR COMMEMORATIVE ARCH

These arches, like the pagoda, do not fulfill any architectural function. They are erected to the memory of inhabitants who have performed notable services to the community, including military leaders, important state officials, men of literary eminence, philanthropists, and men of exceptional virtue. Such arches have been erected in honor of widows who refused to remarry, and virgins who committed suicide to preserve their chastity. Towns and villages have erected them to native sons who succeeded in passing the higher civil service examinations.

They consist of wood or stone or glazed pottery arches which stretch across the street, with three or five openings, and they are occasionally used for decorative purposes—to mark the approach to palaces and temples.

CHINESE GARDENS AND COURTYARDS

Chinese dwellings, whether palaces or private homes, are built around open courtyards. Even modest homesteads usually have more than one courtyard for the use of different branches of the family when they seek rest from the work and cares of the day beneath the open sky.

The courtyard, like the garden, is supposed to resemble a natural landscape as closely as possible, and even the smallest ones will usually have water—if only a fish bowl with some lotus leaves on the surface—a few pots of flowers, and a large rock, to suggest the glories of mountains and streams, of trees and flowers.

The Chinese garden, whether large or small, is intended to be a substitute for rural life and a retreat where the spirit of man can find peace and understanding. Everything must look natural. There are no beds of flowers, no smooth lawns, no regular avenues of trees. The garden is supposed to look as if created by nature, and the Chinese use the most exquisite skill and thought in order to achieve this unstudied effect.

Of course, there must be hills, water, and rocks. There are trees and shrubs, but few flowers, except for the lotuses in ponds and lakes. Such flowers as there are are placed there in pots.

Large gardens are planned like a landscape scene with bridges, pavilions, moon gates, and covered archways. The little winding paths are paved with mosaics of stones laid out in irregular but charming patterns. There will always be rockeries—those large irregular rock formations that are so highly appreciated by the Chinese, and which symbolize the creative force of nature and its strength and endurance.

Some tall rocks in fantastic shapes are set up on end like statues, others are piled up like little hills or are set around the edge of the pool. Stones are valued in accordance with their size and the uniqueness of their shape, but even little rocks are admired and used in some way, for the art of nature is certainly not less appreciated than the art of man. A piece of marble with markings which suggest mountains, streams, and clouds will be hung on the wall and enjoyed as much as a fine painting.

In a large garden there will be a lake with a bridge, the graceful curve of which is completed by its reflection in the water. Then there will be covered walks and galleries, where one can find protection from the sun and rain while enjoying the beauties of nature.

Another feature will be one or more pavilions—those decorative little buildings intended for rest, for study, for the contemplation of nature, and for meditation.

Constructed on the same principle as other buildings, they consist of an ornamental curved projecting roof, sometimes a double roof, supported on pillars which stand on a stone floor or platform. The pavilion may be round, square, octagonal, or polysided, and it may have no walls at all, or only partial walls of wooden lattice work. With its gracefully curved and brightly tiled roof, the pavilion adds a decorative and colorful note to the garden.

Everything must be asymmetrical and in harmony with nature. In the care of gardens and the cultivation of flowers, there is the same realization of the affinity of flowers and trees and birds and insects with the forces of nature—the rain and the wind—as there is in Chinese painting. Dr. O. Sirén quotes a flower lover of the seventeenth century who wrote: "By planting flowers one invites butterflies . . . by planting pines one invites the wind, by planting banana trees one invites rain, and by planting willow trees one invites cicadas."

It is in a garden, or even in a small courtyard, that man is most alive to the importance of living in harmony with the forces of nature, and of the interdependence of man and all living and growing things.

284

A Chinese homestead in pottery (tomb model). Ming, possibly earlier.

Chinese house model in polychrome pottery. Han Dynasty.

"Meeting in Pavilion," by Liu Sung-nien (fl. ca. 1190-1230). Sung Dynasty.

Below: Tympanum of doorway, limestone. T'ang Dynasty. Lucy Maud Buckingham Collection.

Opposite page, top: Detail from a Chinese scroll painting on silk, titled "Ch'ing Ming," or "Spring Festival on the Yellow River." Ming Dynasty copy of a Sung original.

The pavilion.

Marble Pagoda, Peking.

Pottery grave model of ancient chair with round back and footrest bar, and a robe as loose cover. 3 inches high. The ancient dressing table is also very similar to those in use today. 3.5 inches high by 3.3 inches wide. Ming, or possibly earlier.

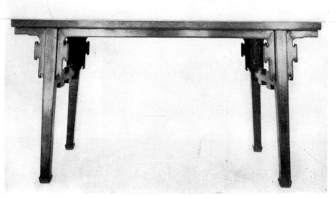

Side table in pterocarpus indicus (huang hua-li of the amber-colored variety), 327/8 by 65 by 28 inches. Yüan or early Ming.

Above: Small sacrificial table in pterocarpus indicus (huang hua-li of the chestnut-colored variety), 31¾6 by 36⅝ by 16⅝ inches. Ming, probably 16th century.
Left: Splay-leg cabinet in chestnut-colored pterocarpus indicus, 48¼ by 29⅛ by 17¼ inches. Ming, 15th or 16th century.

Chapter XI

FURNITURE

DEFINITE PRINCIPLES in regard to the design and the placing of furniture in the home were established in the early Chinese dynasties, and these were closely followed, with only minor modifications, throughout the centuries.

"A simplicity tending towards a severe sobriety, robust and plain forms deriving from the intrinsic nature of the material—those are the eternal virtues of the aesthetic principles of the Far East." This observation, made by Réné Grousset in regard to Kansu neolithic pottery, might equally well have been made about Chinese furniture. The qualities considered essential to the making of furniture, which was strictly architectural in nature, were functionalism, simplicity, strength, and symmetry.

The true nature of Chinese furniture has been the subject of even greater misconception than other forms of Chinese art. A disservice has been done to our appreciation of the essential good taste of the Chinese people by the fact that most of the furniture with which the Western world was familiar fell into two categories.

One was the extremely complicated and luxurious "palace furniture," which was admired more for its costly material and elaborate ornamentation than for its aesthetic quality. The other was the ugly, heavy, intricately carved, teakwood furniture, which was brought back to Europe and America by traders who liked it because it was "quaint" and also because it accorded with the taste of their own period for the massive and ornate.

During the great vogue for *chinoiserie* in the eighteenth century, Chippendale and other English cabinetmakers were inspired by Chinese motifs. In 1754, Chippendale wrote, in submitting designs for some Chinese chairs, "which I hope will improve that taste or manner of work, it having yet never arrived to any perfection." But, although Chippendale understood the use of Chinese fretwork in decoration, he did not know about the Chinese rigid standards of functionalism and simplicity, and his pieces look very strange and foreign to Chinese eyes because of their excess of ornamentation and useless details.

Sir William Chambers, who went to Canton as a supercargo on a Swedish vessel at the age of sixteen, made sketches only of what struck him as most "curious" and most cunningly contrived. He managed to prolong the Chinese vogue but added nothing to the understanding of Chinese taste in furniture.

There was one important influence exercised by China on European furniture, and that was the introduction of the cabriole leg and the claw-and-ball foot, which became popular during the reign of Queen Anne and was used for long afterward. The idea was originally taken, not from Chinese furniture, but from the wooden stands which the Chinese made and exported with their porcelains. The claw-and-ball foot, in its Chinese form, represented the claws of a dragon encircling a pearl.

Another reason why so little has been known about the type of furniture used in Chinese homes is that these things were created solely for use and as an intrinsic part of the house in which they were to be placed. Antique and curio dealers made no attempt to sell such things to travelers from foreign countries, and they were ignored by Western writers on Chinese art.

Many of the Western residents in China seldom left the foreign concessions, and few entered the house of any Chinese who did not live in a Westernized manner. Twenty years ago, in Tientsin, an English resident who saw some old Chinese tables in our house said it was the first time she had seen anyone use "modern furniture." Since that time, however, such works as *Chinese Domestic Furniture* by Gustav Ecke and *Chinese Household Furniture* by George N. Kates have given the outside world information about the furniture actually used by cultured Chinese in their own homes. This has resulted in a great demand in the United States for what is called "Chinese modern furniture"—that is, modern furniture based on designs which may be as much as two thousand years old.

Chinese hardwood furniture appears "modern" to Western eyes, and the older it is the more "modern" it appears, because to the cultivated Chinese taste there could be no elegance without simplicity. This simplicity was studied, and not primitive. It was achieved by the use of the most skilled and careful workmanship. For instance, there is often a barely perceptible tapering in upright pieces, or the least possible rounding of edges, or the mitering of joints a little above the 45-degree angle—all of which add to the grace and symmetry of the lines.

Distinction also lay in the use of handsome woods, superbly worked and polished. The beauty of the plain expanse of fine wood could be emphasized by a slight touch of restrained decoration in the form of mouldings, fretwork, or other carving, but this had to be a part of the basic design and not just an added ornament. In the case of cabinets, chests, and other such pieces, the sole ornamentation might take the form of lock shields, drawer pulls or hinges, usually made of brass. These were often circular in shape and sometimes cut into designs.

The actual carpentry was of the highest order, and entailed the most skillful and intricate joinery. There was no turning. No nails were ever used, and only

290

a minimum of glue. Many tables—legs, braces, and all—were carved out of a solid block of wood like a piece of sculpture.

Wood was more thoroughly seasoned than that used in Europe, and its flawless polish was the result of long and continuous effort. "Done leisurely, done well" runs the Chinese proverb in regard to handicraft.

The little wooden stands which the Chinese use for their bronzes, porcelains, and jades are really miniature wooden tables. The finest of these are carved out of a solid piece of fine seasoned wood, and the greatest care is taken to give them a satinlike polish. A French friend of ours ordered a stand for a porcelain bowl from one of the leading stand makers in Canton. After waiting for some weeks, he went to the shop to ask when his stand would be finished. The carpenter went over to a small chubby child playing on the floor and took something away from him. Then he came back, saying: "Here is your stand. We are working on it."

"Why is that child playing with it then?" the Frenchman asked.

"Every day one of the children plays with it. The oil from their hands soaks into the wood to prepare it for the proper polish. In about six months' time it will be ready for delivery."

The tradition of fine carpentry is a very old one. A famous artisan, Lu Pan, who lived about 500 B.C., was made the patron saint of carpenters; and, if few other cabinetmakers attained fame as individuals, they have worked collectively for many centuries to uphold the standards of their craft. As with other forms of Chinese art, the beginnings of Chinese work in wood are not known, but the Shang scripts and finds have led to the conclusion that the quality of the woodwork of that time was as highly developed as the bronze casting, and that it, too, had its roots in an earlier age.

The Shang people did not sit on chairs. They reclined on mats, using low stools as arm rests, and low tables for setting out dishes of food and for displaying the ritual vessels. In the Metropolitan Museum of Art, New York, there is a bronze stand for ceremonial vessels (part of an altar set from the Tuan-fang collection), which dates back to the latter part of the Shang dynasty. It is of rectangular platform construction and resembles in form many of the low tables, seats, and platforms in reception halls which have been made during the last three thousand years.

It is not certain when chairs were first used, but the Chinese have been described as the only people in the Far East who, in ancient times, sat on stools or chairs or platforms, rather than on the ground. Han documents prove that chairs, stools, armchairs, tables (both low and taller ones), dressing tables, altar tables, and canopy beds were in general use. Pottery grave models excavated from Han tombs show very little difference in general outline between modern Chinese furniture and that used in the second or third century.

Some specimens of the furniture used in the T'ang and Sung dynasties can still be seen in Japan, and they, too, resemble in basic forms much of the work of the cabinetmakers of the Ming and Ch'ing dynasties. These pieces that have survived in Japan are objects of great refinement and sophistication because they were palace pieces which were considered fine enough to be included in imperial collections.

We can read, too, about furniture dating back to the Chou, Ch'in, and Han dynasties which was incrusted with gold and silver, with coral, ivory, jade, and mother-of-pearl, but all this was made for the imperial Court, and not for use in the average Chinese home.

Apart from the Han tomb models and certain paintings, there is little evidence of how the average household was furnished until we come to the Ming dynasty. Yet, because of the continuity of tradition in China, we know that the home of a Ming scholar-official would not be much unlike that of a T'ang or Sung family of culture.

In his book *Chinese Domestic Furniture,* Gustav Ecke gives the following description of a Ming home of the leisured class, which he characterizes as "richness in the garb of grace and measured simplicity."

> The spacious Central Hall was carried on two rows of tall pillars; left and right, east and west, were latticed partitions in cabinet wood, dressed at the back with soft-colored silks. Walls and pillars were papered. The floor was laid with black polished flagstones, and the ceiling finished with cloisons in yellow reed-work.
>
> Against this somber background the furniture was disposed, subject to the discipline of the plan. The amber or purple hues of the rosewood pieces agreed with the subdued tones of costly rugs, chair covers, and cushions in tapestry or embroidered silk.
>
> Pendant scrolls of calligraphies and paintings, blue-and-white porcelains, . . . were distributed with studied care.
>
> Papered lattice windows kept out the glare of the day; open candles and horn lanterns blended the colors at night in subtle harmony.

The above might be a description of a Sung home, and it might equally well describe some of the homes of scholars-collectors, artists, and officials that we visited in many different parts of China. In just such a setting our host would take a painted scroll out of a metal cylinder box, draw it from its brocaded cover, and display it on the long scholars' table, unrolling a few inches at a time.

The furniture would be placed in accordance with fixed standards, almost always along the wall. There was seldom anything in the center of the room, for the effect of order, dignity, and balance had to be maintained in the proportions of the room and the arrangement of its contents. Things did not have to be disposed in pairs, but there did have to be balance between one side of the room and the other. There would not be more than two or three hanging pictures or pieces of calligraphy, and, unless there was a cabinet with antique pieces, there would be very few ornaments in sight. Almost always there would be one vase, or bowl, with carefully arranged flowers or a blossoming branch. All the other ornaments, vases, and pictures belonging to the owner would be stored away in the various cabinets and chests kept in the house for that purpose.

292

Ming furniture was made in more severe and powerful lines; but, if there was a tendency for the cabinetmakers to work in a more graceful and delicate manner in the Ch'ing dynasty, this was not too apparent in homes where the importance of line and balance was never sacrificed to mere decoration, and where much of the furniture had probably been inherited from generations of ancestors.

Next to the structural lines, the most important consideration in the making of furniture was the quality and nature of the wood. Among the favorites were the many species of hua-li (rosewood), with its satin-smooth surface. Even more highly prized was Tzŭ t'an (red or purple sandalwood or palisander), commonly known as blackwood, which is the heaviest of Chinese hardwood and acquires a high luster after years of polishing. Another popular wood was hung-mu, known as red wood, which somewhat resembles mahogany.

Some of the wood used was native to South China, but much of it was imported from India, Burma, Sumatra, the Malay Archipelago, and the Philippines.

The carved teakwood tables—so popular with collectors of Chinese curios—were made chiefly for their benefit. Teak is an exclusively Indian wood, which was not admired by the Chinese and not traditionally used for proper Chinese cabinetmaking.

The Chinese cabinetmakers preferred hardwood which could withstand the radically different climates in different parts of the country. They formerly used only the finest trees with the most beautiful graining and coloring, for the pieces of furniture which were to be so painstakingly worked over for months were expected to last for centuries.

A wood called chang-mu (camphorwood) was employed for making chests and cabinets, but the Chinese did not use the elaborately carved chests which were afterward made for sale to Western travelers. Nor did they make much use of veneer (except in cheap furniture), for they felt that fine wood needed no such extraneous addition.

Rustic furniture was made in native softwood in the same simple traditional forms. Bamboo, frequently employed for this type of work, was used for chairs, tables, stools, couches, and screens. In fact, bamboo was used for everything—food, ornaments, clothing, buildings, and boats, as well as furniture.

The best cabinetwork was made in South China—probably because it was nearer to the main sources of supply of hardwoods—and it was transported to Peking and other places in North China by way of the Grand Canal. The furniture made in the south was inclined to be somewhat more elaborate than that made in the north. Those who have lived in, or visited Canton, are familiar with Blackwood Street, where the cabinetmakers still work in the same tradition, even though they do not maintain the same quality of material and workmanship as in the past.

The furniture most used in Chinese homes includes tables of all types—long, low tables, small high tables, long scholars' tables for writing and painting, long side tables which are set against the wall in the reception room. The Chinese prefer a round table for eating and, sometimes, they put a round wooden top on a smaller square table. This top can be folded in half and put away when not in use. The use of the round table enables the family (perhaps eight or ten persons) to reach the dishes placed in the center of the table with their chopsticks. It also enables the conversation to be general.

Then there are altar tables and lute tables, triangular tables, and special game tables for playing chess and mahjong.

Armchairs are made in various styles with hooped or square backs, and there are several types of chairs without arms. Most chairs have a crossbar or stretcher on which the feet can be placed to keep them off the cold stone floors. Even in warm weather this form of foot rest can be a great comfort.

Stools are very widely used, both indoors and out, and have been in general use for about two thousand years. Some street vendors carry their little stools with them so they can enjoy a rest when tired.

Each home will have tall wardrobes for storing clothes, and these are usually seen in pairs, often with a smaller set of cupboards placed on top of them. Chinese clothes are always made to be folded flat, not put on hangers, and these wardrobes contain shelves inside. Fur coats and heavy padded winter coats may be put away in the long low chests which stand against the wall in the bedrooms.

There is an endless variety of smaller cupboards, cabinets, and sets of open shelves—all of which are designed for some special purpose.

While the fundamental shapes remained the same, there were some variations in the styles of furnishing because of different climates and styles of living. For instance, in the cold climate of North China, a raised brick platform (the k'ang) was built into the room and used as a bed or couch. In winter this could be heated from underneath. A built-in platform of similar type was used for sitting on in the earlier periods and can be seen illustrated in many old pictures.

Because Chinese furniture was designed in accordance with fixed architectural principles the same basic articles were used not only in succeeding dynasties, but also by people—rich or poor—of different classes. The quality of the wood or the workmanship might differ, but most households would have the same tall wardrobes, low chests, tables, chairs, and stools made along the same lines.

Since there was no hereditary aristocracy in China, the fortunes of each family were liable to rise and fall. The tradition of culture was widely diffused, and taste was not confined to any one group. In the simplest home there would be the same desire for plain functional and durable household objects, made according to the same designs as those in rich homes.

Of course, ugly pieces of furniture can be found in secondhand shops in China—great heavy pieces, intricately carved, inlaid, veneered, painted, and incrusted,—which do not conform to any of the accepted standards. Such things are comparatively rare, however, and would probably have been made for a man who had suddenly become rich through business or speculation, and who, to use the Chinese expression, was anxious to "show his money."

In general, however, even modest-priced furniture is of good design and workmanship. It may be looked upon as inferior in China where it has to stand comparison with so much that is superlative, but it can be fully appreciated in the outside world where it has to compete with only mass-produced articles.

One can sum up the Chinese taste in furniture by saying that it has faithfully adhered to the basic requirements established so long ago—dignity, simplicity, structure, and balance.

Chapter XII

LACQUER

CHINESE LACQUER first came to the attention of the West in the form of cabinets, screens, and tables, which were imported in quantity in the seventeenth and eighteenth centuries during the vogue for *chinoiserie*.

The lacquer not only gave a protective covering, but enabled furniture to be made in a variety of colors, such as black, red, yellow, cream, green, and blue. These colors served as a ground for charming and varied decorations, and the pieces were welcomed with rapturous acclaim.

The Jesuit father, Louis le Compte, who arrived in China in 1687 and spent several years there, wrote about lacquer ware as follows: "for Tables and ordinary chairs, it is sufficient to lay on 2 or 3 layers of Vernish which makes it so transparent, that one may discern every Vein of the wood through it. Now if you would hide all the matter—you must do it over and over again, till at length it be nothing but Ice; but so fine at first that it may serve for a Mirror."

This lacquer work was so much admired that Madame de Pompadour made a collection which is now in the Louvre. The European workmen tried to copy the lacquered pieces, but they used copal varnish instead of lac and could not achieve the same luminous quality and finish. Pieces of European furniture were consequently sent to China and Japan to be lacquered there.

In regard to certain Ming lacquered pieces (early seventeenth century), which were exhibited in London in 1936, we find this comment by Frank Davis of the *Illustrated London News*, "as an example of a refinement of taste almost too chaste for most Western eyes, there is a long bench covered in perfectly plain greyish lacquer." The same writer, in commenting on the simplicity of these Chinese pieces, adds: "Indeed they are more than that—they have that harmony of line and of color which we express rather feebly by using the word 'classic.' "

Simplicity, however, was the last quality desired by the devotees of *chinoiserie,* and when they purchased a Chinese lacquered cabinet they would mount it on the most grotesquely carved and gilded legs in place of the plain stand which the Chinese use to show off the lines of a piece to the best advantage.

296

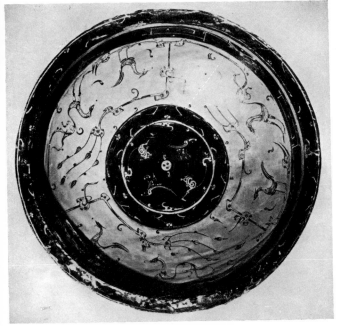

Bowl, painted lacquer, from
Ch'ang Sha. Late Chou Dynasty.
Eugene Fuller Memorial Collec-
tion.

Head of dried lacquer, hollow.
T'ang Dynasty.

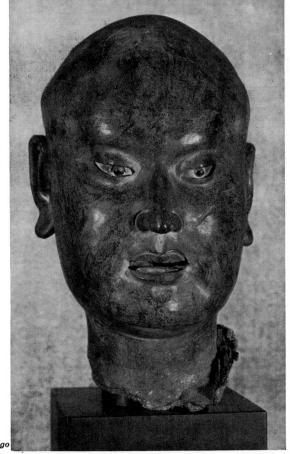

Lacquer box, part of a toilet set.
Han Dynasty.

Seated Bodhisattva, dry lacquer, red and green pigment. T'ang Dynasty. Gift of Mrs. John D. Rockefeller, Jr.

Lacquer Lohan. Sung dynasty.

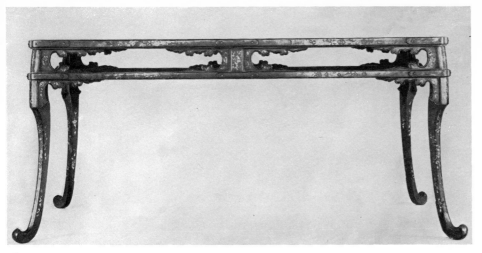

Lacquer table, inlaid with
mother of pearl, top refinished
in the Japanese manner. Sung
Dynasty, probably 12th century.

Dry lacquer figure of a Buddha.
Yüan Dynasty.

Small low table or footstool in
carved cinnabar lacquer. Ming,
reign of Yung Lo.

Philadelphia Museum of Art

Lacquered and gilded wood dragon from ceiling of Chih-hua temple in Peking. Ming Dynasty.

Carved red lacquer box, cinnabar-red on background of dull yellow-ocher color with black lining and base. Narrow brass band set into carving just below one of medallions reads: "Ta Ming Yung Lo Nien Chih." Early 15th century, possibly reign of Yung Lo.

Royal Ontario Museum of Archaeology, Toronto

While some fine plain pieces found their way to Europe, as observed before it was the fantastic that was most in demand. Many "Coromandel" screens, which were believed to be of Indian origin because of their name, were brought to Europe. In reality they had been shipped to the Coromandel coast from China, and from there had been brought to England. These screens were made of hard lacquered wood, usually black but sometimes dark brown and red, with designs finely carved in intaglio. The hollowed-out parts were colored or gilt. This process was chiefly confined to flat work, but when the screens—often twelve-fold—reached England they were cut up and used in the making of cabinets and other pieces of furniture. Their decorative quality was so much admired that attempts to imitate this work became a fashionable handicraft in England and was known as "japanning."

Long before the introduction of lacquer ware to the West, there had been a large export trade in lacquered pieces to all countries of the East. In 1220 it was being exported to Borneo, Cochin China, Java, Sumatra, Malabar, Zanzibar, Persia, Japan, Ceylon, and India, chiefly from the port of Foochow.

Although the use of lacquer ware was so widespread, little was known about its origins. It was not even realized that it had originated in China at the dawn of her history and that it ranked, with silk, paper, printing, pottery, and porcelain, among the great contributions of China to world culture.

Lacquer is a white resinous sap derived from the lac tree of Ch'i Shu (Rhus vernicifera), which is cultivated in Central and South China. When exposed to the air it turns black, and it is recorded that it was first used for writing with a stylus on the bamboo slips which, when tied together, made up the earliest Chinese books.

The Chinese realized very early that lac would make wooden and pottery vessels watertight and would also act as a preservative for wood. After that it did not take them long to find out that it could be used in other ways, both practical and decorative.

According to a Ming treatise on the art of lacquering, written by a Japanese between 1621 and 1628, the Emperor Shun (circa 2255 B.C.) had food utensils made of lacquer, and his successor, the Emperor Yü (famed as the owner of the Nine Bronze Cauldrons), ordered ceremonial articles of black lacquer ware lined with red.

In the Chou dynasty there were official regulations in regard to the lacquering of carriages, leather harnesses, and bows and arrows. Gold and other colors were used in addition to the original black and red. Lacquer was greatly valued for its luster and hardness, and it was accepted in payment of taxes.

All this would once have been regarded as mere legend, and books on Chinese art written twenty-five years ago doubted the existence of lacquer prior to the Ming dynasty. Recently, however, specimens of lacquered objects, and even carved lacquer, have been found in late Chou tombs in North and Northeast China—once more proving that most Chinese records, even if embellished, were based on facts. These excavations have shown that lacquer was applied to pottery and to clay figurines, and that the dry lacquer technique was already in use.

This dry hollow technique was to be much used in the T'ang dynasty and probably as early as the Wei dynasty for the making of Buddhist images. These images, being extremely light in weight, could be carried in religious processions more easily than those made of heavier material. First a wooden mould was made in sections and covered with a mixture containing lacquer, clay, and fiber which was modeled while still wet. This was carefully covered with pressed-down pieces of silk or linen, saturated with fresh lac, which quickly hardened into the desired form. In later periods clay alone was used as the base. When the cloths were completely dry, the wood (or clay) was removed, leaving the cloth shell as a surface for painting in gold or colors. This process, which produced much fine statuary, became popular again during the Buddhist revival in the Yüan dynasty.

Records show that in the early part of the Han dynasty lacquer was much used for armor, writing materials, musical instruments, and other miscellaneous objects. Skepticism in regard to such statements was dispelled when, in 1910, the Japanese found Han lacquered paper pot covers of Chinese make near Port Arthur, Manchuria. This was followed, in 1931, by the discovery of groups of Han lacquered objects in the Lolang tombs of northern Korea, including a painted round lacquer tray (dated A.D. 69) and a woven basket decorated with painted lacquer panels illustrating scenes of filial piety. Han pieces have also been unearthed in Szechüan and in northern Mongolia.

This Han lacquer ware includes small tables, cups, bowls, trays, toilet boxes, pins, combs, mirrors, cosmetic boxes, and pieces of fabric covered with lacquer. They are made in a wide variety of techniques, including inlays of gold and silver foil.

These pieces add to our understanding of the nature of Han art, although most of them were made to be sent outside China and were probably not of the first quality as far as painting is concerned. They are decorated in blacks, reds, and greens, with both bold and delicate designs. The realistic or impressionistic motifs used are similar to those on textiles and bronzes, and include Taoist scenes, symbolic animals, floral patterns, and various other ornamental designs.

Many of them are inscribed and bear the names of the imperial factories where they were made. The object is briefly described and credit is given to each person who participated in the process of manufacture. For example, ten different persons are mentioned on the cover of one small black lacquered Han vessel, as follows:

Painter and lacquerer	Yu
Gilder	Ku
Engraver	Jung
Cleaner	Pao
Finisher	Tsung
Director	Chia
Sub-Director	Kuei
Assistant	Chien
Sub-Assistant	Kuang
Official	Kuei

Lacquer workers appear to have been more greatly esteemed as individuals than many other artisans, since the names of so many of them have been known and recorded throughout succeeding dynasties. There is no doubt that this work at its best was the product of men of infinite patience, remarkable skill, sureness of touch, and a fine artistic sense.

Lacquered furniture, because of the time and talent needed for its manufacture, was classed as a luxury. The home of the average family of culture might have one lacquered table or cabinet, and possibly a tray, a sweetmeat box, and some lacquered bowls, but a whole room would not be furnished with lacquered pieces.

One section of a fourth-century painting by Ku K'ai-chih shows a woman having her hair dressed by a maid, and on the floor around them lie lacquered toilet boxes, these being articles of luxury which would be used in the Imperial Palace.

Similar articles can be seen in the Imperial Treasure House (Shōsōin) at Nara, Japan. Here Chinese T'ang lacquered pieces were deposited, together with many other Chinese art treasures, by the widow of a Japanese emperor who died A.D. 756. This group included musical instruments with inlays of cut-out figures of gold and silver covered with lacquer, mirrors with lacquered backs, and boxes. There are pieces inlaid with mother-of-pearl, others in relief or in fine painted lacquer.

Both the Japanese and the Koreans early learned the art of lacquering from the Chinese, but the exact time when they started this work has not been established.

Although T'ang pieces (with the exception of some Buddhist dry lacquer figures) are very rare outside the above-mentioned group at Nara, we saw a T'ang lacquered lute with a dragon crackle, and a design of nine dragons, in a private collection in Shanghai. It was reputed to have belonged to Yang Kuei-fei. That cannot, of course, be proved, but, since it had obviously been made for the T'ang Imperial Court, it is not impossible that it may have been used by the lovely and unscrupulous T'ang beauty.

Most T'ang and Sung pieces have simple designs, usually of floral subjects, painted on a dark ground. Some have mother-of-pearl inlay and touches of gold and silver. This technique, which the Chinese call "misty brocade," is known in the West as lac *burgautée,* and it was mostly used for small pieces—wine cups lined with silver, small dishes, and, later, snuffboxes and bottles. There was beautiful pierced lacquer work too.

During the Sung dynasty many utensils covered with gold or silver lacquer were made for use in the palace. They had plain uncarved surfaces in accordance with the taste of the time. At the end of the Sung dynasty in 1279 there is a record of a lacquer artist, P'êng Chün-pao, who was renowned for his work decorated with gold.

The chief center for lacquer work in the T'ang and Sung dynasties was at Chia-hsing Fu in the province of Chekiang, halfway between Hangchow and

Soochow, but afterward the best painted lacquer was made in Foochow and Canton, and the finest carved work came from Peking and Soochow.

The two main groups of lacquer work are the painted and the carved. The first—flat lacquer with painted decoration (called Hua ch'i) was made in the following manner:

The wood, well-seasoned and often as thin as a piece of paper, was first planed, then polished. When it was completely smooth, a piece of fine paper (or linen or silk) was pasted over the whole surface which was again sized and polished down until glass-smooth. Then layer after layer of the carefully prepared and colored lac was laid on. Each coat had to dry thoroughly and be carefully polished before the next was applied. When dry, lac becomes extremely hard but not brittle. It dries to a better finish in a damp atmosphere, so objects in process of preparation were kept in a damp place.

A good lacquered piece would probably have twenty or thirty coats of lac, and the preliminary work might take many weeks. Only then was the lengthy process of decoration considered. The artist studied the brilliant surface and considered carefully what design would be most effective. After he had thought it all out, the outline was usually drawn on the lacquer with a lead paste. Then the different colors were filled in. If there was to be gold or silver, this was blown on through a bamboo tube or sieve so that the distribution would be equal. If the pattern called for relief, it was modeled on with a paste of lacquer mixed with other ingredients. One or more coats of transparent lac were again put over the whole piece, and then there would be another period of hardening before the object was completed.

In addition to use on wood this same process of flat lacquer work was sometimes applied to metal or leather. The colors used were gold, silver, vermilion, yellow, turquoise, slate blue, dark blue, brown, green, white, purple, and black. Some of the pieces were encrusted with semiprecious stones, gilt metal, ivory, or jade.

In the fourteenth and fifteenth centuries, literary inscriptions were often cut into the lacquer with a pointed needle or stylus and then filled in with black lac. The pattern was often made wholly or partly in this incised, or pierced, technique and then filled in with black, gold, or colors.

Some of the most beautiful pieces were covered with plain gold and silver, the metallic points shining through the soft brilliancy of the flawless polish.

In the case of carved lacquer (tiao ch'i), the process was similar but it was very much more laborious and more difficult. There were sometimes as many as two hundred or three hundred coats of lacquer built up on the wooden or metal or porcelain base, if the piece was to be of first quality, so as to give depth to the carving. Each layer had to be left to dry, and a fine large piece might take years to prepare and then years to carve. Ten years was not considered excessive.

Sometimes layers of different colors were used, and then the carver had to cut back from the surface to expose each color required by the design. This was done with a V-shaped knife. The idea once prevailed, and was perpetuated even by such a distinguished authority as S. W. Bushell, that the carving was done while the lacquer was "still warm" and hence soft. This was an error readily discernible to those who knew how many months were required to carve even a very small piece. It was the custom to mix the lac with vegetable oil, coloring matter, and other ingredients in the heat of the sun to keep it warm while stirring, but it was seldom warm when applied. By the time the carving was started the piece was completely cold and hard. The work necessitated the utmost precision. A slip of a twentieth of an inch, and the work of years would be ruined, for no correction was possible.

Carved lacquer can be seen in olive green, buff, brown, black, and purple, but the most prized of all was the red lacquer of Peking—the red being derived from cinnabar (or sulphide of mercury). This cinnabar was mentioned in the records of the Shang dynasty as an article of tribute to the Imperial Court.

The designs used might be a landscape, a Buddhist or Taoist subject, birds and flowers, a set of symbols, or one of the other traditional subjects, as in the case of flat lacquer work. There was a wide range of such themes, and each of them could be treated with complete freedom of expression. Often, however, the artist capable of undertaking this most delicate and meticulous work preferred to create designs which were entirely of his own conception.

Lacquer work, both flat and carved, was used chiefly for screens, tables, chairs, boxes, trays, vases, and small ornaments. Beads of carved cinnabar lacquer were very popular.

Once completed, lacquer ware was extremely durable and unaffected even by alcohol. Softwood screens and furniture remained in perfect condition for generations, being able to withstand equally well the excessively damp climate of Canton and the extreme dryness of Peking. A cargo of lacquer that was shipwrecked and salvaged after spending eighteen months in the sea was completely unharmed.

The great length of time required for the making of carved lacquer and the great expense involved led to such later practices as the building up of designs with putty and then lacquering them, or carving wood and then heavily coating it with layers of lacquer.

Lacquer work, both flat and in relief, was being made in Canton as early as the fourteenth century; and an Arabian traveler, Ibn Batuta, wrote about Canton lacquer in 1345, expressing his admiration for its lightness, brilliancy, and solidity and stating that it was already being exported on a large scale to India and Persia. This work was carried on continuously in Canton until the present generation; and, because this was the port of China which had most contact with foreigners, there are many screens with European figures.

The modern work consists chiefly of gold and silver designs on black, but the quality deteriorated mainly because the foreign customers would not wait the required time, so that the artisans found themselves obliged to use substitutes or adulterations and to produce inferior articles which could be turned out more quickly.

The painted Foochow lacquer was considered superior to that of Canton, with its soft colors and bold carving embellished by finely powdered gold. The yellow lacquer was especially fine. The modern style of work was started in the early seventeenth century by a craftsman (Shen Shao An) whose family has continuously carried on the same craft in Foochow ever since.

In the Ming dynasty there was a great interest in lacquer work—especially in the carved lacquer—and the work done in the reigns of Yung Lo and Hsüan Tê was outstanding in technique and design. The color of the Ming cinnabar is darker than that of the Ch'ing, and it is more highly polished. The designs are bold and original, done with great restraint, and there is full appreciation of the importance of blank spaces.

Lacquer work, like all other Chinese crafts, was taken under imperial patronage throughout the reigns of K'ang Hsi, Yung Chêng, and Ch'ien Lung and was manufactured with the greatest technical skill and taste but with less aesthetic feeling and simplicity than in the preceding dynasty.

Even after the gradual deterioration that set in because of the demand for speed in manufacture, to most Western eyes there was not a great difference between Chinese work of the highest and that of lesser quality. Such is the skill of the Chinese artisan that even the pieces made for export or for quick commercial gain continued to be distinguished for their softness of tone, strength of composition, and brilliant surface.

The Chinese connoisseur was so much alive to variations in quality that he was ready to pay a hundred times more for one brand of tea than another, and fifty times as much for a superlative quality of red seal wax. The genius of the Chinese artists and craftsmen was, for long centuries, stimulated and encouraged by the knowledge of the existence of persons of such refined and cultivated taste that it was always worth striving to reach a still higher degree of perfection. The greatest treasure of China has lain in the genius of her art workers; and, even when they have been obliged to lower their standards and hence their pride in their craft, the products that they turn out still retain traces of their old glory.

Chapter XIII

TEXTILES, EMBROIDERY, COSTUMES, AND CARPETS

TEXTILES

THE WHOLE HISTORY of China is interwoven with threads of silk, and these delicate fibers formed China's earliest and strongest links with the outside world.

According to tradition it was the wife of the Yellow Emperor—in the third millenium B.C.—who inaugurated the culture of the silkworm and taught the people how to spin and weave silk so that it could be made into articles of clothing. In Peking there is still a temple dedicated to her memory where every year, as had been done in similar temples for over four thousand years, the empress offered mulberry leaves at the altar and prayed for divine protection for the industry of sericulture. The silkworm became the emblem of industry, and the silk represented delicate purity and virtue.

Silk culture was the special province of women, and there is frequent reference to silk in the early Chou dynasty writings. The last lines of a poem describing silk culture in the Chou "Book of Poetry" run:

> In the eighth month, they begin their spinning—
> They make dark fabrics and yellow.
> Our red manufacture is very brilliant,
> It is for the lower robes of our young princes.

Spinning whorls of stone and pottery, similar to those in use today, were found in the course of the neolithic excavations, and textile patterns were impressed on neolithic pottery. Silk fibers were found in Shang tombs, and in tombs only a little later there were silkworms carved in jade. In the Shang dynasty clothes, cords, and pennants were made of both silk and hemp. At that time the Chinese already wore tailored clothing with sleeves and small buttons, as well as furs.

Silk was exported to other countries which were eager to obtain this fine fabric. To the Greeks the fiber was known as *ser,* from the Chinese word "ssŭ," and they called the Chinese people the *Seres,* and the woven silk *serikon.* Thus it was as the people of silk that China was first known to the Western world.

307

All the way across Asia from China to Rome the silk was carried along the caravan routes, and it was also carried in all directions by sea. The famous Silk Route was said to have been opened up late in the second century, but silk had been carried abroad long before that time.

Aristotle mentioned silk weaving in the fourth century B.C., and silk had been carried to India even earlier. It was after the opening of the Silk Route, however, that the export trade with the West reached its fullest expansion. It was a source of great wealth to China, and Pliny complained of its tremendous cost in Rome where "it was worth its weight in gold," a fact which appears to have done little to discourage the purchasers. Most of the silk reached Europe through intermediaries in the Near East, where it was often unpicked and rewoven into designs which conformed to changing Roman fashions.

Of course the Chinese took precautions to guard the secret of the silk culture which had proved so profitable, and the various attempts made to steal it from them provided the plots for many tales of adventure. One of the most famous stories is about the Chinese princess who, in the first century after Christ, carried eggs of silkworm moths, hidden in her headdress, to Khotan. From there it is said that the culture of silkworms spread to India and Persia.

About the third century, Japan acquired the desired knowledge through Korea. There is also the story of the two Persian monks who studied the art of sericulture while in China, and left for home A.D. 550, carrying with them silkworm eggs concealed in a hollow cane. They are said to have brought these to Constantinople, from which city the method of producing silk fibers spread all over Europe.

During the Han dynasty the Chinese still were the only people who could weave the precious fabric, and their trade in figured silks, quilts, tapestries, and embroideries assumed tremendous proportions. In addition to silk, the caravans carried furs and spices westward, the Chinese receiving wool and cotton textiles in exchange.

It is to China that the world owes the development of the art of using silk in weaving and embroidery. Their patterns permeated the whole of the Near East, and textile finds in Egyptian graves of the Hellenistic and Christian periods show Chinese decorative motifs. Some of the Chinese floral, linear, and other designs were taken over so long ago that their origin has been forgotten, and they are generally believed to have originated in France, Italy, or the Near East.

From the annals of the Han dynasty and from the contemporary historical records of Ssŭ-ma Ch'ien we learn that it was the necessity of assuring an open passage westward for the export of silk textiles which led the Han Emperor Wu Ti, in the last quarter of the second century B.C., to seek the expansion of Chinese political and military control into Central Asia along the great caravan route in Chinese Turkestan.

It was on this silk caravan route that Sir Aurel Stein, in the course of his third expedition to Chinese Turkestan (1913-1916), found many fragments of figured silks which are the oldest known surviving examples of Chinese textiles. This is how he described the excavation of the grave pits: "Here rapid but systematic clearing yielded a rich antiquarian haul in quite bewildering confusion. Mixed up with detached human bones, and fragments of wooden coffins, there emerged in abundance objects of personal use, such as decorated bronze mirrors, etc. . . . Chinese records on wood and paper, and, above all, a wonderful variety of fabrics which even in their ragged dirt-encrusted condition delighted my eye. Among them were beautifully woven and colored silks; torn pieces of polychrome figured fabrics, damask, tapestry and embroidery work, all in silk; fragments of fine pile carpets, by the side of plentiful coarse materials in wool and felt."

In 1924-1925 the Kosloff expedition unearthed, in the region of Lake Baikal, many more fragments of figured silks. Further specimens of Han silks—plain and figured and embroidered—have been found in tombs in northern Mongolia, Siberia, Palmyra, Afghanistan, and the Crimea.

The high quality and complicated techniques of all these silks—which included moiré, damask, gauze, quilting, and embroidery—show the prosperity and refinement of the age and they are obviously the result of a long history of development in the weaving of textiles.

Most of these fragments date from about the first century B.C. In some cases there is a small-scale intricate design, while on others there are simple diaper patterns. The term "diaper" is used to designate a small pattern repeated continually and uniformly all over a surface. In the case of Chinese textiles it may refer to geometrical patterns, conventional floral forms, or such designs, among others, as thunder-and-cloud, recumbent silkworms, trellis work, mystic knots, fish roe, coins, herringbone, honeycomb, whorls, or various written characters.

On certain specimens the strong whorls, the elongated animal forms of horses and dragons, and the complicated patterns seem to combine the elegance of style of the Warring States with the naturalistic features of the Han dynasty.

Among the Aurel Stein pieces there are patterns of heraldic beasts in combat, horsemen, horses at flying gallop (a typical Han motif), floral decorations with curved leafy stems, geometrical designs, and cloud scrolls. On these fragments of silk the decoration is similar to that seen on the bronzes, ceramic wares, and bas-reliefs, of the Han dynasty.

Alan Priest and Pauline Simmons of the Metropolitan Museum of Art say of these Han silks: "In fragments that show no decorative figuring, a variety of plain cloth weave is always used, corresponding to what is technically known as a rib of rep weave. The figured silks with the exception of a few specimens in monochrome, described as damasks, and a single example of gauze, are all polychrome, the colors rich and harmonious, and the weaves of exquisite texture. The warp twill is used in all of these polychromes."

China first conceived the idea of weaving figured silk, and, about the end of the third century, the Roman monk, Dionysius Periegetes, wrote: "The Seres make precious figured garments, resembling in color the flowers of the field, and rivalling in fineness the work of spiders." This figured silk was called "diaspron" or "diaper" from the name given to it in Constantinople, but, after the twelfth century when Damascus became famous for its weaving of silk, the name "damask" was given to all patterned silks, including the Chinese.

It is recorded that the Emperor Ming-ti of the Wei dynasty presented to the empress of Japan, who sent an embassy to the Chinese Court in 238, five rolls of brocades with dragons woven on a crimson ground. Silk was much used throughout this era of the growth of Buddhism for religious banners and vestments.

Many examples of T'ang textiles are still in existence, including some which show Persian and other designs, for Chinese products were in great demand throughout the Mohammedan world. Fine fragments of T'ang figured silk, plain silk, embroideries, tapestries, brocades, and gauzes were excavated from various sites in Chinese Turkestan. The figured textiles include conventional floral patterns, vines, tendrils, animals, birds, and dragons. In some cases the pattern is set in circular rosettes. Similar designs appear on the T'ang examples of silks and embroideries which can be seen in the Imperial Treasury in Nara, Japan.

During the T'ang dynasty, the textile arts reached their fullest development, and many important artists made designs for textiles, embroideries, and tapestries.

In a Sung book, over fifty brocade patterns of the T'ang dynasty which were still in use were recorded. Among them we find such subjects as: "Dragons Coiling through a Hundred Flowers," "Lotus Flowers and Reeds," "Cherries," "Squares and Medallions of White Flowers on Colored Grounds," "Lotus and Tortoises," "Floral Emblem of Longevity," "Musical Instruments," "Panels with Eagles surrounded by fine Sprays of Flowers," "Water-weeds and Playing Fish," "Sprays of Rose-Mallow," "Tree Peonies," "Wild Geese flying in the Clouds," "Peacocks," "Lions sporting with Balls," "Dragons in Water," "Dragons and Phoenixes," "Argus Pheasants and Storks," "Palaces and Pavilions," "Tortoise-shell Grounds," "Pearls and Grains of Rice," and "Dragons in Medallions pursuing Jewels." In addition there are striped and diapered designs of more simple character, groups of symbols, and combinations of Chinese written characters. The damasks and transparent gauzes were woven in similar patterns.

A "General Survey of Art Objects" (Po wu yao lan), written in the Ming dynasty, devotes one volume to the subject of ancient silks under the headings: "Brocades" ("chin") and "embroideries" ("hsiu"). The writer points out that many of the ornamental designs still in use, such as "Dragons and Phoenixes," "Birds and Flowers," "Peachstones and Grapes," originated in the Han dynasty. Silk weavers are known as the most conservative of craftsmen, and these same motifs were still being used in the present century.

Textile designs supplied the basis for the decoration of many other art forms, and it was estimated that two-thirds of the decorations used on Ming porcelains—such as the foliated panels and medallions on brocaded grounds surrounded by bands of diaper, or the borders of waves around the base of vases—were derived from ancient textile designs, while the other third were based on the patterns used on old bronzes.

If the silk weavers clung to the old traditions when it came to selecting designs, they were equally bound to the past in their looms, which have remained unchanged except for their increase in size. Throughout the centuries the silk has been woven on the same upright loom worked by two artisans. The weaver is seated below, while his assistant, perched on top of the frame, works the treadles and helps to change the threads. There is a Chinese saying in regard to silk weaving that: "The warp symbolizes the immutable forces of the world, and the weft the transient affairs of man."

Although there was little export trade during the Sung dynasty, that period saw the development of large silk workshops in Soochow and Hangchow, which turned out figured silks, brocades, velvets, and tapestries (K'o ssŭ). Examples of Sung brocades have survived in the mountings on Sung paintings, the designs being mostly of a floral nature, with free scattered naturalistic flowers.

K'O SSŬ—SILK TAPESTRY

The making of K'o ssŭ tapestry is almost as old as the art of silk weaving. Han specimens brought back from Chinese Turkestan by Sir Aurel Stein showed the complete development of this complicated technique (which was not known by the name K'o ssŭ until the Sung dynasty). It was much used in the weaving of imperial robes and Palace hangings, and sometimes such tapestries necessitated years of work—perhaps a whole lifetime for a single piece. Many of the silk tapestries were mounted on scrolls in the same way as paintings, and it often required close scrutiny to determine whether they were painted or woven.

In the T'ang dynasty this woven tapestry was used to make covers for important literary documents and painted scrolls, a custom which was continued throughout the Sung period when the weavers of K'o ssŭ worked in cooperation with the artists. They wove copies of original documents by famous calligraphists, and they reproduced in silk the paintings of the outstanding masters of the period. The names of the foremost Sung master weavers were recorded, and they include Chou K'o-chou, Shen Tzŭ-fan, Wu Chiu, Wu To, and Chou Hsiang-tung. The looms used may have been of the most primitive, but they allowed the greatest freedom of action, and many artists said that their woven works surpassed in beauty the famous paintings which they took as their models. Some of the most minute details were filled in with a paint brush.

In many cases these tapestries have outlasted the original paintings and have served to show how many famous, but now lost, paintings looked. One important Sung artist, Wen Yen-k'o, said he could manipulate the silk threads with the same facility as a great calligraphist could handle his brush.

The delicacy of this K'o ssŭ tapestry has never been equaled in any other country. When it is compared with the fine French Gobelins tapestry, we find that Chinese K'o ssŭ shows as much as 20/24 warp threads per centimeter and up to 116 weft threads on a centimeter of warp, whereas the best Paris Gobelins tapestry shows 8/11 warp and 22 weft threads per centimeter.

Only silk was used for both warp and weft, and such care was exercised in this work that the weavers spun their own silk threads and dyed them themselves so they could be certain of the quality and color. Gold thread was often interwoven with the silk, and, in this connection, we were surprised when we were in Paris to notice how the gold in Gobelins tapestries, less than two centuries old, had already tarnished, whereas in pieces of Chinese K'o ssŭ woven six or seven hundred years ago the gold is still bright.

The gold and silver tinsels of China were so superior that, at the end of the eighteenth century a weaver was sent out with Lord Macartney's embassy to China to discover the secret of these metallic threads which did not tarnish or discolor. The weaver died before he was able to complete his investigation.

TEXTILES IN THE LATER DYNASTIES

During the Mongol conquest there was a great expansion of trade with other countries, and the silk trade flourished both for export and for domestic consumption. Many Chinese woven and embroidered textiles in the cathedral treasuries of Europe date from this period. They are different in design from those made for Chinese use and were doubtless woven according to orders and patterns sent from Europe and the Near East. For this reason it has not always been realized that they are of Chinese origin.

In spite of an attempt by the first Ming rulers to retreat behind the Great Wall, foreign trade continued to expand in the Ming and Ch'ing dynasties. In England, a proclamation issued in 1631 by King Charles I mentions "satins, taffetas and embroidered carpets from China." Many church vestments were made and sent to Europe during the eighteenth and nineteenth centuries.

In addition to every type of silk tissue, gauze and brocade, which were characterized by their brilliant colors, gold thread, and floral patterns, the weavers excelled in making velvet with raised flowers, cutting the pile with a very deep edge and filling in the ground with gold thread.

Hung Wu, the Ming emperor who overthrew the Mongols, had a passion for austerity and he prohibited the use of K'o ssŭ, but later it flourished again under Hsüan Tê, who summoned to Peking the outstanding weavers of South China and ordered them to reproduce in K'o ssŭ the great pictures of the T'ang dynasty.

In the Ming and Ch'ing dynasties as many as two hundred and three hundred different kinds of silk fabrics were made, including brocades, velvets, Canton crepes, satin, and gauzes. Pongee silks were made in Shantung, often woven in homes on crude hand looms.

There was also large-scale cotton culture in China in the early part of the Ming dynasty, and by the fifteenth century China became one of the greatest cotton-growing areas of the world.

EMBROIDERY

The beauty of Chinese woven textiles and tapestries was rivaled by the exquisite embroideries, called Hsiu hua. This work was done entirely by hand with a needle and required infinite patience and skill. No loom was used, but the silk was stretched on a frame placed on pivots. The design was drawn on the plain material.

The art of needlework seems to have been practiced from the earliest periods, and the Chou "Book of Rites" discusses silk banners and Court costumes embroidered with the Twelve Ancient Ornaments. Few very early specimens have survived, but some first century pieces were found in northern Mongolia. Sir Aurel Stein also discovered embroideries made prior to the tenth century in the hidden chapel of the Caves of the Thousand Buddhas at Tun Huang, including a large embroidered Buddhist picture which he brought back to England. These pieces are similar in technique and design to those made many centuries later.

Although embroidery was one of the handicrafts practiced by a large body of professional artisans, it was also considered as the special domain of women of all classes. We read of one T'ang princess who "worked with her needle 3000 pairs of mandarin ducks on a single coverlet of silk, filling in the intervals with fine sprays of rare flowers and foliage. To complete the dazzling effect she strewed it with beads of precious stones."

Every Chinese girl was taught to embroider and, just as a man's learning and intelligence were judged by his technique in calligraphy, so were a woman's judged by her skill with the needle. In former times when a girl became engaged she had to present pieces of embroidery to all the relatives and friends of her prospective bridegroom for their critical appraisal.

CROSS-STITCH EMBROIDERY

In the remote province of Szechüan and in the rural districts of other provinces the country women specialized in cross-stitch embroidery on white homespun cotton and grass cloth. The thread was dyed in indigo and the design was made in blue. In order to express beauty in their lives they wove and embroidered hangings for their beds and squares of cloth (like handkerchiefs) to be pinned in front of their dresses. The latter were given by brides to the families of their husbands.

Cross-stitch designs included the usual subjects, such as fishes (for happiness and fertility), lotuses (for purity) in pieces made for a bride, and the dragon with a pearl to denote riches and good luck.

Other designs in geometrical patterns express old historical stories and family scenes. The favorite subject, however, was that of the native son, who had taken a high degree in the official examinations, returning in triumph to his town or village on a prancing horse.

SILK EMBROIDERY

As early as the Sung dynasty, there were books of woodcuts which illustrated traditional designs for embroideries. Similar books have been published right up to the present time. They include special motifs for embroideries for the

Court, the temple, and the theater. The work done by women artists in their own homes was, however, often made entirely according to their own original designs.

The work was done with silk thread, braid, or floss in every variety of stitch —satin stitch, long and short stitch, stem stitch, and Peking stitch (French knot). In the treatment of gold and other thick thread, couching and laidwork were much used. There was one type of embroidery in which the design looks exactly the same back and front. The stitches used in the Ch'ing dynasty were the same as those found on Han textiles.

In the seventeenth and eighteenth centuries, large quantities of embroideries were made for the European market, and it was the Chinese who originated and sent to Spain and Portugal the type of shawl which became widely known as the Spanish shawl. Embroidery was used for screens and wall hangings, clothes, shoes, fans, banners, bed covers, tobacco pouches, and spectacle cases.

The finest old specimens of embroidery, mounted on brocade and used as hanging scrolls, are absolutely smooth and glossy, like paintings. There was a Chinese saying that "in painting a portrait you must reproduce the sound, and in painting a flower you must show its brilliance." This was what the embroiderer strove to achieve, giving more life to leaves and flowers, or the plumage of a bird, by the brilliance of the silk threads than they could with a brush and paint.

The Sung painter Kuo Hsi said: "Unless I dwell in peace and sit at leisure . . . ten thousand worries drowned and subdued, I am not able to get at the mood and meaning of beautiful lines . . ." That is how it was with every artist and craftsman, and that is how it was when a Chinese woman took up her embroidery frame, and cast aside the ten thousand worries of her daily life. In the work of her hands and her eyes and her mind there was healing and peace. And this peace and serenity, which were so essential a part of its creation, are what are communicated through the centuries when one holds in one's hands, or even sees in a case in a museum, specimens of Chinese pictures, porcelains, jade, or embroidery.

The most famous of all embroidery artists were the ladies of the Ku family of Shanghai. In the middle of the fifteenth century the women of this family became known for their incomparably beautiful pictures, and their fame continued to grow through the centuries. In our time many embroidery shops in the provinces of Chekiang and Kiangsu engraved the words Ku Hsiu (Ku embroidery) on their signboards as a symbol of superlative quality, even when they had no pieces actually made by the Ku family.

The place where the Ku ladies worked was called the Garden of the Fragrance of Dew, and they had complete freedom in regard to subject. They had unique methods of dyeing their silk and of combining their colors so that, whether they were depicting birds and flowers, mountains and streams, or horses and riders, their embroidered pictures were of extraordinary delicacy and beauty. The eminent Ming artist and critic Tung Ch'i-ch'ang said, when he saw one of their embroidered panels: "This is surely one of the wonders of the world."

According to a Chinese treatise on the subject: "The technique of the stitches is only one of the qualities of Ku Hsiu. Even more important are the composition, the coloring and the resemblance." "The resemblance," it is explained, "is not of the body, but also of the soul. Flowers have different positions in different weathers, animals make different movements under different conditions, and people have varying expressions in changing circumstances."

The husband of one of the Ku ladies explained to Tung Ch'i-ch'ang: "During days too hot or too cold, too windy or rainy, my wife would never dare to touch her embroidery frame. Only when the weather was fine and the sun bright, birds happy and flowers sweet, then she would catch the atmosphere and stitch it into the silks."

The rare remaining specimens of Ku Hsiu embroidery still retain the atmosphere of bright sunshine, singing birds and sweet flowers, which were so exquisitely woven into the delicate fabric.

COSTUMES

All the textile arts—silk weaving, K'o-ssŭ tapestry, and silk embroidery—figured prominently in the making of costumes, and so did the symbolism which was so inseparable from every expression of Chinese art or handicraft.

It is recorded that the Emperor Shun (circa 2255-2205 B.C.) wore silk clothing, and arranged to have the Twelve Ancient Ornaments * woven into his sacrificial robes. From that time onward these emblems were woven, painted, or embroidered on all the robes of ceremony of the Chinese emperors.

The imperial robes had to be symbolic in every detail—in quality of textile, in form, in color, and in ornament—because the ruler was the Son of Heaven, the symbol of the Supreme Power, the father and mother of the people. He personified the laws of the universe and all its elements—the sun, the moon, the stars, the sea, and the mountains. All this had to be represented on his robes, as well as the different systems of Chinese philosophy.

The imperial garments worn on state occasions were magnificent in texture, color, and pattern, but they were not designed primarily to be decorative. Every detail conveyed a meaning to those who looked at them. When Westerners talked of illiteracy in China, the Chinese might very well have pointed out (but were too polite to do so) that it was the foreigners who were illiterate because they were unable to read the messages plainly set forth on every piece of figured silk, embroidery, porcelain, jade, wood carving, or painting.

Not only the ornament but every detail of the imperial robe had some meaning. In the ancient classic writings we read that: "The roundness of the sleeves reminded the wearer that, when he raised his hands while walking, his manners should be elegant (like the shape of a circle). The straightness of the seam at the back, and the rectangles of the embroidered collar reminded the wearer that his administration should be impeccable and his justice incorruptible. The lower

* Described in Chapter XV.

315

edge of the robe, which was horizontal, like the beam of a balance, signified that the will was firm and the heart always calm."

In addition to the Twelve Ancient Ornaments, the earth was represented by a square, and heaven by a circle. The lower border of the robes, which symbolized the sea, was worked with waves. In addition, there were various Buddhist and Taoist symbols, as well as the motifs used to express happiness, long life, conjugal felicity, abundant posterity, and so forth.

Although there have been many variations in the shape, sleeves, and color, of the imperial robes in different dynasties, the symbolic ornaments were never omitted. Only the emperor could have all the Twelve Ancient Ornaments on his robes of ceremony; the nobles of first rank could use the sun, moon, and stars; those of the next rank, mountains and dragons. Only the emperor could have a dragon with five claws, but high officials (mandarins) could have dragons with four claws, and ordinary citizens could have them with three. There were five sets of varying robes for officials of different ranks.

The rules laid down in regard to the robes worn by the emperor, the empress, the princes and princesses, and the other Court officials and their women at different seasons of the year and for different ceremonial occasions were entirely remodeled in the reign of the Emperor Ch'ien Lung. Court etiquette necessitated a complete change of costume for each of the twenty-four periods (two weeks each) of the Chinese calendar. The weight of the silk varied according to the season, and the fur linings (fur was worn inside, not outside, the silk) ranged from white lamb and squirrel to fox which, considered the warmest, was used in midwinter. For summer there were thin transparent silk gauzes lined with thin silk.

Just as magnificent, and perhaps even more beautiful than the imperial robes, were the ceremonial garments worn by the highest Buddhist and Taoist priests. The Buddhist robes are usually made in rectangular shapes, with all the important Buddhist symbols. Some of them are made of the richest tapestry or the heaviest brocades, yet they always consist of small squares sewn together or else are woven to represent squares, symbolizing the tattered rags worn by Buddha.

The Taoist robes are almost square in shape, some of them with very wide sleeves. They are equally impressive. On the back—woven or inserted like a large patch—there is a square piece representing the earth, or a round one which may represent heaven. This will more often take the form of a T'ai Chi (the Source of Existence) which contains the yang-yin symbols, and is usually surrounded by the Eight Trigrams. In addition, scattered about the robe are other Taoist symbols usually denoting longevity or immortality.

Equally spectacular are the old stage costumes made to be worn by the important theatrical companies in Peking and other large cities. The designing of stage costumes was a carefully studied art, and through this medium were depicted historical periods, ranks, styles, professions, and even character—since a villain would not wear the same type of garments as a hero. In order to achieve the necessary effect, the clothes worn on the stage were somewhat exaggerated

316

Above: Chinese temple hanging —leaf green brocaded satin. Ming Dynasty.

Top right: Fragment of polychrome figured silk. Horseman and grotesque among clouds. Han Dynasty, about 1st century B.C. Excavated in Chinese Turkestan by Sir Aurel Stein.

Buddhist scroll—silk K'o ssŭ in many colors. 29 feet by 16¾ inches. Reign of Ch'ien Lung (1736-1795) and originally in the collection of the emperor.

Group of Ch'ing Dynasty costumes.

Bottom, left: Embroidered panel made by the Ku Hsiu family of Shanghai. Ming Dynasty.

Bottom, right: Blue K'o ssŭ Imperial Ceremonial robe with the twelve Imperial symbols. Reign of Yung Chêng (1722-1735).

Ancestor portrait, showing costume worn by high official. Ch'ing, dated 28th year of Ch'ien Lung.

Above: Ancestor portrait, showing costume worn by wife of official. Ch'ing Dynasty.

Left: "Beauty of South China." Ch'ing Dynasty. Portrait showing type of dress that might be worn at home by any woman of the Ch'ing Dynasty.

Taoist priest's robe, showing Taoist symbols. 19th century (?). *Below:* Chinese carpet—sage green and red cut velvet. 18th century.

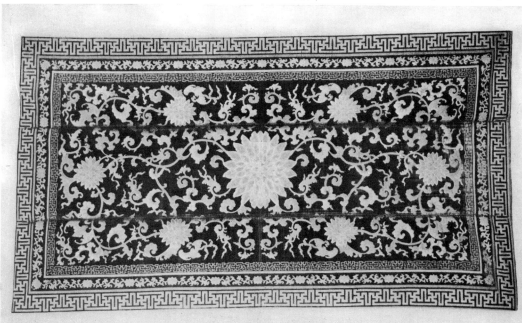

—the colors were more brilliant, the patterns and symbols larger, the lines more extreme, the sleeves and skirts longer and more sweeping. All the differences were sharper than in real life. While the Chinese spent little on stage scenery, the costumes worn by leading actors were tremendously costly. The headdresses were particularly varied and elaborate, both for male and female characters, and these often included the fêng huang (feathers of the Argus pheasant) which ran six to eight feet long, and which swayed gracefully as the actors moved.

The Chinese classic dramas were usually set in the period of the Three Kingdoms, or in the Han, T'ang, and Sung dynasties. Although many of the plays were written in the Yüan dynasty, when China was under Mongol rule, they dramatized the great men and events of the earlier periods.

The flowing robes, the very wide skirts, the full sweeping sleeves, the handsome headdresses, all of which can be seen more clearly on the stage than in contemporary paintings, show that the clothes worn by the Chinese in these earlier periods were more graceful and elegant in outline than those worn in the Ming and Ch'ing dynasties, although the latter are remarkable for their texture, color, and ornament.

The use of silk was by no means confined to persons of the official class in the later dynasties, but could be worn by all who were able to purchase it. In various cities of China, even in the south far removed from the Court and its influence, we have been shown chests filled with exquisite silk garments which have been treasured by families for generations. In these middle-class homes there were satin jackets in the most delicate colors—pearl gray, pale blue, and lilac—which had been woven, embroidered, or appliquéd, in every possible technique. The design was often limited to the borders and the collar and cuffs, with perhaps a few sparsely scattered flowers on the fabric itself. These garments were more in keeping with the Chinese ideal of sophisticated simplicity than were the elaborate imperial costumes, which were designed to be awe-inspiring.

The same restraint was shown in the graceful silk skirts with their loose floating panels at the back and front and intricate accordion pleating at the sides. These were of every color, including some "rainbow" or multicolor ones.

We did not see many baby garments, perhaps because they more easily became stained or damaged. However we did find a few little jackets which had obviously been lovingly embroidered by some mother a century or more ago, with all the symbols for good luck, long life, health, wealth, and happiness, in miniature designs with the tiniest of stitches.

RUGS AND CARPETS

Chinese rugs were almost unknown to us in the West before the present century, and there is little information available about their origins. Practically nothing has been written on the subject in China, since rug weaving was mostly carried on in remote northwest regions.

Wool had to be obtained from the districts where there were herds of sheep or camels—from Mongolia, Kansu, or Turkestan. That was the reason why the practice of weaving wool into rugs was carried on, until fairly modern times at least, chiefly by the people of the regions of Ninghsia and Paotou, and around Yarkand and Kashgar in Chinese Turkestan. The finest wool was said to come from Ninghsia but there was never enough to meet the demand.

Some authorities claim that the Chinese were the first to weave rugs with a thick pile and that they were made as early as the Hsia dynasty. On the other hand experts of the school that is firmly convinced that nothing could possibly have originated in China (in spite of such trifling inventions as silk, lacquer, porcelain, paper, and printing) insist that the idea of weaving woolen carpets was introduced into China only a few centuries ago.

It is possible, as has been suggested, that the idea of rug weaving may have come from Central Asia to Turkestan, and from there to China. There are equally good reasons for believing that the idea of rugmaking may have been indigenous to China, and that the Chinese people in the far northwestern regions conceived the idea of weaving rugs of wool for the same purpose as the people of Mongolia and Turkestan—in order to keep themselves warm. Rugs were originally woven to cover the k'angs (the raised, built-in platforms, heated from underneath in winter, and used for sitting and lounging on in the daytime and for sleeping on at night). They were also made to serve as bed covers, to be hung over the door to keep out the cold winds, and to be used as saddle covers and horse trappings.

One basis for assuming that they may have been of native origin is that the designs on even the oldest known rugs are Chinese and are similar to those on their ceramics and textiles. An even more important piece of evidence is that the Chinese technique differed from that used by the rugmakers of Central Asia and the Near East. There is the additional fact that colored rugs and decorated carpets are mentioned in Han records, and that, in the course of his excavations in Chinese Turkestan along the old Silk Route, Sir Aurel Stein found "fragments of Chinese fine pile carpets by the side of plentiful coarse materials in wool and felt," which were being carried from China to the Near East in the first century.

So far no other examples of very early rugs have been found, but in that treasure trove of the T'ang arts of China in the Shōsōin at Nara (Japan) there are fine examples of Chinese rugs of the eighth century, with grayish white grounds, brown border, and designs worked in brown and indigo blue. These were not made by the method of tied knots, as used in the other rug-weaving countries, but by a process of felting which has since been lost.

This opens up the possibility that the idea of rug weaving was indigenous to China, but that, at some later date—perhaps during the Mongol occupation, at which time there are records of exchanges of weavers between Persia and China—the Chinese may have substituted the use of the Persian knot for their own earlier method. Even then the Chinese rugs did not closely follow those of Persia and other countries of Near East and Central Asia, for they were much more loosely knotted, with a shaggier pile, perhaps because they were not intended to be placed on the floor.

The number of colors used was not as varied as in the Near East, being limited, for the most part, to the Five Sacred Colors—black, blue, red, white, and yellow. Vegetable dyes, of the same type as those employed in the textile and ceramic industries from the earliest periods of Chinese history, were used exclusively until the present century. The majority of the old Ninghsia rugs were made in two colors only—yellow and blue.

In northwestern villages, along the basin of the Yellow River, whole families worked in their homes on these rugs, and this custom continued, with exactly the same simple looms, materials, designs, and vegetable dyes right into the present century. They used chiefly the wool of sheep and lambs, most of which came from Mongolia. Primarily these rugs were made as important family possessions and for brides to carry with them to their husband's home. In the course of time, however, a few surplus rugs were woven and sold.

Eventually a small number of rugs were transported to the large centers of China along the old Silk Route. They were greatly admired by members of the imperial household, high officials, and persons of wealth, and these competed with each other to possess a more beautiful rug than anyone else. The result was that the weavers strove to produce finer and finer rugs in the hope that they might be able to make one so splendid that it would please the emperor himself.

While a great vogue had arisen for their products, the makers still had to compete with the weavers of Persia who supplied most of the rugs used in the Imperial Palace. Gradually, as the general demand for rugs increased, looms were set up in Peking as well as in other large centers, but the region around Ninghsia and Paotou continued to turn out the rugs which were the most highly prized.

There are very few specimens of Chinese carpets older than the Ming dynasty. Marco Polo spoke of the carpets and hanging wall rugs of many different colors made of camel's hair which he saw in Peking, but few of these appear to have survived the general destruction which ended the Mongol occupation.

In the Ming dynasty the rugs were usually quite small, and they were either square or rectangular, never round. They were not put on the floor except in Buddhist temples, where, in addition to serving as hangings, they were used for deadening the sound of walking feet and for kneeling on when in prayer.

During the Ming and Ch'ing dynasties rugs were made under imperial patronage, and they were seldom seen south of Peking. In such southern cities as Canton, for instance, where the climate made such things unnecessary, and which was so far removed from the wool-raising districts, carpets remained almost unknown. This perhaps explains why the early European and American traders, who were confined to that port, did not export Chinese rugs.

In the T'ang, Sung and Yüan dynasties the designs were geometrical and conventional. By the Ming dynasty they became more elaborate. Geometrical patterns predominated in the borders, and the central design consisted of medallions or an all-over geometric pattern or both. There were not more than about 80 to 90 knots per foot, and even the finest Chinese rugs never approached the Persian in the tightness of the knotting. In this dynasty "metal and silk" rugs were made, the silk pile being woven into a warp of gold and silver threads.

These famous "palace silk rugs" were woven in beautiful soft colors and striking patterns. Most of them were small, and they were intended to be placed on furniture or used as a hanging.

Ming woolen carpets were mellow and subdued in color. Yellow and blue, with some brown and perhaps a suggestion of red, were the only colors used. One distinctive technique employed in Chinese carpets was the cutting out of the pile to soften the angularity of the designs, which gave a carved effect to the rug and enhanced its appearance.

During the early part of the reign of the Emperor K'ang Hsi, there was the same limited color range as in Ming and the same sparseness in decoration. Later, naturalistic floral motifs became more popular than the geometric patterns, with the medallions predominating. The rugs tended to be more ornate, and new colors were introduced. The texture grew firmer, increasing to as much as 120 knots per foot. Many pure silk rugs, and some metal and silk ones, were woven.

Under the Emperor Ch'ien Lung the weavers became more skilled in their technique and they wove elaborate rugs of all sizes. For the first time large carpets, and rugs of circular shape, made their appearance. While blue and yellow remained dominant there was a wider range of additional colors. Red was more popular, white was frequently used, and green was introduced. The colors were harmoniously blended, and the weave tightened to range from 80 to 150 knots. Many rugs had two borders—one geometric and one floral.

The finest rugs still continued to be those made around Ninghsia and Paotou, which grew to resemble tapestry woven in wool, with delicate shadings of color. Those of Paotou came to be considered even finer than those of Ninghsia because of their close texture, often 160 knots to the foot, and the range and richness of their coloring. The colors were usually dull shades of blue, red, and brown, with touches of yellow and green. The subjects of these "picture rugs," in addition to the usual Chinese subjects and symbols, often took the form of some pastoral or local scene. These were not intended to be placed on the floor.

In general the designs on old rugs include borders of key pattern, scroll pattern, T pattern, or "cash" pattern (small rounds). The center may show an all-over diaper pattern, a geometrical pattern, medallions of flowers, Chinese characters for long life, happiness, good luck, or prosperity, as well as any of the Buddhist, Taoist, or other symbols. Frequently used were animals—stork and deer for longevity, tigers, Fo dogs, and horses. On Imperial Palace rugs there would appear the five-claw dragons.

Nature symbols were very popular with the rug weavers. A calm sea was represented by semicircles placed one above the other. If the water was rippled, the semicircles would be slightly distorted or broken. To indicate waves, the circles became lines meeting at the top in an acute angle, and for a rough sea there would be small dots or circles or small clouds, representing spray which continued from the crest of the waves. Small straight lines descending a short distance from the clouds indicated that there was a storm and that rain was falling.

Another nature symbol took the form of mountains, which denoted strength and firmness. With both water and mountains there might be bridges, boats, and pavilions.

While Chinese rugs did not achieve the same high standard of material or workmanship as did those of Persia and other parts of the Near East, the simplicity, restraint, and clarity of the designs and the cool blues and yellows in which they were woven render them more suitable for modern homes. Once they were seen they became exceedingly popular. In 1903, Chinese rugs obtained the first prize at the St. Louis International Exhibition, and they began to be made commercially in large quantities, in all sizes, shapes, colors, and with all types of decoration—traditional and modern, to satisfy the orders from the United States and Europe.

At the same time the demand for antique Chinese rugs was so great that more of them can now be found in other countries than in China itself.

The T'ai Chi. Yang and yin symbols surrounded by the Eight Trigrams, the Pa Kua.

Chapter XIV

ENAMEL, METALWORK, AND JEWELRY

THERE IS A TYPE of work known as T'ieh hua (iron flower), much of which was made in early times from simple sheet iron by monk artists. Among the finest old examples surviving are the sixteen windows in the old Buddhist monastery of Ling Yin (Soul's Retreat), near West Lake, Hangchow.

This ironwork usually took the form of sprays of flowers, such as those of the Four Seasons, or simple landscapes. It was set in a wooden frame with no back, the wall on which it was hung serving as a background.

Whether factual or not, the story told about the origin of this art is worth repeating because it is so typical of the attitude of the Chinese toward all arts and crafts. In the T'ang dynasty, a poor wandering artist was suddenly taken ill and fell down in the road outside a forge. The blacksmith carried the sick man into his house and nursed him until he had recovered his health. Having no money, the artist expressed his gratitude to his benefactor by painting a picture which the smith hung up on the wall opposite his anvil. As he worked he found himself unable to take his eyes from the painted picture, and he soon felt compelled to try and copy it in beaten iron. When he was finally satisfied with the result of his efforts, he presented the finished iron work to the artist, saying: "You work in your medium with brush and paint, I work with my good iron. Have we not both an equal chance of being remembered by posterity?"

The artist was so much impressed by the strong effective lines of the iron flowers that he joined forces with the blacksmith to design and forge the iron pictures, the demand for which has continued until the present time.

The creative urge of the Chinese has been so compulsive that they have expressed their art in whatever medium was available to them. Those who could not express themselves in the great arts of calligraphy and painting, or in such important crafts as pottery, sculpture, lacquer ware, jade carving, or silk weaving sought to create beauty out of such materials as were available to them.

326

ENAMELWARE

One of the arts which the Chinese have practiced but did not invent was that of enamelware. It was never as highly regarded as the porcelain which it attempted to rival because it lacked the qualities of translucency and resonance, but many craftsmen have excelled in this medium.

There are three main types of enamelware—cloisonné, champlevé, and painted.

CLOISONNÉ ENAMEL

It was assumed that the art of cloisonné enamelware was introduced into China in the Yüan dynasty by the Arabs. Then in 1910 the Japanese government issued an album with 150 plates, illustrating some of the examples of T'ang art which had been deposited in the Imperial Treasury at Nara (Japan) in the eighth century. Among them were specimens of Chinese mirrors decorated on the back with finely executed floral designs in Chinese cloisonné work.

The Chinese believe that the art of cloisonné ware was introduced from Byzantium and that the name "Fa-lin," by which it was known, was a corruption of the old name "Fo-lin" for the Roman empire. The derivation of this word is mainly conjectural, and other meanings are claimed, such as that "Fa-lan" was derived from the name for Frank or France.

There is definite evidence, however, that the art of cloisonné ware was practiced from ancient times in Western Asia and in various parts of Europe, including Ireland. China was not so isolated from the rest of the world in the early centuries of our era as has sometimes been thought. There was constant commerce along the Silk Route, as well as by sea. Considerable intercourse existed during the T'ang dynasty between Byzantium and China, and there are records that Syrian traders managed to reach Yunnan and from there penetrated farther into China. They were followed by a large group of Arabs who settled in Canton in the eighth century.

The Byzantines, who excelled in this art, worked on plates of gold, but the Chinese usually used copper as a base for their cloisonné work, and it was gilded only after the pieces had been completed.

The word *cloison* means cell or partition. After the copper base was formed to the desired shape, the pattern was carefully outlined in little cells made with narrow strips or partitions of gold, silver, or copper, which were then soldered on edgewise.

The enamel itself was a glasslike substance, which came in blocks from Shantung province, and had to be finely powdered, sifted, and mixed with water in one of the many little bowls, perhaps fifteen or twenty, which represented the different colors to be used. These were then filled into the cells by means of a Chinese writing brush.

After the first filling, the piece was baked for a few minutes in a small kiln. This caused the enamel to contract to about one-third of its original bulk, and the cells had to be filled and baked again, and yet again, so they would be full and free from pitting. Then the surface was filed and polished, until the piece was ready for gilding. The final effect was that of a mosaic of colored enamels outlined in gold.

Whether introduced into China by the Persians or by the Arabs or by any other of the Middle Eastern craftsmen who worked in the Chinese capital in the early T'ang dynasty, the T'ang cloisonné pieces in the Shōsōin collection in Nara are as fine as any that were made later, and the designs had already taken on an unmistakably Chinese aspect.

Perhaps the most interesting feature of the introduction of this art into China is that the Chinese used the same technique to apply the designs in different colors of enamel to their pottery in the T'ang period, separating one color from another by strips of clay, or by incised outlines, or else by hollowing out depressions in the body of the piece to prevent one color from running into another. The latter process was similar to the type of enamelwork known as champlevé, which had probably been introduced into China at the same time as cloisonné. It is thus possible that the introduction of enamelwork into China was responsible for the whole idea of decorating pottery and porcelain with varicolored enamels.

The making of cloisonné seems to have ceased completely during the Sung dynasty, and so did the application of colored enamels to ceramic wares. This would appear to confirm that the two techniques were interrelated; it also emphasizes the fact that the austere Sung scholars, who were the arbiters of elegance, did not care much for colored decorations. What they admired was the simplest perfection of form and cool monochrome glazes, so it is easy to understand that even the finest cloisonné, with its mosaic of colored enamels, would not appeal to their taste.

This is not set forth in any spirit of criticism, for it was the exquisite and sophisticated taste of the Chinese connoisseur which maintained the high standards of true Chinese art and restrained the craftsmen, with their tremendous creative energy, from those excesses in decoration and ornament which marred some of the work done in periods when the power of the scholars was in decline.

The Yüan dynasty was one of the times when the Court was not dominated by the Chinese scholar, and there was a great demand for luxury and for elaborately decorated objects. At the end of the regime, if not before, cloisonné work again appeared on the scene, perhaps being made by some of the Arabic artisans who settled in China at that time. There are pieces in existence which are marked with the seal (the nien hao) of Chih-chêng (1341-1367), the last Mongol emperor.

It was not until the Ming dynasty that cloisonné work reached its full stature, both in quantity and quality. The art of cloisonné enameling again developed at the same time as did the practice of decorating porcelain ware with colored enamels—the same type of vitrifiable enamels being used on both mediums.

While, as we have already seen, there has always been controversy about the actual meaning, derivation, and correct form of the name Fo-lan, or Fo-lin, used

Cloisonné enamel dish. General all-over pattern
of fret designs on turquoise ground. Ming, reign
of Chia Ching.

Garden seat. Cloisonné. Ming Dynasty.

Pair of Imperial enamel vases with *famille rose* floral decoration, and Imperial enamel plate with Dragon medallion and ruby back. Both reign of Ch'ien Lung.

Pair of silver bowls. Sung Dynasty. Eugene Fuller Memorial Collection.

Imperial Fêng Huang (phoenix) crown for Empress. Composed of thirty or forty separate ornaments of gold wire, transparent coils, sprays of flowers, birds, butterflies, phoenixes, and other symbols, sparkling with uncut rubies, pearls, and cats' eyes. Late T'ang or early Sung Dynasty.

331

Pair of Chinese silver-gilt hairpins. Head consists of pierced floral motif from which two phoenixes, studded with paste in imitation of coral and jade, rise on stiff wires. From bill of each bird depends a chain and flower basket ending in a flower with gold leaves. 17th century or earlier.

Detail of Chinese Imperial crown. Late T'ang or Early Sung Dynasty.

to designate cloisonné, it later came to be commonly known by the name of Ching T'ai lan (Ching T'ai enamel) because the Emperor Ching T'ai (1450-1457) took it under his special patronage, ordering many temple vessels to be made. The small incense burners in the Palace museum in Peking made in that reign were considered among the finest objects in the collection.

It is suggested that the great advance in the quality and popularity of cloisonné in the reign of Ching T'ai was due to the arrival of many of the Greek artisans who had worked on Byzantine enamels and who sought refuge in China when Constantinople was taken by the Turks in 1453.

Ming cloisonné is bold and free in design, and the colors are pure and vivid. The principal enamels used are two shades of blue—dark lapis lazuli and turquoise—and coral red and deep yellow. Grass green occasionally occurs. The least successful colors were black and white.

Later, when the Emperor K'ang Hsi established his series of imperial factories, workshop No. 6 was devoted to the manufacture of enamels. Here the technique greatly improved, while, at the same time, the early forcefulness of design and brilliant coloring were retained. Many of the pieces were made in archaic bronze forms.

The Ch'ien Lung pieces showed still further refinements of technique, with complete elimination of the pitting that occurred in earlier specimens, and skillful blending of colors. On the other hand, the forms and designs are less bold and the colors less deep and lucid. Much heavy gilding was used on the accessories, as well as on the piece itself.

In contrast, the modern products are of a purely commercial type, with sparse gilding of poor quality.

Another method of enameling is champlevé (the oldest of all), already referred to, in which depressions are made in the solid metal to be filled in with enamel colors. Then there is repoussé work, in which decorations in gilt may be hammered into relief, with the colored enamel as background, or the cloisons filled with enamel colors may stand away from the gilt surface in relief. Sometimes these different techniques are combined on the same piece.

PAINTED ENAMELS

The art of enamel painting dates back no further than the end of the fifteenth century. At that time the craftsmen of Limoges, France, found that they could dispense with cloisons and depressions, and paint directly on the flat metal surface. First the whole surface was covered with a layer of opaque enamel (usually white); and, after that had dried, additional enamel colors could be added in the same way as a picture is painted. This technique developed into the magnificent Limoges enamels of the sixteenth century, and was afterward used in England in the making of what was called Battersea enamel.

It was at the end of the seventeenth century, in the reign of K'ang Hsi, that French missionaries brought pieces of Limoges enamel to China to be copied, and many orders for enamels for the Court of Louis XIV were executed. The French enamels were closely copied in regard to both technique and subject.

The Chinese referred to this painted enamel as yang tz'ŭ (foreign porcelain), and for some time they were not much interested in it, apart from filling the European orders. Many of the armorial porcelain services made for England included copper winepots, teapots, or hot-water pitchers, which were enameled and decorated in Canton with the same designs as the porcelains. Some of the French pieces had religious designs, while others had more frivolous European subjects of the Watteau type.

Much of the painted enamel work was done in Canton. Porcelain "in the white" was sent to that city from Ching-tê Chên to be decorated for the export trade with the same colored enamels as were used on the copper, but the porcelain was called yang ts'ai (foreign colors). The colors used for yang tz-ŭ and yang tz-ai were those of the *famille rose* palette, including the rose-pink made from gold chloride ("purple of Cassius").

In addition to the export ware, a finer form of painted enamel was made in Peking in the pure Chinese taste, including many landscape panels for the Imperial Court. The Emperor Ch'ien Lung wrote poems on some of the pieces extolling their beauty.

In spite of this imperial encouragement, few Chinese showed much enthusiasm for the "foreign porcelain." The author of a Chinese book on porcelain ("Wên fang ssǔ k'ao"), published in the reign of Ch'ien Lung, writes: "One often sees incense-urns and flower vases, wine cup and saucers, bowls and dishes, wine-ewers and boxes painted in very brilliant colors; but, although vulgarly called porcelain, they have nothing of the pure translucency of the true material, and are fit only for the service and ornament of the ladies' apartments—not for the chaste decoration of the library of a scholar or official."

Other Chinese collectors have always admired, and still do admire, fine specimens of enamelware, both cloisonné and painted. Those alive today admit that these objects lack translucency and resonance, but point out that they have another outstanding quality—that of permanence. They are less liable to breakage than porcelain, and, unless there is actual destruction, a piece of enamel can be depended on to retain its brilliant coloring unimpaired by the passing of time.

GOLD AND SILVER

The Chinese do not appear to have accorded the same place of honor to gold as have many other peoples. They use the same character for metal and gold, and it represents the chief of the five elements—metal (or gold), wood, fire, water, and earth—in the fêng-shui or the yang-yin system of divination.

Cubes of gold were used as currency from the eleventh to the third centuries B.C.; and, before China had foreign intercourse, gold and silver had the same value. Until the Han dynasty gold was quite cheap, but afterward foreign trade and the demand for the metal in making Buddhist images greatly increased its value.

The Chinese made beautiful vessels of gold, but very few early specimens survived for the obvious reason that they could too easily be converted into money. The same may be said about the silver vessels, even though more of these are still in existence.

Gold was used not only in the making of vessels and Buddhist images, but also as inlays in bronze, for gilding other substances, and for the famous gold thread. In the T'ang dynasty and earlier, women wore finely wrought gold ornaments, often of filagree work, in their hair. Gold and silver and silver gilt were used for making hairpins, bracelets, finger rings, necklaces, and belt buckles. Existing specimens of silver, which date back to the late Chou dynasty, include pole ends, a silver gilt cup inlaid with precious stones, and a hairpin with glass-paste inlay. The range of silver objects made in the early dynasties comprises ritual objects, toilet accessories, household utensils—bowls, cups, ladles—and even a silver funerary mask of the Han period.

Many T'ang and Sung bowls were made of silver (sometimes washed with gold), and they were intended for the use of the living. These were decorated with freely drawn designs in scroll work, naturalistic flowers, and, sometimes, elaborate patterns.

Hardly anything has been written on the subject of the superb gold and silver work done by the Chinese in their early history, and this lack of knowledge has contributed to the general failure to recognize the high degree of culture which prevailed in China.

When, in 1786, the ship *Grand Turk* returned from Canton with fine Chinese porcelains, Paul Revere was so impressed with their simplicity and delicacy that he used some of the bowls as models for his silverwork. It is an interesting comment on the interrelationships of art that the same shapes he copied from the Chinese porcelains, and which are still being copied in silver today, were also made in silver by the Chinese many centuries earlier.

JEWELRY

Antique Chinese jewelry was highly decorative and usually of a symbolic nature. The work itself was considered more important than the material. For instance, with the exception of pearls, the stones used were usually of the semi-precious type, such as jade, coral, amber, and lapis lazuli. The stones were not cut but merely polished and set *en cabochon*.

We have mentioned the fine gold and silver gilt filagree ornaments worn by Chinese women in the T'ang dynasty. The men wore jewelry as well as the women—jeweled belt hooks, beads, finger rings, and jade pendants. Beads were worn by both men and women from the time of the Yellow Emperor, and they continued to be popular up to the present time. In cold weather beads of jade, coral, and agate were worn; in summer these were replaced by beads of cedar and ivory.

Birds, flowers, and butterflies were carved from jade and other semiprecious stones and set in fine gold surrounded by pearls. An unusual substance used in

Chinese jewelry and headdresses consisted of kingfisher feathers, which were appliquéd on silver or copper. The bright blue plumage was said to resemble the sky, and the blue-green tints the distant hills. While the azure, sapphire, turquoise, green-blue, and other tints of these feathers are beautiful in themselves, jewelry of this type is hardly up to the standards of most Chinese art. This explains the fact that the word for these feathers is also used to designate a gaudily dressed woman.

The Chinese craftsmen worked in so many different mediums that one could go on and on describing their metalcraft work in copper, brass, and pewter, the designing and painting of wallpaper, the making of glass pictures, the folk carvings from roots of trees, and the expressive soapstone figures.

Throughout the long history of China the ultimate concern of the whole people, and the faith which gave purpose and meaning to their lives, was to make something where there had been nothing—to create art.

And this faith fully justified itself because all that remains of the many towns and villages which have disappeared are a few of the things fashioned by the hands of their artists and craftsmen. These things are what exist when all else has vanished, and they speak of the past with a clear voice that can still be heard around the world.

VII: *MEANINGS IN CHINESE ART*

Chapter XV

SYMBOLISM AND SUBJECTS

THE BEST WORKS of Chinese artists and craftsmen can meet the basic challenge of great art by their ability to stand alone, to remain admirable even when completely separated from the time, place, civilization, and atmosphere in which they were created.

They can reveal their beauty, their strength or delicacy, their perfect sense of balance, and their fine proportions to every beholder. But, in addition to its artistic quality, every Chinese work of art, as we have already seen, was intended to convey a meaning. Every picture contains an idea, and it is this meaning, this idea, which gives us an insight into a civilization of over fifty centuries, and some measure of understanding of the hopes, fears, desires, aspirations, and beliefs of its people.

The delicate loveliness of a piece of carved jade may look as unsubstantial and as devoid of serious intent as a dew drop. Yet behind it lies not only the long years of hard work spent in acquiring the skill to create it, but also a definite message to be conveyed to the recipient.

The symbolism expressed is always beneficent. It implies a belief in a Supreme Power that can grant human beings their highest desires. No art object conveys any evil intent. Besides this form of symbolism, decoration will often show some character—legendary or historical—who embodies admired characteristics or illustrates some tale of love, heroism, or virtue. These tales, even when told about real persons, may not be completely true. They often vary in different parts of the country, and sometimes the same story is attributed to different characters.

These symbols, the love of nature, the religious and philosophical concepts, the stories of heroes and saints and great beauties have endowed Chinese art with its vitality and spirit. Stripped of its folklore, Chinese art would lose not only its meaning and charm, but would be reduced to an accumulation of life-less—even if still beautiful—pieces of bronze, pottery, porcelain, jade, silk, and paper.

Symbolism is so intrinsic a part of Chinese art that reference to it has been made in every section of this book, but it is still essential to list some of the most commonly used symbols, as well as some of the favorite subjects.

THE ORIGIN OF ALL THINGS

Perhaps the oldest symbolic form is that known as the T'ai Chi, the Creative Principle, or Origin of all Things. This is depicted by the symbol known as the yang and yin, which represents the male and female element, the duality from which all existence is derived. Yang represents the positive elements—heaven, sun, light, masculinity—and yin all the passive, receptive elements, such as earth, moon, darkness, femininity.

This symbol of the Source of Existence is frequently shown surrounded by the Eight Diagrams (or Trigrams), the Pa Kua. These consist of a series of combinations of lines (the straight ones representing the yang, and the broken ones the yin principles) upon which a whole system of geomancy and divination, and even, it has been claimed, the science of mathematics and the art of writing characters, was built up. It is used in decoration as a design of good omen.

THE FIVE ELEMENTS

The whole scheme of Chinese philosophy (according to the "Shu Ching"—the classic "Book of History") was based on the Five Elements, or active principles of Nature. These were: Water, Fire, Wood, Metal, and Earth, all of which were in harmony with, or antagonistic toward, each other. From the operations of these Five Elements derived the Five Atmospheric Conditions, the Five Kinds of Grain, the Five Planets, the Five Metals, the Five Colors, the Five Tastes, et cetera.

THE FOUR SACRED ANIMALS

Among these oldest of Chinese symbols, dating back to the beginnings of their civilization, are the Four Sacred Animals. These are the Tortoise, the Dragon, the Phoenix, and the Unicorn, which, the legend runs, helped the first Chinese man (P'an Ku) to bring order out of chaos.

The Dragon, which symbolizes the renewal of life because it controls the much-needed rainfall, rules over the east and influences the spring. The Tortoise, symbol of longevity, strength, and endurance, controls the north and influences winter. The Phoenix, which is seen only when the land is at peace, and which stands for joy and warmth, rules over the south and influences summer. The Unicorn (which is often replaced by the White Tiger) was supposed to have power over the west and to influence the maturity and fulfillment of autumn.

All these animals have had varying symbolic meanings at different times. The meaning intended to be conveyed often depended on the setting and the rest of the decoration.

THE TWELVE ANCIENT ORNAMENTS

The Twelve Ancient Ornaments, symbols of authority and power, are so old that in the "Book of History," the first of the Five Classics, we read that the Emperor Shun (circa 2255-2205 B.C.) called them "The Ancient Symbols" and had them woven into his sacrificial robes.

"I wish," the Emperor Shun is quoted as saying, "to see the emblematic figures of the ancients—the sun, the moon, the stars, the mountain, the dragon, the pheasant—depicted on the upper garment; the ritual cups, the aquatic grass, the flames, the grains of rice, the axe and the symbol of distinction embroidered on the lower garments; I wish to see all these displayed with the Five Colors, so as to form the official robes; it is yours to adjust them clearly."

The Emperor Shun pointed out the symbolism in these things:

The sun, moon and stars indicate the knowledge we should possess to govern well (by understanding Nature).

The mountains indicate the constancy and firmness needed by a good and wise ruler; and, because they distribute clouds and rain, they symbolize his concern for the welfare of his people.

The dragon, with its infinite variety of forms, symbolizes the need for adaptability and shows that a good and wise ruler should use all methods necessary to inspire his people with virtue.

The beauty and variety of the colors of the pheasant remind us of the good example we should give by practicing all the virtues and accomplishments.

On the upper garment we see six different kinds of embroidery to remind us of the virtues which should be engraved on our hearts.

The ritual cups (on which are depicted the tiger and the long-tailed monkey), which we are accustomed to see in the halls of our ancestors, symbolize purity and disinterestedness. They denote that a good ruler should use spiritual force to quell disturbances in the same way as the tiger can subdue things with courage and strength.

The flames, which fire pottery, melt metals, and cook food, symbolize the constant renewal of zeal and love of virtue in the good and wise ruler.

The water weeds (aquatic plants), which yield to the movement of the water, show that we should adapt ourselves to changing times.

The grains of rice (or millet) indicate the abundance we should provide for the people.

The axe is a symbol of the resolution with which the emperor must meet every situation.

And the symbol of distinction (Fu)—consisting of two "chi" characters back to back—show how we must distinguish between good and evil, and also that there must be co-ordination between the ruler and his ministers.

The first of the Ancient Ornaments, the Sun, represents the yang, or generative principle. In the Sun is seen a cock—heralder of daylight and activity.

339

The second, the Moon, represents the yin, or receptive principle. Inside the Moon is a hare mixing the Elixir of Immortality, with pestle and mortar, representing the female element preparing and preserving life. This symbol of the Moon, and the hare preparing the Elixir of Life, has remained one of the most popular and is much used at the time of the Moon Festival in autumn even in the decoration of cakes and sweetmeats.

While these symbols are first mentioned in connection with the weaving and embroidery of official robes, they are used, singly or in groups, on porcelain, lacquer, and other objects. Many of them have become interwoven with Taoist mythology.

THE TWELVE SIGNS OF THE ZODIAC

Another set of ancient symbols is the Twelve Signs of the Zodiac—one for each month—which, unlike ours, are all represented by animals: the rat, ox, tiger, hare, dragon, serpent, horse, goat, monkey, cock, dog, and bear. It was important for every Chinese to know under which animal he was born because of the influence it was believed that animal would have on the course of his life.

OTHER ANCIENT SYMBOLS

One of the oldest and most used forms of decoration is the thunder and cloud, or the meander, fret, or key pattern, seen so frequently on Shang bronzes. This important symbol (for the clouds brought the rain) is used in spiral forms and in angular forms. It is seen in simple and in intricate designs, and has been used for thousands of years as a border design on bronzes, pottery, fabrics, and all other forms of art.

Other popular designs for diaper patterns and borders, particularly on fabrics and porcelains, are formed of cash (round or square coins with a hole in the center), which symbolize riches. In later dynasties these often take the form of little round flowers which have the same significance. Then there are the Ju-i scepter (or fungus) designs, the diamond pattern, designs of fishes' scales, grains of rice, herringbone, honeycomb, the letter *T*, silkworms, cicadas, and octagonals.

CONFUCIAN SYMBOLISM

The different religions and philosophies of China have contributed subjects for artists and craftsmen, and each has had its own symbols. Confucius, opposed to all formal religious forms, contributed no gods or immortals and no distinct emblems, but the pictures and objects which pertain to filial piety and to culture and learning have been considered as his symbols.

The twenty-four Symbols of Filial Piety consist of a series of examples of excessive devotion to parents.

Then there are the Four Accomplishments; which stress the importance of learning and culture. Music is represented by a lute, games of skill by chess, art by paintings, and scholarship by books.

Figure of Kwan Yin in polychromed wood. Sung Dynasty.

eated porcelain figure of the Taoist Immortal,
hung-li Ch'üan. Ming Dynasty. Chia Ching pe-
od (1522-1566). Underglaze blue. Eli Lilly Col-
ction.

ight: Porcelain group of Twin Genii of Peace
d Harmony in the Household, called Ho-Ho.
ecorated in *famille rose* colors. Ch'ien Lung
riod (1736-1795). Figure of Kwan Yin, in poly-
romed wood. Sung Dynasty.

"Two Geese," by Lü Chi (ca. 1500). Ming Dynasty.

Detail from twelve-panel lacquer screen by Fong Long Kou of Fatshan (1690), showing five children watching fighting birds.

Opposite page:
The Twelve Ancient Ornament (see text). This set is taken from an Imperial twelve-symbol rob of yellow K'o ssŭ, Ch'ien Lung period (1736-1795). From left to right, starting at the top, the represent the sun, the constella tion (stars), the moon, the drag on, the mountain, the wate weeds (aquatic grass), the mille (or grain of rice), the pheasan the flames, the ax, the ritual cups the symbol of distinction. Th order in which these symbols ar depicted varies.

Courtesy Time Magazine, May 1952

Newark Museum

Above.

Left: Glazed pottery roof tile in form of Yen Lo, The Decider of Life in Hades. Three-color glaze. Ming Dynasty. *Right:* Roof tile in form of figure of Shen I, the Divine Archer, astride the Bird of Dawn. Usually leads the procession of roof tiles. Three-color glaze. Ming Dynasty. Royal Ontario Museum of Archaeology, Toronto.

Left:

Group of blue and white porcelains. *Left:* Water cup used in painting. Family scene in Chinese garden. Yung Chêng period (1722-1735). *Right:* Blue and white vase with design of rocks and flowers. K'ang Hsi period (1662-1722). *Center:* Blue and white water cup used in painting. Design of Ju-i scepters, or fungus, around top, and the trigrams of the Pa kua around the body. K'ang Hsi period (1662-1722). Herman and Paul Jaehne Collection.

Another set of symbols attributed to Confucius is the Four Treasures of the Room of Literature: the writing brush, the ink block, the ink slab, and paper.

A fourth group of so-called Confucian symbols used widely on porcelain and embroidery is known as the Hundred Antiques. This includes the Four Accomplishments, the Four Treasures of the Room of Literature, and various other objects connected with literary, official, and artistic life—musical instruments, ritual objects, written characters, vessels, vases, brush pots, and flowers. Also included, and in most general use, are the Eight Precious Things (or Eight Ordinary Symbols):

The Sonorous Stone. Used as a bell. Symbol of good judgment. Emblem of good luck.

The Pair of Books. Emblem of learning. Charm against evil spirits.

Pair of Rhinoceros' Horns. Carved as drinking cups. Emblem of happiness.

Artemisia Leaf. Symbol of happiness. Charm to cure illness.

Pearl. A charm to avert fire, flood, and other disasters. Also denotes feminine purity and beauty.

Coin. Emblem of wealth.

Painting or Mirror. Symbol of conjugal felicity. Charm to ward off evil spirits.

Lozenge. An ancient musical instrument. Symbol of victory.

All these symbols are usually drawn with interweaving ribbons.

TAOIST SYMBOLISM

In the field of Taoism we find every type of symbolism and legend, ranging from simple fairy tales to historical stories, from superstition to philosophy, and from amusing folly to impressive wisdom.

Frequently seen in all forms of art are the figures of the Eight Taoist Immortals, the Pa Hsien. These were historical or legendary figures who lived at different times, and who were said to have achieved immortality through their understanding of the secrets of Nature. Sometimes in groups, and sometimes singly, each with a special emblem, they are often depicted crossing the sea in fragile boats, walking over a bridge on their way to the Taoist paradise, or standing against a background of mountains and wild scenery.

Between them they represent all the conditions of human life—masculinity and femininity, poverty and wealth, age and youth, scholarship and lack of education.

The Chief of the Eight Immortals is Chung-li Ch'üan, said to have lived in the Chou dynasty. He is usually shown as a statesman with a fan in his hand. With this instrument he was supposed to have had the power of reviving the souls of the dead. This association derives from the following story:

Chung-li Ch'üan married a beautiful young wife and retired to his native place to lead the life of a philosopher. Once, while he was out for a walk, he noticed a young woman in deep mourning sitting near a recently dug grave, fanning the soil. In response to his questions she explained that her late husband had asked her to wait at least until the earth around his grave was entirely dry before marrying again. She had already found another man who wanted to marry her and was trying to make the earth dry more quickly by fanning it.

The philosopher offered to help her. He invoked the aid of spirits and, taking her fan, struck the ground with it. It immediately became quite dry. The woman begged him to keep the fan as a token of her gratitude.

When he returned to his home, his wife asked about the fan. He told her the story, whereupon she became very angry, saying she would never behave in such a disgraceful manner as that widow who was a person devoid of all decent human feelings.

In order to test her, Chung-li Ch'üan feigned death, and at the same time he assumed the form of a handsome young man who wooed the supposed widow. In a few days she agreed to marry him; and, when the suitor told her he needed the brains of her late husband to concoct a powerful medicine, she opened up the coffin without hesitation. To her horror, her husband suddenly came to life and sat up, while the young man vanished into thin air. Unable to survive such humiliation, the young wife hanged herself, and Chung-li Ch'üan set fire to his house. He then walked out of it, taking with him only the sacred book of Taoism—the Tao-tê Ching—and the fan which he always carried.

Another of the Eight Immortals is Chang Kuo-lao, a famous magician of the seventh to eighth centuries after Christ. He is usually accompanied by his white mule which he rode backward and which, when he did not need it, he could make small and fold away in his bag. His emblem is a type of musical instrument made of a bamboo tube.

The third Taoist Immortal, Lü Tung-pin, the patron saint of barbers and of the sick, is a scholar and recluse living in the eighth century. In his right hand he holds a fly brush, and his emblem is a sword, generally worn slung across his back. With this sword Lü Tung-pin traveled around the world for more than four hundred years, ridding it of various forms of evil.

Ts'ao Kuo-chiu, son of a military commander of the tenth century and brother of an empress of the Sung dynasty, is another of these Eight Immortals. He wears official robes and Court headdress and is the patron saint of actors. His emblem is a pair of castanets.

The fifth is Li T'ieh-kuai, an intimate friend of Lao Tzŭ, who often sent for Li to come and visit him in the Taoist paradise. When his spirit went on these visits to the other world, he left his body, apparently dead, in the care of a disciple. On one occasion his spirit stayed away longer than usual, and the disciple, who had been called to attend his mother's sickbed, decided he must be really dead this time and burned the body.

Eventually the spirit of Li T'ieh-kuai returned to earth and could not find his body, so he searched around wildly for some dead body to enter. The first he came across was that of a lame beggar, and for this reason he is always represented as a beggar with an iron crutch and a pilgrim's gourd as his symbol. He is sometimes seen standing on a crab or accompanied by a deer.

346

Han Hsiang-tzŭ, who lived in the ninth century, was the nephew of the famous scholar Han Yü. He was supposed to have the power of making flowers grow from the earth instantaneously. Han Hsiang-tzŭ was the favorite pupil of Lü Tung-pin, who carried him to the top of the Magic Tree where grew the peaches of immortality. Falling off this tree, he became an immortal himself. The patron of musicians, his symbol is the flute. He never knew the value of money, and, if given any, would scatter it on the ground.

The seventh of the legendary Taoists, Lan Ts'ai-ho, is of uncertain sex but is often represented as a woman dressed in a tattered blue gown, with only one shoe and the other foot bare. She waves a wand as she strolls along, earning her living by singing in the streets. Her emblem is a basket of flowers and she is the patron saint of gardeners.

The eighth of this group, Ho Hsien-ku (seventh century), was the daughter of a shopkeeper of Hunan. She was honored for the long distances she used to walk to obtain delicate bamboo shoots for her sick mother. She would wander alone in the hills, living only on powdered mother-of-pearl and moonbeams, which gave her immortality. She was summoned to the Court of the Empress Wu (A.D. 625-705) but disappeared on the way. Her special province is the management of the home, and she carries a lotus flower or seed pod in her hand.

In addition to carrying his own emblem, certain of the Eight Immortals may often be seen with the other Taoist symbols—the Ju-i scepter and the fly whisk. The first is carried by Shun Lao, who is the deification of Lao Tzŭ himself, and another favorite subject with artists. He is often seen resting under a pine tree, accompanied by a deer.

The fly whisk, which is both a Taoist and a Buddhist symbol, is carried by Lü Tung-pin. Since no living creature could be killed, it was used to drive off the mosquitoes and flies.

Other Taoist figures include the Three Star Gods—Shou Shing, the God of Longevity, who carries a peach and a scroll; Lu Hsing, God of Wealth and Rank, who wears official robes and carries a Ju-i scepter; and Fu Hsing, God of Happiness, depicted with a child on his back reaching for a peach of immortality.

The Taoist paradise is known as the Hills of Longevity, depicted in paintings and decorations as a region of mountains, with lakes and streams, bridges, pavilions, and pine and peach trees, where the Taoist immortals, fairies, and cranes float through the air. For food they eat the fruits and gems of immortality and they drink the water of the fountain of life which flows from a lofty rock of jade.

Another figure popular with artists is Hsi Wang Mu, the Queen Mother of the West, who rules over the immortals from her palace on the shore of the Lake of Gems. She is depicted as a beautiful, richly clad woman, attended by two young girls, one of whom holds a large fan and the other a basket of the symbolic peaches.

Then, of course, Lao Tzŭ himself is often represented in stone, wood, ivory, and jade, sometimes riding on a buffalo. He seems far removed from all the fables that have grown up around his teachings. The Way (Taoism) that he advocated was a return to Nature, a spiritual cleansing, the abolition of artificial restraints, the discarding of social institutions and of superfluous possessions. He held that human beings could be happy only if they became like little children and lived again in simplicity and goodness.

Probably the most popular of all Taoist figures, and the ones who seem to have the most connection with the philosophy of Lao Tzŭ, are the Twin Genii of Mutual Peace and Harmony (the Shuang Hsien). One of them carries a lotus and the other a covered box, each of which is called ho in Chinese. Because this forms one of those pictorial rebuses of which the Chinese are so fond, these twins are usually referred to as Ho-ho. They are the symbols of harmonious union, of peace and love in the household. Consequently, objects in which they figure are popular as wedding gifts.

These Ho-ho are usually shown as two charming, smiling children, embracing each other or standing close together. They are supposed to have originally represented two T'ang hermit poets who were such inseparable friends that they were referred to as "two in body but one in spirit."

The legend runs that "they ate of the fruit of immortality" and so gained eternal youth. There is, however, a Chinese belief that couples who live in harmony will prolong their youth and their life; and possibly behind the words of the tale is the implication that because they lived in accordance with the teachings of Lao Tzŭ "in simplicity and goodness as little children" they remained eternally youthful and happy.

The Chief of the Eight Taoist Immortals, Chung-li Ch'üan, is said to be an immortalization of the Taoist philosopher Chuang Tzŭ, who lived from the fourth to the third centuries B.C. Chuang Tzŭ wrote of men with miraculous powers and prepared the way for the Taoist perpetual search for the elixir of immortality and all the superstition that gradually grew up around this religion. The following stories in which he figures have been used by artists in every century as subjects for paintings and decoration.

In one of them, Chuang Tzŭ says: "Once I dreamed that I was a butterfly flying about, and feeling enjoyment as I did so. Suddenly I awoke. Then I did not know if I had dreamed I was a butterfly, or whether I was now a butterfly dreaming that I was Chuang Tzŭ."

The other story, which lies behind the many paintings named "The Pleasure of the Fishes," runs:

When Chuang Tzŭ stood watching fishes in a river, he said to his friend: "Look at the fishes darting hither and thither. That is how they take their pleasure."

"Since you are not a fish," replied the friend, "how can you know what gives pleasure to the fishes?"

"And since you are not I," answered Chuang Tzŭ, "how can you know what I know?"

The above represent examples of the dual relativity of knowledge, which is said to be the basis of Taoism. They also show the complete identification of the Taoist, and of the Chinese artist in general, with every form of life. The highest praise an artist could receive was for him to be told that "When he painted a horse he was a horse," or "When he painted an insect he thought he was an insect."

BUDDHIST SYMBOLS

Besides the most popular Buddhist figure, the Kwan Yin, Goddess of Mercy, numerous representations of the Buddha himself are to be found, both as an infant and as an adult.

The early disciples of Buddhism, the Eighteen Lohans, are seen again and again in Chinese art. There were originally sixteen of them, but two have been added. One, Ho Shang, known as the Laughing Buddha (although he is not a Buddha but a Bodhisattva), is represented as a very corpulent man with breast and abdomen uncovered. He laughs broadly, denotes kindness and gentleness, and is often surrounded by little children. The other is Dharmatrata, an author who lived in the first century, shown with long hair, a fly whisk, a vase, and a bundle of books.

Much used in decoration, either singly or in groups, are the eight Buddhist symbols of good luck, or Eight Happy Omens:

State Umbrella. The emblem of official authority and reward of good government, given to the most popular officials on their retirement.

Canopy. Symbol of official rank, held over high officials on ceremonial occasions.

Covered jar or vase. Vessel in which ashes of Buddhist priest were placed. It represents triumph of Supreme Power over death, is also a symbol of perpetual harmony.

Conch Shell. Represents the voice of Buddha because of the murmur heard if held to the ear, and is an omen for a successful journey.

The Lotus Flower. An emblem of purity and perfection. "It grows out of mud, but is not defiled." The petals of the lotus blossom suggest the spokes of a wheel, and symbolize endless cycles of reincarnation.

The Wheel of the Law. Symbol of truth and life—of Buddha himself. It has the power to destroy superstitions.

Pair of Fishes. Emblem of conjugal happiness and fidelity, also of fertility and plenty. Charm against evil.

Endless Knot. Emblem of Longevity because it has no end. It also represents the Eight Admonitions of Buddha—"Do not kill, do not steal, do not fornicate, do not bear false witness, do not drink wine." The other three refer to old age, sickness and death. This symbol is also known as the Mystic Knot of Everlasting Happiness, and is sometimes said to represent the intestines.

Another set of Buddhist symbols, known as the Seven Buddhist Treasures, consists of the golden wheel, a beautiful female consort, horses, elephants, divine guardians, ministers, and the wonder-working pearl.

The swastika is a Buddhist symbol too, but it is of even more ancient origin than Buddhism. It is the most auspicious of emblems, the seal of Buddha's heart, and stands for resignation. It is also used as a sign which represents ten thousand.

SYMBOLISM IN TREES, FLOWERS, PLANTS, BIRDS, AND INSECTS

From the time of the Five Dynasties onward, Chinese artists have been interested in painting flowers and birds. This interest has been not merely for their decorative qualities. Each flower was painted to emphasize some step in the rhythm of nature—the bud, the hardy blossom which first defies the cold of winter, the glorious fullness just before the fall of autumn, and the relation between the flower and the bird or insect. Frail blossoms are shaken to the ground by the wind, but there is the constant promise of renewal.

Then, too, many flowers have been endowed with special symbolic messages. For instance, the narcissus is the winter flower, known as the water fairy; the prunus (plum) blossom denotes courage and hope because it is the first to brave the frosts of winter; the magnolia signifies feminine sweetness and beauty; the lotus, fruitfulness and purity, "growing out of the mud and remaining undefiled." Two lotus flowers on a single stem denote a happy marriage. The peony represents opulence and good fortune.

The chrysanthemum, flower of mid-autumn, stands for pleasure and good cheer. The last flower to bloom before winter sets in, it is like a man who maintains his integrity in an era of corruption and confusion. It also symbolizes a life of ease and retirement from public office.

There are the Twelve Floral Symbols—one for each month of the year. These vary slightly in different regions, but usually consist of the following:

January	Prunus blossom	July	Lotus
February	Peach blossom	August	Pear blossom
March	Peony	September	Mallow
April	Cherry blossom	October	Chrysanthemum
May	Magnolia	November	Gardenia
June	Pomegranate blossom	December	Poppy

Another classic subject in art decoration consists of the Flowers of the Four Seasons:

Winter	Prunus blossom
Spring	Tree peony
Summer	Lotus
Autumn	Chrysanthemum

The flowers most beloved by gardeners, poets, artists, scholars, and craftsmen are those known as the Four Gentlemen (Ssu Chün-tzŭ). They are the prunus blossom, the wild orchid, the bamboo, and the chrysanthemum. In the

350

West we might hesitate to call the bamboo a flower, but the Chinese include the bamboo, the fungus, and the artemisia leaf in their lists of flowers.

The wild orchid symbolizes humility and modest worth, a retiring nature, and great refinement. Confucius called this flower the emblem of the Superior Man, saying: "The orchid is not easily distinguished from the grass around it: one must look carefully in order to find it. Thus the Superior man resembles the Common Man in appearance, and, if men wish to know him, they must seek out his hidden virtue and excellence."

The bamboo denotes uprightness and dependability. It bends before the storm but never breaks. It typifies endurance and truth.

The plum and bamboo together symbolize friendship throughout life, and the bamboo, plum, and pine tree together are called the Three Friends of Winter (faithful to each other even in adversity). They also denote the harmony between Buddha (bamboo), Confucius (pine), and Lao Tzŭ (prunus).

There is meaning, too, in the way different birds and flowers are combined in the same picture. Chrysanthemums and grouse together indicate good luck and official promotion, the phoenix and the peony represent riches and opulence. Plum blossoms and magpies denote winter, while the stork and pine signify longevity. The wild goose is the symbol of love and constancy and inspiration. When flying in pairs they symbolize happy married life because the wild goose takes only one mate.

The duck, usually shown together with the lotus, denotes faithfulness in marriage. Often seen on porcelains, are pictures of cocks and hens amid artificial rockery in a garden of peonies. These testify to the pleasures of country life.

The flying bird is a symbol of freedom, and the Chinese ideal was to be as pure as a prunus blossom, free as a bird, strong as a pine tree, and pliant as a bamboo.

Butterflies indicate joy and happy marriage, and the bat stands for happiness. This is because the character for "bat" has the same sound as the word for "happiness." A common design consists of five bats around the character "Shou" (longevity). This represents the Five Blessings—old age, wealth, health, love of virtue, and natural death.

Fishes are symbols of abundance, wedded happiness, and harmony. A single carp leaping in water augurs success in passing the official examinations. Just as the carp has the perseverance to struggle upstream against the current, so the student will overcome all obstacles.

The willow tree is often seen together with the swallow and is the tree of poets and writers. The peach tree denotes long life and happy marriage. It also signifies the virtue, promise, and grace of a young bride who is compared to a blossoming peach tree. The cassia tree is the emblem of literary success.

The persimmon, because of its bright festive color, is a token of joy; and the pomegranate with its numerous seeds represents abundant posterity. The finger-shaped citron, known as Buddha's hand, is an emblem of happiness, and the fungus means longevity and immortality.

351

ANIMALS

Most of the animal symbols have been covered earlier in this book—the dragon and the tiger, for instance; the unicorn (Ch'i-lin), "which has the body of a deer, the hoof of a horse, the tail of an ox, and a head like a dragon" and which is a symbol of good government; the tortoise, which is a sign of longevity; and the hare, which lives in the moon and prepares the elixir of life.

The horse is the symbol of wisdom, dignity, speed, faithfulness, and courage. The Eight Horses are a familiar art form. They represent the chariot horses of the Chou Emperor Mu Wang on his celebrated Journey to the West (circa 1000 B.C.), which has become a Taoist legend.

The popular Buddhist Dogs of Fo are like small playful lions, often shown with a ball under one foot. This ball is called a pearl—a gem which averts fire, floods, dust storms, and disturbances within a city. To lose this pearl would cost the Fo Dog his life.

The bull, or water buffalo, is often seen with a boy on his back. In Buddhist symbolism this means that there are dominant human qualities that can be used for good or evil. If understood and properly controlled, they will carry men upward and onward. Otherwise, having a horn, they will turn and gore their victim.

The deer, frequently seen with the God of Longevity, is, by itself, a symbol of official promotion. This is because the sound of the word for deer (lu) and the word for increased emolument sound the same.

The rebus, the pun, and the play on words are very popular with the Chinese. Often a whole message or piece of symbolism takes the form of objects having names similar in sound to certain virtues or qualities.

SYMBOLISM IN CHARACTERS AND WORDS

Chinese written characters are so decorative and so greatly revered that the decoration on an art object frequently takes the form of a written symbol or saying. Such words as Hsi (joy) are often seen in pairs (double joy) on objects intended for bridal gifts. Equally popular are the characters for long life, happiness, good luck, wealth, and congratulations. These can be written in many different ways—in square, seal, grass, and various other types of script. In our collection is a birthday scroll on which the character "Shou" (long life) is written in a hundred entirely different ways by a hundred different artists and poets.

Sometimes the symbolism is written out plainly. For instance, a cup may be marked "Ever full," meaning "May you ever be prosperous," or there may be a poetic phrase, such as: "Dew is fragrant in the middle of autumn." An autumn scholar is one whose talents were recognized late in life, and this might be inscribed on a gift presented to a man who had finally passed his official examinations after many unsuccessful attempts.

CHILDREN

A type of collection which was popular with Chinese women was formed entirely of objects depicting children. These paintings, and other objects, do not show portraits of individual children, but they seek to convey the spirit of childhood, its charm, playfulness, and innocence. A favorite theme is that of mothers bathing and dressing small children or playing with them in their houses or gardens. We see children playing games of all kinds—blind man's buff, flying kites, kicking shuttlecocks, spinning tops, catching locusts, dragon-flies, or butterflies.

Other pictures show children at the Lantern Festival holding little lotus lamps, at the Dragon Boat Festival, or playing with bows and arrows, riding hobby horses, and playing at weddings and funerals. One very popular subject is that of the Toy Vendor. The man is standing in the street, while a group of small children gaze admiringly at his wares.

These drawings and figures are always delightful in themselves, but they are also intended to convey some inner meaning, probably that fond desire, "May you have many children," or the equally hoped-for blessing, "May your sons be successful in passing the official examinations."

The theme of the Hundred Children design so frequently encountered in fabrics and porcelains indicates that it was meant to be offered to a newly married couple, and implies the wish that their progeny be numerous. Again, the subject, often seen, of children playing by a lotus pool means: "I wish that you may have many, many children, coming one by one as the lotus blossoms open one by one." Then there is the Buddhist motif of two little boy babies—drawn back to back—surrounded by lotus blossoms. It is intended to emphasize that the heart and disposition of a small child are as good as the lotus is pure and spotless.

Another favorite subject is a group of small children fishing or playing with fish in a fish bowl. This means, "May the fish you catch turn into dragons," which is a way of expressing the hope, "May your children grow up to attain great success in the examinations and become high officials." A scene that is frequently depicted shows a playmate rescuing a small boy who has fallen into a large porcelain fish bowl, deep enough for him to drown in, while trying to reach a frog. The playmate is too small to lift him out of the water, but he has the presence of mind to seize a large stone and make a hole in the side of the bowl so that the water will run out. His conduct is contrasted with that of the other children who ran away in their fright and would have left him to drown. This favorite theme is based on a true story. The rescuer was Ssŭ-ma Kuang (1009-1086), who grew up to become one of the most distinguished statesmen and historians of the Sung dynasty.

The family unit has meant more to the Chinese than to any other people, and a break in its continuity has been regarded as the greatest calamity. Sons were more ardently desired because it is the son who continues the family line, the daughter becoming part of the family of her husband. That does not mean that the little girls were less loved; in fact Chinese poetry makes many allusions to the appeal of little girls as well as boys.

However it was the boys who were liable to become high officials and confer great honor upon the family, so that is the motif that occurs again and again. Usually there will be five little boys playing together, for the Chinese ideal family was "Five sons and two daughters."

In the screen panel illustrated in this book, five children are shown watching two fighting roosters. This expresses the wish that the children may have the five virtues ascribed to the birds:

1. Culture (training).
2. Strength.
3. Bravery.
4. Loyalty to companions.
5. Being true to one's word.

It also implies the wish that the recipient may have five sons who have all these qualities, and who will all compete for honors in official life.

KUAN TI, THE GOD OF WAR

Perhaps the most popular historical figure, and the one most often carved, moulded, painted, and embroidered is that of Kuan Ti (also called Kuan Yü), the God of War. He was not beloved because of his warlike qualities but because he hated war and used his spiritual power to avert war and protect the people from its scourge. Among his titles is one meaning: "Prince of War-Won Peace."

However it was not enough for a popular character to be God of War. A great man had to be a scholar as well as a warrior, so Kuan Ti was given the added title of God (or Patron) of Literature, because he was a devoted student of the Spring and Autumn Annals of Confucius. He is often depicted reading from this book while still wearing his armor.

Kuan Ti lived in the chaotic time of the Three Kingdoms and helped to unify the country again. Associated with him in his romantic adventures were two lifelong friends, with whom he was united by the blood brotherhood oath: "One to another we shall be brothers now, henceforth and until death," and he is usually shown with one or both of these comrades.

A popular saying about him runs: "A warrior bold enough to stroke the tiger's beard, and yet one who always acted in a chivalrous manner."

THE FAMOUS BEAUTIES

The woman considered the loveliest in all Chinese history is Hsi Shih, who has remained a symbol of feminine beauty for twenty-five centuries. One still hears the remark: "Every woman is a Hsi Shih to the man who is in love with her."

354

Hsi Shih was the daughter of humble parents and made her living by washing silk in the stream. While engaged in this work she was seen by the Minister Fan Li, who rode by and was overcome with her grace. This scene of the maiden washing silk in the stream is the one most often depicted by artists, and is usually accompanied by a poem, such as:

When Hsi Shih steeped her yarn
Beside the running brook,
Like mosses on her washing stone
Men's hearts with yearning shook.

But since she went to Ku-su
And thence returned no more,
For whom do Peach and Plum trees bloom
Along the vernal shore?

Although he loved her, the Minister Fan Li was seeking to destroy the king of the rival state of Wu, and he decided to use Hsi Shih as his instrument of destruction. He had her trained in all feminine accomplishments, dressed her in the most exquisite garments, and then sent her to the Court of Wu. The king of Wu fell completely under her spell, neglected the affairs of state, and finally lost his kingdom and his life.

The melancholy end of the tale is told by the T'ang poet, Li Po, in his poem: "The ruins of the Ku-su Palace":

"In the deserted garden among the crumbling walls
. . . .
Nothing remains but the moon above the river—
The moon that once shone on the fair faces
That smiled in the King's palace of Wu."

Among the earliest portraits mentioned is that of Li Fu-jên, the outstanding beauty of the Han dynasty. It was said that "One of her glances would overthrow a city, and two would destroy an empire." She was the favorite of the Emperor Wu Ti (140-86 B.C.) and, after her death, he remained inconsolable the rest of his life.

The tale of the beautiful Chao Chün is one of the most familiar themes of Chinese folklore, opera, and art. The Emperor Yüan Ti (48-32 B.C.) issued a proclamation requesting all the most beautiful girls in the country between the ages of fifteen and twenty to come to the Palace and have their portraits painted so that he could select a bride. The fairest maiden of all was Chao Chün, and the Court painter told her that if she paid him enough he would see that she was chosen as empress. But she was the daughter of poor parents who were unable to bribe the artist, so he painted a very ugly picture of her and, although she stayed on in the Palace among the other concubines, the Emperor never sent for her or set eyes on her.

When the Tartar Khan demanded that the Chinese send him a bride, the emperor selected Chao Chün because, judging by her portrait, he thought she was so ugly that he would never want her. Only when everything had been arranged did the emperor see her, and he then fell violently in love with her. He wanted to send another bride in her place; but the Tartar Khan, who had seen a true portrait, painted and sent to him by the same Court artist, threatened to make war if she were not handed over. Chao Chün, who loved the emperor, said it was her duty to sacrifice herself for her country, as the Chinese army was not strong enough to fight the Tartars.

The emperor had the scheming Court artist beheaded, and he sent camels laden with gold to try and buy Chao Chün back, but the Khan refused to let her go, and he made her his queen.

On the bank of the Amur River, Chao Chün felt she could go no farther, so she threw herself into the water, crying that she would wait for her emperor in the next world. The Khan was so moved by her death that he made peace with China, but he refused to let her body be carried home and had a tomb built for her on the banks of the Amur River. To this day the earth over her grave is said always to be green, although the surrounding country is bare of vegetation.

White chrysanthemums streaked with red symbolize the journey of the lovely Chao Chün into the snowy wastes of Central Asia.

Equally well-known is Yang Kuei Fei, the peerless beauty of the T'ang dynasty, with "the radiance of a flower on her face." Scenes of her life and death have been made the subject of countless paintings, poems, operas, decorative motifs on porcelain, screens, embroideries, and carvings in jade and ivory.

Particularly popular with carvers of jade and ivory, perhaps because so many of them are Mohammedans, is another famous beauty, Hsiang Fei (Fragrant Concubine), the wife of a Mohammedan prince. Her husband was killed in battle, and Hsiang Fei was brought a prisoner to Peking to be a concubine to the Emperor Ch'ien Lung. Ch'ien Lung fell in love with her and did everything he could to win her, but she would not respond to his advances because, she said, she must remain faithful to the memory of her slain husband.

In the hope that she would feel less homesick, the emperor built a replica of a Mohammedan city, with mosques, bazaars, and people from her own land, where she could see it from her windows. But he could not win her love and she committed suicide. She is usually shown as a Western type of woman, wearing Western clothes.

Another woman, who is not known as a beauty but is still a popular subject with artists, is Hua Mu-lan, the girl warrior—usually depicted in a coat of mail like a Chinese Joan of Arc. She was a Tartar girl of the people. Her father, who had been conscripted into the army, fell ill; and, to save him from punishment, Hua Mu-lan put on male clothes and took his place. For twelve years she fought in the wars. Nobody suspected that she was a woman, and she was able to preserve her chastity. Once the fighting was over, she returned home, saying that her only desire was to take off her armor and again put on the clothes of a woman.

OTHER SUBJECTS USED IN PAINTINGS AND DECORATION

In an essay on the origin of painting (written by Sung Lien 1310-1381) there is the following comment: "Among the ancients, those who were skilled in painting illustrated the Odes, or the Classic of Filial Piety . . ., the Analects of Confucius, or the Book of Changes . . . so that the contents of those works might not be obscured by time. Gradually, however, there came a falling away, and artists were attracted by the glories of chariots, horses, soldiers and women; they then turned their thoughts to the beauties of flowers, birds, insects and fishes; and they gave play to their emotions in painting mountains, forests, streams and rocks, until the old conception of the pictorial art was entirely lost."

The earliest Chinese painting took the form of portraits, depiction of important events, and illustrations of moral precepts. An example of the latter type is the painting by Ku K'ai-chih (fourth century), now in the British Museum, which is called "The Admonitions of the Imperial Preceptress to the Ladies of the Palace." It consists of a series of nine illustrations of a poem by the poet Chang Hua (circa 232-300). Each section shows a scene of domestic life in the Palace, and bears an inscription which points a moral. One section, for example, shows a lady of the first century B.C. refusing to ride in the same palanquin as the emperor because "she does not want to distract his thoughts from the affairs of state."

On another there is a hunter, kneeling at the foot of a mountain, who is about to draw his bow at a pheasant. On this is inscribed: "There is nothing in Nature that is high that will not soon be brought low. When the sun is at its zenith it begins to sink; when the moon is fullest it starts to wane. To rise to glory is to build a mountain with grains of sand. To meet with calamity is as easy as for a tense spring to rebound."

A third section shows a lady seated before her toilet table, having her hair dressed. The legend reads: "Men and women know how to ornament their persons, but few know how to beautify their souls." Then another illustration shows a man seated beside a bed. To a young woman lying in it he says: "If your words are good, people for a thousand leagues around will trust you, but if your heart is not sincere even your bed companion will lose confidence in you."

A well-known picture (much copied by later artists) was first painted by another of the Four Patriarchs of Painting, Chan Tzŭ-ch'ien (Sui dynasty). It is called "Chu Mai-ch'en spilling the water." Chu Mai-ch'en's wife left him because he was poor. In the course of time he became rich and powerful, while she sank into the depths of poverty. Then she came to him and asked to be taken back. The picture shows Chu spilling water from a bowl onto the ground and saying: "If you can pick up this water again then you can come back."

LANDSCAPE PAINTING

From the T'ang dynasty onward, while artists continued to illustrate Buddhist themes, stories of filial piety, "The Nine Songs," Palace scenes, and all the other traditional subjects, the main emphasis was on landscape painting.

357

The leading artists preferred what was called "Shan Shui" (mountains and streams) to all other subjects. They painted landscapes in varying weather, in different seasons, at dawn and at dusk. They experimented with new ways of depicting what they felt about trees, stones, clouds, mist, and water. If they did not try to point a moral, or tell a tale, they did strive to express an emotion or an idea. The idea was the relationship of man to nature, his place as an integral part in the scheme of life, and his oneness with all living creatures, even the smallest of insects.

Sung Ti, an artist of the Sung dynasty, originated the Eight Views of the Hsiao and the Hsiang, and these became traditional subjects for artists of later periods. They were: "wild geese alighting on a sandy beach," "sailing toward home again," "a mountain inn at twilight," "snow on the banks of the lake," "moonlight night in autumn," "evening rain on the river," "the tolling of a bell at eventide from a distant temple," and "sunset glow over a fishing village."

Other traditional subjects were "gathering storm in the mountain," "fine weather after a storm," "snow on the mountains," "gazing at clouds," "autumn in the hills," and "discussing the philosophy of life in a straw-thatched hut" (sublime thoughts in simple surroundings). Each artist painted these subjects in his own way, and expressed his own feelings at the wonders of nature and of life.

Sometimes the artists combined landscape painting with some scene from a favorite poem or story. Li Lung-mien (Sung dynasty) was the first to paint the picture "Returning Home," which was to become another classic subject. This was inspired by the poem of T'ao Yüan-ming (365-427), who retired from his official position, after only eighty-three days in office, because "he was unwilling to bend the hinges of his back to his superiors in order to gain security from cold and hunger."

Another Sung artist, Liu Sung-nien, painted a picture called "Visit Amid Mountain Gloom." This is a mountain scene, with a man in a small boat which is pulling away from a house beside a mountain stream. The man had felt a great urge to visit his friend, but when he reached the house he turned back because the desire had left him. This is not only a popular subject but has given a proverb to the language.

Many artists complained that it was hard to do justice to certain scenes because of the difficulty of conveying sound. "Oh, if I could but paint a dying groan," said one painter. Others pointed out that without sound it was a problem to express a waterfall, or such subjects as "listening to the wind in the pine trees," "hearing the murmur of spring," or "autumn winds and breaking waves."

Expressing the same idea, the monk-painter Shih-t'ao wrote on one of his pictures a poem which began:

> There is music in this landscape
> And those who grasp it feel it in their hearts.
> (Translated by O. Sirén)

Many scrolls were painted as gifts to friends, and these would symbolize some special sentiment or wish. For instance, there is a picture that was painted by the Ch'ing artist, Kao Ch'i-p'ei, to be presented to an old friend whom he had met again after many years. The man in the painting is watching water flow past his house, as have the years since he and his friends were young students together.

In the Ming dynasty there was a great vogue for figure painting. Scholar-artists painted each other in their homes, gardens, or other typical settings. A hermit would be shown in his mountain hut, a retired official on his country estate, or a mother directing her household. The figures were quite small, and the "transmission of spirit" lay chiefly in the environment which was intended to reveal the character of the sitter.

In briefly outlining the symbolism and the subjects preferred by Chinese artists and craftsmen, one realizes again and again how universal their appeal is. The differences are superficial—based on strange names, different costumes and customs—but the emotions and ideas expressed belong to all people and to all times. Although her clothes may be foreign, a painting of a lonely young wife whose husband has gone off to war is something that can be understood in every language, as can the beauty of distant hills, or the charm of children at play.

The triumph of the inner spirit over external differences is well illustrated in another popular subject with artists called "The Judge of Horses." This is a story of the Chou dynasty. A feudal duke, whose ruling passion was his love of thoroughbreds, employed an official, Po Lo, a renowned judge of horses. Po Lo was advanced in years, and wanted to retire, but the duke was afraid that he would not be able to find a worthy successor.

The official informed him that he had already found a man—a humble hawker of fuel and vegetables—who was fully his equal. So the hawker was summoned to court, and, in the course of conversation with the duke, talked about a wonderful horse he had seen in a distant land. When asked about the sex and color, he said, after some hesitation, that it was a dun-colored mare. The duke ordered him to try and procure this unique animal. He went away and, some months later, returned triumphantly leading a beautiful black stallion.

The duke flew into a rage and stormed at Po Lo: "What kind of a rogue or fool is this man you recommended so highly? A judge of horses who cannot even distinguish sex or color!"

Po Lo scrutinized the horse, and exclaimed in wonder: "Has he really got as far as that? Then he far outclasses me in his ability to judge horses. He sees only the spirit and the inner quality. He looks only at the things he ought to see, and ignores that which does not interest him. Has there ever been any horse in this country as fine as this one?"

The duke admitted that it was a superlative horse, and appointed the hawker to be the keeper of the palace stables.

These are just a few of the favorite subjects, characters, tales, and legends which have, for many centuries, been written about, handed down by parents to their children, related by the story tellers who went from village to village, and enacted in the theaters or by traveling groups of puppet and shadow players. They are an essential part of the fabric out of which Chinese art, culture, and philosophy have been woven.

The Four Accomplishments.

The Emblems of the Eight Immortals (in the order described in the text, from left to right and from top to bottom; this order, however, may vary).

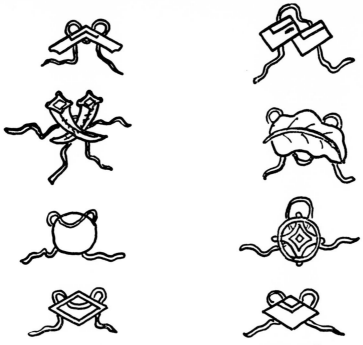

The Eight Precious Things, or the Eight Ordinary Symbols.

The Eight Buddhist Symbols of Good Luck. (The order of both of these is that described in the text, from left to right and from top to bottom. This order, however, may vary.)

TABLE OF DYNASTIES, PERIODS, AND REIGNS

Dynasty and Rulers	Legendary Dates
NEOLITHIC PERIOD	**3000-2500 B.C.**
Fu Hsi	2852-2737

Reputed discoverer of the Eight Trigrams and of writing. Said to have taught people hunting, fishing, and cooking.

Shên Nung	2737-2697

Reputed to have invented the plough, founded the art of agriculture and use of medicinal herbs. God of Agriculture and Medicine.

Huang Ti	2697-2597

Yellow Emperor. Reputed discoverer of bronze casting and system of weights and measures. Made first roads, carts and vessels. Invention of potter's wheel. His empress started silk culture.

Yao	2357-2255
Shun	2255-2205

The ideal rulers of China's Golden Age, extolled by Confucius. Said to have inaugurated calendar, organized government and music.

Traditional Dates

Dynasty and Rulers	Traditional Dates
HSIA	**2205-1766 (1994-1525[a])**
The Great Yü (founder)	2205-2197
SHANG-YIN	**1766-1122 (1525-1028[a])**

Dynasty and Rulers	Traditional Dates
CHOU	**1122-221 (1027-222[a])**
Early Chou (Western)	1122-947 (1027-ca. 900[a])
Middle Chou (Western)	946-770 (ca. 900-600[a])
Late Chou (Eastern)	770-256 (ca. 600-256 [Huai style][a])
(Period of the Spring and Autumn Annals)	722-481
(Period of the Warring States)	481-222 (255-222 [Interregnum][a])
"Huai"—Interregnum	770-206

	Dates
CH'IN	**221-206**
Shih Huang Ti	221-210
HAN	**206 B.C.-A.D. 220**
Western Han (Earlier or Ch'ien Han)	206 B.C.-A.D. 25
Liu Pang, founder	206 B.C.-
Wu Ti	140-86 B.C.
Wang Mang	A.D. 9
(Hsin dynasty	A.D. 8-23)
Eastern Han (Later or Hou Han)	A.D. 25-220
Ming Ti	A.D. 58

[a] These newest dates follow the latest findings of Dr. Bernhard Karlgren, director of the East Asiatic Collections, the Museum of Far Eastern Antiquities, Stockholm. They are always subject to modification in the light of future research and excavations.

Dynasty and Rulers	Dates	Dynasty and Rulers	Dates
THREE KINGDOMS	A.D. 220-280	**LIAO**	907-1125
Wei	220-265	(Western Liao)	1125-1211
Shu Han	221-263	**SUNG**	960-1279
Tung Wu	222-280	Northern Sung	960-1127
SIX DYNASTIES	222-589	T'ai Tsung	976
Tung Wu, Eastern Chin, Sung, Ch'i, Liang, and Ch'ên		Ching-tê	1004
		Shên Tsung	1068
(All these dynasties had their capital on the site where Nanking now stands.)		Chê Tsung	1093
		Hui Tsung	1101
		Southern Sung	1127-1279
CHIN (Western Chin and Eastern Chin)	265-420	Kao Tsung	1127
		Western Hsia (Hsi Hsia)	1032-1223
		Chin (Nü-chen Tartars)	1115-1234
NORTHERN and SOUTHERN		**YÜAN**	1280-1368
dynasties	386-589	Kublai Khan	1280
Northern dynasties:	386-581	**MING**	1368-1644
Northern Wei	386-557	Hung Wu	1368-1398
(includes		Chien Wên	1399-1402
Western Wei	535-557)	Yung Lo	1403-1424
Eastern Wei	534-550	Hung Hsi	1425
Northern Ch'i	550-577	Hsüan Tê	1426-1435
Northern Chou	557-581	Chêng T'ung	1436-1449
Southern dynasties:	420-589	Ching T'ai	1450-1457
Sung (Liu)	420-479	T'ien Shun	1457-1464
Southern Ch'i	479-502	Ch'êng Hua	1465-1487
Liang	502-557	Hung Chih	1488-1505
Ch'ên	557-589	Chêng Tê	1506-1521
		Chia Ching	1522-1566
SUI	589-618	Lung Ch'ing	1567-1572
		Wan Li	1573-1619
T'ANG	618-907	T'ai Ch'ang	1620
Wu Tê	619-626	T'ien Ch'i	1621-1627
T'ai Tsung	627-649	Ch'ung Chêng	1628-1643
Kao Tsung	650-683	**CH'ING**	1644-1912
Empress Wu	682	Shun Chih	1644-1661
Ming Huang	713	K'ang Hsi	1662-1722
Tai Tsung	763	Yung Chêng	1722-1735
Tê Tsung	780	Ch'ien Lung	1736-1795
Wu Tsung	844	Chia Ch'ing	1796-1820
Hsüan Tsung	849	Tao Kuang	1821-1850
		Hsien Fêng	1851-1861
FIVE DYNASTIES	907-960	T'ung Chih	1862-1873
Liang	907-923	Kuang Hsü	1874-1908
T'ang	923-936	Hsüan T'ung	1909-1912
Chin	936-946	**CHINESE REPUBLIC**	1912-
Han	947-950		
Chou	951-960		

BIBLIOGRAPHY

This bibliography covers the whole field of Chinese art and, at the same time, it gives some idea of the wide range and expanding knowledge of the subject. While the early pioneers made a valuable contribution to knowledge, later discoveries and study have entirely changed many of their conclusions. Consequently, it is always advisable to note the date of material and compare it with more recent contributions on the same subject.

Some of the most important writings on Chinese art are to be found in periodicals, museum bulletins, and monographs. While many of these have been discontinued or are now out of print, most of them can be consulted in art reference libraries.

GENERAL

Ashton, Leigh (edited by). *Chinese Art.* Written on the occasion of Royal Academy Exhibition of Chinese Art. London, 1935.

——, and Basil Gray. *Chinese Art.* London, 1935.

Arts of the Ming Dynasty. Catalogue of Exhibition of the Detroit Institute of Arts. 1952.

Ayscough, Florence. *Tu Fu—The Travels of a Chinese Poet* (translation). New York and Boston, 1934.

——. *Chinese Women Yesterday and Today.* Shanghai, 1937.

Bachhofer, L. *A Short History of Chinese Art.* New York, 1946.

Burling, Arthur and Judith H. "Collecting in Wartime Shanghai," *Antiques* (New York), February, 1944.

——. "Chinese Art, True and False," *Antiques* (New York), July, 1944.

——. "Antique Market in China Today," *Apollo,* December, 1946.

——. "Buying Antiques in China," *Apollo,* January and February, 1948.

Bushell, S. W. *Chinese Art.* 2 volumes, first edition. London, 1904.

Bynner, Witter, and Kiang Kang-hu. *The Jade Mountain.* A Chinese anthology of T'ang poems. New York, 1929.

Carter, Dagny. *Four Thousand Years of Chinese Art.* New York, 1948.

Chavannes, Edouard. *Les Mémoires Historiques de Sé-ma Ts'ien.* Paris, 1895-1905.

Cohn, William. *Chinese Art.* London, 1930.

Cranmer-Byng, L. *The Vision of Asia.* London, 1947.
Fenollosa, E. F. *Epochs of Chinese and Japanese Art.* 2 vols. London, 1913.
Ferguson, John C. *Survey of Chinese Art.* Shanghai, 1940.
———. *Outlines of Chinese Art.* Chicago, 1919.
Fitzgerald, C. P. *China, a Short Cultural History.* London, 1935.
Getty, Alice. *The Gods of Northern Buddhism.* Oxford, 1914.
Giles, H. A. *China and the Chinese.* New York, 1902.
———. *The Civilisation of China.* London, 1911.
———. *Chinese Biographical Dictionary.* London, 1898.
———. *A History of Chinese Literature.* New York, 1901.
———. *Religions of Ancient China.* London, 1905.
———. *Gems of Chinese Literature.* Shanghai, 1922.
Goodrich, Prof. L. Carrington. *A Short History of the Chinese People.* New York, 1943.
Granet, Marcel. *La Civilisation Chinoise.* Paris, 1929.
Grousset, René. *The Civilisations of the East* (translated by C. A. Phillips). New York, 1941.
———. *Histoire de l'Extrême Orient.* Paris, 1929.
Hirth, Frederick. *The Ancient History of China to the End of the Chou Dynasty.* New York, 1908.
Hobson, R. L. *Chinese Art.* London, 1927.
Hu Shih, Dr. *Religion and Philosophy in Chinese History.* Shanghai, 1931.
International Exhibition of Chinese Art, Catalogue of. London, 1935-1936.
Jayne, Horace H. F. "In Defense of the Ming Dynasty," *Parnassus,* February, 1930.
Johnson, S. *Oriental Religions and their Relation to Universal Religion.* 1877.
Johnston, R. F. *Lion and Dragon in Northern China.* New York, 1910.
Latourette, K. S. *The Chinese. Third edition.* New York, 1946.
Legge, James. *The Chinese Classics* (translations). Hong Kong, 1861-1877.
———. Religions of China. London, 1880.
Li Ung Bing. *Outlines of Chinese History.* Shanghai, 1914.
Marco Polo. *The Travels of Marco Polo, the Venetian.* Translated and edited by Sir Henry Yule. London, 1929.
Maspero, Henri. *La Chine Antique.* Paris, 1929.
Munsterberg, Hugo. *A Short History of Chinese Art.* New York, 1949.
Nourse, Mary A. *A Short History of the Chinese.* Philadelphia, 1944.
Obata, Shigeyoshi. *The Works of Li Po, the Chinese Poet.* Tokyo, 1935.
Silcock, Arnold. *Introduction to Chinese Art and History.* New York, 1947.
Sirén, O. *History of Early Chinese Art.* London, 1929.
Strong, Hilda A. *A Sketch of Chinese Arts and Crafts.* Peking, 1933.
Tizac, H. d'Ardenne de. *L'Art Chinois Classique.* Paris, 1926.
Waley, Arthur C. *The Temple and other Poems.* London, 1923.
Wieger, Léon. *Bouddhisme Chinois.* 1910.
———. *Taoism.* Paris. 1911-1913.

Chinese and Japanese Books

Ku Ying-t'ai. *General Survey of Art Objects, (Po-wu-yao-lan)* 1621-1627.
Ts-ao Chao. *Essential Discussion of the Criteria of Antiquities, (Ko-ku-yao-lun.)* 1387; enlarged and rewritten in 1388-1397, 1459, 1596, and later.
Toyei Shuko. An illustrated Catalogue of the Ancient Imperial Treasury called Shōsōin (Nara). 3 vols. Tokyo, 1909.

Barr, Alfred H., Jr. *Matisse: His Art and His Public.* New York, 1951.

Binyon, Laurence. *Painting in the Far East.* London, 1923.

———. *Spirit of Man in Asian Art.* Cambridge, Mass., 1935.

———. *Flight of the Dragon.* London, 1922.

———. *Catalogue of the Chinese, Corean and Siamese paintings in the Eumorfopoulos Collection.* London, 1928.

———. "A Chinese Painting of the Fourth Century" *Burlington Magazine,* January, 1904.

Burling, Arthur and Judith H. "Wu Li, Great Chinese Christian Painter," *China Journal,* April, 1941.

———. "Chinese Finger Painting," *China Journal,* June, 1941.

———. "Seals on Chinese Paintings," *Apollo,* December, 1948.

———. "Contemporary Chinese Painting," *Magazine of Art,* October, 1949.

Chavannes, E., et R. Petrucci. "La Peinture Chinoise au Musée Cernuschi," *Ars Asiatica, 1,* 1914.

Chiang Yee. *The Chinese Eye.* London, 1935.

———. *Chinese Calligraphy.* London, 1938.

Cohn, William. *Chinese Painting.* London, 1948.

Contag, Victoria. *Die beiden Steine.* Brunswick, 1950.

———, and Wang Chi-ch'üan. *Maler- und Sammler-Stempel aus der Ming- und Ch'ing Zeit.* (Work on Chinese Seals). Shanghai, 1940.

Contemporary Chinese Paintings. Catalogue of Metropolitan Museum of Art Exhibition, 1943-1944.

Dubosc, Jean-Pierre. *Great Painters of the Ming and Ch'ing Dynasties.* Exhibition at Wildenstein Galleries, New York. With foreword by Laurence Sickman. 1949.

Duthuit, Georges. *Chinese Mysticism and Modern Painting.* Paris, 1936.

Ferguson, J. C. *Chinese Painting.* Chicago, 1927.

Fischer, O. *Chinesische Landschaftsmalerei.* Munich, 1921.

Fogg Art Museum. *Masterpieces of Chinese Bird and Flower Painting.* 1951.

Fry, Roger, et al. *Chinese Art.* London, 1935.

———. *Vision and Design.* London, 1920.

Giles, H. A. *An Introduction to the History of Chinese Pictorial Art.* Shanghai, 1918.

Hackney, Louise Wallace. *Guide Posts to Chinese Painting.* Boston, 1927.

———, and Yau Chang-foo. *A Study of Paintings in the Collection of Ada Small Moore.* New York, 1940.

Harada, J. *A Pageant of Chinese Painting.* Tokyo, 1936.

Hirth, F. *Scraps from a Collector's Note Book.* New York, 1905.

———. *Anniversary Volume.* London, 1920.

Hummel, A. E. *Eminent Chinese of the Ch'ing Period.* 2 vols. Washington, 1943-1944.

Hu Shih, Dr. "Development of Zen Buddhism in China," *The Chinese Social and Political Science Review,* January, 1932.

Jenyns, R. Soames. *A Background to Chinese Painting.* London, 1935.

Lee, Sherman E. "The Story of Chinese Painting," *Art Quarterly,* 1948.

Lin Yutang. *The Gay Genius.* New York, 1947.

Liu Hai-su. *A Brief History of Chinese Painting.* Written as introduction to collection of Chinese paintings. The Shanghai College of Fine Arts, 1940.

Loo, C. T. *Exhibition of Authenticated Chinese Paintings.* New York, 1948.

March, Benjamin. *Linear Perspective in Chinese Painting.* Philadelphia, 1931.

Okakura, Kakuzo. *The Book of Tea.* Edinburgh, 1919.

Pelliot, Paul. *Les Grottes de Touen-Huang.* Paris, 1920-1924.

Petrucci, Raphael. *Philosophie de la Nature dans l'Art de L'Extrême Orient.*

——. *Encyclopédie de la Peinture Chinoise.* Paris, 1918. (Translation of the Chinese Manual of Painting—*The Mustard Seed Garden*—with notes.)

——. *Chinese Painters.* New York, 1920.

Roth, James. "The Separation of Two Layers of Ancient Wall Painting," *Artibus Asiae,* Vol. XV, 1/2, MCMLII.

Rowley, G. *Principles of Chinese Painting.* Princeton, 1947.

Rudolph, Richard C., in collaboration with Wen Yu. *Han Tomb Art of West China.* Berkeley and Los Angeles, 1951.

Sakanishi, S. *The Spirit of the Brush.* London, 1939.

——. *Translation of an Essay on Landscape Painting by Kuo Hsi.* London, 1935.

Sickman, Laurence. "Notes on Later Chinese Buddhist Art," *Parnassus,* April, 1939.

Sirén, O. *History of Early Chinese Painting.* London, 1933.

——. *History of Later Chinese Painting.* London, 1938.

——. *Chinese Paintings in American Collections.* Paris, 1928.

——. *The Chinese on the Art of Painting.* Peking, 1936.

Stein, Sir Aurel. *Sand-Buried Ruins of Khotan.* London, 1903.

——. *Ancient Khotan.* London, 1907.

——, and L. Binyon. *The Thousand Buddhas.* London, 1921.

Suzuki, D. T. *Essays in Zen Buddhism.* London, 1948 and 1950.

——. *A Brief History of Early Chinese Philosophy.* London, 1924.

Taki, Seiichi. *Three Essays on Oriental Painting.* London, 1910.

Tomita, Kojiro. *Portfolio of Chinese Paintings in the Boston Museum.* Cambridge, 1933; Boston, 1938.

——. "Brush Strokes in Far Eastern Painting," *Eastern Art,* 1931.

Tschang Yi-Tchou et J. Hackin. *La Peinture Chinoise au Musée Guimet.* 1910.

Waley, Arthur. "Yün Shou-p'ing called N'an-t'ien," *The Year Book of Oriental Art and Culture.* 1924/25.

——. *Introduction to the Study of Chinese Painting.* London, 1923.

——. *Zen Buddhism and its Relation to Art.* London, 1922.

——. *Chinese Poems.* London, 1948.

Warner, Langdon. *Buddhist Wallpainting at Wan Fo Hsia.* Cambridge, 1938.

Watts, Alan. *The Spirit of Zen.* London, 1936.

Wenley, A. G. "A Note on the so-called Sung Academy of Painting," *Harvard Journal of Asiatic Studies,* June, 1941.

White, Bishop William C. *Tomb Tile Pictures of Ancient China.* Toronto, 1940.

——. *Chinese Temple Frescoes.* Toronto, 1940.

Chinese Books

Chêng Ch'ang. *Chung Kuo Hua Hsüeh Ch'üan Shih.* (History of Chinese Painting.) Shanghai, 1929.

Ch'in Chung-wên. *Chung Kuo Hui Hua Hsüeh Shih.* (History of Chinese Painting.) 1934.

Hsü Ch'in Ming Hua Lu. (Biographies of Ming Painters.) 1817.

Hsüan Ho Hua P'u. (Sung Catalogue of Imperial Paintings.) 20 vols. 1119-1126.

Hu Chêng-yen. *The Ten Bamboo Studio Book on Painting.* (Shih Chu Chai Shu Hua P'u.) First edition 1627; often reprinted.

Ku Kung Shu Hua Chi. (Calligraphies and Paintings in the Palace Museum.) Peking, 1930 et seq.

Li Chih. *Hua p'in.* (Book of Art Appreciation.) Written in late eleventh or early twelfth century.

Lu Tsun. *Sung Yüan I Lai Hua Jên Hsing Shih Lu.* (Dictionary of Painters from eleventh to eighteenth centuries.) 1829.

Mi Fei. *Hua Shih.* (History of Painting.) 1051-1107.

P'ei Wên Chai Shu Hua P'u. (Imperial Encyclopaedia of Calligraphy and Paintings.) 1708.

Wang Kai. *The Mustard Seed Garden. (Chieh Tzŭ Yüan Hua Chüan.)* 17 vols. First edition 1679; many later editions.

Pottery and Porcelain

Andersson, J. G. "Prehistoric Sites in Honan," *Bulletin of the Museum of Far Eastern Antiquities,* vol. 19, 1947.

———. *Children of the Yellow Earth.* London, 1934.

Arne, T. J. "Painted Stone Age Pottery from the Province of Honan, China," *Palaeontologica Sinica,* Peking, 1925.

Bahr, A. W. *Old Chinese Porcelain and Works of Art in China.* London, 1911.

Beath, S. S. "Black Pottery of the Liang Chu Site near Hangchow," *China Journal,* December, 1939.

Bishop, Carl Whiting. "The Neolithic Age in Northern China," *Antiquity,* 1933.

Bluett, E. E. *Ming and Ch'ing Porcelains.* London, 1933.

Brankston, A. D. *Early Ming Wares of Ching-tê Chên.* Peking, 1938.

Brinkley, F. *China: its History, Arts and Literature. Porcelain,* vol. 9. London, 1904.

Burgess, F. W. *Old Pottery and Porcelain.* London, 1916.

Burling, Arthur and Judith H. "In Search of the Origins of Kuangtung Pottery," *Antiques,* August, 1946.

———. "Chinese Teapots and Winepots," *China Journal,* September and October, 1941.

Burling, Judith, and Mabel Irene Huggins. "Pots for Celestial Beverages," *Antiques,* April, 1942.

Bushell, S. W. *Oriental Ceramic Art.* (Collection of W. T. Walters.) New York, 1899.

———. *Description of Chinese Pottery and Porcelain* (A translation of the T'ao Shuo by Chu Yen). Oxford, 1910.

Cole, F. C. *Chinese Pottery in the Philippines.* Field Museum Publication. Chicago, 1912.

Cox, Warren E. *The Book of Pottery and Porcelain.* New York, 1944.

D'Entrecolles, Père. Two letters dated 1712 and 1722, published in *Lettres Edifiantes et Curieuses....* Translated in part by S. W. Bushell.

Farley, Malcolm F. "The White Wares of Fukien and the South China Coast," *Far Eastern Ceramic Bulletin,* September, 1949.

Franks, A. W. *Catalogue of a Collection of Oriental Porcelain.* London, 1879.

Grandidier, E. *La Ceramique Chinoise.* Paris, 1894.

Gulland, W. G. *Chinese Porcelain.* London, 1898.

Hannover, Emil. *Pottery and Porcelain: The Far East* (translated from the Danish), edited by Bernard Rackham. London, 1925.

Hedley, Geoffrey. "Yi-hsing Ware." *Transactions of the Oriental Ceramic Society.* February, 1937.

Hentze, Carl. *Chinese Tomb Figures.* London, 1928.

Hetherington, A. L. *The Early Ceramic Wares of China.* London, 1922.

———. *The Pottery and Porcelain Factories of China.* London, 1921.

———. *Chinese Ceramic Glazes.* Cambridge, England, 1937.

Hippisley, A. E. *Sketch of the History of Ceramic Art in China.* Washington, 1902.

Hirth, F. *Ancient Porcelain.* Leipzig, 1888.

Hobson, R. L. and A. L. Hetherington. *Art of the Chinese Potter from the Han Dynasty to the end of the Ming.* London, 1923.

Hobson, R. L. *The Eumorfopoulos Collection Catalogue of Chinese, Corean and of Persian Pottery and Porcelain.* Vols. i-vi. London, 1927/1928.

368

——. *A Catalogue of Chinese Pottery and Porcelain in the Collection of Sir Percival David.* London, 1934.

——. *A Guide to the Pottery and Porcelain of the Far East in the British Museum.* London, 1937.

——. *Chinese Art.* London, 1927.

——. *Chinese Pottery and Porcelain.* London, 1915.

——. *The Wares of the Ming Dynasty.* New York, 1923.

——. *The Later Ceramic Wares of China.* London, 1925.

Hobson, R. L., Bernard Rackham, and William King. *Chinese Ceramics in Private Collections.* London, 1931.

Honey, W. B. *The Ceramic Art of China and Other Countries of the Far East.* London, 1945.

——. *Guide to Later Chinese Porcelain.* (Victoria and Albert Museum.) London, 1927.

——. "Early Chinese Glass," *Burlington Magazine,* November, 1937.

Jacquemart, A. and E. Le Blanc. *Histoire artistique, industrielle et commerciale de la porcelaine.* Paris, 1862.

Julien Stanislas. *Histoire et Fabrication de la Porcelaine Chinoise* (translation of part of the Ching-tê Chên T'ao Lu 1815). Paris, 1856.

Jenyns, R. Soames. *Later Chinese Porcelains.* London, 1951.

Karlbeck, O. "Notes on the Wares from the Chiao Tso Potteries," *Ethnos,* July-September, 1943.

Laufer, B. *Beginnings of Porcelain in China.* Chicago, 1917.

——. *Chinese Pottery of the Han Dynasty.* Leyden, 1909.

Lee, George J. "Numbered Chün Ware." *Transactions of the Oriental Ceramic Society.* 1945/1946.

Lee, J. G. "Ming Blue and White," *Philadelphia Museum Bulletin,* Autumn, 1949.

Lee, S. E. "Sung Ceramics in the Light of Recent Japanese Research," Artibus Asiae, 1948.

Monkhouse, Cosmo. *A History and Description of Chinese Porcelain.* London.

Paléologue, M. *L'Art Chinois.* Paris, 1887.

Peat, Wilbur D. *Chinese Ceramics of the Sung Dynasty.* The John Herron Art Institute, Indianapolis.

Plumer, J. M. "The Place and Origin of the World-famous Chien Ware Discovered," *Illustrated London News,* October 26, 1937.

——. "The Source of the Celebrated Sung Secret Color Ware Discovered," *Illustrated London News,* March 20, 1937.

Pope, John A. *Fourteenth Century Blue and White; a Group of Chinese Porcelains.* Washington, 1952.

Shirae, Shinzo, and Warren E. Cox. "The Earliest Blue and White Wares of China," *Far Eastern Ceramic Bulletin,* September, 1949.

Trubner, Henry. *Chinese Ceramics.* Catalogue of Exhibition at Los Angeles County Museum. 1952.

——. "Tz'ǔ Chou and Honan Temmoku," *Artibus Asiae,* Vol. XV, 1/2 MCMLII.

Vasselot, J. J., Marquet de, et Marie-Juliette Ballot. *La Céramique Chinoise.* (Musee du Louvre.) Paris, 1922.

Wu Ching-ting. *Prehistoric Pottery in China.* London, 1938.

Chinese Books

Kao Lien. *Tsun Shêng Pa Chien* Ming work on wares of Sung Dynasty. 1591.

Ku-chin-t'u-shu (Pottery Section). *Encyclopaedia of Emperor K'ang Hsi.* 1662-1722.

Ts'ao Chao. *Essential Discussion of the Criteria of Antiquities.* (*Ko-ku-yao-lun.*) 1387; enlarged and rewritten in 1388-1397, 1459, 1596, and later.

BRONZES

Bishop, C. W. "The Bronzes of Hsin-chêng Hsien." Annual report, Smithsonian Institution. Washington, 1926-1927.

Creel, H. G. *The Birth of China.* New York, 1937.

——. "Dragon Bones," *Asia Magazine,* March, 1935.

Hentze, C. *Frühchinesische Bronzen und Kulturdarstellungen.* Antwerp, 1937.

——. *Sakralbronzen und Ihre Bedeutung in den Frühchinesichen Kulturen.* Antwerp, 1941.

Karlgren, B. *A Catalogue of the Chinese Bronzes in the Alfred F. Pillsbury Collection.* Minneapolis, 1952.

——. "Yin and Chou in Chinese Bronzes," *Bulletin of the Museum of Far Eastern Antiquities,* 1936.

——. "New Studies in Chinese Bronzes," *BMFEA,* 1937.

——. "Huai and Han," *BMFEA,* 1941.

Kelley, C. F., and Chen Meng-chia. *Chinese Bronzes from the Buckingham Collection.* The Art Institute of Chicago.

Koop, A. J. *Early Chinese Bronzes.* London, 1924.

Legge, James. *The Chinese Classics* (translations).

Lodge, J. E., A. G. Wenley, and J. A. Pope. *A Descriptive and Illustrative Catalogue of Chinese Bronzes.* Washington, 1946.

Priest, Alan. *Catalogue of the Bronze Exhibition.* Metropolitan Museum of Art. New York, 1938.

Rostovtzeff, M. *The Animal Style in South Russia and China.* Princeton, 1929.

Sirén, O. *History of Early Chinese Art.* London, 1929.

Tizac, H. d'Ardenne de. *L'Art Chinois Classique.* Paris, 1926.

Waterbury, F. *Early Chinese Symbols and Literature.* New York, 1942.

White, Bishop William C. *Tombs of Old Loyang.* Shanghai, 1935.

Yetts, W. Perceval. *The George Eumorfopoulos Collection of Chinese and Corean Bronzes, Sculptures, Jades, Jewelry and Miscellaneous Bronzes.* Vol. 1. London, 1929.

——. *Catalogue of the Cull Collection of Chinese Bronzes.* London, 1939.

SCULPTURE

Ashton, Leigh. *Introduction to the Study of Chinese Sculpture.* London, 1924.

Chavannes, Edouard. *Mission Archaeologique dans la Chine Septentrionale.* Paris, 1909-1915.

——. *La Sculpture sur Pierre en Chine.* Paris, 1893.

Grousset, René. *In the Footsteps of Buddha.* London, 1932.

Karlbeck, O. "Anyang Marble Sculptures" and "Anyang Moulds," *Bulletin of the Museum of Far Eastern Antiquities,* No. 7, 1935.

Priest, Alan. *Chinese Sculpture in the Metropolitan Museum of Art.* New York, 1943.

Pelliot, Paul. *Les Grottes de Touen-houang; peintures et sculptures bouddhiques des epoques des Wei, des T'ang et des Soung.* Paris, 1914-1924.

Reichelt, K. L. *Truth and Tradition in Chinese Buddhism.* Shanghai, 1928.

Sirén, O. *Chinese Sculpture from the Fifth to the Fourteenth Century.* London, 1925.

Segalen, V., G. de Voisins, and J. Lartigue. *Mission Archaeologique en Chine.* Paris, 1926 and 1936.

Stein, Sir Aurel. *Ruins of Desert Cathay.* London, 1912.

Tizac, H. d'Ardenne de. *La Sculpture Chinoise.* Paris, 1931.

——. *Les Animaux dans l'Art Chinois.* Paris, 1923.

Warner, Langdon. *The Long Old Trail in China.* London, 1938.

JADE

Bishop Collection of Jade. Handbook No. 10. Metropolitan Museum of Art, New York.

Goette, John. *Jade Lore.* Shanghai, 1936.

Jenyns, R. Soames. *Chinese Archaic Jades.* London, 1950.

Laufer, B. *Archaic Chinese Jades collected in China by A. W. Bahr.* New York, 1927.

———. *Jade, a Study in Chinese Archaeology and Religion.* The Field Museum. Chicago, 1912.

Nott, Stanley Charles. *Chinese Jade throughout the Ages.* London, 1936.

———. *Chinese Jades.* 1942.

Pelliot, Paul. *Jades Archaiques de Chine appartenant à M. C. T. Loo.* Paris and Brussels, 1925.

Pope-Hennessey, Dame Una. *Early Chinese Jades.* London, 1923.

———. *A Jade Miscellany.* London, 1946.

Salmony, Alfred. *Carved Jades of Ancient China.* Berkeley, 1938.

———. *Far Eastern Jades* (Charles M. Pratt Collection, Vassar College Art Gallery). 1941.

Walter Art Center. *Catalogue of Jades.* Foreword by D. S. Defenbacher, text and description by J. Leroy Davidson. Minneapolis, n.d.

IVORY

Laufer, B. *Ivory in China* (pamphlet). Chicago, 1925.

Sowerby, Arthur de Carle. Ivory number of *China Journal,* September, 1936.

ARCHITECTURE

Bulling, Annaliese. "Two Models of Chinese Homesteads," *Burlington Magazine,* September, 1937.

Chu Chi-ch'ien. "Architecture." *Symposium of Chinese Culture.* Shanghai, 1930.

Inn, Henry, and S. C. Lee. *Chinese Houses and Gardens.* New York, 1949.

Miriams, D. G. *Chinese Architecture.* Shanghai, 1940.

Sirén, O. *The Walls and Gates of Peiping.* London, 1924.

———. *Imperial Palaces of Peking.* Paris, 1926.

———. *A History of Early Chinese Art and Architecture.* Vol. 4. London, 1930.

———. *The Gardens of China.* New York, 1949.

FURNITURE

Burling, Arthur and Judith H. "Chinese Furniture," *Apollo,* August, 1948.

Cescinsky, Herbert. *Chinese Furniture.* London, 1922.

Ecke, Gustav. *Chinese Domestic Furniture.* Peking, 1944.

Kates, George N. *Chinese Household Furniture.* New York, 1948.

Le Compte, Louis. *Memoirs and Observations made in a late journey through the Empire of China* (English translation). London, 1697.

Roche, Odilon. *Les Meubles de la Chine.* Paris. n.d.

LACQUER

Low-Beer, Fritz. "Chinese Lacquer of the Early Fifteenth Century," *Bulletin of the Museum of Far Eastern Antiquities,* 1950.

Strange, Lt. Col. Edward F. *Chinese Lacquer*. London, 1926.

——. *Catalogue of Chinese Lacquer*. Victoria and Albert Museum. London, 1925.

Voretzsch, E. A. "Ancient Chinese Lacquer," *Eastern Art,* Vol. 3. 1931.

TEXTILES, EMBROIDERIES, COSTUMES, AND CARPETS

Andrews, F. H. *Ancient Chinese Figured Silks excavated by Sir Aurel Stein at ruined sites of Central Asia*. London, 1920.

Arlington, E. *The Chinese Drama*. Shanghai, 1930.

Brief Guide to the Chinese Woven Fabrics. Victoria and Albert Museum. London, 1925.

Fernald, Helen. *Catalogue of Ch'ing Dynasty Robes*. Exhibit, Royal Ontario Museum. Toronto, 1946.

Hackmack, Adolf. *Chinese Carpets and Rugs*. Tientsin, 1924.

Hedin, Sven. *The Silk Road*. London, 1938.

Hsu Wei-nan. *A Few Words on Ku Hsiu Embroidery*. Shanghai, 1940.

Johnston, R. F. *The Chinese Drama*. Shanghai, 1921.

Kendrick, A. F. "Textiles," *Burlington Magazine* monograph. 1925.

Leitch, Gordon B. *Chinese Rugs*. New York, 1928.

Po-wu-yao-lan. *General Survey of Art Objects*. (Ming Dynasty work in Chinese), 1621-1627.

Priest, Alan. *Catalogue of an Exhibition of Imperial Robes and Textiles of the Chinese Court*. The Minneapolis Institute of Arts, 1943.

——. *Costumes from the Forbidden City*. Metropolitan Museum of Art. New York, 1945.

——, and Pauline Simmons. *Chinese Textiles*. New York, 1934.

Simmons, Pauline. *Chinese Patterned Silks*. New York, 1948.

Stein, Sir Aurel. *Serindia. Report of Explorations in Central Asia and Westernmost China*. Oxford, 1921.

Vuilleumier, Bernard. *Symbolism of Chinese Imperial Ritual Robes*. London, 1939.

Yetts, W. Perceval. "Discoveries of the Koslov Expedition," *Burlington Magazine,* April, 1926.

CLOISONNÉ ENAMEL, PAINTED ENAMEL, JEWELRY, SILVER

Bushell, S. W. *Oriental Ceramic Art*. New York, 1899.

——. *Description of Chinese Pottery and Porcelain*. A translation of the T'ao Shuo by Chu Yen. Oxford, 1910.

Priest, Alan. "Chinese Jewelry," *Bulletin of the Metropolitan Museum of Art,* December, 1944.

Rienacker, Victor. "Chinese Cloisonné Enamel," *Apollo,* August and September, 1948.

Watts, W. W. "English Silver with Chinese Influence," *Antiques,* May, 1952.

Wên fang ssu k'ao. (Book on Porcelain.) A Ch'ien Lung publication.

SYMBOLISM AND SUBJECTS *

Chavannes, Edouard. *De l'Expression des Voeux dans l'Art Populaire Chinois*. Paris, 1922.

Dyson, V. *Forgotten Tales of Ancient China*. Shanghai, 1927.

* Although there are few books on the subject, every book on Chinese art is permeated with references to Chinese symbolism.

Werner, E. T. C. *Myths and Legends of China.* London, 1922.

Williams, C. A. S. *Chinese Symbolism and Art Motives.* Shanghai, 1941.

Yetts, W. Perceval. *Symbolism in Chinese Art.* Chinese Society, London, 1912.

Relations Between China and the West

Burling, Arthur and Judith H. "Western Influences in Chinese Art," *Apollo,* January, 1946.

———. "Western Influences in Chinese Art," *China Journal,* April, 1941.

———. "Notes on the McCann Collection of Chinese Lowestoft," *Apollo,* February, 1947.

———. "George Chinnery," *Antiques,* February, 1948.

———. "Early Contacts with China recorded in ill-fated Chater Collection." *Apollo,* June, 1949.

The China Trade and Its Influence. Metropolitan Museum of Art, New York, 1941.

Cordier, Henri. *La Chine en France au Dixhuitième Siècle.* Paris, 1910.

Davidson, Ruth Bradbury. "Chinoiserie," *Antiques,* May, 1952.

Dulles, Foster Rhea. *The Old China Trade.* Boston, 1930.

Hirth, F. *China and the Roman Orient.* 1885.

Hudson, G. F. *Europe and China.* London, 1931.

Hunter, W. C. *Bits of Old China.* Originally published 1882; reprinted, Hong Kong, 1911.

———. *The Fan-Kwae at Canton before Treaty Days, 1825-1844.* Published 1882; reprinted, Hong Kong, 1911.

Hyde, J. A. Lloyd. *Oriental Lowestoft.* New York, 1936.

Orange, James. *The Chater Collection.* London, 1924.

Reichwein, A. *China and Europe: Intellectual and Artistic Contacts in the Eighteenth Century.* New York, 1925.

Ridge, W. Sheldon. *When the West Came to the East.* Peking, 1936.

Schmidt, Robert. *Porcelain as an Art and a Mirror of Fashion* (translated and edited by W. A. Thorpe). London, 1932.

Periodicals

Antique Collector (London)

Antiques (New York)

Apollo (London)

Archives of the Chinese Art Society, (New York)

Art Bulletin (Quarterly of the College Art Association of America)

Art Digest (New York)

Artibus Asiae, edited by Alfred Salmony (Switzerland)

Art News (New York)

Art Quarterly (Detroit Institute of Arts)

Asia Magazine (New York), afterward called *Asia and the Americas.*

Bulletins and publications of various museums, including:
   Art Institute of Chicago
   Boston Museum of Fine Arts
   British Museum, London
   Brooklyn Museum
   Carnegie Institute, Pittsburgh
   Cincinnati Art Museum

City Art Museum of St. Louis
Cleveland Museum of Art
Detroit Institute of Arts
Fogg Art Museum, Cambridge
Freer Gallery of Art, Washington
Honolulu Academy of Arts
John Herron Art Institute, Indianapolis
Los Angeles County Museum
Metropolitan Museum of Art, New York
Minneapolis Institute of Arts
Musée Cernuschi, Paris
Musée Guimet, Paris
Musée du Louvre, Paris
Museum of Far Eastern Antiquities, Stockholm
Newark Museum
Philadelphia Museum of Art
Royal Ontario Museum of Archaeology
Seattle Art Museum
Toledo Museum of Art
University of Michigan Museum of Art
University Museum, Philadelphia
Victoria and Albert Museum, London
Walters Art Gallery, Baltimore
William Rockhill Nelson Gallery of Art, Kansas City
Worcester Art Museum, Massachusetts

Bulletin de l'Ecole Française (Hanoi, Indochina)
Bulletins of the Geological Society of China, 1934/35
Burlington Magazine (London)
China Journal (Shanghai), 1924 to November 1941
Connoisseur (London)
Eastern Art (Philadelphia)
Far Eastern Ceramic Bulletin
Gazette des Beaux Arts (Paris)
Harvard Journal of Asiatic Studies
Illustrated London News
Journal of Oriental Studies of the Catholic University of Peking
Journal of the Royal Asiatic Society, North China Branch (Shanghai)
Kokka: a Monthly Journal of Oriental Art (Tokyo)
Ko Kung: Monthly Publication of Imperial Palace Museum (Peking 1929-1936)
La Revue de l'Art, Paris
Magazine of Art (Washington and New York)
Monumenta Serica
Ostasiatische Zeitschrift (Berlin)
The Studio (London 1893-   )
T'ien Hsia Monthly (Shanghai)
T'oung Pao (Leiden, 1890-1899; Series I, Reprinted Peking 1941; Series II, 1900 onwards)
Transactions of the Oriental Ceramic Society (London 1921-   )
The Year Book of Oriental Art and Culture, 1924-25, edited by Arthur Waley

INDEX

Academic School of Painting, 60, 84
"Admonitions of the Imperial Preceptress to the Ladies of the Palace," 55, 357
Afghanistan, 309
agate, 172, 197, 335
Ai Hsüan, 72
album leaves, 48, 85, 88
Alexander the Great, 234
Altar of Heaven, 250, 281
altar tables, 291, 294
Altman, Benjamin, 23
amber, 197, 335
"American Eagle" design, 205
amethyst, 34
ancestor worship, 210, 211
An Ch'i, 22
Andersson, Dr. J. G., 129, 252
an hua (secret design), 154
animals and grapes, 229
Annam, 273
Anne, Queen, 290
Anyang, see Shang-Yin
apple-green, 168
Arabs, 134, 327-328
architecture, 71, 137, 277-284
Argus pheasant, 321
Aristotle, 308
Armorial services, 203-205, 334
artemisia leaf, 170, 345, 351
Art News, 88
astronomical motifs, 220
Attiret, Père, 98, 282
aubergine (egg-plant), 169, 199
"autumn scholar," 352
Avalokiteshvara, 235, 247
Ayscough, Florence, 58
"Azure Dragon," 229

baby garments, 321
Baltimore, Walters Art Gallery, 23
bamboo, 24, 68, 70, 80, 89, 92, 279, 293, 351
"Bamboo in Monochrome," 79
barium, 172
baroque, 25, 201
Barr, Alfred H., Jr., 40

barrel garden seats, 153
bas-reliefs, 53, 209, 218, 231, 235, 281
base of vessels, 35, 36
bats, 351
Battersea, 333
battle axes, 211, 217, 253, 339
beads, 172, 296, 335
bears, 230, 260
Beginnings of Porcelain, 136
belt hooks, 217, 260, 270, 335
Binyon, Lawrence, 83
birds, 42, 63, 65, 66, 72, 73, 81, 84, 88, 92, 97, 135, 198, 199, 201, 212, 220, 253, 310, 335, 351
"birthday plates," 169
Birth of China, 128, 214
biscuit, enameling on, 157, 169
Black Pottery, 130, 131
"Black Serpent," 229
"Black Tortoise," 229
Blackwood Street, 293
blanc de chine porcelain, 35, 161
blood brotherhood oath, 354
blue, deep, 168, 199
blue-and-white, 22, 152, 155, 156, 157, 160, 170, 199, 203, 205
Bodhidharma, 76
Bodhisattvas, 219, 234, 246, 247
"boneless method," 64, 95
Book of Changes, 217, 357
Book of Etiquette and Ceremony, 217
Book of History, 217, 338, 339
Book of Poetry, see Shih Ching
Book of Rites, Chou, 251, 253, 255, 313
Boston Museum of Fine Arts, 53, 78, 86
Böttger, Dresden, 163
Boxer Uprising, 55, 126, 206
Bow, 162
bows and arrows, 211, 273
Brankston, A. D., 30, 152
brass, 336
Brass Street, 282
bridges, 277, 279, 280, 281, 284
British Museum, 15, 22, 55, 357

brocade patterns, 310
brocades, 310
bronze animal forms, 212, 216, 220, 221, 229
bronze-green, 199
bronze inscriptions, 211, 217
bronzes, 129, 208-229
    forms, 211, 212
    method of casting, 212, 213
    motifs, 213, 214
    symbolism, 213, 214, 219, 220, 229
brown, 168, 199, 206
brushes, 47, 52, 270, 273
brush pots, 47, 270
"Buccaro," 163
Buddhism, 51, 54, 80, 134, 148, 219, 233, 236, 245, 310, 316, 349, 350
Buddhist art, 56, 58, 63, 64, 71, 76, 77, 232-236, 245-250, 270
Buddhist sculpture, 29, 232-234, 245-250, 302
Buddhist steles, 232, 245
Buddhist symbols of good luck, 349, 350, 361
bull, or water buffalo, 213, 260, 352
burgautée lacquer, 197, 199, 303
Burma, 257, 273, 293
Bushell, S. W., 200, 304
butterflies, 73, 89, 157, 198, 206, 335, 348, 351, 353
Byng, L. Cranmer, 65
Byzantium, 327, 333

cabriole leg, 290
cabinets, 293, 294, 296
California, 23
calligraphy, 26, 36, 40, 44, 49
Cambaluc (Peking), 80
"camelia-leaf" green, 199
canopy, 349
canopy beds, 291
Canton, 22, 78, 94, 100, 125, 162, 201-203, 205, 257, 289, 304, 305, 327, 334
carp, 258, 351
carpets, 321-325

"cash" pattern, 309, 324, 340, 345
cassia tree, 351
castanets, 346
Castiglione, Père, 98, 125
Cathay (China), 80
Caughley Pottery Works, 204
Caves of the Thousand Buddhas, 56, 234, 313
celadon, 142-144, 156
Centennial Exhibition, Philadelphia, 22
Cézanne, 89
Ch'a Ching (Tea Classic), 136, 163
Chaffers, William, 204
chairs, 291, 293, 294
Ch'ai ware, 140, 147
Ch'a Lu, 148
Chambers, Sir W., 201, 289
Ch'ang (jade emblem), 253
Chang-an, 132, 134, 246
Chang Hsüan, 61
Chang Hua, 357
Chang Ku, 66
Chang Kuo-lao, 346
chang-mu (camphorwood), 293
Chang-nan, 135, 141
Chang Sêng-yu, 56
Chang Tsao, 99
Chang Yen-yüan, 45
Ch'an (Zen) painting, 72, 76, 77, 81, 91, 92, 148, 248
Chantilly, 162
Chan Tzŭ-ch'ien, 56, 357
Chao Ch'ang, 72
Chao Chün, 355, 356
Chao Mêng-fu, 79, 81
Chao Po-chü, 74
Chao Po-su, 74
Chao School of Painting, 79
Chao Ta-nien, 67, 72
Chardin, 89
chariot fittings, 211, 217, 273
Charles I, 312
Chekiang province, 314
Chelsea, 162
"ch'êng," 277
Ch'êng Hua reign, 156
Chengtu, 64
Ch'ên Hung, 60
Ch'ên Jung, 77, 78
Ch'ên Ju-yen, 83
Ch'ên Shu, 97
Ch'ên stone pillars, 231
cherry blossom, 350
"cherry-red," 168
Chê School of Painting, 84
chests, 293, 294
Chia (bronze form), 212
Chia Ching (Ming), 160
Chia Ch'ing (Ch'ing), 125, 205
Chia-hsing, painters of, 89
Chia-hsing Fu, 303
Chia-ting, painters of, 89
"Chiang t'ai," 170
Chicago, 23
Chi Chou, 146
chicken cups, 157
Chien (bronze form), 212
Ch'ien Hsüan, 81
Ch'ien Lung, 198, 199, 201, 207, 269, 316, 324, 333, 334, 356

Chien yao, 147, 148, 163
Chih-chêng, 328
Ch'ih Yu, 49
children, 24, 155, 157, 159, 353
Ch'i-lin (unicorn), 260, 352, 388
chimeras, 230, 245
"chin" (*brocade*), 310
Ch'in dynasty, 51, 52, 218, 255, 280
Building of Great Wall, 51
burning of books, 51
Chinese Art Society of America, 37
"Chinese Domestic Furniture," 290, 292
Chinese Export Porcelain, 22, 202, 204, 205
Chin T'ien, 129
Chin Yüeh, 97
Ch'ing dynasty, 25, 27, 91, 98, 100, 128, 138, 167
carpets, 323, 324
costume, 321
enamel, 333, 334
furniture, 291, 293
ivory, 25
jade, 25, 269
lacquer, 306
painting, 25, 92-126
porcelain, 25, 128, 167-207
textiles, 312
Ching Hao, 63, 64
Ching Tai, 333
Ching T'ai lan (enamel), 333
Ching-tê, 141
Ching-tê Chên, 30, 133, 135, 141, 142, 146, 152, 153, 167, 203, 206
Chinnery, George, 125
chinoiserie, 90, 98, 201-204, 289, 296
Chins (*see also* Nü-chen Tartars), 78, 140
Chio (bronze form), see *Chüeh*
Chippendale, 25, 201, 289
Ch'i Shu (lac), 301
Chiu (bronze form), see *Kuei*
Chiu, A. Kaiming, 86
Ch'iu Ying, 87
chopsticks, 272, 273, 274
Chou Ch'ên, 87
Chou dynasty, 14, 132
architecture, 278-280
bronze, 25, 31, 215-218
family system, 215
feudal system, 215
ivory, 273
jade, 254, 255
lacquer, 301
literature, 215-217
love of learning, 215
painting, 50
political economy, 215
religion, 215-217
women, 215
Chou Fang, 62
Chou Hsiang-tung, 311
Chou K'o-chou, 311
Chou Li, see *Book of Rites*
Chou Tan-ch'üan, 146, 147, 160
Chou Wen-chü, 64
Christ, 233

Christians, 80, 245, 308
chrysanthemum, 71, 169, 350, 351, 356
Chuang Tzŭ, 67, 348
Chüeh (bronze form), 212, 216
Chu Hsi, 29, 75, 77
Chü Jan, 65
Chü-lu, 147
Chu Mai-ch'ên, 357
Chün yao, 15, 144, 149, 150
Chung (bronze form), 212
Ch'ung Chêng, 91
Chung-li Ch'üan, 345, 346
Chu Yüan-chang (*see also* Hung Wu), 83
cicada, 172, 213, 253, 260, 340
Cincinnati, 23
cinnabar lacquer, 197, 210, 272, 305, 306
circular medallions, 310
cire-perdue method, 213
citron (Buddha's hand), 351
Civil Service examinations, 73, 75, 76, 86, 201, 313, 353
Civilisation on Trial, 201
clair-de-lune, 145, 198
claw-and-ball foot, 290
Cleveland, 23
cloisonné, 327-329
cock, 339, 354
Co-hong system, 125, 202
combs, 217
compound, 277
Compte, Louis le, 296
conch shell, 349
Confucius, 50, 51, 54, 55, 58, 69, 77, 80, 84, 100, 132, 137, 217, 220, 233, 245, 255
Constantinople, 308, 309, 333
contemporary painting, 126
copies and imitations, 13, 25, 27-39, 146, 198, 206
copper, 336
coral, 34, 197, 335
coral red, 169, 205
Coromandel screens, 301
costume, 84, 307, 315, 361, 321
cotton culture, 312
courtyards, 282-284
cowrie shells, 213, 272
crackle on porcelain, 144, 145, 147
Creel, H. G., 129, 214, 219
Crimea, 309
cross-stitch embroidery, 313
Crown Prince of Sweden, 16
crystal, 34, 172, 197

dagoba, 283
Damascène, Jean, 98
Damascus, 309
damask, 309
David, Sir Percival, 16, 21, 29, 30, 143
Davis, Frank, 296
deer, 161, 212, 324, 346, 347, 352
Delft pottery, 156, 203
Denver, 23
Detroit, 23
"devil's work balls," 275
"devil's work" porcelain, 160
Dharmatrata, 349

Diamond Sutra, 57, 87
diaper patterns, 309, 324, 340
"diaspron," 309
Directoire, 200
Discourses of the State, 217
Doctrine of the Mean, 51
Document Classic, (see *Shang Shu*)
"Dog of Fo," *see* Fo dogs
doorways, 279
Dordogne region, 273
dove chariots, bronze, 219
dragon, 49, 56, 77, **169**, **213**, **216**, 230, 253, 254, 255, 258, 260, 272, 310, 316, 338, 339, 352
Dragon Boat Festival, 157, 353
"Drunken Buddhist priest," 56
ducks, 88, 351
Dutch East India Co., 202
Dwight (Fulham), 163

Early Chou, 216
East India Companies, 156, 202
Ecke, Gustav, 137, 279, 290, 292
eel-skin yellow, 168
eggshell porcelain, 130, 160, 198
Egyptian graves, 308
eight Buddhist symbols of good luck, 349, 350, 361
Eight Happy Omens, 349
Eight Horses, 352
Eight Immortals, 71, 162, 219, 246, 274, 345-348, 360
Eight Masters of Nanking, 96
Eight Ordinary Symbols, 345, 361
Eight Precious Things, 345, 361
Eight Trigrams, 49, 316, 325, 388
Eight Views of the Hsiao and the Hsiang, 358
Eight Wonders of Yangchow, 96
elephants, 211, 212, 213, 273
Elers Brothers, 163, 164
Elixir of Immortality, 340
Elizabeth, Queen, 202
"Emaciated Horse," 79
embroidery, 312-315
embroidery stitches, 314
emerald-green, 198, 199
"Empress of China," 204
Empress Wu, 246, 347
enamel, 35, 158, 167, 197, 203, 326-328, 333, 334
    champlevé, 327, 328, 333
    cloisonné, 35, 158, 167, 197, 327, 328, 333
    painted, 35, 167, 197, 203, 327, 333, 334
Encyclopaedia Britannica, 99
Endless Knot, 349
English East India Co., 202
Entrecolles, Père d', 153, 168, 170, 203
equipment of painters, 47, 48
Essay on Landscape Painting, 66
Eumorfopoulos, George, 14, 15, 16
European figures, 161, 200, 305, 334
export trade, 142, 143, 156, 162, 167, 202-205, 301, 308, 312, 314, 333, 334

Fa Hsien, 234
"fa hua," 157
"fa-lin" (*Fo-lan*), 327, 328
famille jaune, 169
famille noire, 23, 169
famille rose, 164, 171, 197, 198, 199, 200, 204, 206, 334
famille verte, 23, 169, 197, 206
Famous Beauties, 198, 354-356
Fan K'uan, 65
Fan Li, 355
Fans, 48, 273, 275, 345-347
Fatshan, 165
"feathers and fur," 72
"fên Ting," 146
fêng huang, 321
"fêng-shui" (wind and water), 277, 334
Fenollosa, E. F., 23
fertility symbols, 213
finger painting, 99
fish bowls, 153, 198
fishes, 42, 59, 135, 198, 213, 253, 254, 349, 351, 353
"Fish Roe" design, 309
"Fish Scale" design, 340
Five Blessings, 351
Five Classics, 339
five-clawed dragon, 169, 316, 324
Five Dynasties, 63, 64, 139, 249, 350
Five Elements, 334, 338
Five Gentlemen, 96
Five Metals, 338
Five Sacred colors, 323, 338, 339
Five Tastes, 212, 338
flambé reds, 166, 168, 198
flames, 339
floral medallions, 229, 324
floral patterns, 24, 308, 309, 310, 311, 324
flowers, 42, 63, 65, 72, 73, 76, 81, 84, 92, 94, 95, 155, 159, 169, 198, 199, 200, 206, 335, 350, 351
Flowers of Four Seasons, 326, 350
Flower Street, 282
flower vases, 200, 270, 279, 292, 334, 349
fly brush, 346, 347
Fo dogs, 159, 258, 324, 352
Foochow, 301, 304, 305
Forbidden City, 250, 281
"foreign colors," 204
foreign influences, 90, 156
Fou-liang, 135
Four Accomplishments, 340, 360
"Four Gentlemen, The," 70, 350, 351
"Four Great Masters," 86-88
Four Great Masters of Anhui, 96
"Four Masters of Yüan Dynasty," 81, 83, 88
"Four Patriarchs of Painting," 56, 357
Four Sacred Animals, 338
"Four Treasures of the Room of Literature," 47, 340
"Four Wangs," 93, 94
France, 308, 334
Freer, Charles Lang, 23

Freer Gallery of Washington, D.C., 23
Fry, Roger, 40
fu (bronze form), 212, 216
Fu (Symbol of Distinction), 339
Fu Hsi, 209
Fu Hsing, 347
Fukien porcelain, 35, 147, 161
fungus, 259, 340, 351
furniture, 84, 273, 274, 289-295
Furniture Street, 282

Gandhara, 234
gardenia, 350
gardens, 84, 277, 281, 283, 284
Garden of the Fragrance of Dew, 314
"Gathering of Scholars," 71
"Gay Genius," 70
Genghis Khan, 152
geometric patterns, 213, 220, 229, 260, 273, 309, 323
Gide, André, 10
Giles, Herbert A., 68
Gill, Eric, 127
gilt bronze images, 236, 245, 250
ginseng, 205
glass, 132, 167, 171, 172, 197
glass pictures, 336
Gobelins tapestry, 311
God of Happiness, 347
God of Longevity, 347
God of Wealth, 347
gold, 168, 171, 198, 199, 205, 206, 213, 219, 303, 334, 335
gold thread, 311, 312
good luck, eight Buddhist symbols of, 349, 350, 361
Goodrich, L. C., 83
gourd, 279
grains of rice (or millet), 339
Grand Canal, 293
"Grand Turk," 335
grave pottery, 130, 131, 135, 141, 151
"graviata" bowl, 200, 206
Great Deluge, 209
Great Wall, 52, 280, 281, 312
Greek influence, 135, 140, 229, 234
Greeks, 307, 333
greenish-yellow, 169
grouse, 351
Grousset, R., 289
Guardians of Four Cardinal Points, 247
Gupta School, 246
Gutenberg, 90

hair pins, 217, 260, 270, 273, 335
hand scrolls (chüan), 47, 48
Han dynasty:
    architecture, 280, 281
    bas-reliefs, 53, 231
    bronzes, 219
    carpets, 322
    jade, 259, 260
    lacquer, 302, 303
    mirrors, 220, 229
    painting, 52, 53, 54, 137
    pottery, 25, 133, 134, 136
    silk, 308, 309

tomb figures, 15, 29, 137, 138
tombs, 53
Hangchow, 60, 64, 73, 74, 77, 78, 80, 130, 311, 326
hanging scrolls (chou), 47, 48
Han Hsiang-tzŭ, 347
Han Kan, 41, 60
Han Lin Academy, 65, 206
Han yü, see tomb jades
Han Yü, 248, 347
Hao Shih-chiu, 160
hares, 253, 340, 352
hawthorne jar, 170
Haydon, Benjamin R., 99
Hellenistic period, 308
heraldic beasts, 309
"hermit" painters, 82, 83, 84, 91
"herringbone" pattern, 309
"Hills and Water" (landscape), 252, 271, 284, 357
hill-shape incense burner, 133
Hills of Longevity, 347
Hindu religion, 233, 234
Hippisley, Alfred E., 197, 200
historical figures, 274
Ho (jade of), 27, 28
Ho Chü-p'ing, 231
Ho-Ho, see Twin Genii
Ho Hsien-ku, 347
homestead, 277
Honan, 29, 129, 137, 143, 147, 148, 150, 208, 231, 235, 282
Honey, W. B., 161
honeycomb pattern, 309
Honolulu, 23, 72
Hopei, 279
horses, 60, 71, 79, 135, 138, 211, 219, 231, 246, 260, 324, 349
horses at flying gallop, 309
Ho Shang (Laughing Buddha), 162, 349
hsi (bronze form), 212
Hsi (joy), 352
Hsia Dynasty, 129, 209, 210, 322
Hsia Kuei, 37, 75
Hsiang Fei, 356, 357
Hsiang Shêng-mo, 89
Hsiang Yüan-p'ien, 21, 22, 89
Hsiao T'ang Shan (Shantung), 53, 54, 231
Hsieh Ho (see also Six Canons), 37, 45
"hsieh i" (thought writing), 89
"hsieh-pi," 60
hsien (bronze form), 212
Hsien Fêng, 206
Hsing-chou, 136
Hsin-p'ing, 135
Hsi Shih, 354, 355
hsiu hua (embroidery), 310, 312, 313, 314
Hsi Wang Mu, 347
hsü (bronze form), 212
Hsüan Ho Hua P'u, 63, 65, 72
Hsüan Tê (Hsüan Tsung), 84, 153, 312
Hsüan Tê porcelain, 36, 155
Hsüeh T'ao (notepaper), 62, 66
Hsü Hsi, 64
Hsü Lin, 88
Hsü Wei (Wên-ch'ing), 89, 90
hu (jade emblem), 253

hu (bronze form), 212
Hu, 172, 173
Hua ch'i (lacquer), 304
Huai period, 216, 255
Hua Mu-lan, 356
"hua shih," 170
huang (jade emblem), 253
Huang Chü-ts'ai, 65
Huang Ch'üan, 64
Huang Kung-wang, 81, 82
Huang Ti, 49, 129, 208, 209, 307, 335
Hua p'in, 48
Hu Ch'üan, 51
Hui-hsien, 137
Hui Tsung, 72, 73
Hundred Antiques, 345
Hundred Children, 353
Hundred Deer, 199
Hundred Flower design, 199
Hundred Horses, 199
"Hundred Wild Geese," 72
hung-mu (red wood), 293
Hung Wu, 83, 152, 281, 312
Hu Shih, Dr., 22
Hu tablets, 272

I (bronze form), 212, 216
Ibn Batuta, 305
"I Ching," 49, 217, 251
"icicle" pattern, 279
Ih, see I
"I Li," 217
Illustrated London News, 296
Imperial Academy of Painting, 58, 65, 72, 73
Imperial Encyclopaedia of Calligraphy and Painting, 94, 97, 98
Imperial Palace, 80, 250, 277, 280, 281, 303, 323, 324
Imperial robes, 311, 315, 316
Imperial Workshops, 167, 172, 261, 274, 333
India, 76, 134, 136, 233, 234, 246, 273, 293, 308
Indianapolis, 23
Indian influence, 234-236, 246, 248, 282, 283
Ingres, 45
ink blocks, 47
ink slabs (ink stones), 47, 270
insects, 45, 66, 72, 76, 97, 198, 349
interior decoration, 25
Ireland, 327
iron, 129
iron dust, 168
iron-red, 168, 171, 200
ironwork, 326
Italy, 308
I Tsing, 136
ivory, 35, 167, 197, 254, 272-276, 335
ivory concentric balls, 275
Ivory Street, 282
I-Yin, Viceroy, 49
I Yüan-chi, 72

jade, 34, 129, 167, 172, 197, 251-260, 269-271, 335
analysis of, 256

beads, 260
bracelets, 260, 270
jadeite, 256
Jade Mountain, 269
jades, musical, 255, 256
Jade Seal of State, 256
Jade Street, 270, 282
jade writing tablet, 254
Japan, 62, 81, 86, 126, 163, 249, 279, 291, 302, 308, 310
japanning, 301
jasper, 34
Jen-hui (Yen Hui), 81
Jên Jên-fa, 79
Jên-wu (Men and Things), 50
"Jesuit china," 203
Jesuits, 90, 98, 99, 197, 201, 296
jewelry, 335, 336
Jews, 80, 134, 245
Johnson, Captain, 55
Ju Chou yao, 147
Judge of Horses, 359
Ju-i scepter, 259, 279, 340, 347

K'ai-fêng Fu, 58, 64, 73, 140, 144
kakemono, 47, 48
k'ang (platform), 291, 294, 322
K'ang Hsi, 97, 98, 100, 282
enamels, 333
painting, 98
porcelains, 23, 94, 167-170
Kansas City, W. Rockhill Nelson Art Gallery, 23, 78, 255
Kansu, 56, 129, 234, 289, 321
Kao Ch'i-p'ei, 99, 358
Kao K'o-Kung, 79
Kao Lien, 13
kaolin (China clay), 134, 142, 145
Kao Tsung, 73, 246
Karlgren, Dr. B., 208, 216, 217
Kashgar, 322
Kashing, 89
Kates, George N., 290
Keizer, A. Cornelis de, 203
Khotan, 308
Kiangsi, 135, 148, 314
kingfisher feathers, 336
"kinuta," 143
knots per foot (carpets), 323, 324
Ko Chêng-ch'i, 97
Ko Chiu-ssŭ, 80
Ko-ku Yao Lun, 154
Korea, 22, 62, 302, 308
Kosloff expedition, 309
K'o Ssŭ (tapestry), 311, 312
Ko yao, 13, 144
Ku (bronze form), 212, 216
Ku An, 80
Kuang (bronze form), 212
Kuang Hsü, 206
Kuangtung pottery, 36, 150, 164-167
Kuan-hsiu, 63, 71
Kuan Tao-shêng, Lady (Kuan Tao-jên), 79
Kuan Ti, 159, 162, 354
Kuan T'ung, 63
Kuan yao, 13, 144, 145, 147
Kublai Khan, 79, 82, 152
Kuei (bronze form), 212
Kuei (jade emblem), 253, 254
"kuei kung" (devil's work), 160

Ku Hsiu (embroidery), 314, 315
Ku K'ai-chih, 21, 45, 55, 56, 274, 303, 357
Kung Ch'un, 162, 163
Kung Hsien, 96
Kung K'ai, 79
"kung-pi" (meticulous), 60
Ku Ning-yüan, 89
K'un-ts'an, 92, 93
Ku Yüeh-hsüan type porcelain, 30, 171, 172, 197, 206
Kuo Hsi, 42, 65, 66, 72, 314
"Kuo Yü," 217
Kwan Yin, 29, 58, 72, 162, 219, 235, 247-249, 270, 349
Ky-lin, 260, 338, 352
Kyoto, 279

lac burgautée, 197, 199, 203
"lacework" porcelain, 200
lacquer, 24, 25, 137, 167, 245, 254, 296, 301-306
  carved, 303, 304
  dry, hollow, 301, 302
  painted, 303, 304
  pierced, 303, 304
La Farge, Henry A., 88
Lake Baikal, 233, 309
Lake of Gems, 347
Lama Temple (Peking), 248
Lamaism, 248-250
Lam Qua, 125
Lang Shih-ning see Castiglione
Lang T'ing-tso, 168
Lang yao, 168
Lantern Festival, 353
Lanterns, porcelain, 198
Lantern Street, 282
Lan Ts'ai-ho, 347
Lao Tzŭ, 11, 54, 55, 76, 77, 182, 217, 233, 346-348
lapis lazuli, 335
lattice work, 279, 282
Laufer, B., 136, 172
Laughing Buddha, 162, 349
lavender, 198
lei (bronze form), 212
Leonardo da Vinci, 41, 51, 90
Lettres Edifiantes, 282
"li" (inner spirit), 69, 70
li (bronze form), 211
Liang Dynasty, 245
Liang K'ai, 77, 99
Li Chên, 62
Li Ch'êng, 65
Li Chi, 251, 253, 255, 313
Li Chieh, 280
Li Chih, 48
Li Ch'ing-ch'ao, 58
Li Fu-jên, 355
Li Jih-hua, 89
Li K'an, 68, 79
Li Liu-fang, 89
Li Lung-mien (Li Kung-lin), 41, 67, 71, 358
Limoges, 33
Lin Chüan Kao Chih, 66
Ling Yin (Soul's Retreat), 326
Lin Liang, 88, 248
Lin Yutang, 69
Li Po, 229, 355
Li Ssŭ-hsün, 59, 60

Li Sung, 74
Li T'ai-po, 60
Li T'ang, 74
Li T'ieh-kuai, 346
Li Tzŭ-chêng, 91
Liu Chün, 88
Liu-ju ("Six Likes"), 87
liu-li (opaque glass), 172
Liu Pang, 219
Liu Sung-nien, 74, 358
Li Yin, 97
Lohans, 63, 71, 138, 234, 247, 250, 274, 349
Lolang tombs, Korea, 302
London Exhibition, 15
lotus, 169, 279, 348, 349, 350, 351, 353
Louis XIV, 200, 201, 334
Louis XV, 200, 201
Louis XVI, 200
Louvre, 296
Lowestoft, 22, 162, 204
Loyang, 14, 50, 53, 132, 218, 235, 255
lozenge, 345
Lü Chi, 88
Lu Hsing, 347
Lung Ch'ing reign, 160
Lung-ch'üan yao, 142-144
Lung Mên caves, 235, 246
Lu Pan, 291
Lu T'an-wei, 56
Lu Tê Chih, 89
Lu Tung-pin, 346, 347
Lü Yü, 136-163

Macao, 90, 95, 125
Macartney, Lord, 312
Ma Ch'üan, 97
Ma Fên, 72
magnolia, 350
magpies, 351
Mahayana Buddhism, 233, 234, 247
Maitreya, 235
makemono (hand scrolls), 47
malachite, 34, 219
Malay Archipelago, 293
mallow, 350
mallet-shaped vase, see kinuta
mammoth ivory, 273
Manchus, 88, 92, 125, 126, 167
Mandarin porcelain, 204
Manicheans, 245
marble pictures, 284
marble sculptures, 211, 230
Marco Polo, 80, 90, 151, 154, 281, 323
"Marks and Monograms on Pottery and Porcelain," 204
marks and seals, 28, 35, 47, 133, 141, 144, 147, 154, 155, 161, 166, 167, 170, 269, 328
masks, 217, 230, 335
Matisse, 40
Matisse, His Art and His Public, 40
Ma Yüan, 37, 75
meander pattern, 279, 340
meanings in Chinese Art (see also symbolism), 12, 24, 25, 203, 315, 316, 337-340, 345-359

"medallion" bowl, 200, 206
medicine bottles, 197
Meissen, 162
Mencius, 54, 132, 217
"metal and silk" rugs, 323, 324
metal rims, 145, 146, 147
metalwork, 326-328, 333-335
Metropolitan Museum of Art, 23, 37, 78, 232, 273, 291, 309
"Mi dot" (pointillism), 68
Middle Chou, 216
"Middle Kingdom," 201
Mi Fei, 26, 41, 67, 68
Ming Dynasty, 13, 25, 139
  architecture, 281, 283
  carpets, 323, 324
  cloisonné, 328, 333
  costumes, 321
  furniture, 291, 292
  ivory, 274
  jade, 269
  lacquer, 305, 306
  painting, 83-91
  porcelain, 128, 152-167
  sculpture, 250
  statues, 30
  textiles, 312
Ming Huang, 60, 61
Ming Ti, 233
Ming-ti (Wei), 310
Ming tombs, 250, 281
Minneapolis, 23, 269
mirror-black, 168, 171
mirrors, 217, 219, 220, 229, 327
"misty brocade," 303
"Mohammedan blue," 155, 157
Mohammedans, 80, 245, 310, 356
Mo-ku hua ("boneless method") 64, 95
Mongolia, 76, 78, 80, 97, 248, 302. 309, 313, 321, 323
Mongols, 54, 58, 73, 78, 79-82, 91
"monk" painters, 91, 92
monochrome glazes, 159, 168, 198, 199
Mont-Corvin, Jean de, 80
moon, 95, 96, 339, 340, 352
Moon Festival, 340
moon-gates, 279, 284
mother-of-pearl, 197, 199
Mo Tï, 217
mountains, 65, 84, 93, 95, 325, 339
Mu-ch'i, 77
multi-colored porcelains, 156, 157
Musée Cernuschi, Paris, 236
musical instruments, 84, 211, 229, 302, 303
Mustard Seed Garden, 50, 96
Mu Wang, 352
mystic knots, 309, 349
Nanking, 83, 96, 153, 281, 282
Nanking Porcelain Pagoda, 154, 282
nan mu (wood), 279
Nara, see Shōsōin
narcissus, 350
nature worship, 210, 252
Near East, 308, 322
Neo-Confucianism, 75

neolithic pottery, 129, 130, 131, 289
neolithic sites, 14, 209
nephrite, 256
Nestorian Christians, 245
Nevers, 156
nien-hao, 141, 155, 170, 197
Nien Hsi-yao, 198
Nine bronze tripods, 209, 301
"Nine Famous Emperors," 49
"Nine Songs," 357
Ninghsia, 322, 323, 324
Ningpo, 80
Ni Tsan, 81, 82
Northern celadons, 143
Northern Chou, 236
Northern School of Painting, 59, 60, 84, 87, 88, 94
Northern Sung Dynasty, 145, 249
painting, 64-73
Nü-chen Tartars, 64, 73, 78, 80, 140

Oderic, Friar, 260
old men, 43, 63, 274
Ontario, Canada, 23
onyx, 172, 197
oracle bones, 130, 131, 210, 278
orchid, 70, 79, 350, 351
Ou Tzŭ-ming, 164
Ou-yang Hsiu, 67
owl, 213, 230
ox, 230

pagodas, 201, 277, 280, 282-284
Pa Hsien, *see* Taoist Immortals
P'ai-lou (arch), 283
painting, 11, 21-24, 36-39, 40-126, 357-359
  agriculture and sericulture, 74
  animal, 54, 57, 84
  bird and flower, 57, 64, 65, 72, 81, 84, 88, 97, 350
  bird and insect, 64, 72, 89, 92, 97, 350
  Court scenes, 60, 63, 64, 71, 87
  devils and spirits of the underworld, 79, 81
  flowers and vegetables, 63, 72, 89, 94, 95, 350
  genre, 57, 71, 87
  historical scenes, 74, 84
  landscape, 25, 41, 50, 54, 57, 63, 64, 65, 74, 75, 82, 84, 85-88, 93-95, 97, 357, 358
  legends in regard to, 59
  portrait and figure, 49-53, 54, 57, 63, 87, 88, 99, 100, 274, 359
  religious, 57, 80, 90
"pai Ting," 146
Pa Kua, *see* Eight Trigrams
Palladio, Andrea, 25
Palmyra, 309
"palace furniture," 289
"palace silk" rugs, 323, 324
p'an (bronze form), 212
P'an Ku, 338
Pao-ting, 211
Paotou, 322, 323, 324
paper, 47, 52

Pa Ta Shan Jên (Chu Ta), 92, 93
patina, 31, 32, 214
pavilions, 71, 284
peach, 347
peach-bloom glaze, 168, 198
peach blossom, 274, 350
Peaches of Immortality, 347, 348
peach tree, 351
peacock-green, 168
pear blossom, 350
pearls, 335, 345, 349, 352
pegmatite, 170
Peking, 60, 78, 80, 91, 172, 257, 277, 281, 303, 323, 333
"Peking" bowl, 200, 206
Pelliot, Paul, 37, 53
pendants, 217, 253, 255, 274, 335
P'êng Chün-pao, 303
peony, 169, 350, 351
Percival David Foundation of Chinese Art, London, 21
Periegetes, Dionysius, 309
Persian influence, 135
Persian knot, 322
Persians, 134, 308, 310, 322, 323, 328
persimmon, 351
petuntse, 134, 142
pewter, 9, 336
pheasant, 213, 339
Philippines, 293
phoenix, 229, 338, 351
pi (jade emblem), 172, 253, 255
picture mounting shop, 48
Pien Wên-chin, 84
Pi Fa Chi (Records of Brushwork), 63
pilgrim's gourd, 346
Pillsbury, Alfred F., 23
pine trees, 278, 347, 351
pi-sê (secret color), 139
"playing with ink" ("mao hsi"), 70, 71
"Pleasure of the Fishes," 348
Pliny, 308
pole finials, 217, 335
Po Lo, 359
pomegranate, 351
pomegranate blossom, 350
Pompadour, Madame, 201, 290
Poon Yok Hsi, 166
poppy, 350
Porcelain Administration, 135
"Porcelain de Medici," 156
porcelain figures, 158, 159, 161, 162, 166, 169
Port Arthur, Manchuria, 302
Portuguese, 202
Po-shan Hsien, 172
potter's wheel, 129, 130, 134, 135
pottery and porcelain, 127-207
  origins of pottery, 129
powder blue, 168
Po-wu-yao-lan, 149, 156, 310
Priest, Alan, 37, 246, 309
priests' robes, 315
proto-porcelain, 133
prunus (plum) blossom, 70, 84, 161, 169, 350, 351
"purple of Cassius," 171, 334

Pu-tai (Laughing Buddha), *see* Ho-Shang

Quinsay (Hangchow), 80

Rackham, Bernard, 127
"rainbow" skirts, 321
Raleigh, Sir Walter, 256
Raphael, 86, 90
relations between East and West, 100, 201-205, 308, 327, 333, 334
religious vestments, 310, 312
Remarks on the Masterpieces of Chinese Paintings, 95
Rembrandt, 38, 41
"Returning Home," 358
Revere, Paul, 335
Revolution of 1912, 91, 126, 206
rhinoceros horn, 274, 345
rhus vernicifera (lac), 301
Ricci, Matteo, 90
"rice grain" vessels, 200
ritual cups, 339
Ritual of the Chou, 132, 278
robin's egg, 199
rock-cut temples, 234-237
rockeries, 284
rococo, 25, 201, 202, 207
Roman Empire, 171
Rome, 52, 308
roofs, 278, 279-282
roof tiles, 158, 160, 278, 281, 282
  figures, 158, 160
root carvings, 336
rose-pink, 171, 198, 206, 334
rose quartz, 34
rosewood (hua-li), 292, 293
Rouen, 156
"ruby-backs," 171
ruby-red, 198, 199
rugs, 321-325

St. Cloud, 162
St. Louis, 23
St. Louis Exhibition, 325
Salting, George, 15, 16
Samarra, 136
sang de boeuf (ox blood), 168
san ts'ai, 157-159, 166
"Scarlet Bird," 229
scholar's table, 47, 48, 143, 144, 153, 164, 270, 274
screens, 293, 305
sculpture, 54, 230-250
Scythians, 214
sea horses, 229
seals, *see* marks and seals
Seattle, 23
ser (ssŭ), 307
Seres, 307
serikon, 307
Sesshu, 86
Seven Buddhist Treasures, 349
sgraffito decoration, 151
"shadowy blue," *see* ying-ching
Shanghai, 86, 314
Shang Lin, 280
"Shang Shu," 217
Shang-Yin Dynasty, 131, 132
  architecture, 278
  bronzes, 25, 31, 49, 208-229

culture, 209, **210**
furniture, 291
ivory, 272, 273
jades, 252, 253
marble sculpture, 230
painting, 49
pottery, 25, 129, 131, 132, 211
religion, 210
sacrifices, 211
silk, 307
"Shan Shui," 73, 357
Shansi, 129, 137, 231, 234, 236
Shantung, 129, 137, 172, 231, 236, 312, 327
Shekwan (*see also* Kuangtung pottery), 164-167
Shên Chou, 85, 86
Shên Hao, 91
Shên Nung, 209
Shen Shao An, 306
Shensi, 129, 134, 137, 234
Shên Tê-fu, 153
Shen Tzŭ-fan, 311
"Shih Ching," 217, 252, 273, 307
Shih Huang Ti, 51 137, 218, 255, 280
Shih K'o, 64, 99
Shih-t'ao, 92, 93, 358
Shih Tsung, 139
Shihwan, *see* Shekwan
Shōsōin, Nara (Imperial Treasury), 303, 310, 322, 327, 328
"Shou," 351, 352
Shou Shing, 347
Shuang Hsien, 348
"Shu Ching," 338
"Shu fu" porcelain, 152
Shu-hua-p'u (Imperial Encyclopaedia of Calligraphy and Painting), 94, 97, 98
Shun, Emperor, 50, 129, 132, 301, 315, 339
Shun Lao, 347
Siam, 273
Sian-fu, 277
Siberia, 273, 309
Sichelbarth, Père, 98
silk, 47, 52, 156, 202, 307-313
    secret of culture, 308
silk designs, 308
Silk Route, 52, 308, 322, 323, 327
silkworms, 213, 307, 309, 340
silver, 197, 199, 213, 219, 303, 334, 335
Silver Street, 282
Simmons, Pauline, 309
Sirén, O., 284, 358
"sitting at royal ease," 248
Six Canons of Painting, 44-46
Six Cosmic Forces, 253, 254
Six Dynasties, 54, 134, 229, 245
"Six Greatest Masters" (Ch'ing), 93, 94, 95
slanting "T" pattern, 220, 324
snake, 213, 216, 220
snuff bottles, 170, 172, 197, 198
soapstone, 34, 336
"Society of the Cincinnati," 205
Soleyman, 136
Son of Heaven, 210, 252, 315
sonorous stone, 345
Soochow, 60, 74, 151, 304, 311

Source of Existence, 316, 338
Southern School of Painting, 59, 60, 64, 65, 71, 72, 85, 88, 93
Southern Sung Dynasty, painting, 74-79
Spanish shawls, 314
spear heads, 211
spirals and whorls, 213, 216, 220, 273, 279, 309, 340
"Spirit Road," 250
"spotted" celadon, 144
Spring and Autumn Annals, 354
Ssŭ Chün-tzŭ, 70, 350
Ssŭ-ma Ch'ien, 52, 53, 308
Ssŭ-ma Kuang, 67, 69, 353
stage costumes, 316, 321
stars (constellation), 339
State Umbrella, 349
steatite (soapstone), 170
Stein, Sir Aurel, 308, 309, 311, 313, 322
stilt marks, 147, 149
stone sculpture, 230-249
stork, 324, 351
stupas, 282, 283
Su Han-ch'ên, 74
Sui Dynasty, 56, 134, 150, 236
Sumatra, 293
Summer Palace, Peking, 202, 281
sun, 339, 340
Sung Culture and Ideals, 64
Sung Dynasty, 10, 11, 47
    architecture, 280
    carpets, 323
    embroidery, 313, 314
    furniture, 291, 292
    ivory, 274
    jade, 260
    K'o ssŭ, 311
    lacquer, 303
    painting, 25, 64-78, 83
    porcelains, 25, 140-151
    sculpture, 249
    silk, 311
    silver, 335
Sung Lien, 357
Sung Ti, 358
Sun Yat-sen, 126
Su Tung-p'o (Su-shih), 43, 67, 68, 69, 70, 71, 88
swallow, 351
swastika, 349, 350
symbolism (*see also* meanings in Chinese art), 213, 214, 216, 217, 219, 220, 229, 252, 259, 260, 315, 316, 337-340, 345-359
Symbols of Filial Piety, 340
Syrians, 327
Szechüan, 64, 136, 231, 236, 302, 313

"T'ai" (towers), 279, 280, 282
T'ai Chi, 316, 325, 338
Tai Chin, 84, 85
T'ai P'ing rebellion, 126, 154, 206
T'ai Sung, 61
T'ai Tsu, 64
T'ai Tsung, 57, 65, 245, 246
"ta kuei," 253

T'ang Dynasty, 57-62, 134-136, 140, 145
    carpets, 322, 323
    embroidery, 313
    furniture, 291
    gold, 335
    "Golden Era," 57, 134
    horses, 25
    jade, 260
    jewelry, 335
    lacquer, 303
    mirrors, 229
    painting, 56, 57-62
    pottery, 135, 136
    sculpture, 245-247
    silver, 335
    tomb figures, 15, 25, 29, 137, 138, 321, 328
Twilight of T'ang, 63, 139
T'ang Yin (liu-ju), 41, 86, 87
T'ang Ying, 197-199, 207
Taoism, 11, 14, 51, 55, 63, 64 76, 77, 80, 91, 219, 220, 229, 246, 316, 345-349
Taoist Immortals, 71, 162, 220, 246, 269, 274, 345-349
Taoist sculpture, 246
Tao Kuang, 205
"T'ao Lu," 161
"T'ao Shuo," 149, 172, 200
Tao-tê Ching, 346
T'ao-t'ieh mask, 213, 214, 216, 220, 260
T'ao Yüan-ming, 358
Tartar City, 281
Tartars, 54, 61, 143, 249
Ta Shou (ancestor portrait), 100
Ta-yi kilns, 136
tea, 162, 163
tea ceremonies, 135, 148, 149
Tea Classic, 136, 163
tea-dust glaze, 168, 199
teakwood, 289, 293
teapots, 162-164
"temmoku," 148
Temple of Heaven, 159, 250, 281
Ten Bamboo Studio Books on Painting, 96
"Ten Saints," 96
textiles, 307-312
"The Four Gentlemen," 70, 350, 351
Thesée, 10
"The Way" (Taoism), 347
Three Friends, 155, 351
Three Kingdoms, 54, 134, 321, 354
Three Star Gods, 347
thumb-rings, 253, 260
thunder and cloud pattern, 213, 216, 220, 279, 309, 340
"tiao ch'i" (lacquer), 305, 314
Tibet, 76, 80, 97, 248
T'ieh hua (iron flower), 326
T'ien Lung Shan caves, 236, 246
Tientsin, 22, 290
tiger, 49, 56, 112, 135, 213, 253, 260, 324, 352
ting (bronze form), 212, 216
t'ing, 277
Ting Chou pagoda, 282
Ting Chou yao, 145, 146

Tizac, M. d'Ardenne de, 236
Tokyo, 64, 77
Toledo, 23
tomb animal sculpture, 231, 232, 245
tomb homesteads, 281, 290, 292
tomb jades, 252-254
tomb pottery figures, 137-139, 151
tomb violations, 31, 128
Tomita, Kojiro, 86
Tomlinson, H. M., 13
tools, agricultural and hand, 211
tortoises, 230, 272, 338, 352
tortoise shell, 197
t'o-t'ai porcelain, 152, 154, 155
tou (bronze forms), 212
tou ts'ai, 157, 199, 206
Toynbee, Arnold J., 201
Toy Vendor, 353
"transmission of spirit," 359
"trellis" diaper pattern, 309
Ts'ai Hsiang, 148
Ts'ang Ying-hsüan, 167, 198
Ts'ao Kuo-chiu, 346
Ts'ao Pu-hsing, 55
Tsinan-fu, 130
Tsou Fu-lei, 84
Ts'ui Ko, 72
Ts'ui Po, 72
tsun (bronze form), 212, 216
ts'ung (jade emblem), 253
Tsun Shêng Pa Chien, 13
Tuan-fang altar set, 291
Tu Fu, 66, 136
Tung Ch'i-ch'ang, 86, 88, 89, 93, 314, 315
T'ung Chih, 206
Tung Yüan, 65
Tun-huang caves, 56, 57, 234, 235, 246, 313
Turkestan, 56, 97, 98, 134, 234, 257, 308, 311, 321, 322
Turks, 333
Turner, Thomas, 204
turquoise, 34, 172, 197, 213, 217, 219
turquoise blue, 168, 199, 206
"t'u Ting," 146
"TVL" pattern, 221
Twelve Ancient Ornaments, 313, 315, 316, 339, 340
Twelve Floral Symbols, 350
Twelve Signs of Zodiac, 340
Twin Genii of Peace and Harmony, 348
Tz'ŭ Chou (north of Anyang), 132, 135, 144, 150
Tzŭ Hsi (Empress Dowager), 126
Tzŭ t'an (sandalwood), 293

underglaze red, 155
unicorn, 260, 338, 352
University of Pennsylvania Museum, 232, 245

Velasquez, 89
vermilion paste for seals, 47, 306
Versailles, 202
Victoria and Albert Museum (London), 15, 16, 260

violet-blue, 169
"Visit Amid Mountain Gloom," 358
votive shrines, 234, 245

Waley, Arthur, 70
Walker, Thomas Barlow, 23
Walker Art Gallery, Minneapolis, 269
wallpapers, 24, 202, 336
Walters, W. Thompson, 22
Wang An-shih, 67, 69, 71
Wang Chien, 93
Wang Fu, 84
Wang Hsi-chih, 44
Wang Hui, 93, 95
Wang Kai, 96
Wang Mêng, 81, 82, 83
Wang Mien, 84
Wang Mo-ch'i, 66
Wang Ping, 166
Wang Shih-min, 93, 94
Wang Wei, 60, 61
Wang Yüan-ch'i, 93, 94, 97, 98
Wan Li, 128, 153, 160
wardrobes, 294
"Warham bowl," 142
Warring States, 133, 216, 217, 255, 309
warriors' helmets, 211
"Washing the Elephant," 56
Washington, George, 22
water containers, 47, 143, 171, 269
water weeds (aquatic plants), 33
Watteau, Jean Antoine, 334
Wa-wa cups, 157
"Way, The" (Taoism), 347
Wei Dynasties, 54, 134, 137, 138, 246
   Northern Wei, 234, 235
   sculpture, 234, 235, 302
Wei Lu, 171
Wên Chêng-ming, 86
Wên fang ssŭ k'ao, 334
wên jên (literary painters), 52, 60, 65, 66, 71, 72, 82, 88, 92
Wenley, A. G., 65
Wên Shu, 89
Wên T'ung, 67, 68
Wên Yen-k'o, 311
West, impact of China on, 201, 202
West China, 53, 213
Wheel of the Law, 349
Whistler, James, 23
"White Tiger," 229
wild geese, 88, 351
willow-pattern plate, 204
willow tree, 351
windows, 279, 282
winepots, 149, 154, 163, 164, 165
winged animals, 220, 229
winged lions, 231, 245
women artists, 79, 89, 94, 97
woodcuts, 74, 96
wooden stands, 290, 291
wood sculpture, 230, 236, 245, 249, 250
writing wrist-rest, 47, 270, 273

Wu Chên, 81, 82
Wu Chiu, 311
Wu Li, 41, 95
Wu Liang tombs (Shantung), 53, 54, 209, 218, 231
Wu School of Painting, 85
Wu Tao-tzŭ, 41, 58, 59, 61, 247
Wu Ti, 133, 236, 308, 355
Wu To, 311
wu ts'ai, 157, 158, 159, 160, 167
Wu Wei, 85

Xavier, François, 90

Yang Chiang, 165
Yangchow, 60
Yang Kuei-fei, 61, 260, 303, 356
Yang-Shao (Honan), 14, 252
yang-ts'ai (foreign colors), 334
Yang tz'ŭ, 334
yang-yin, 12, 55, 210, 252, 316, 325, 334, 338, 339, 340
yao (pottery or wares), 142
Yao, Emperor, 50, 129
Yao Ho, 66
"yao p'ing," 197
Yarkand, 257, 322
"ya shou pei" cups, 154
yellow, 168, 198, 205
"Yellow Dragon," 229
Yellow Emperor, *see* Huang Ti
Yellow River, 147, 209, 214, 323
Yellow Temple, 248
Yen Hui, 81
Yen Li-pên, 61, 246
Yen Li-tê, 61
Yetts, W. P., 212, 214, 229
Yi, see I
Yi-hsing pottery ware, 36, 150, 162-164
yin, *see* yang-yin
Yin, *see* Shang-Yin
ying ch'ing, 139, 140, 147
Yü (*see also* Hsia Dynasty), 209, 301
Yü (*see also* jade), 256
Yü (bronze form), 212, 216
Yüan Dynasty, 79-82, 139, 151-152, 249, 250, 260, 274, 322, 323, 327, 328
   ivory, 274; jade, 260
   painting, 81, 82
   porcelain, 152
   sculpture, 249, 250
Yüan Ming Yüan, 202
Yuan Ti, 56, 355, 356
Yüeh-chou, 136, 139
Yung Chêng, 100, 171, 172, 197-199
Yung-lo, reign of, 84, 152, 153, 154, 281
Yün Kang caves, 234
Yunnan, 236, 327
Yün P'ing, 94
Yün Shou-p'ing, 94, 95

Zen (*see also* Ch'an), 72, 76, 77, 148, 248
Ziccawei, 95
Zoraostrians, 245

LIST OF ILLUSTRATIONS
[Arranged chronologically]

COLOR PLATES
Paintings
"Blue Hills of Spring," Sung, 105
"Magpie on a Flowering Branch," Sung, 110
"Spring Play in a T'ang Garden," attr. to Emperor Hsüan Tsung (Hsüan Tê), 117
"Ode to the Pomegranate," by Shên Chou, Ming, 120

Porcelains
Bowls of Chün yao ware, Sung, 182
Vase of Tz'ŭ Chou ware, Sung, 182
K'ang Hsi Vase, *famille noire*, 195

Glazed Pottery Roof Tiles
Ming, 344

Sculpture
Kwan Yin in polychromed wood, Sung, 341

BLACK AND WHITE ILLUSTRATIONS
Paintings
Ink Squeeze of Loyang tile, 3rd century B.C., 101
Painted Loyang tile, Han, 101
Ku K'ai-chih: detail of scroll, 102
Yên Li-pên: detail of scroll, 102
Wall painting of Kwan Yin, 102
"Scholars Collating Classic Texts," 103
Fan K'uan: "Mountains in Snow," 104
attr. Li Lung-mien: "Realm of Immortals," 104
Hui Tsung: "Silk beaters," 103
attr. Chou Wên-chü: "Spring Morning," 105
attr. Chou Wên-chü: "Emperor and Musicians," 107
attr. Chao Ch'ang. "Yellow Roses and Bees," 109
Hsü Tao-ning. "Fishing in a Mountain Stream," 106
"The Sleeping Man," unknown artist, Sung, 107
Ma Fên. "The Hundred Geese," Sung, 110
Su Han-ch'ên. "Lady Before Mirror in Garden," 106
"Women Bathing Children," Sung fan, 111
Hsia Kuei. "Landscape," 109
Ma Yüan. "Bare Willows and Distant Mountains," 111
Li Sung. "Boat on a Stormy Sea," 111
Liu Sung-nien. "Meeting in Pavilion," 286
Ch'ên Jung. Detail "Nine Dragon" scroll, 113
Kao K'o Kung. "Mountains in Clouds," 112
Kung K'ai. "Gathering of Philosophers," 112
Kung K'ai. "Chung K'uei, the Demon-Queller," 113
Chao Mêng-fu. "A Goat and a Sheep," 114
Kuan Tao-shêng. "Bamboo Study," 114
Li K'an. "Ink Bamboo," 115
Chao Yung. "A Horse and a Groom," 115
Hsia Chang. "Clear Wind in the Valley," 117
T'ang Yin. "A Winding Stream," 116
Lü Chi. "Two Geese," 342
Tung Ch'i-ch'ang. Album sketch, 118
"Spring Festival on Yellow River," 286

Pa Ta Shan Jên (Chu Ta). "Bird," 119
Wu Li. "Landscape," 118
Yün Shou-p'ing. "Flower Study," 119
Kao Ch'i-p'ei. "Two Ducks," 121
Lu Tê Chih. "Black Bamboos," 122
Wang Shih-min. "Landscape," 124
Wang Chien. "Landscape," 123
Wang Hui. "Landscape," 122
Wang Yüan-ch'i. "Mountain scene," 124

Pottery and Porcelain
Neolithic Kansu funerary urn, 173
Late neolithic black pottery stem bowl, 173
Prehistoric pottery jar, 173
Shang white pottery jar, 174
Black pottery amphora, ca. 1500 B.C., 175
Black pottery jar, Chou, 175
Round pottery box with cover, Chou, 175
Two tomb figures, Late Chou, 176
Black pottery covered Tou, Late Chou, 176
Large jar, ca. 3rd century B.C., 176
Pottery facsimile of bronze bell, Late Chou, 177
Detail of vase in shape of bronze Hu, Han, 177
Pair of pottery horses, Wei or Six Dynasties, 178
Pottery Horse, Wei Dynasty, 178
Tomb figurine of woman, T'ang or earlier, 18
Pottery camel and rider, T'ang, 179
Equestrienne dismounting, pottery, T'ang, 179
Female dancers and musicians, T'ang, 180
Merchant holding wine-skin vessel, T'ang, 180
Covered jar, glazed, T'ang, 180
Covered jar and small water pot, T'ang, 181
Clay tomb figure of warrior, T'ang, 181
Dish on three legs, colored glazes, T'ang, 181
Pottery dog, T'ang, 183
Ying Ch'ing vase, late T'ang or early Sung, 183
Vase, spotted Yüeh ware, Six Dynasties, 182
Lotus-shaped Southern kuan yao bottles, Sung, 183
Pair of gallipots, Tz'ŭ Chou ware, Sung, 17
Peach-shaped cup, kuan yao, Sung, 17
Ying Ch'ing ewer, Sung, 184
Vase, Tz'ŭ Chou ware, Sung, 184
Tz'ŭ Chou pillow, Ju-i or cloud-shape, Sung, 184
Tz'ŭ Chou rice bowl, vase, and wine-pot, Sung, 185
Jar with cover, Tz'ŭ Chou ware, Sung, 185
Tz'ŭ Chou tall, wide-lipped, vase, Sung, 185
Lung-ch'üan celadon vase, Sung, 186
Lung-ch'üan celadon vase, Sung, 186
Chien yao stoneware jar and bowls, Sung, 186
Tz'ŭ Chou, Black Chien, and Chün yao bowls, Sung; and Shu Fu bowl, Yüan, 187
Northern celadon bell, Sung, 187
Kinuta shaped celadon vase, Sung, 187
Southern Ting ivory-colored bowl, Sung, 188
Ko yao bowl, Sung, 188
Cup stand with underglaze lavender, Ming, 189
White ewer, Ming, Yung Lo, 189
Blue-and-white bowl, Ming, Hsüan Tê, 191
Blue-and-white conical bowl, Ming, 20
Blue-and-white bowl, Ming, 191
Small eggshell porcelain bowls, Ming, 191
Blue-and-white vase, double gourd, Ming, 188
Blue-and-white bowl, Hsüan Tê, 190
Figure of Chung-li Ch'üan, Ming, 341

Three-color beaker-shaped vase, Ming, 192
Wan Li blue-and-white dish, 192
Yi-hsing teapot, Ming, 192
Blue-and-white box with lid, Wan Li, 193
Tê-hua teapot, blanc de chine, Ming, 192
Group of Ming roof tiles, 193
Ching-tê Chên white vases, Ming and Ch'ing, 193
Tê-hua stem cup, blanc de chine, Ch'ing, 193
Shekwan figure of poet, Li Po, 18th century, 194
Shekwan yellow glazed bowl, Ming, 194
Porcelain plate, *famille verte*, K'ang Hsi, 194
Kwan Yin, *famille verte*, K'ang Hsi, 194
Blue-and-white vase, magnolia design, Ch'ing, 17
Three-color vase, *famille jaune*, K'ang Hsi, 19
Peach bloom flower vase, K'ang Hsi, 19
Blue-and-white covered jar, K'ang Hsi, 196
Blue-and-white vase and water cups, Ch'ing, 344
Covered bowl, white on dark blue, K'ang Hsi, 194
Three-color tall vase, Ch'ing, 196
Twin Genii, Ho-Ho, *famille rose*, Ch'ing, 341
Export porcelain plate, dinner service George Washington, Order of Cincinnati, 1785, 19

Glass

Bowl, engraved, probably Sung Dynasty, 196
Ku-yüeh Hsüan bowl and snuff bottle, Ch'ien Lung, 196

Bronzes

Covered jar, "Lei," Shang-Yin Dynasty, 221
Wine vessel, "Ku," Shang-Yin, 221
Upright gong bell, "Chung," Shang-Yin, 221
Bronze vessel, "Kuang," Shang-Yin, 222
Ceremonial wine vessel, "Chia," Shang-Yin, 222
Bronze vessel, "Ting," Shang-Yin, 222
Elephant form wine vessel, "Huo," Early Chou, 223
Ceremonial vessel, "Fang Tsun," Early Chou, 223
Vessel, "P'an," Shang-Yin or Early Chou, 223
Wine beaker "Tsun," Early Chou, 224
"Kuei" on stand, Early Chou, 224
Pole end, Middle Chou, 224
Owl, or pheasant, form wine vessel, Chou, 225
Buffalo form wine vessel, Middle Chou, 18
Wine vessel, "Yi," Middle Chou, 225
Bronze animal mask, Western Chou, 225
Wine flask, "Hu," 481-205 B.C., 226
Bronze "Ch'ien," Late Chou, 226
Vessel in form of stag, Late Chou, 227
Toilet box, "Lien," Han, 227
Bronze lion, A.D. 386-557, 227
Bronze gilt figure of Buddha, T'ang, 228
Bronze mirrors, Han and T'ang, 228

Sculpture

Chimera, stone, 4th-5th century, 237
Colossal head of Buddha, Wei, 237
Buddhist votive stele, Wei, 238
Seated Maitreya from Lung Mên, A.D. 512, 238
Colossal head of Bodhisattva, 6th century, 239
Head of a Buddha, stone, Northern Wei, 240
Sakyamuni Buddha, marble, ca. A.D. 600, 240
Group of four Bodhisattvas, wood, Sui, 240
Guardian King, stone, 8th century, 241
Head of a Bodhisattva, stone, T'ang, 242
Kwan Yin, wood, 13th or 14th century, 243
Pottery figure of Lohan, Ming, 244
Cantonese wooden figures, 244

Jades

Plain "pi," Shang-Yin, 261
Jade mask of human face, Shang-Yin, 261

Ts'ung, probably Middle Chou, 261
Bird-dragon, white, Middle Chou, 262
Pi, spinach green, Late Chou, 262
Scabbard tip, Late Chou, 262
Green jade stags from Honan, Chou, 263
Jade disk, "Pi," Warring States, 263
Carved jade ornament, Late Chou, 263
Dragon pendant, Late Eastern Chou, 264
Horse's head, green, Han or 3rd century, 264
Reclining water buffalo, dark green, Sung, 265
Pillow in form of baby, K'ang Hsi, 265
Nephrite screen, Ch'ien Lung, 265
Greenish-white jade mountain, Ch'ien Lung, 266
Amethyst cups and green coupe, Ch'ien Lung, 266
Brush holder, 18th-19th century, 266
White vase in form of lotus, Ch'ing, 20
Jadeite Kwan Yin, 19th century, 18

Ivory

Dignitary, and Shou Shing, Ming, 267
Kuan Ti, Ming, 268
Three Buddhist female deities, Ming, 268
Rhinoceros horn cup, early 18th century, 268

Architecture, Furniture and Lacquer

Chinese homestead in pottery, Ming, 286
Pottery house model, polychrome, Han, 286
Tympanum of doorway, limestone, T'ang, 286
The pavilion, photograph Long Chin San, 287
Marble Pagoda, Peking, 287
Pottery grave model of chair and dressing table, Ming, 288
Side table, Yüan or early Ming, 288
Small sacrificial table, Ming, 288
Splay-leg cabinet, Ming, 288
Bowl, painted lacquer, Late Chou, 297
Head of dried lacquer, hollow, T'ang, 297
Lacquer box, part of toilet set, Han, 297
Seated Bodhisattva, dry lacquer, T'ang, 298
Lacquer Lohan, Sung, 298
Lacquer table, Sung, 299
Dry lacquer figure of Buddha, Yüan, 299
Cinnabar lacquer low table, Yung Lo, 299
Carved red lacquer box, early 15th century, 300
Detail from 12-panel lacquer screen, 1690, 342

Textiles, Embroideries, Costumes and Carpets

Fragment polychrome figured silk, Han, 317
Temple hanging, Ming, 317
Buddhist scroll—silk K'o ssǔ, Ch'ien Lung, 317
Group of Ch'ing Dynasty costumes, 318
Ku Hsiu family embroidery, Ming, 318
K'o ssǔ Imperial robe, Yung Chêng, 318
Ancestor portrait of official, 1764, 319
Ancestor portrait, woman, Ch'ing, 319
"Beauty of South China," Ch'ing, 319
Taoist priest's robe, 19th century, 320
Chinese carpet, 18th century, 320
Twelve Ancient Ornaments, Ch'ien Lung, 343

Enamels

Cloisonné dish, Chia Ching, 329
Garden seat, Ming, 330
Imperial vases and plate, Ch'ien Lung, 330

Silver and Jewelry

Pair of silver bowls, Sung, 331
Imperial Fêng Huang crown, T'ang or Sung, 331
Pair of silver-gilt hairpins, 17th century, 332
Detail of Imperial crown, 332